Political Parties
in the Regions of Russia

Political Parties
in the Regions of Russia

DEMOCRACY UNCLAIMED

Grigorii V. Golosov

LYNNE
RIENNER
PUBLISHERS

BOULDER
LONDON

Published in the United States of America in 2004 by
Lynne Rienner Publishers, Inc.
1800 30th Street, Boulder, Colorado 80301
www.rienner.com

and in the United Kingdom by
Lynne Rienner Publishers, Inc.
3 Henrietta Street, Covent Garden, London WC2E 8LU

Library of Congress Cataloging-in-Publication Data
Golosov, Grigorii.
    Political parties in the regions of Russia : democracy unclaimed / Grigorii V. Golosov.
    Includes bibliographical references and index.
    ISBN 1-58826-217-0 (alk. paper)
    1. Political parties—Russia (Federation)   2. Russia (Federation)—Politics and
government—1991–   3. Political culture—Russia (Federation)   4. Democracy—Russia
(Federation)   5. Democratization—Russia (Federation)   I. Title.
JN6699.A795G565   2003

                           2003047047

British Cataloguing in Publication Data
A Cataloguing in Publication record for this book
is available from the British Library.

Printed and bound in the United States of America

∞   The paper used in this publication meets the requirements
of the American National Standard for Permanence of
Paper for Printed Library Materials Z39.48-1992.

5 4 3 2 1

To the memory of my mother,

Tamara Sergeevna Golosova

Contents

Tables

Acknowledgments

This book would not have been possible without the financial support of the Woodrow Wilson International Center for Scholars in Washington, D.C., which granted me a fellowship from September 2002 to May 2003. Of the organizations that supported this decade-long project in the earlier phases of its implementation, I would like to extend my gratitude to the John D. and Catherine T. MacArthur Foundation, the Research Council of Norway, and the Central European University, Budapest. I also wish to acknowledge the advice and assistance provided to me at my home institution, the European University at St. Petersburg. I am particularly indebted to Vladimir Gel'man, who gave unstintingly of his profound knowledge of Russia's regional politics, and to Iulia Shevchenko, who helped me both as a scholar, by giving me valuable advice, and as my wife, by supporting me throughout the project. I would also like to thank two anonymous manuscript readers for their suggestions, and my research assistants at the Woodrow Wilson Center, Bram Caplan and Caroline Savage, for their help. Those errors of fact and interpretation that remain in the book, as well as the views expressed, are entirely mine.

Acronyms of Political Parties

APR	Agrarian Party of Russia
ChR	Honor and Motherland
DPR	Democratic Party of Russia
DVR	Democratic Russia's Choice
KPRF	Communist Party of the Russian Federation
KPRSYa	Communist Party of the Republic of Sakha–Yakutia
KPRT	Communist Party of the Republic of Tatarstan
KPS	Kuznetsov–Polozov–Savitskii: Together for the Sake of the Future
KPSS	Communist Party of the Soviet Union
KRO	Congress of Russian Communities
LDPR	Liberal Democratic Party of Russia
NDNG	Our Home Is Our City
NDR	Our Home Is Russia
NPRF	People's Party of the Russian Federation
NPSR	Popular Patriotic Union of Russia
OKS	All-Russian Coordination Council
PES	Party of Economic Freedom
PPR	Orthodox Party of Russia
PRES	Party of Russian Unity and Accord
PST	Party of Workers Self-Government
RDDR	Russian Movement for Democratic Reforms
RiZ	Equal Rights and Legality
RKRP	Russian Communist Workers Party
RNRP	Russian Popular Republican Party
ROS	Russian All-People's Union
RPRF	Republican Party of the Russian Federation
SDPR	Social Democratic Party of Russia
SPP	Social Help and Support
SPS	Union of Right Forces
VR	Russia's Choice
ZPN	For Genuine People's Power, Civil Peace, and the Interests of the Man of Toil
ZVU	For the Rebirth of the Urals

Regions of the Russian Federation

1. Adygeia	16. Chuvashia	31. Kahbarovsk
2. Aginskoe Buriat	17. Dagestan	32. Khakasia
3. Altia territory	18. Evenk	33. Khanty-Mansi
4. Altia republic	19. Ingushetia	34. Kirov
5. Amur	20. Irkutsk	35. Komi
6. Arkhangel'sk	21. Ivanovo	36. Komi-Permiak
7. Astrakhan	22. Jewish autonomy	37. Koriak
8. Bashkortostan	23. Kabardino-Balkaria	38. Kostroma
9. Belgorod	24. Kaliningrad	39. Krasnodar
10. Briansk	25. Kalmykia	40. Krasnoiarsk
11. Buriatia	26. Kaluga	41. Kurgan
12. Chechnya	27. Kamchatka	42. Kursk
13. Cheliabinsk	28. Karachaevo-Cherkesia	43. Leningrad
14. Chita	29. Karelia	44. Lipetsk
15. Chukotka	30. Kemerova	45. Magadan

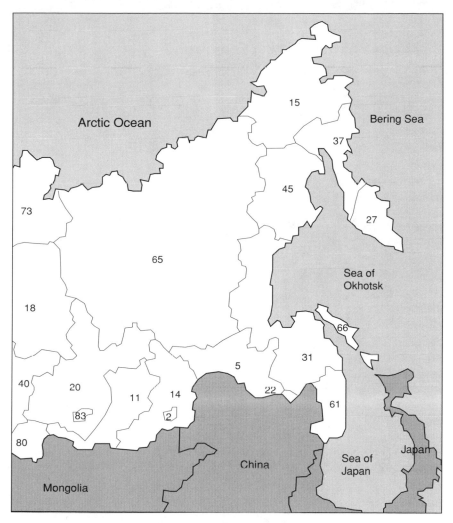

I

Introduction

The purpose of this book is to examine the systemic disincentives to party formation in the regions of Russia. An influential approach in political science stipulates the indispensability of political parties for democratic development (Lipset 2000: 48) by equating "modern democracy" to "party democracy" (Katz 1980: 1). In a similar vein, many scholars contend that parties are essential to the process of democratic consolidation (Pridham 1990: 2). Weakly institutionalized party systems seriously impede democratic development, because without institutionalized political parties, democracies tend not to fare well on such important parameters as citizen involvement, policy stability and accountability, leadership recruitment and turnover, political legitimacy, and democratic survivability in general (Mainwaring 1999: 323–341). Yet more than ten years after the collapse of authoritarian rule, and well after the arrival of relatively free and fair subnational elections, the very existence of political parties in the regions of Russia remains questionable. From this point of view, democracy in the regions of Russia remains unclaimed.

Outline of the Book

My definition of "political party" ultimately descends from the categorization of Downs (1957: 25): a party is "a team of men [and women] seeking to control the governing apparatus by gaining office in duly constituted elections." Epstein (1966: 104) clarified this definition by adding that "the recognizable label . . . is the crucial defining element." The model of party competition advanced by Downs assumes that voters are motivated exclusively by policy considerations. At the same time, however, they are rational individuals who want to minimize costs entailed by electoral choice, which means that they are not inclined to waste their time examining party programs and scrutinizing candidate profiles. They need information shortcuts from their policy preferences to individual candidates. Downs himself was inclined to believe that such information shortcuts were, in fact, ideologies (Hinich and Munger 1994), which was an entirely plausible assumption given that Downs limited his analysis to two-party competition. In multiparty competition, however, party labels not only signify divergent ideologies but also play the role of information shortcuts. In other words, they serve as coordination devices that allow voters to coalesce on their policy preferences. Thus in this book, a political party is any group that contests elections under its own label.

From this perspective, party formation means that instead of contesting elections as independents, politicians either join existing parties or coalesce to form new ones. This fairly self-explanatory concept, however, is rarely used in comparative political research. Instead, a large and increasing number of scholars prefer to speak of party institutionalization, which, as defined by Huntington (1965: 394), is the process by which parties become established and acquire value and stability. In Russia and the majority of other post-Soviet countries, at least on the subnational level, the central question is not the degree of parties' ideological or organizational cohesion but rather the lack of important parties as such. In other words, what matters in these democracies is not why political parties have or have not managed to acquire value and stability, but why they have or have not become established. Ironically enough, the few studies that have examined party formation empirically have so far dealt not with new democracies that produce massive evidence on the subject, but rather with fairly old democracies in the early times of their existence, such as Victorian Britain (Cox 1987) and the pre–Civil War United States (Aldrich 1995).[1] My study, while heavily relying on this work for theoretical insight, deals with very contemporary social settings characterized, for instance, by the presence of the electronic mass media. Thus it is intended to add the present to the small body of research on party formation that is already in existence.

When approaching the principal question of my study, I assume that political parties emerge as a product of politicians' self-interest. As Aldrich (1995: 24) put it, "politicians turn to their political party—that is use its powers, resources, and institutional forms—when they believe doing so increases their prospects for winning desired outcomes, and they turn from it if it does not." This assumption leads me to a strongly elite-centered perspective on party formation in Russia. In an influential strain of literature on democratic transitions, elites emerge as principal actors who ultimately determine both the direction of political transformations and their outcomes (Higley and Burton 1989). From this perspective, the major difference between Russia and many other new democracies, including postcommunist ones, is a remarkably low level of elite change after political regime transformation (Gel'man and Tarusina 2000). As demonstrated by Cox (1986), political parties started to command the majority of the vote in Britain not earlier than the power of the individual members of parliament eroded. In a similar vein, it may be expected that the vast resources inherited by the post-Soviet elite from the past, when successfully converted into electoral advantages, emerged as an obstacle to party formation. Leaving the empirical elaboration and refinement of this expectation for further analysis, at this moment I would like to emphasize its importance for the overall explanatory framework employed in this study. If political parties were the only kind of agencies that could be successfully employed for securing individual electoral success, then their emergence simultaneously with the arrival of electoral institutions could be taken for granted. If, however, elites can rely upon alternative resources that can be utilized in the electoral arenas, this creates a situation where the costs and benefits of party affiliation are weighted against those of nonpartisanship.

While following Downs (1957) and Aldrich (1995) in identifying electoral success as the major goal of politicians and thereby as the primary incentive for party formation, I extend the set of incentives to be analyzed by introducing an additional dimension that concerns the regions' institutional design. Indeed, as rules that constrain political behavior (Carey 2000), institutions determine the scope of available means and thereby shape the goals of politicians. The vast majority of Russia's regions use constitutional models that involve separation of powers between directly elected chief executives and legislative assemblies. Correspondingly, my analysis deals with two principal kinds of political actors, the executives and the legislators. For the executives, to maximize power means to maximize control over the legislature. For the legislators, to maximize power means to maximize legislative autonomy. I also discuss electoral system effects and current efforts by Russia's federal authorities to "engineer" the development of party systems at the regional level.

The logic described above determines the organization of this book. In Chapter 2, I describe and analyze Russia's national political parties and party system. I begin with an examination of the origins of Russia's political parties in the period when they were not able to participate in elections. Then I analyze the activities of individual political parties that were active in Russia in 1993–2003. My analysis demonstrates that in 1993–2003, the institutional and political conditions of Russia remained unfavorable for party formation. The set of factors that, in one way or another, suppressed party formation included presidentialism, the lack of party-structured elections coincidental with the event of regime change ("founding elections"), certain characteristics of the electorate, and the ban on Communist Party activities imposed by the national executive in 1991. Thus when placed into a cross-national perspective, Russia's party system can be characterized as excessively fragmented and excessively volatile, while the influence of national political parties over the presidency and federal government seems to be negligible. At the same time, political parties seem to be rapidly developing in the electorate, and they did manage to emerge as principal agencies of democratic decisionmaking in the national legislature. In both capacities, they have strong incentives for territorial penetration. Thus the lack of territorial penetration suggests the existence of region-level factors that effectively resist it.

Chapter 3 systematically presents empirical evidence on the lack of party penetration. The regularity of Russia's regional elections, both executive and legislative, was established in parallel with the country's slow drift toward symmetrical federalism. The pattern of holding regular regional legislative elections was evident already over 1993–1995 and remained stable since then, while regional executive elections were being held on a relatively regular basis starting in 1995. Detailed information on regional elections presented in the chapter includes aggregate evidence on the levels of activity and success of political parties. Then I present and analyze the data on individual parties. The analysis demonstrates that the role of political parties in regional elections remained small throughout the whole period, and it tended to decrease in 1999–2003. The overall pattern of party activity in the regions seems to gradually stabilize, but is supplemented with a high degree of changeability in the compositions of individual political parties present in the regions. Overall, the evidence presented in the chapter suggests that in the majority of Russia's regions, the services offered by political parties remain out of demand.

I begin Chapter 4 by testing a possible alternative interpretation of the data, according to which the services of political parties are unavailable rather than out of demand. Given the low level of their electoral success, political parties may be simply absent in the regions. The chapter demonstrates that such an explanation is not valid. In fact, what is observable in the regions is the oversupply of party labels. I argue that oversupply effectively inflates the cost of affiliation with political parties, thus undermining the process of party formation. Then I proceed to demonstrate that even those parties that are generally viewed as strong enough to provide valuable support to their candidates are not actually in capacity to contest every elected office. This happens for a constellation of reasons involving the relatively low social standing of party activists, the organizational properties of parties, and coalition politics. Finally, I briefly examine services offered by political parties to candidates in regional elections. I demonstrate that while party affiliations may be useful for the majority of candidates, there are numerous and easily available alternatives to the services parties can offer. In this connection, I analyze the role of money and paid campaign organizers in Russia's regional elections. The general conclusion of the chapter is that party labels are quite in supply, but few of them are in demand; those party resources that are actually demanded are in scarce supply; and there are viable alternatives to almost anything a party can offer.

Chapter 5 shifts the focus of my analysis to the demand side. Proceeding from the assumption that political parties are valued as means of achieving electoral success, I examine the utility of political parties in Russia from this specific standpoint. I start with the argument that political parties cannot be expected to be very useful under conditions when electoral outcomes are predetermined. For parties to exist, a certain level of uncertainty is a necessary condition. Uncertainty, in turn, stems from conflicts within the elites. Thus intraelite conflicts emerge as the first topic of the chapter. My analysis demonstrates that they do indeed serve as basic preconditions for party formation. However, the principal participants in the majority of such conflicts tend to rely upon superior resources provided by their institutional affiliations. In executive elections, these resources substitute for party affiliations in two senses. First, by ensuring the organizational and financial superiority of their holders, they allow them to conduct electoral campaigns without party assistance. Second, information conveyed to the voters by the labels attached to institutions and businesses is at least as valuable as information conveyed by party labels. The same applies to regional legislative elections, where party affiliation is most likely to be skipped by those categories of candidates who have something else to rely upon. In fact, in these smaller and less important electoral arenas, available substitutes for party affiliation tend to proliferate, as the advantages of administrative and economic power become complemented with the advantages of social capital.

Chapter 6 examines the second aspect of party utility, the use of political parties for maintaining and maximizing power within varying institutional contexts. I begin with a description and analysis of the formal institutions in the regions of Russia. The analysis demonstrates that while clear manifestations of presidentialism can be found in some of the regions, this is not the case in many others, and that the most widespread constitutional model on the regional level of Russia's politics is semipresidentialism. Rather than facilitating party development, this exacerbates the regional executives' will to place legislatures under their political control and thereby makes conditions for party formation even worse. On the one hand, regional executives find institutional ways of preventing party development, as exemplified by the use of bicameralism and administrative-territorial electoral districts in many of the republics. On the other hand, the political mechanisms of establishing executive control over the assemblies involve political parties only rarely. While prone to external political control, the regional assemblies are nevertheless capable of achieving certain degrees of legislative autonomy. Politically loyal deputies do not necessarily lack their own policy agendas. Quite the reverse, the opportunity to pursue these policy agendas motivates them to seek legislative seats, with political loyalty to the executive being delivered in exchange. My analysis demonstrates that the policy domain within which such agendas can be set and pursued is the economy. Yet for this to be achieved, regional legislatures develop committee structures rather than party structures, which makes party affiliation irrelevant on the assembly floor.

In Chapter 7, I examine how different modifications of individual candidacy-based plurality-majority rules, as well as combinations of these rules with proportional representation, influence party formation in the regions. I begin by providing factual information about the history of the adoption, technical characteristics, and relative spread of different electoral formulas in the regions of Russia. Then I analyze some of the findings established in comparative electoral system research and juxtapose them with Russia's political reality, which leads me to a number of theoretical expectations regarding the effects of different electoral formulas upon party formation. Findings presented in the chapter suggest that that proportional representation supports party formation not only mechanically, by excluding independents from the electoral arenas, but also, in mixed systems, by way of the interaction of their plurality-majority and proportional tiers. At the same time, each of the observable modifications of plurality-majority rules is more favorable for party formation than the dominant system, single-member plurality. I explain this phenomenon by developing a model that incorporates these systems' ability to set lower effective thresholds and to enhance the information value of party labels, thus facilitating the entry of party candidates and their electoral success. Thus it is not by accident that by 2003 single-member plurality established itself as a prevalent system in regional legislative elections.

In Chapter 8, I bring different causal factors together by developing and statistically testing a comprehensive explanatory model of party underdevelopment in the regions of Russia. The model incorporates intraelite conflicts, electoral system effects, voter preferences, and a number of control variables commonly featured in ecological analyses of Russian politics. On this basis, I proceed to discuss the prospects of inducing party formation by means of political engineering. First, I identify incentives that drive national political actors to pursue strategies aimed at accelerating party formation in the regions. These incentives, while different for the executive and for the legislature, are nevertheless sufficiently strong and mutually compatible to make them coalesce. In this connection, I examine two major innovations, party reform and regional electoral system reform. While political engineering is a persistent topic of certain strains of political research, to my knowledge there are few studies of actual cases of political engineering. From this perspective, many aspects of the interrelated party and electoral system reforms in contemporary Russia—the formation of proreform coalitions, the resistance of antireform actors, and their early attempts at adaptation to the changing institutional environments—are of primary theoretical interest. I conclude the chapter with a brief speculation on the directions that can be taken by party system development in Russia upon the implementation of reforms.

Methodology and the Data

Political parties in the regions of Russia have received relatively little scholarly attention. The initial stage of party formation in the regions has been described in a number of publications (Fish 1995; Gel'man and Senatova 1994; Golosov 1995; Luchterhandt 1998; Brown 1998), but these works are outdated simply because they deal with the preelectoral phase of the process. Indeed, the advent of full-scale electoral politics to the regions of Russia starting in the period from late 1993 to early 1994 drastically changed the environment within which political parties had existed and brought about a completely new set of incentives and counterincentives for party formation. Since that time, however, research on political parties has been largely divorced from research on Russia's regions. While political parties continued to be viewed as national political phenomena scarcely related to regional life, regional studies justly paid little attention to influences as insignificant as political parties appeared to exert (McAuley 1997; Stoner-Weiss 1997; Kirkow 1998; Treisman 1999; Gel'man, Ryzhenkov, and Brie 2000). This, in combination with the low accessibility of empirical evidence, has made regional party life almost a terra incognita of contemporary Russian studies. Even findings reported in papers focused on electoral processes in the regions normally indicated little more than that party candidates were relatively few and relatively weak (Petrov 1996; Solnick 1998). Exceptions are few. In particular, it has been demonstrated that the electoral strength of administrative and economic managers impedes party development (Slider 1996; Golosov 1997; Hughes 1997). Taking a different but still elite-centered perspective, Matsuzato (1997) related regional party development in Russia to the "split and reconfiguration of ex-Communist party factions." This theory, while being quite insightful in the sense that it indicated a possible direction of party formation under the conditions of elite persistence, is empirically irrelevant to the actual process of party formation in the regions. The work of Stoner-Weiss (2001, 2002) arrives at interesting conclusions regarding the consequences of party underdevelopment, such as the lack of political accountability of regional political elites and central government incapacity. Several findings that will be elaborated further in this analysis have been reported in my previous publications (Golosov 1997, 1999a, 2001; Gel'man and Golosov 1998).

One of the shared characteristics of the earlier research on political parties in the regions of Russia is its limited empirical reach. Some of the analyses mentioned above were based on case studies. Slider (1996), Golosov (1999a), and Stoner-Weiss (2001) have employed aggregate data on the levels of party representation attained as a result of the regional legislative elections of, respectively, December 1993 through the first half of 1994, 1995 through 1998, and 1995 through 1997. The data used by Slider, however, were less than sufficient in the sense that he used aggregates calculated by the analytical department of Russia's presidential administration (Smirniagin 1995) without having access to such essential information as the levels of representation of individual parties, not to mention the scope of electoral involvement of those parties that did not actually win seats. For certain cognitive purposes, case studies and studies relying on incomplete information are fully legitimate research strategies. However, the methodological properties of this study make it imperative to rely upon complete and rather detailed information. In general, the methodology employed here can be characterized as cross-regional analysis with a strong emphasis on quantitative comparison. From this perspective, the regions of Russia provide their students with an almost ideal research setting. On the one hand, there are as many as eighty-nine of them, which allows for using standard statistical techniques such as bivariate analysis and multiple ordinary least squares (OLS) regression. On the other hand, being located in the same country during a limited time span, they have numerous shared characteristics, which allows for a drastic reduction in the number of independent variables that have to be entered into analysis.

One of the advantages of cross-regional comparisons is that there is no need to invest much effort into the "conceptual homogenization of the field" (Dogan and Pelassy 1990)—that is, into replacing proper names of the phenomena under observation with concepts of general validity. However, a certain amount of clarification remains indispensable. I understand "regions of Russia" to mean the eighty-nine constitutional units of the Russian Federation.[2] I understand "party candidates" and "party deputies" to mean those candidates and deputies who are nominated by parties. Empirically, this notion is restrictive. A wider notion would have included a rather miscellaneous set of options. For instance, there are cases when individual party leaders publicly express their support to individual candidates. Such cases can be disregarded because, normally, such endorsements are motivated solely by the party's desire to increase its own visibility in the electoral arena, and they add little if anything to the candidates' electoral success. In other cases, however, the association between parties and party-supported candidates may be stronger. An important form of party affiliation rather widely employed in the regions of Russia, often as a consciously chosen alternative to nomination, is stating party affiliation on the ballot paper. A technical problem is that such a provision became widespread only by the middle of the second electoral cycle, and even if it existed continuously, the official sources rarely reported relevant information. A substantive consideration that made me exclude this form of stated party affiliation from my analysis is that unlike party nomination, parties themselves do not control it. There are instances when candidates who actually compete against preferred party nominees state that they are party members too in order to increase their electoral appeal and to split their rivals' electorates. In Russia, political parties are generally not in position to prevent it. Indeed, to receive a party card in order to show it to the members of the regional electoral commission is easy for any candidate, while to oust this candidate from the party and make the electoral commission change the ballot paper is a difficult and time-consuming procedure often involving the courts. For a study focused on party formation, not individual candidates' strategies, party nomination appears to be the only appropriate grounds for distinguishing between party candidates and independents. Correspondingly, I understand "independents" to mean all candidates who secure nominations in different ways.

One more instrumental concept that has to be introduced at this moment is that of electoral cycles. I employ it to reflect the temporal sequences of different-level elections, and to do so in a way that allows for identifying different stages of party formation. While the first task could be fulfilled by taking any national elections as dividing points, with the overwhelming political importance of presidential elections suggesting them as most likely candidates for this role, the second task requires taking into account additional considerations. As demonstrated in Chapter 2, political parties are not important actors in Russia's national presidential elections, but they have managed to assume a rather salient role in national legislative races. Moreover, the fortunes of individual parties, including the prospects for territorial penetration, crucially depend on the numbers of seats they manage to win in the lower chamber of the national legislature, the Duma. Thus the natural dividing points in a study of party formation in Russia are actually the Duma elections of 1993, 1995, and 1999. Furthermore, it has to be taken into account that not only electoral returns as such but also the conduct of national legislative campaigns influenced the political life of the regions in a variety of profound ways. In particular, new entrants into the national political arena were naturally motivated to participate in regional electoral campaigns that were held concurrently with the national ones. For this reason, I locate the starting point of any given electoral cycle not in December, when national legislative elections actually took place, but in August, when the corresponding electoral campaigns actually started. Thus the first electoral cycle embraces the period of August 1993 to July 1995, the second from August 1995 to July 1999, and the third from August 1999 to July 2003. A detailed chronology of regional elections by cycle and year is provided in Chapter 3. Here, it is sufficient to say that holding different types of elections concurrently is not a very widespread practice in Russia's regions, and that the most commonly met sequence within the second and third electoral cycles was thus: national legislative elections, national executive elections, regional executive elections, and regional legislative elections. At the same time, the number of regions that in one way or another deviate from this sequence is quite substantial. The first electoral cycle is unusual not only in the sense that it was very brief but also because it did not involve executive elections in Russia as a whole and in the vast majority of regions.

The notion of electoral cycles is essential for the temporal organization of data presentation and analysis. It would be simply impossible to examine party formation without tracing the dynamics of the process. Meanwhile, none of the previously published studies on the subject were based upon a set of systematically organized diachronic evidence. The technical reason for this narrowness of empirical focus is clear, but it concerns not so much methodology as the availability of the empirical evidence. This brings me to a final topic, data sources. To start with, the Central Electoral Commission of Russia has never officially published any data on the 1993–1994 regional legislative elections, even though these data were accumulated in Moscow and the commission did occasionally release them to organizations as influential as Russia's presidential administration, which explains the origin of the aggregates published by Slider (1996). For other audiences, however, these data were largely unavailable because they remained dispersed in the regional sources, mostly in the official newspapers published by regional authorities. This led me to undertake an extensive library search focused primarily on the regional printed media.[3] The most important data derived from the regional newspapers were the lists of candidates by electoral district. Normally published two or three weeks prior to elections, they contained the names of candidates, their birth dates, and their professional occupations. The form of nomination was mentioned in the majority of regions but not in all of them, and party membership was mentioned only in a few cases. Sometimes, the lack of the data on the form of nomination made it imperative to examine all the issues of the given newspaper that came to print in the course of a month or two before the elections, and such an examination was also useful for identifying political stances taken by some of the regional parties. Of course, official electoral returns provided the second piece of essential information for each of the regions under examination. Some of the regions published district-level electoral returns. In the majority of regions, however, regional electoral authorities provided only the lists of winners. Information about the basic characteristics of electoral systems such as formulaic structures was easily retrievable from the lists of candidates and other sources.

In 1997 the Central Electoral Commission of Russia started to make the results of regional elections available to a wide audience by publishing volumes of regional electoral statistics. As of mid-2003, three such volumes had been published. They cover the gubernatorial elections held from 1995 to the first half of 1997,[4] the legislative elections held from 1995 to 1997,[5] and both kinds of elections held from the second half of 1997 to the end of 2000.[6] In addition, the Central Electoral Commission copublished with a commercial think tank, the Mercator Group, a compact disc on the 1991–1998 elections.[7] While the contents of the CD largely coincide with the books mentioned above, they contain certain useful additions too. The publications of the Central Electoral Commission are very valuable sources. In particular, they invariably present information about the forms of nomination embarked upon by the successful candidates, even if such information is not retrievable from the regional sources.[8] Speaking of the executive elections, these publications contain all information necessary and sufficient for statistical analysis: candidate lists, the lists of winners, and detailed electoral returns. Speaking of the legislative elections, there are more omissions due to the more complex nature of the data. On the one hand, the staff of the Central Electoral Commission produced very useful data on the numbers of parties that contested individual elections, the numbers of party candidates in each of them, and the numbers of party nominees among the winners. It also published very useful data on the composition of electoral blocs. On the other hand, the numbers of candidates nominated by each of the parties and even the names of these parties could be only retrieved from the chapters on individual regions prepared by the regional electoral commissions on the request of the central body. While it does seem that the regional election organizers did have a sort of questionnaire that allowed for presenting the data in relatively uniform ways, the quality of the regional information varies tremendously. While it invariably contains the lists of winners with their forms of nomination, information about the role of parties in candidate nomination ranges from quite comprehensive to absent. In addition, the publications of the Central Electoral Commission do not contain district-level results of regional legislative elections, even though they do indicate the percentage shares of the vote received by the winners.

The continuous presence of the Central Electoral Commission of Russia on the Internet provides an additional source of valuable information. The first official site of Russia's electoral authorities, that of the Federal Center for Informatization (FCI), started to function in 1998.[9] For a long time, while containing quite comprehensive information about regional executive elections, it was of little utility for the study of legislative elections. This situation changed in March 2002 after the Central Electoral Commission opened its own site, which took over much of the functions previously performed by the FCI site.[10] At the same time, the site of the FCI was charged with performing a number of new functions, one of which was publishing the lists of candidates in all regional elections, detailed returns of the executive elections, and partial returns of the legislative elections (normally, the shares of the vote received by the winners and second-runners). This drastically improved the state of accessible information on regional elections. Still, detailed district-level results of regional legislative elections remain retrievable only from regional sources. In this respect, the spread of the Internet in the regions was of great help too. Regional Internet sites that provide information about elections can be broadly divided into four categories: the official sites of regional electoral commissions, the official sites of regional administrations (and much more rarely, regional legislatures), the sites of the regional newspapers, and unofficial electoral sites.[11] Despite the apparent difference between the statuses of the official and unofficial Internet publications, for the principal kind of information of interest to me, candidate lists, this difference is insignificant. Candidate lists, if published at all, are invariably published in a standard form determined by the regional law. The same applies to district-level electoral returns. The obvious and inherent shortcoming of the Internet sources is that they do not stay for long. Electoral databases are massive, and few hosts can afford to maintain pages containing them for more time than they are perceived to be practically relevant. Even the FCI maintains complete candidate lists for approximately one month prior to elections and then replaces them with the lists of the winners. Regional sources tend to be short-lived too. Even if the Internet site remains, pages containing relevant information may pass away. However, given that they are often exclusive sources on regional elections, and that information provided by them is sometimes as rich in detail as the collected biographies of all individual candidates, it would be scarcely affordable to ignore them. Also, an obvious advantage of the Internet publications for the purposes of quantitative analysis is that the data come in computer-readable form.

While the publications described above provided a bulk of information used in this study, I also employed the materials collected and analyzed by several individual scholars and think tanks. First, I made an extensive use of the publications of the Moscow Carnegie Center and, prima facie, of the voluminous handbook on regional politics covering the period 1989–1997 (McFaul and Petrov 1998). For the narrow purposes of my analysis, the data presented in the handbook are often less than sufficient not only because the depth and accuracy of coverage of individual regions varies, which is only natural for a publication of such scope, but also because many of the distinctions that are important for my study, such as between party support and party nomination, are irrelevant from the point of view of the authors. Still, McFaul and Petrov's work provided me with a lot of information irretrievable from elsewhere, and with a lot of explanatory insight in the process. A Moscow political scientist, Yurii Abramov, placed on the Internet a source of similarly wide scope in the course of the 1999 national legislative campaign.[12] A very important piece of information on the 1997 legislative elections in twenty-two regions of Russia has been published on the Internet by a Moscow-based think tank, Panorama.[13] While the quality of entries on individual regions varies, some of them contain very detailed information, including candidate lists and district-level returns. Judging from the specific form of data presentation, they have been derived from the local official publications. A very important source of information on the 1997–1998 regional legislative elections has been produced by another Moscow-based think tank, the Institute for the Humanities and Political Studies (IGPI). The regional experts of the institute were undoubtedly well-informed and objective insiders who had complete access to the official publications of the regional electoral commissions. The publications of the IGPI contain not only detailed factual information, sometimes including candidate lists and district-level returns, but also valuable analyses of the electoral processes in the regions.[14] Finally, local political scientists or observers provided me with official information on some of the regional legislative elections.[15]

Thus the scope of sources from which I derived information for statistical analysis is fairly wide. Since data collection involved a lot of cross-checking,[16] in this book I avoid references to the individual sources described above. In particular, I do not cite sources for tables containing aggregate information or statistical analysis results. While fully realizing that such omissions are less than desirable from the point of view of the standards of scholarship, I also understand that full exposition of sources for each of the tables would have increased the length of the book. My qualitative analysis heavily relies on factual information and empirical generalizations derived from a wide range of national and regional journalistic and scholarly sources. These sources are properly cited in the endnotes.[17] In addition, my analysis involved not only electoral data from the regions but also the data on national electoral returns and socioeconomic statistics. The data of the former category have been derived from the official publications of the Central Electoral Commission.[18] The 1993 national legislative elections are exceptional in the sense that comprehensive information on them cannot be derived from a single printed source, even though it can be compiled from a number of official publications.[19] In particular, the number of invalid ballots was revealed well after the elections.[20] The source of socioeconomic statistics is a publication of the State Statistics Committee of Russia.[21]

*   *   *

The major conclusions arrived at in this book are thus. The underdevelopment of political parties in Russia, while caused by a number of important nation-level political and institutional factors, has an additional important source in region-level obstacles to party formation. Political parties do have incentives to penetrate the peripheries in the country, and they are generally capable of recruiting the regional cadres of activists to participate in their territorial penetration efforts. These cadres, however, tend not to belong to the administrative and economic managerial elites of the regions, which explains the lack of credible party-affiliated candidates in regional elections. The vast resources of the regional elites, both inherited from the Soviet past and acquired in the process of transformation, allowed them to monopolize the electoral arenas of the regions without making use of party labels and other party-related resources. Instead, they rely upon the advantages of political and social incumbency as manifested in institutional affiliations and occupational statuses, and make use of their material resources to engage commercial political consulting as an alternative to political parties. The regional elites also succeeded in developing nonparty mechanisms that allow for the political control of the executives over the legislatures and, simultaneously, for relative legislative autonomy. At the same time, few of the regional electoral systems are permissive enough to support party-nominated candidates. Under these conditions, political parties do not form not so much because their formation confronts resistance, even though such cases can be registered, but rather because they are not in demand. Hence the conscious attempt of the federal authorities to restructure Russia's regional politics by means of political engineering.

Notes

1. Studies of the formation of individual parties focused on organizational structures and incentives are not rare (see, for instance, Hopkin 1999). However, I believe that organizational development arrives only after systemic incentives for party building are in place.

2. The complex official taxonomy of Russia's regions, including republics *(respubliki)*, territories *(kraia)*, provinces *(oblasti)*, federal cities *(goroda federal'nogo znachenia)*, the autonomous province *(avtonomnaia oblast)*, and autonomous districts *(avtonomnye okruga)*, are briefly discussed in Chapter 3. Here, it is important to mention that while it is gradually becoming conventional to use the Russian denominations of the types of regions, or some of them at least, such as *kraia* and *oblasti,* I prefer to use English wording for the sake of smoother narration. With several exceptions (Moscow city, Moscow province, St. Petersburg, North Ossetia, and the Jewish autonomous province), the proper names of the regions used in this study are based on the transliterated Russian spellings of the names of their capitals (for the majority of territories and provinces), "titular nationalities" (for all republics and the majority of autonomous districts), or geographic locations from which their official Russian names are derived (such as Amur,

Kamchatka, and Taimyr). Throughout the book, I use the transliteration system of the Library of Congress with the following minor modifications: I write *ya, yu* rather than *ia, iu* at the beginning of words; I write *ia* rather than *iia* at the end of words; I omit the soft and hard signs at the end of words; and I use the conventional spellings of the following terms and personal surnames: Chechnya, Yeltsin, Zhirinovsky, and Yavlinsky.

3. The regional newspapers studied are: *Amurskaia pravda* (Blagoveshchensk), October 1994; *Belgorodskaia pravda* (Belgorod), March 1994; *Birobidzhanskaia zvezda* (Birobidzhan), February–March 1994; *Brianskie izvestia* (Briansk), March–April 1994; *Cheliabinskii rabochii* (Cheliabinsk), April–May 1994; *Kaliningradskaia pravda* (Kaliningrad), March–April 1994; *Kamchatskaia pravda* (Petropavlovsk-Kamchatskii), March 1994; *Kirovskaia pravda* (Kirov), February–March 1994; *Krasnoe znamia* (Tomsk), March 1994; *Krasnoiarskii rabochii* (Krasnoiarsk), March 1994; *Krasnyi sever* (Vologda), March 1994; *Kurskaia pravda* (Kursk), March 1994; *Magadanskaia pravda* (Magadan), March–April 1994; *Mariiskaia pravda* (Ioshkar-Ola), November–December 1993; *Novgorodskie vedomosti* (Novgorod), March 1994; *Omskaia pravda* (Omsk), March 1994; *Orlovskaia pravda* (Orel), February–March 1994; *Penzenskaia pravda* (Penza), January–February 1994; *Pravda severa* (Arkhangel'sk), November–December 1994; *Podmoskovnye izvestia* (Moscow), December 1993; *Poliarnaia pravda* (Murmansk), March 1994; *Priokskaia gazeta* (Riazan), March–April 1994; *Prizyv* (Vladimir), March 1994; *Pskovskaia pravda* (Pskov), January 1994; *Rabochii krai* (Ivanovo), March 1994; *Rabochii put* (Smolensk), February–March 1994; *Respublika Sakha* (Yakutsk), December 1993; *Severnaia pravda* (Kostroma), February–March 1994; *Severnyi krai* (Yaroslavl), February–March 1994; *Sovetskaia Chuvashia* (Cheboksary), February–March 1994; *Sovetskii Sakhalin* (Yuzhno-Sakhalinsk), March–April 1994; *Sovetskoe Zaural'e* (Kurgan), March 1994; *Stavropol'skaia pravda* (Stavropol), March 1994; *Tambovskaia zhizn* (Tambov), March–April 1994; *Tul'skie izvestia* (Tula), November–December 1994; *Tuvinskaia pravda* (Kyzyl), November–December 1993; *Tverskaia zhizn* (Tver), March 1994; *Ural'skii rabochii* (Ekaterinburg), March–April 1994; *Utro Rossii* (Vladivostok), October 1994; *Volga* (Astrakhan), February–March 1994; *Volgogradskaia pravda* (Volgograd), November–December 1993; *Volzhskaia kommuna* (Samara), March 1994; *Vostochno-sibirskaia pravda* (Irkutsk), March–April 1994; *Yuzhnyi Ural* (Cheliabinsk), March 1994; *Zabaikal'skii rabochii* (Chita), March 1994; and *Zvezda* (Perm), March 1994. I only rarely relied on the regional printed media for information on elections that took place in 1995 and thereafter. Notable exceptions include the lists of candidates derived from *Sovetskaia Adygeia* (Maikop), November 11, 1995; *Brianskoe vremia* (Briansk), December 5, 2000; *Volga* (Astrakhan), October 12, 2001; and *Severnyi kur'er* (Petrozavodsk), April 30, 1998; and electoral returns published in *Tverskie vedomosti* (Tver), December 21, 2001. After trying a variety of sources including the publications of the Central Electoral Commission of Russia, I found that adequate information about the 1998 elections in Tyva could be only retrieved from *Tuvinskaia pravda* (Kyzyl), March–April 1998. Of other regional printed sources used in this study, I would like to mention a uniquely comprehensive publication of the electoral commission of Tambov province, *Vestnik Tambovskoi oblastnoi izbiratel'noi komissii* no. 2 (14), 2001, and three research monographs, Sungurov (1996), Tsygankov (1998), and Liubarev (2001).

4. *Vybory glav ispolnitel'noi vlasti sub"ektov Rossiiskoi Federatsii, 1995–1997: Elektoral'naia statistika* (Moscow: Ves Mir, 1997).

5. *Vybory v zakonodatel'nye (predstavitel'nye) organy gosudarstvennoi vlasti sub"ektov Rossiiskoi Federatsii, 1995–1997: Elektoral'naia statistika* (Moscow: Ves Mir, 1998).

6. *Vybory v organy gosudarstvennoi vlasti sub"ektov Rossiiskoi Federatsii, 1997–2000: Elektoral'naia statistika,* 2 vols. (Moscow: Ves Mir, 2001).

7. *Vybory v Rossiiskoi Federatsii, 1991–98: Elektoral'nyi spravochnik dlia monitoringa, analiza i prognoza* (Moscow: Federal'nyi tsentr informatizatsii and Mercator Group, 1999), compact disc.

8. For instance, after investing a lot of effort into trying to fulfill my request to find out what parties nominated their candidates in the 1995 legislative elections in Komi, a local political scientist, Viktor Kovalev, came to the conclusion that such information was never aggregated on the regional level, while the documents on which such an aggregation could be performed were most probably destroyed soon after the elections. The Central Electoral Commission, however, published the list of winners that indicated their forms of nomination.

9. www.fci.ru.

10. www.cikrf.ru.

11. The regional Internet sources employed in my study, by region, are: Adygeia, www.golos.maykop.ru; Altai Republic, www.altai-republic.com/media/official_news_rus_2.htm; Altai territory, altaipress.altai.ru/kurs/negr/00_03_22_03.shtml; Amur, elect28.amur.ru:980; Arkhangelsk, www.foris.ru/vibori/viboff.htm, www.dvinaland.ru/russian/vedomstwa/izbirkom; Bashkortostan, www.bashinform.ru/resultat.html; Belgorod, izbirkom.bel.ru; Buriatia, electoral.buryatia.ru; Cheliabinsk, www.uralexpert.ru/analyt/anpolz.htm; Chuvashia, www.gs.chuvashia.net; Irkutsk, www.admirk.ru/vib_zs.htm; Ivanovo, izbirkom.indi.ru; Kamchatka, ritm.kamchatka.ru/choise; Karelia, www.elect.karelia.ru; Khanty-Mansi, www.hmao.wsnet.ru/power/izcom; Komi, www.rkomi.ru/izbirkom; Koriak, www.palana.ru/documents/election2000/dum2000–04.asp; Krasnodar, nair.kuban.ru/election, zsk-kuban.ru, krasnodar.cikrf.ru; Krasnoiarsk, vybor.24rus.ru; Kurgan, ikko.nm.ru; Leningrad, lenobl.ru/parliament10; Magadan, www.obl_izbirkom.magadan.ru/files/map33.htm, www.kolyma.ru; Moscow, mik.mos.ru, show.mgik.mos.ru; Murmansk, www.ikmo.ru; Nenets, nao2000.narod.ru/vibor.htm; Nizhnii Novgorod, www.s52.fci.ru; Novosibirsk, www.sibforum.ru/vibor, www.adm.nso.ru/election; Orenburg, www.elect.orb.ru; Perm, elect.perm.ru; Primorskii, www.primorsky.ru/prim/izbirkom; Pskov, www.pskov.ru/izbirkom; Rostov, www.ikro.aaanet.ru; Sakha, www.ykt.ru/izbirkom; Samara, www.adm.samara.ru, gas.samtel.ru/2001, election.samara.ru; Saratov, www.sarvest.ru/show_article.phtml?id=8119&psid=13&dat=, www.ikso.saratov.gov.ru; Smolensk, province.smolensk.ru; St. Petersburg, www.elections.spb.ru, www.election.spb.ru, www.spbik.spb.ru; Stavropol, www.vibor.stavropolie.ru; Sverdlovsk, www.e-reliz.ru/govern, www.midural.ru/izbircom, www.rossel.ru/Rus/election/ppzs.htm; Tambov, izbirkom.tmb.ru; Tatarstan, izbircom.bancorp.ru; Tiumen, www.t-l.ru/digest.shtml?themesfolders/elections/candidates_info/index2.htm; Tomsk, elect70.tomsk.ru; Tver, netra.fci.ru/~iksrf69; Udmurtia, www.udmurt.ru/cgi-bin/udm.pl?id=4; Ul'ianovsk, ck.ul.ru/rga1999/nov/simk_183_11.shtml; Vladimir, www.vladobladm.vtsnet.ru/izbircom/2000/v_dzs/index.shtml, avo.ru/izbircom; Vologda, www.vologda.ru/~izbircom; Voronezh, www.ikvo.vrn.ru; and Yaroslavl, citizen-y.chat.ru/d_itogi2000.htm, www.yar.fci.ru.

12. socarchive.narod.ru.

13. www.panorama.ru.

14. In this analysis I used the following publications of IGPI (*PM* stands for *Politicheskii monitoring*): S. Akkieva, Kabardino-Balkarskaia Respublika v dekabre 1997 g., *PM*, 1997, no. 12; T. Barandova, Vybory Sobrania deputatov Arkhangel'skoi oblasti vtorogo sozyva, 1996–1998 gg., *PM*, 1998, no. 3; T. Drabkina, Vybory deputatov Zakonodatel'nogo sobrania Leningradskoi oblasti vtorogo sozyva, 14 dekabria 1997 g., *PM*, 1998, no. 3; M. Evdokimov, Vybory deputatov Smolenskoi oblastnoi dumy vtorogo sozyva, 21 dekabria 1997 g., *PM*, 1998, no. 3; D. Faritov, Vybory deputatov Saratovskoi oblastnoi dumy vtorogo sozyva, 31 avgusta 1997 g., *PM*, 1998, no. 3; D. Faritov, Saratovskaia oblast v avguste 1997 g., *PM*, 1997, no. 8; A. Gandeev, Vybory deputatov Astrakhanskogo oblastnogo pred stavitel'nogo sobrania vtorogo sozyva, 26 oktiabria 1997 g., *PM*, 1998, no. 3; S. Glushkov, Vybory deputatov Zakonodatel'nogo sobrania Tverskoi oblasti vtorogo sozyva, 14 dekabria 1997 g., *PM*, 1998, no. 6; E. Kislova, Respublika Buriatia v iiule 1998 g., *PM*, 1998, no. 7; E. Lapshova, Vybory deputatov Samarskoi gubern skoi dumy vtorogo sozyva, 7 dekabria 1997 g., *PM*, 1998, no. 3; R. Pyrma, Vybory deputatov Belgorodskoi oblastnoi dumy vtorogo sozyva, 12 oktiabria 1997 g., *PM*, 1998, no. 5; N. Raspopov, Vybory deputatov Zakonodatel'nogo sobrania Nizhegorodskoi oblasti vtorogo sozyva, 29 marta 1998 g., *PM*, 1998, no. 3; V. Rukhliadev, Vybory deputatov Novosibirskogo oblastnogo soveta vtorogo sozyva, 21 dekabria 1997 g., *PM*, 1998, no. 3; V. Rukhliadev, Vybory deputatov Gosudarstvennoi dumy Tomskoi oblasti vtorogo sozyva, 21 dekabria 1997 g., *PM*, 1998, no. 3; O. Senatova and A. Yakurin, Vybory deputatov Novgorodskoi oblastnoi dumy vtorogo sozyva, 19 oktiabria 1997 g., *PM*, 1998, no. 3; V. Slatinov, Vybory deputatov Oblastnogo soveta Orlovskoi oblasti vtorogo sozyva, 22 marta 1998 g., *PM*, 1998, no. 6; G. Titov, Vybory deputatov Zakonodatel'nogo sobrania Penzenskoi oblasti vtorogo sozyva, 7 dekabria 1997 g., *PM*, 1998, no. 3; P. Tkachev, Vybory deputatov Kurskoi oblastnoi dumy vtorogo sozyva, 29 iiunia 1997 g., *PM*, 1998, no. 3; A. Tsepilov, Vybory deputatov Zakonodatel'nogo sobrania Omskoi oblasti vtorogo sozyva, 22 marta 1998 g., *PM*, 1998, no. 3; V. I., Vybory deputatov Zakonodatel'nogo sobrania Rostovskoi oblasti vtorogo sozyva, 29 marta 1998 g., *PM*, 1998, no. 3; V. K., Vybory v Komi, *PM*, 1998, no. 3; V. Vagin and V. Okhota, Vybory deputatov Pskovskogo oblastnogo sobrania vtorogo sozyva, 29 marta 1998 g., *PM*, 1998, no. 3; S. Vladimirov, Vybory deputatov Riazanskoi oblastnoi dumy vtorogo sozyva, 30 marta 1997 g., *PM*, 1998, no. 3; A. Vul'fovich, Tiumenskaia oblast: godovshchina vyborov gubernatora i vybory oblastnoi dumy, *PM*, 1998, no. 2; V. Zhelezniak, Lipetskaia oblast v mae 1998 g., *PM*, 1998, no. 5; and M. Zherebiat'ev, Vybory deputatov Voronezhskoi oblastnoi dumy vtorogo sozy va i munitsipal'nogo soveta Voronezha, 23 marta 1997 g., *PM*, 1998, no. 3.

15. Rustam Bikmetov on the 1999 elections in Ul'ianovsk province, and Vladimir Avdonin, Natalia Mel'nikova, Dmitrii Sel'tser, and Vladimir Nechaev on the 2001 elections in Riazan, Kirov, Tambov, and Kursk provinces, respectively.

16. In fact, my cross-checking revealed that while none of these sources or groups of sources contained comprehensive and entirely accurate information, their combination produces a highly reliable data set on regional elections.

17. When making references to newspapers, I do not indicate the place of publication for two categories. First, I always omit Moscow as the place of publication. Second, for newspapers published elsewhere, I omit the place of publication only if it is stated in the name of the newspaper in the unchanged grammatical form. For example, I write *Saratovskie vesti* (Saratov) but *Vechernii Saratov.*

18. *Vybory deputatov Gosudarstvennoi Dumy Federal'nogo Sobrania Rossiiskoi Federatsii, 1999: Elektoral'naia statistika* (Moscow: Ves Mir, 2000);

Vybory Prezidenta Rossiiskoi Federatsii, 2000: Elektoral'naia statistika (Moscow: Ves Mir, 2000); *Dopolnitel'nye vybory i zameshchenie vakantnykh mandatov deputatov Gosudarstvennoi Dumy Federal'nogo Sobrania Rossiiskoi Federatsii, 1996–1998: Elektoral'naia statistika* (Moscow: Ves Mir, 1999); *Vybory Prezidenta Rossiiskoi Federatsii, 1996: Elektoral'naia statistika* (Moscow: Ves Mir, 1996); and *Vybory deputatov Gosudarstvennoi Dumy Federal'nogo Sobrania Rossiiskoi Federatsii, 1995: Elektoral'naia statistika* (Moscow: Ves Mir, 1996).

19. *Rossiiskaia gazeta,* November 11, 1993; *Rossiiskaia gazeta,* December 28, 1993; and *Biulleten Tsentral'noi Izbiratel'noi Komissii Rossiiskoi Federatsii* no. 1 (12), 1994.

20. Grigorii Belonuchkin, www.cityline.ru/politika/fs/gd1rezv.html.

21. *Regiony Rossii* (Moscow: GKS RF, 1997).

2

National Political Parties in Russia

This chapter provides basic factual information about Russia's political parties within the context of national political developments. Primary attention is paid to those parties that managed to penetrate the peripheries of the country, thus assuming certain levels of importance in the regional political arenas. In this chapter, however, their activities in the regions will not be discussed at length. Detailed information about many other parties that contested national elections in 1993–1995 can be found elsewhere (Korguniuk and Zaslavskii 1996; Golosov 1999b). Proceeding from the assumption that "the characteristics of a party's origin are in fact capable of exerting a weight on its organizational structure even decades later" (Panebianco 1988: 50), the first section of the chapter examines the origins of Russia's political parties in the period when they were not able to participate in elections. The second section describes individual political parties that were active in Russia in 1993–2003. The third section illuminates the systemic properties of party competition in Russia by placing them into a wider comparative perspective.

The Preelectoral Period of Party Formation

Up to 1990, fully independent political associations could not exist in the Soviet Union. During the summer and fall of 1986, Mikhail Gorbachev broke sharply with the policies pursued earlier and initiated his new strategy, perestroika. One of the important steps in implementing this strategy was to support the growth and spread of informal groups. By this, Gorbachev apparently sought to create a nonparty support base for his reformist agenda, which would enhance his positions vis-à-vis powerful competitors in the Communist Party leadership. Some of the informal groups became politically active as early as 1987 (*Neformal'naia Rossia* 1990; Sedaitis and Butterfield 1991), while others gradually shifted from nonpolitical activities to full-scale political engagement (Urban and Gel'man 1997). In his public rhetoric, Gorbachev initially presented himself as a neo-Leninist who wanted to update and modernize the system but at the same time wanted to keep it indisputably socialist, in vigorous competition with the West (Dunlop 1993). By the end of 1988, however, neo-Leninism as the ideological basis of the informal movement had been almost totally replaced with a different variety of political discourse that can be dubbed the "mainstream democratic ideology." Narrative expositions of this ideology may be found in the programs of several parties that emerged from the informal movement (Koval 1991). For the sake of brevity, it might be quite illuminating to cite a Moscow journalist who, when asked about his political goals, referred to the necessity of building a normal society, "one founded on human rights, civil liberties and granting to people of economic freedom" (Kullberg 1994: 941). This formulation revealed the core element of the mainstream democratic ideology: it was imbued with references to the central tenets of Western liberal philosophy, such as the universality of fundamental human rights, with the West itself representing the way in which these rights had to be protected. Soviet communism, in contrast, had been viewed as an abnormal, totalitarian system.

Many students of these processes notice that ideologically, the emerging parties were practically indistinguishable from one another (Urban 1991). This is quite understandable, taking into account that the mainstream democratic ideology defined their identity sets in a basically uniform way. Why, then, did several—not just one—democratic parties emerge? Unfortunately, the survey data and other firm evidence that could clarify this problem are scarce. The available data, however, unambiguously point at the fact that, being defined by their rejection of the Soviet order, the informal groups viewed the intensity of this rejection as a major basis for party building (Fish 1995: 88–93). For this end, it apparently did not matter to what extent potential political partners distanced themselves from the regime in their public rhetoric. Commitment to the mainstream democratic ideology could be safely taken for granted. What really mattered was the intensity of antiregime attitudes as expressed in the life trajectories of the members of the groups. From this perspective, the informal movement fell into two distinctive categories. On the one hand, there were those who during the informal phase of their political careers retained membership in the Communist Party of the Soviet Union (KPSS), thus not breaking completely with the past. This group of the informals formed a network of party discussion clubs, which transformed itself into the Democratic Platform within the KPSS and eventually, into the Republican Party of the Russian Federation (RPRF). On the other hand, many informals never joined the KPSS, or left it long before it was safe to do so, thus displaying a perceivably stronger commitment to the cause of democracy. These people formed the basis of the Social Democratic Party of Russia (SDPR) (Pribylovskii 1992; Sungurov 1994). The union between the RPRF and the

SDPR, widely advocated by some of the leaders of both parties, never materialized.

Despite its label, which was somehow reminiscent of socialism, the SDPR—at least initially—was in no means a socialist party. When the party was still in embryo (1988), the very idea of creating an alternative party was generally considered to be adventurously dangerous, with the very term "social democracy" being employed as a relatively safe umbrella. In February 1989 a number of informal groups throughout Russia created the Social Democratic Confederation. When in May 1990 this entity was transformed into the SDPR, it maintained the name as a tribute to its own tradition but failed to include anything meaningfully reminiscent of socialism into its program.[1] In fact, the party explicitly committed itself to "social partnership" and to the creation of a "new middle class" in Russia. The prehistory of the RPRF took less time. It was only in June 1990 that the Democratic Platform within the KPSS decided to split off from the party; in November the RPRF was officially established and adopted a program quite similar to that of the SDPR. Many informal groups joined neither the SDPR nor the RPRF but preferred to operate on their own instead. Such groups were often referred to as "sofa parties"—those whose whole membership could comfortably sit on a single sofa.

From 1987 through early 1989 the informals remained a dominant form of independent political activism in Russia. This situation started to change with the arrival of electoral politics. The March 1989 elections to the Congress of People's Deputies of the Soviet Union were held in the country where only one political party, the KPSS, was officially recognized, and under a system that allowed the noncompetitive allocation of a significant share of seats (Brovkin 1990). By holding these elections, Gorbachev further strengthened his position vis-à-vis the party apparatus (Sakwa 1990: 18–19). At the same time, the 1989 elections dramatically increased the scope of opportunities available to independent political actors, even though it is clear that in 1989 the new structure of opportunities was in its very initial phase. Independent associations did not even have the right to nominate candidates for office (Urban 1990: 37–43). The vast majority of the candidates, including the democratic ones, ran under the KPSS label. Some of them, however, were actively supported by the informals. All over the country, a plenitude of voter clubs and citizen committees were organized to promote the democrats striving for the congressional mandates. In Moscow and Leningrad, these efforts resulted in a number of impressive victories by democrats (Kiernan and Aistrup 1991). This led to two important organizational developments. Within the newly elected body, the democrats created their own faction, the Interregional Deputies Group. The first meeting of the group took place in June 1989. On the grassroots level, voters clubs and electoral support teams united to form a nationwide electoral alliance, Democratic Russia, directly connected with the Interregional Group (Brudny 1993).

The March 1990 elections to the Congress of People's Deputies of the Russian Federation further increased the incentives for independent political activism. This time, there was no noncompetitive seat allocation at all, while the level of competitiveness increased along with the visibility of major ideological tendencies. Democratic Russia emerged as the major challenger to the candidates supported by the KPSS. The elections were generally successful for the democrats, especially in large cities (Remington 1994). As a result, the representative of the democrats, Boris Yeltsin, was elected as the chairman of the congress.[2] This, however, did not lead Democratic Russia to organizational consolidation. In fact, the alliance effectively ceased to exist after the elections. Voters clubs and citizens committees, as well as the informal movement as a whole, did help a sufficient number of candidates to win elections. Many of the elected deputies, however, had little reason to view the support of such groups as a crucial factor of their success. Individual efforts, popularity, and media exposure were generally more important. The very fact of electoral success further increased the winners' independence from their support teams. Even the leaders of informal groups who gained election to legislative bodies acted without responsibility toward their organizations, and contributed little if any effort to sustain these groups (Fish 1995: 134). Instead, they preferred to accommodate to their new institutional environments. This included the creation of parliamentary factions. While in the Union Congress, the Interregional Group for a long time remained the only faction, the Russian Congress was better structured along partisan lines (Remington et al. 1994). These lines, however, did not have their continuation in the emerging extraparliamentary organizations. Those deputies who were supported by Democratic Russia during their campaigns created several factions, including Communists for Democracy, and others.

The real meaning of the 1989–1990 campaigns for party formation in Russia was that this experience had made a lot of individuals who contemplated launching political careers aware of the new structure of opportunities. Lacking either personal popularity or access to the media, these people sought alternative vehicles of promotion. At the same time, some of the members of the new political class that emerged within the new legislatures sought to strengthen their power bases by means of party building (Golosov 1998). As a result, the idea of creating a mass democratic party, capable of removing the KPSS from power, soon gained popularity. An ardent proponent of this idea, Nikolai Travkin, launched the Democratic Party of Russia (DPR) in May 1990. Travkin held that to fight an effective trench war against the KPSS, his party had to be organized along similar lines, with a single leader and strict discipline exercised over the activities of its members.[3] After a brief period of associating itself with the independent workers movement, DPR accepted the mainstream democratic ideology. It is worth mentioning that the first three parties officially registered by Russia's Ministry of Justice in 1991 were the DPR, the RPRF, and the SDPR.[4]

The party-building efforts of Travkin were viewed not entirely favorably by those democratic leaders, especially among the elected people's deputies, who started to feel themselves unexpectedly deprived of any access to the channels of political mobilization. Lacking organizational bases of their own but enjoying instead enormous personal popularity, they sincerely feared the emergence of what had been referred to as a populist dictatorship within the democratic movement (Brudny 1993). In order to counterbalance this perceived danger, the Moscow and Leningrad democrats initiated the formation of a new political movement, once again labeled Democratic Russia. In contrast to the DPR, the organizational structure of Democratic Russia was designed as a loose coalition of democratic parties, groups, and individuals, directed by several cochairs and not imposing any kind of discipline over its participants. Obviously, such an organizational basis was quite acceptable for earlier democratic formations, and indeed the SDPR and the RPRF provided Democratic Russia with many local branches. For the DPR, however, the emergence of Democratic Russia posed a formidable challenge.[5] Not surprisingly the debate between Travkin and his opponents in the organizing committee of Democratic Russia resulted in his withdrawal from the movement. Travkin's position, however, was strongly resisted by the largest local branches of the DPR. Under these conditions, Travkin apparently realized that not to join Democratic Russia meant to threaten the very existence of the DPR, and he reluctantly reversed his initial stance.

More than the 1990 Congress of People's Deputies elections, the June 1991 presidential election in Russia was conducted along partisan lines. However, competing parties as such were largely absent. Several parties, including Democratic Russia, the DPR, the SDPR, the RPRF, and a plethora of smaller groups adhering to the "mainstream democratic ideology" endorsed the candidacy of Yeltsin. Hence he emerged as the joint candidate of the democratic opposition (Urban 1992). The KPSS produced as many as four candidates, representing different trends within the disintegrating party, or as some analysts argued, a conscious strategy aimed at splitting the electorate in the first round of the elections, which would have rendered the necessity of holding a second round. The only explicit party candidate was Vladimir Zhirinovsky, whose campaign, however, exposed neither "mainstream democratic" nor communist ideological commitments. In fact, it represented a third ideological pole of the perestroika-era ideological spectrum, nationalism. With the emergence of the informal movement, groups of nationalists started to make their appearance in major Russian cities, often adopting the name of Pamiat (Memory). Some of these groups were as moderate as many of the early proreform informals, while others displayed a xenophobic and occasionally anticommunist attitude, viewing the regime as a marionette of a worldwide Judeo-Masonic conspiracy (Verkhovskii and Pribylovskii 1996). In contrast to the democrats, the nationalists viewed the very idea of a multiparty system with suspicion (Orttung 1992). Thus Pamiat never constituted a unified organizational entity. Rather, it was a collection of groups using the same label.

Seemingly, Zhirinovsky was able to capitalize on the organizational impotence of the nationalists. After trying several parties of the "mainstream democratic" orientation, he established his own group, officially founded in May 1990 and labeled the Liberal Democratic Party of the Soviet Union.[6] At first glance the party did not differ much from other "mainstream democratic" organizations. Zhirinovsky himself, when asked to sum up his political credo, exclaimed: "My program? It is like everybody else's: perestroika, free market, and democracy!" (Pribylovskii 1992: ix). Soon it became clear that the new party, as well as a number of other previously unknown groups, enjoyed a quite extraordinary degree of attention at the top of the Soviet hierarchy.[7] For the Communists, Zhirinovsky's party could be viewed as a safe coalition partner under the conditions of the emerging multiparty system. For Zhirinovsky himself, the support of the authorities was essential for maximizing his political gains in these strongly competitive environments. After joining the 1991 presidential race, Zhirinovsky based his rhetoric on promising to defend Russians and the Russian-speaking population over the whole territory of the Union of Soviet Socialist Republics (USSR) (Kartsev 1995). Indeed, it was difficult to challenge Yeltsin on the grounds of the mainstream democratic ideology originally accepted by Zhirinovsky's "liberal democrats." Embracing nationalism instead was a risky strategy, but as demonstrated by electoral returns, it paid off.

Yeltsin won the 1991 presidential election with 57.3 percent of the vote. Procommunist candidates fared poorly: the best of their results was a low 16.9 percent. Surprisingly for many observers, Zhirinovsky managed to capture the third place in the election with 7.8 percent. As a result of the election, Russia apparently entered a new phase of political development. With the largest of the former republics of the USSR controlled by a proreform president, the credibility of the Communists as a potential ruling party sharply declined. In particular, Yeltsin's victory helped him to garner the loyal support of the old political, managerial, and administrative elites in the periphery of the country. Strongly reluctant to join the democratic movement, which appeared to be too radical and thus hostile to their own interests, they sought alternative political organizations. One such option was the proreform wing of the KPSS, which in 1991 started to break off as the Democratic Party of Russian Communists, led by Aleksandr Rutskoi.[8] Later it was renamed the People's Party Free Russia, and still later the Russian Social Democratic People's Party. Another, the Movement for Democratic Reforms, was originally intended to serve as an umbrella organization for those communists who wanted to join the winner without leaving the KPSS.[9]

The attempted coup of August 1991 changed the whole structure of opportunities available to major political actors. The leaders of the democratic movement were among the first to come out in support of Yeltsin's decree banning the KPSS, yet the collapse of that aging organization meant that the task of the democratic parties had been largely accomplished (Weigle 1994). Upon the receipt of extraordinary powers from the Congress of People's Deputies, Yeltsin invited none of the leading democrats to participate in drafting and implementing the program of economic reform. Instead this task had to be accomplished by a team of individuals who owed their promotions exclusively to their connections and personal loyalties to Yeltsin (Sakwa 1993: 74). Within the Russian legislature elected in March 1990, the role of parties remained modest if not negligible. Only one of the factions claimed to be party-based (Sobianin 1992: 11).

As a result of these developments, both the leaders and the activists of the political parties found themselves in a rather ambiguous situation. On the one hand, the cause they were fighting for had apparently won. On the other hand, their political gains were, as a rule, miserable, and if they were not, this was scarcely related to their party affiliations. As a result, to cite one example, the estimated membership of the DPR had fallen from 50,000 in early 1992 to barely 15,000 by the end of that year (Sakwa 1993: 148). Moreover, the initially centralized structure of the DPR had largely disintegrated. Travkin concentrated his efforts primarily on coalition building on the elite level, joining a coalition of the "moderate opposition" to Yeltsin sponsored and effectively led by an influential representative of the military-industrial complex, Arkadii Vol'skii of the Civic Union (Lohr 1993). At the same time, local party organizations became increasingly independent from Moscow and often preferred to act on their own. This resulted in what was sometimes referred to as the "two-story" structure of the DPR, with local organizations being neither effectively connected to the Moscow leadership nor represented in that leadership. The RPRF and the SDPR confronted a different kind of problems. For these parties, their democratic identity was something that could not be compromised under any circumstances. One possible option was to support Yeltsin unconditionally, and another was to keep distance from the government and criticize it for being "insufficiently democratic." The SDPR was continuously divided over which of the options was more consistent with its ideological foundations. The RPRF, even though it displayed a higher degree of organizational stability, also witnessed the emergence of deep internal divisions. Correspondingly, Democratic Russia started to rapidly lose its members. In many regions, the democratic movement effectively reverted to the state of affairs typical of 1987–1988 (Sungurov 1994: 21).

New attempts to create democratic parties were few and generally unsuccessful. The Party of Economic Freedom (PES), created and actively sponsored by the president of the Moscow Stock Exchange, Konstantin Borovoi, did succeed in luring some of the democratic activists into its network,[10] but no new democrats arrived. Yet another attempt had been undertaken by one of the original founders of the stillborn Movement for Democratic Reforms, Moscow mayor Gavriil Popov. His entity, called the Russian Movement for Democratic Reforms (RDDR), pursued a different strategy. Apparently, Popov was not very optimistic about the prospects of building his party from the grassroots. Instead, he tried to attract those peripheral administrative managers who fared well under the new regime but still lacked political connections to the Moscow elite. It was expected that they would invest some of their resources in party building. Even though one of the senior regional executives, Konstantin Titov of Samara province, did join the RDDR,[11] Popov's strategy generally failed, perhaps due to the lack of his own influence.

The attitude of the government toward its potential political supporters remained ambiguous throughout the period. On the one hand, it often bluntly ignored the remaining democrats. On the other hand, the idea that it might be useful to create a "governing democratic party" was not entirely out of circulation, if only because the situation in the country could bring about fresh elections at literally any time. In 1992–1993, Russia witnessed several attempts to create such a party. One of these attempts had been undertaken in July 1992 at a meeting called the Forum of Democratic Forces. The forum brought together two kinds of participants. On the one hand, the forum included some of the national leaders of Democratic Russia, so-called pragmatists who tended to unconditionally support the government. On the other hand, the government itself had been represented by a number of senior officials, such as the principal drafter of the reform program and the acting prime minister, Egor Gaidar (McFaul 1993: 66–72). In June 1993 the process of the formation of the governing party culminated in signing a declaration that proclaimed the establishment of a new coalition named Russia's Choice.

At the same time, the rival ideological tendencies started to gradually revitalize. The nationalists were quicker in their attempt to gain the momentum. In addition to the remnants of Pamiat, new organizations started to emerge. One of them was the Russian All-People's Union (ROS), led by Sergei Baburin. Baburin was elected to the Congress of People's Deputies of Russia as a representative of the democratic forces, but later he started to advocate views emphasizing Russian nationalism and chauvinism (Pribylovskii 1992: 85). In this capacity, he joined and led one of the anti-Yeltsin parliamentary factions, Russia. Some of the members of the faction, mostly recent communist party members, joined Baburin to form ROS in October 1991. One of them was Gennadii Ziuganov, the future leader of the Russian Communists. The program of ROS stated such goals as the territorial unity of Russia, the rejection of pro-Western foreign policy, the revival of the state sector of the economy, and the limiting of the market.[12] In 1992, different nationalist and communist groups created a coalition of the radical opposition that was called the National Salvation Front.[13] The ideology of the coalition was predominantly nationalist, even though it seemed that communist groups provided the bulk of its members (G. Hahn 1994).

Among the first measures accomplished by Yeltsin after the failure of the 1991 coup were moves to suspend and then to ban the Communist Party and to transfer its vast assets to the state. While no hard data on the matter are available, it seems that most former members left the party with little regret. However, a representative survey held in early 1992 demonstrated that about 2 percent of the sample population still identified themselves as Communist Party members (White and McAllister 1996: 113). An option available to the steady Communists was to join the Russian Communist Workers Party (RKRP), created in November 1991. Rather than belonging to the upper layers of the former KPSS hierarchy, the leaders of the RKRP originated from a number of groups that already in the late 1980s criticized Gorbachev for concessions made to procapitalist forces (Orttung 1992). The RKRP advocated establishing a dictatorship of the proletariat based on worker self-management, Marxist-Leninist ideology, and a planned economy.[14] Organizationally, the RKRP claimed to have essentially the same structure as the disbanded KPSS. In particular, the statute of the party emphasized that party cells must be at the workplace, not residential. In fact, the activities of the RKRP and its close affiliate, the Workers Russia movement, more closely resembled Democratic Russia of the previous phase of the country's political development than they did the KPSS. By mid-1992, the RKRP claimed to have 150,000 members, which if true would have made it the largest party in Russia (Sakwa 1993: 41).

In late 1992 the Constitutional Court of Russia upheld Yeltsin's action banning the KPSS with regard to the central organs of the party but not to those at the local level. This decision ignited a comprehensive campaign to revive the Communist Party. The RKRP took part in that campaign, but without success. The majority of the former party members in the periphery simply restored their party committees on the grassroots levels.[15] This process culminated in the revival/unification of the Congress of Communists in February 1993. The representatives of more than 500,000 newly registered party members attended. The organizational basis for the

Communist Party of the Russian Federation (KPRF) was provided not by the RKRP or any other previously established group but rather by independent party organizations and local left-wing movements. The leaders of the RKRP sharply criticized the KPRF leadership for, in particular, "deviations from the class position." Such an accusation was not entirely unrealistic, given that the new party's elected leader, Ziuganov, had a long history of flirtation with noted nationalists (Vujacic 1996). The appeals of the RKRP leaders to class consciousness, however, did not help save their organization. Local branches of the RKRP started to disintegrate, with large groups of their members joining the new party. Yet another organization established in 1993 was the Agrarian Party of Russia (APR). It so closely allied itself with the Communists that it was often characterized as a rural subdivision of the KPRF (Schneider 1995: 31), even though the leaders of the party rejected such a characterization.[16] At the same time, it is worth mentioning that the top leaders of the APR, Mikhail Lapshin and Ivan Rybkin, were communist party members at the time when the APR was founded.[17]

Political Parties Within the Context of National Electoral Politics

On September 21, 1993, Yeltsin dissolved the Congress of People's Deputies by decree. The legislature responded by impeaching Yetsin and electing Rutskoi as an acting president. On October 4 the army seized the parliament building. Rutskoi and some other leaders of the opposition were put in jail. In the interim between these two events, on October 1, Yeltsin issued a decree that set rules for electing a new parliament. The parliament, now named the Federal Assembly, was to consist of two chambers. The 450 members of the lower chamber, the State Duma, were to be elected by a mixed electoral system: half of them by proportional representation in a single, nationwide district, and the other half by plurality in single-member districts. A 5 percent barrier was used to prevent the proliferation of small parties. The upper chamber, the Federation Council, was to consist of 178 deputies delegated by the executive and legislative authorities of Russia's regions.[18] Proportional representation elections were by far the most important innovation brought about by Yeltsin's decrees. Moser and Thames (2001) provide a detailed factual account of the public debate and policy choices that jointly contributed to the introduction of the mixed electoral system in Russia. It seems that an adequate concise formulation has been suggested by McFaul (2001: 1179–1180), who calls it an "accident of history." In the midst of a constitutional crisis, a group of trusted yet not politically powerful deputies who were previously involved in debates about the electoral law, especially Viktor Sheinis, managed to convince the president that proportional representation would be good for securing his political control over the legislature. Indeed, it could be argued that elections in single-member districts would benefit the KPRF with its allegedly vast territorial network (Remington and Smith 1996; Belin and Orttung 1997). However, the primary motivation of Sheinis seemed to be normative, stemming from his conviction that viable political parties were essential for the consolidation of democracy in Russia, and that, as put by Sheinis himself, "no proportional representation, no parties."[19]

One of the major problems with holding proportional representation elections was, of course, the lack of a political party that could represent Yeltsin and the executive in general. It was only in October 1993 that the founding congress of such a party (or, to be precise, a "public movement"), Russia's Choice (VR), was assembled. The newly established movement served as an axis of the simultaneously formed electoral bloc of the same name. In addition to democratic activists and government leaders, the new coalition included local heads of administration and other officials.[20] Initially, some of the officials, especially Egor Gaidar, who was elected as a leader of the bloc, sought to turn Russia's Choice into a fully professional and well-organized political party. Although supportive of the government, the leaders of Democratic Russia thoroughly rejected the idea. Instead, they favored preserving a loose organizational framework, and this position prevailed. The excessive number of prominent personalities in the leadership of Russia's Choice was naturally disadvantageous for the activists of Democratic Russia, as their chances to be placed high on the party list were reduced at this juncture. In fact, only 7 percent of the names on the list of Russia's Choice were those of party activists.[21] It is therefore not surprising that the national leaderships of two major constituent parts of Democratic Russia, the RPRF and the SDPR, refused to join the new entity.

Thus even though the VR did absorb a good deal of individuals who were previously active in the "democratic movement," as well as in Democratic Russia as its forefront organization, it would not be fair to consider it as a direct organizational continuation of the Gorbachev-era political mobilization. The core component of the VR was the government itself. That is why the VR can be viewed as an early manifestation of the phenomenon that thereafter persisted in Russia. Journalists were quick to dub this phenomenon "the party of power." While accepting this wording, I would like to clarify it conceptually. The parties of power are not parties in power. Throughout the 1993–2003 period, Russia's presidents were not members of any parties, and the same applies to the majority of other senior officials within the federal executive. Rather, the parties of power are electoral vehicles. The specific purpose pursued by them is to bring to the national legislature politicians who are loyal to the federal executive. The ultimate rationale for their existence is therefore to provide the executive with certain levels of legislative support without sharing power or responsibility. In fact, despite Gaidar's urgings, Yeltsin never associated himself with the VR. Moreover, in addition to the VR, the federal executive generated a second party of power, labeled the Party of Russian Unity and Accord (PRES). Unlike the VR, the PRES entirely lacked any roots in the democratic movement. Created by Sergei Shakhrai, head of the State Committee for Nationalities, on the eve of the campaign, the PRES based its organizational structure almost exclusively on the regional centers of that rather powerful committee. Probably the most important asset of the PRES, however, was the role played by Shakhrai in distributing federal subsidies among the republics of Russia. As a result, the minister of nationalities enjoyed fairly cozy relations with many leaders of the republics.[22] The two parties of power exposed different ideologies. The VR advocated free-market liberalism and speedy economic reforms. In contrast, the PRES, while not advancing any alternative economic program, rhetorically distanced itself from the mainstream democratic ideology. As put by Shakhrai, "some people often call our party provincial and conservative, and well, we agree with that; we advocate a strong Russian statehood, order and legality in the country, federalism and the defense of national dignity."[23]

This brings us to the important problem of the composition of Russia's party spectrum in 1993 and thereafter. The principal ideological alternatives of the previous period of party development, the mainstream democratic ideology and Soviet-style communism, became irrelevant after the collapse of the communist regime. The latter became not only ideologically discredited but also organizationally demolished with the dissolution of the KPSS. The former, with its contents being largely defined by the rejection of the communist regime, became irrelevant because the object of rejection disappeared. With the start of economic reform, the major policy issue in the country, like in all other postcommunist polities, was the direction and speed of transformation. The ideological polarization on this issue easily fits into the common pattern of egalitarian distribution and state intervention on the left versus free-market principles and justified inequality on the right (Zaller 1992; Hinich and Munger 1994). During the perestroika period, this distinction in Russia was largely blurred, so that it was not unusual to describe the "mainstream democrats" as "the left," and the KPSS as a "right" or "conservative" force (Evans and Whitefield 1998). By 1993, however, principal economic policy alternatives became all too salient to allow for this idiosyncratic wording. Insofar as promarket versus antimarket positions emerged as one of the major dimensions of Russia's political spectrum (Oates 1998), the proponents of the market ceased to call themselves "the left." Even though the word "democrats" had a longer life, by the end of the 1990s it assumed a largely derogatory meaning, which apparently prompted free-market liberals to assume the label "right forces" in the

1999 national legislative elections. In parallel, the KPRF and the RKRP claimed the label "the left" for themselves and were increasingly referred to in this way by their political opponents.[24] In further analysis, I will follow this conventional terminology.

The parties of power, however, do not fit well into the conventional left-right continuum because their policy choices are defined not by ideological commitments but by their positions as the contenders in multiparty elections most closely tied to the executive incumbents (Colton and McFaul 2000: 203; Smyth 2002). From this perspective, the VR's commitment to free-market liberalism was not as important as the fact that it included senior government officials and used its affiliation with the executive as a source of its electoral appeal. In fact, the vague ideology of the PRES was a lot more typical for the parties of power to come. The PRES, however, was less clearly associated with the incumbent executive. Yet another ideological category outside the left-right dichotomy is nationalism. A sophisticated model of the ideological structuring of postcommunist party systems developed by Kitschelt (1992) allows for placing nationalism at one of the extremes of the liberal cosmopolitan versus authoritarian nationalist continuum. Urban (1997) presents a different yet quite convincing theoretical explanation of how nationalism found its distinctive place in the political spectrum of contemporary Russia, which is all the more valuable because it allows for understanding why, in contrast to the mainstream democratic ideology, nationalism survived into the current phase of Russia's political development. Many empirical studies (Byzov 1995; White, Rose, and McAllister 1997; Oates 1998) point to the distinctiveness of nationalism on the basis of such "hard" evidence as survey data or content analysis of party platforms. Thus, without going into substantive discussion of the matter, I find it cognitively expedient to agree with Simonsen (2001: 263) that "some political actors are simply better categorized by their nationalism than by their position on, say, an economic (state vs. market) or political (liberal vs. authoritarian) scale." Nonideological interest advocacy groups are the fifth component of Russia's political spectrum.

As demonstrated by Oates (1998: 85), the best-articulated right-wing ideological standing in the 1993 campaign was exposed by an organization that was officially called "Electoral Bloc: Yavlinsky, Boldyrev, Lukin" and that came to be known as Yabloko (Apple) after the acronym of the surnames of its leaders. The official founders of Yabloko were the RPRF and the SDPR. Practically, as reflected in its label, the coalition was dominated by a number of prominent personalities including Grigorii Yavlinsky, an economist who owed his popularity to a program of market reforms published in 1990. In October 1993, Yavlinsky and a number of other high-profile individuals formed their own list and then invited the democratic parties to join.[25] After some hesitation, especially evident in the case of the RPRF, the founders accepted the invitation. Yet another right-wing party that contested the 1993 elections was the RDDR. Both the DPR and the RDDR tried to find their own electoral niches by differentiating themselves from the main competitors for the promarket vote, the VR and Yabloko. To achieve this, both advocated models of economic development that would support industrial production rather than nonproductive sectors of the economy.[26] While the RDDR apparently had little to add to this attractive but vague programmatic stance, the DPR heavily supplemented its campaign with the rhetoric of fighting crime and corruption voiced by a prominent filmmaker, Stanislav Govorukhin.[27] Several other right-wing groups, including the PES, planned to participate in the 1993 elections but failed to collect enough signatures to get their lists nominated.

Speaking of the opposition, several parties confronted difficulties in collecting signatures against the background of widespread fear engendered by the violent dissolution of the previous parliament (Urban 1994: 137). The ROS claimed that the police had raided its offices and stolen 20,000 signatures.[28] In fact, none of those five nationalist groups previously associated with the anti-Yeltsin opposition that announced their intentions to participate in the elections were able to join the campaign,[29] as a result of which Zhirinovsky's party emerged as the only representative of this ideological tendency. The Liberal Democratic Party was, in fact, the only political party ever registered by the ministry of justice of the Soviet Union. While this registration became void with the extinction of the Soviet Union,[30] in 1992 Zhirinovsky managed to gain a new registration with Russia's Ministry of Justice, this time, promptly, under the label Liberal Democratic Party of Russia (LDPR). Zhirinovsky continued to receive a lot of media attention throughout 1992–1993. This happened not because the media outlets were very sympathetic to him, but because the progovernment newsmakers tried to make a popular image of a "Russian fascist" out of Zhirinovsky, who after all had already gained some name recognition in the 1991 presidential election.[31] This dubious popularity among the journalists was quite productively employed in Zhirinovsky's 1993 campaign. Much of the campaign visibility of the Liberal Democrats had to be attributed to Zhirinovsky's excellent media campaign, as well as to the fact that the LDPR most successfully combined an unmistakably nationalist ideological stance with a well-articulated antigovernment position (Golosov 1996: 65–67) and to the lack of ideologically similar competitors.

Several political parties were banned from participation in the elections as a result of their involvement in the October 1993 events. These included Rutskoi's party, then the People's Party Free Russia, the RKRP, and initially the KPRF.[32] While individual members of the banned parties could run in single-member districts, the RKRP boycotted the 1993 elections, calling for a campaign of civic disobedience instead. In this, it was joined by a number of smaller radical communist sects.[33] The KPRF, in contrast, easily collected the required number of signatures and was added to the list of registered parties. Still, running an effective vote-maximizing campaign in the aftermath of the October events was a difficult task for the Communists, who were widely portrayed in the media as the "party of civil war." As a result, the party's preelection rhetoric, as expressed in Ziuganov's speeches, was overcautious, obscured with quasi-academic terminology, and generally vague. Consciously avoiding sharp issues, Ziuganov placed major emphasis on "strengthening the state and defending its vital interests," which, he said, was a precondition for "any debates on what path of reforming the economy would be preferable."[34] In contrast to the LDPR, the KPRF did not run any significant media campaign (Kholmskaia 1994). The overcautious position of the KPRF leadership was clearly reflected in the fact that, in its deliberate rejection of a vote-maximizing strategy, it practically abstained from conducting any campaign activities in the countryside. Instead, it encouraged the communists there to campaign on behalf of the APR. Programmatically, the APR was not very different from the KPRF. One idea more articulated in the Agrarian program was a rejection of the "uncontrollable" sale of land.[35]

Of the interest advocacy groups that contested the 1993 elections, the most important was a movement called Women of Russia. The movement was based on the remnants of the vast network of *zhensovety* (women's councils) that emerged in 1988 as part of Gorbachev's social mobilization effort. Curiously enough, there was almost nothing gender-specific (in fact, nothing specific at all) in the program of the movement.[36] Its major slogan was "democracy for all irrespective of gender, nationality, social standing, religious beliefs, and political convictions." Many observers speculated that the true rationale beyond the creation of Women of Russia was to prevent the politically indifferent but "conservative" female electors from voting for the KPRF. Allegedly, the organization was supported by the presidential administration, but evidence on that remains largely anecdotal. It is true, however, that the movement's leader, Ekaterina Lakhova, was a long-term associate of Yeltsin brought by him to Moscow from Sverdlovsk province to work as his adviser on the issues of women, family, and children.[37] In addition to the nine parties and blocs described above, four other groups took part in the 1993 elections.

Table 2.1 summarizes the 1993 electoral results.[38] In contrast to the expectations voiced by the drafters of the electoral law, the LDPR, not the VR, emerged as an undisputed winner in the party-list competition. Ironically, it was only due to the plurality tier of the system that the party of power was able to form the largest legislative faction in the end. Yet another group whose success in the 1993 elections surprised many observers was

Women of Russia. The parties of the left, the KPRF and the APR, jointly gained 19 percent of the vote, followed by Yabloko, the PRES, and the DPR. Almost two-thirds of the deputies elected in single-member districts were independents, which suggests that Sheinis was generally right when he contended that without a proportional tier, the 1993 elections would have produced a parliament without political parties. The leaders of the VR perceived the 1993 election results as disastrous. Indeed, there was nothing of the outright victory that the government was so confident in on the eve of the campaign. Soon after the elections, Gaidar resigned from the government and proposed to transform Russia's Choice into a disciplined and centralized political party, Democratic Russia's Choice (DVR).[39] The party was indeed established under Gaidar's leadership, but this move alienated the leaders of Democratic Russia. At the same time, Gaidar's attempt to create a more centralized organization left outside of Russia's Democratic Choice some of the democratic celebrities and state officials who joined the VR in 1993. Hence by the beginning of the 1995 campaign, Gaidar's organization was just a shadow of the vast political machine created in 1993. It still claimed the role of the main party of the right for itself, but these claims were scarcely substantiated. To make them look more credible, Gaidar launched an electoral bloc, Democratic Russia's Choice–United Democrats. The bloc, however, largely coincided with its major participant, Gaidar's party.

Table 2.1   Results of the 1993 Elections to the State Duma of Russia

Party	Share of Party-List Vote (%)	Number of Party-List Seats	Number of District Seats	Overall Number of Seats	Overall Share of Seats (%)
LDPR	21.4	59	5	64	14.4
VR (including Democratic Russia)	14.5	40	30	70	15.8
KPRF	11.6	32	16	48	10.8
Women of Russia	7.6	21	2	23	5.2
APR	7.4	21	12	33	7.4
Yabloko (including SDPR and RPRF)	7.3	20	3	23	5.2
PRES	6.3	18	1	19	4.3
DPR	5.1	14	1	15	3.4
RDDR	3.8	—	4	4	0.9
4 other parties	4.3	—	4	4	0.9
Independents	—	—	141	141	31.8
Against all	3.9	—	—	—	—
Invalid votes	6.8	—	—	—	—
Total	100.0	225	219	444	100.1[a]

Note: a. Does not sum to 100.0 percent because of rounding.

The disintegration of Russia's Choice produced several new parties. Most of them were quite reminiscent of the "sofa parties" of 1989–1991. One of the VR's former leaders, Boris Fedorov, created his own movement, Forward, Russia! The movement was ideologically distinctive from other right-wing parties in that it emphasized "democratic patriotism" and a strong albeit liberal state.[40] The famous ophthalmologist Sviatoslav Fedorov abandoned the RDDR to create the Party of Workers Self-Government (PST). In its rhetoric, the PST combined liberal ideas (it took a firmly antibureaucratic stance) with a specific version of "people's capitalism" derived from the management routines of Fedorov's vast network of eye-surgery clinics.[41] In addition, eleven smaller right-wing groups contested the 1995 election. Many of these groups advocated one or another version of "democratic opposition" to Yeltsin. The proliferation of such parties was all too bad for Yabloko. In the course of 1994 the leaders of all three original founding members of the bloc left it, apparently because their own roles in Yabloko remained very modest in comparison to that of Yavlinsky and his "near circle." Many activists of the RPRF and some SDPR members, however, preferred to stay. This allowed Yabloko to start constructing its own organizational network. In January 1995, Yabloko declared itself an "all-Russian public association" with provision for membership extended to individuals, national parties, and regional parties (Gel'man 1999b). Programmatically, Yabloko adhered to its long-established line of democratic opposition to Yeltsin.

The disintegration of Russia's Choice and its moderate opposition to the government once again left Russia without a "governing democratic party." In April 1995, Prime Minister Viktor Chernomyrdin announced that he would lead a new "center-right" movement pretentiously labeled Our Home Is Russia (NDR). The movement, joined by several cabinet members and other key figures in the government apparatus, as well as by high-ranking officials in most regions of the country, had been unanimously identified as a reincarnation of the party of power by Russian political observers.[42] Indeed, much like Russia's Choice of 1993, Our Home Is Russia effectively combined state administration with private capital. But in contrast to its predecessor, the NDR's ideological adherence to the right was not very articulated. In fact, it lacked any coherent ideology, substituting it with vague calls for "stability" and a government of "professionals" who would lead without "shocks" and "experimentation." In many regions, the organizations of the NDR practically coincided with state administrative offices. But there was also some influx of the break-off groups and whole regional branches of Russia's Choice into the new movement.[43] The formation of the NDR led to a series of struggles for leadership within the new movement. For instance, Sergei Shakhrai was initially active in this party-building effort. Later—apparently as a result of his dissatisfaction with the scope of his influence—he withdrew his Party of Russian Unity and Accord from the movement and joined the 1995 campaign independently from the NDR.[44]

In the 1993 Duma, Zhirinovsky's LDPR was the only representative of the nationalist segment of Russia's political spectrum. In 1995, however, Zhirinovsky found many imitators (Simonsen 1996). One of them was the former vice president of Russia, Aleksandr Rutskoi, who transformed his Russian Social Democratic People's Party into a new organization of a radically nationalist orientation, the Derzhava (Great Power) Social Patriotic Movement (Solovei 1996). In order to extend the organizational basis of the movement, Rutskoi tried and initially succeeded in attracting under its banners a variety of preexisting nationalist groups, including a breakaway group of the LDPR, almost all nationalist groups that participated in the National Salvation Front, and some of the descendants of Pamiat.[45] Another attempt to invade into the ideological space of the LDPR had been undertaken by the Congress of Russian Communities (KRO). The KRO emerged from political obscurity when in early 1995 its leadership was joined by three high-profile personalities at once—a noted representative of the military-industrial complex, Yurii Skokov, Lieutenant-General (retired) Aleksandr Lebed, who had received immense publicity for his defense of the Russian-speaking minority in Moldova, and one of the leaders of the DPR and a former minister in Gaidar's government, Sergei Glaz'ev. A charismatic leader with dynamic oratorical skills, Lebed was expected to complement Skokov's political experience and financial resources, while the presence of Glaz'ev was to symbolize the coalition's commitment to the strategy of gradual economic reforms. In general, however, the ideology of the KRO was nationalist, based on an irredentist commitment to the reunification of all Russians in an enlarged state (Ingram 1999).

The ideological evolution of the leadership of the KPRF in 1994–1995 was characterized by its gradual rejection of Marxist orthodoxy, accompanied by the shift toward a more nationalist stance (Urban and Solovei 1997; Vujacic 1996; Flikke 1999). Hence the intention to invade the ideological niche occupied in 1993 by Zhirinovsky was quite evident. This trend was viewed with suspicion by some of the regional branches of the party. Indeed, a majority of KPRF members and activists based their notion of the Communist Party on its explicit commitment to Marxism-Leninism (Golosov 2000). Such tacit disagreements, however, did not lead to any significant splits. In part, this can be explained with reference to the skillful leadership of Ziuganov (Ansell and Fish 1999). At the same time, it seems that as the KPRF consolidated its position of the major party of Russia's left, party members increasingly perceived belonging to it as an important asset despite their disagreements with the party leadership on the issues of ideology. The electoral platform of the KPRF in the 1995 elections mentioned the word "socialism" only once, in connection with the August 1991 events. The bulk of the document was dedicated to the defense of the Russian nation and statehood against their alleged destroyers in power.[46] At the same time, the continuing presence of the RKRP was an important contextual factor. In 1995 the party of the radical left opted for electoral participation. After uneasy negotiations, the RKRP refused to enter a coalition with the KPRF, accusing the latter of unwillingness to provide proper representation to the workers (which, to put it in more pragmatic terms, meant that the KPRF claimed no less than 90 percent of the positions on the list for itself).[47] As a result, the RKRP, joined by a couple of minor organizations, formed its own bloc under a lengthy label, Communists–Workers Russia–For the Soviet Union. The APR also remained in the electoral arena. In the course of the 1995 campaign, the leaders of the APR were so confident in its success that they rejected any coalition strategy. The party tried to dissociate itself from the KPRF by claiming to represent the interests of rural Russia.[48] Yet another challenge to the KPRF came from Power to the People. The leaders of Power to the People were Sergei Baburin, a long-standing leader of the nationalist ROS, and former Soviet prime minister Nikolai Ryzhkov. The programmatic stance of the alliance was ambiguous in the sense that one of its leaders and many activists were nationalists, but in the rhetoric of the main spokesman for the bloc, Ryzhkov, nostalgic socialist-era sentiment definitely prevailed.[49]

With as many as forty-three parties taking part in party-list elections, the number of the participants in the race more than tripled in comparison with 1993. In part this can be explained with reference to the fact that the 1993 campaign was brief, started unexpectedly, and could not be contested by some of the parties because they were banned, otherwise excluded, or deliberately chose to boycott the elections (Sakwa 1995). In combination, these factors raised the level of uncertainty regarding the chances of individual participants in the 1995 elections. In particular, the success of Women of Russia apparently motivated a plethora of new interest advocacy groups to join the campaign claiming to represent different societal constituencies, from deceived investors to beer lovers. Yet another factor that contributed to party proliferation in the 1995 elections was the disintegration of the VR, which did not produce any credible claimant for the right-wing vote. Table 2.2 reports the results of the 1995 elections. This time, the KPRF emerged as the biggest winner both in terms of gaining votes and in terms of converting votes into seats. With only four parties that jointly received slightly more than 50 percent of the vote crossing the 5 percent threshold, each of their votes assumed a double value. At the same time, the KPRF gained more than a quarter of the single-member seats. The level of representation achieved by the KPRF not only made it the strongest party in the Duma, but also allowed it to delegate some of its members to join

Table 2.2   **Results of the 1995 Elections to the State Duma of Russia**

Party	Share of Party-List Vote (%)	Number of Party-List Seats	Number of District Seats	Overall Number of Seats	Overall Share of Seats (%)
KPRF	22.3	99	58	157	34.9
LDPR	11.2	50	1	51	11.3
NDR	10.1	45	10	55	12.2
Yabloko	6.9	31	14	45	10.0
Women of Russia	4.6	—	3	3	0.7
RKRP (in bloc)	4.5	—	1	1	0.2
KRO	4.3	—	5	5	1.1
PST	4.0	—	1	1	0.2
DVR (in bloc)	3.9	—	9	9	2.0
APR	3.8	—	20	20	4.4
Derzhava	2.6	—	—	—	—
Forward, Russia!	1.9	—	3	3	0.7
ROS (in bloc)	1.6	—	9	9	2.0
30 other parties	13.6	—	14	14	3.1
Independents	—	—	77	77	17.1
Against all	2.8	—	—	—	—
Invalid votes	1.9	—	—	—	—
Total	100.0	225	225	450	99.9[a]

Note: a. Does not sum to 100.0 percent because of rounding.

deputy groups created on the basis of the APR and Power to the People, the Agrarian deputy group and People's Power respectively.[50] Jointly, the faction of the KPRF and deputy groups sponsored by it controlled almost a half of seats in the Duma. The LDPR performed half as well as in 1993, which did not prevent it from placing second in the party-list competition. The ill-conceived party of power, the NDR, was able to form only a minority faction, while Yabloko emerged as the only right-wing party in the Duma. Thus the Russian right paid a dear price for fragmentation, as well as for the poor quality of its campaigns (Fish 1997).

Political parties were not important actors in the 1996 presidential election (Brudny 1997). Mainly this resulted from the fact that the incumbent president, Boris Yeltsin, ran as an effectively independent candidate. His campaign, heavily supported by the administrative machinery of the state and by the progovernment media and financed in part by a group of financial tycoons (Gel'man 1998), owed little to those parties that officially supported him. They abounded, though. In addition to the NDR, the majority of the right-wing parties supported Yeltsin. To present Yeltsin as a "national" candidate defying partisan loyalties, the collection of his supporters was supplemented with a number of artificially created "centrist" and "left-wing" organizations. Of the remaining ten candidates, political parties officially nominated only two, Yavlinsky and Zhirinovsky. The major challenger, Ziuganov, was naturally endorsed by the KPRF, but he ran as an independent candidate supported by a loose coalition of the left and nationalists, including the APR, the RKRP, Derzhava, and the ROS.[51] Paradoxically enough, the 1995 elections virtually destroyed the KRO but boosted the personal popularity of Lebed. Soon after the Duma elections, Lebed broke any ties with Skokov and started to campaign on his own. Some factions of the KRO and the DPR, as well as his own small movement, Honor and Motherland (ChR), supported Lebed, who however ran as an independent candidate.[52] In May 1996, Lebed's public appearances started to receive a lot of favorable coverage in the generally propresidential media. After Yeltsin himself equivocally recognized Lebed as his "legitimate heir," it became clear that Lebed found his role in Yeltsin's campaign.[53]

This was, of course, the role of vote-splitter. Lebed's campaign exploited his oratorical skills to send quite an ambiguous yet generally attractive message to the voters of all political inclinations, from nationalists, with their longing for a "strong power," to right-wingers, who were expected to embrace his free-market economic program. In the first round of the 1996 elections, Yeltsin placed first with 35.3 percent of the vote, closely followed by Ziuganov with 32.0 percent. Lebed, with his 14.5 percent, emerged as a third-runner. Party candidates Yavlinsky and Zhirinovsky fared poorly with their 7.3 and 5.7 percent of the vote, respectively. The remaining five candidates jointly collected 2 percent of the vote. In the interim between the two rounds of the elections, Lebed (as well as Yavlinsky and Zhirinovsky) endorsed the candidacy of Yeltsin, who won with 53.8 percent of the vote.

In the aftermath of the 1996 elections, Lebed enjoyed his status of a crown prince and immense popularity among the populace. Not only did his tiny movement start to attract massive following, but he also proceeded to create a political party of his supporters, the Russian Popular Republican Party (RNRP). In the course of time, however, Lebed's popularity started to fade away. First he was dismissed as a secretary of Russia's Security Council, a position of ill-defined responsibilities granted to him as a reward for the masterfully conducted campaign. Then, as it became clear that Yeltsin was not going to die or resign in the near future, the status of his most probable successor also became less than credible. Lebed himself contributed to this process by participating in the scandal-ridden 1998 gubernatorial elections in Krasnoiarsk territory. He won the elections but had to leave the national political arena. The second major development came in May 1998 when Yeltsin unexpectedly fired Chernomyrdin as a prime minister and, after a standoff with the Duma, forced it to approve the candidacy of Sergei Kirienko. Kirienko, however, did not occupy the post for long. The August 1998 financial and economic crisis not only ousted him from office but also, for the first time in the history of postcommunist Russia, resulted in the Duma's refusal to approve a candidate nominated by Yeltsin. Instead, the legislature opted for the candidacy of Evgenii Primakov, who formed a government that included several representatives of the KPRF and the APR as key ministers. The mayor of Moscow, Yurii Luzhkov, allegedly played an important role in coordinating political activities that led to Primakov's appointment.[54] After the 1998 crisis it became clear that Yeltsin, whose popularity as measured by public opinion polls plummeted to near zero, would not run for the third term. At the same time, Luzhkov, previously regarded as Yeltsin's supporter, effectively launched his bid for Russia's presidency.

Naturally, these events made the NDR irrelevant as the incumbent party of power. With Chernomyrdin out of the prime-ministerial chair and little if any chance to win the presidency, the NDR could only survive as a pro-Yeltsin parliamentary faction. A new pro-Yeltsin party was out of the question, for any association with the outgoing president became a liability. With no credible alternative emerging from outside the left-wing camp, it was only natural to view Luzhkov as the forthcoming president. This invited the creation of a pro-Luzhkov party of power, and such a party did not take long to arrive. Luzhkov's movement, Fatherland, was officially founded in December 1998. In addition to the presidential hopeful himself, the leadership of the movement included the leaders of several small nationalist and left-leaning organizations, including what remained of the KRO and Derzhava, and Women of Russia. Fatherland also absorbed almost two dozen even smaller groups of different ideological leanings.[55] Indeed, the programmatic message of Fatherland was about as vague as that of the NDR. Apparently, its primary appeal to the voters was generated by the personality of Luzhkov. The members of Yeltsin's administration viewed the party-building efforts of the presidential hopeful with understandable anxiety. One of the particularly disturbing aspects of these developments was Luzhkov's success in luring many regional leaders under the banners of Fatherland. In order to counterbalance this trend, Yeltsin's administration encouraged several influential regional leaders to launch their own movement, All Russia. Rather than participating in parliamentary elections on its own, the movement was expected to join an anti-Luzhkov coalition, which remained to be formed.[56] However, things turned out differently. In August 1999, Fatherland and All Russia created an electoral bloc led by Evgenii Primakov. After being dismissed by Yeltsin in May 1999, Primakov emerged as a potentially strong claimant for the Russian presidency. It was widely alleged that prior to entering the bloc, he reached an agreement with Luzhkov, who consented to postpone his own bid in exchange for the position of prime minister and Primakov's successor. The bloc, labeled Fatherland–All Russia, also included the APR. Thus it emerged as quite a formidable political machine.

Yeltsin's administration remained in desperate need of its own party of power. After the project to use All Russia as a component of such a party failed, there was an equally ill-conceived attempt to merge the NDR with the DVR and several other parties of the right.[57] However, the new party of power could hardly be created without a credible presidential candidate. Such a candidate emerged only on the eve of the 1999 parliamentary elections. After being appointed prime minister, Vladimir Putin started to swiftly gain political credit primarily because of his tough stance against Chechen secessionists (Rutland 2000; Shlapentokh 2001). His popularity steadily rose in September and October 1999, which made Yeltsin's aides hope that Primakov and Luzhkov could be prevented from taking a legislative majority. Thus the new party of power came into existence after all. Labeled the Interregional Movement Unity, or Medved (Bear), it was an electoral bloc officially formed by six small and politically impotent groups, but which were legally entitled to participate in national elections, and led by a group of prominent personalities including Sergei Shoigu, the respected federal minister for emergency situations. The NDR held negotiations on joining the new entity but eventually refused because of the "unsatisfactory conditions" offered to the old party of power, which wanted the second and third positions on the party list of Unity for its leaders.[58] Ironically, at that moment Shoigu remained a member of the NDR too. During its brief and manifestly nonideological campaign, Unity delivered three principal messages. First it posed itself as a party of youthful, energetic, and professional leadership. Second it placed major emphasis on Russia's territorial integrity and national greatness. Third it firmly and increasingly associated itself with Putin, even though it was only in early December that it explicitly recognized a pro-Putin majority in the Duma as its principal political goal (Colton and McFaul 2000).

Deprived of its status as the party of power, the NDR effectively degenerated into a minor right-wing group. The principal party of the right in the 1999 elections, the Union of Right Forces (SPS), was an electoral bloc that formally included the DVR and several other groups, including a party of Sergei Kirienko, New Force. Kirienko, not Gaidar, occupied the top position on the bloc's list. On a less formal basis, the bloc absorbed more than ten previously existing right-wing organizations.[59] Thus the right did learn a lesson from the disastrous consequences of excessive fragmentation in the 1995 elections. However, Yabloko did not join the SPS and proceeded on its own. The only noteworthy nationalist organization that took part in the 1999 campaign was the LDPR. After the Central Electoral Commission refused to register its list for a number of alleged violations of the electoral law, the LDPR managed to reenter the race under the label

Zhirinovsky Bloc. Interest advocacy groups in the 1999 elections included Women of Russia and a new formation, the Pensioners Party. A communist observer was probably correct in his contention that the rationale behind the latter party was a deliberate attempt to split the communist vote.[60]

It was not by accident that a long-standing component of the left, the APR, joined Fatherland–All Russia in the 1999 campaign. In November 1998, Ziuganov announced that the "patriotic forces" would participate in the 1999 elections "in three columns," one of them being formed by the KPRF itself, another by the APR, and the third by "patriots"—that is, by those nationalists who allied themselves with the left. In this regard, Ziuganov wittingly noted: "You catch more fish if you skillfully use three nets [rather than one]."[61] In fact, the three tendencies already coexisted under the umbrella of the Popular Patriotic Union of Russia (NPSR), a movement created in the aftermath of the 1996 elections. Since the activities of the NPSR were largely confined to regional electoral arenas, they will be treated at some length in Chapter 3. Here, it is sufficient to say that Ziuganov's proposal came as a heavy blow to the NPSR. The APR had already lost the 1995 party-list elections, and there was little reason to believe that it would do any better in 1999. As for the "patriots," the continuous existence of the LDPR made the electoral success of their "column" quite implausible. The true reason for Ziuganov's proposal was to economize on KPRF list seats that had to be offered to the party's insignificant partners. After a long period of negotiations, the APR effectively broke its alliance with the Communists to join Fatherland–All Russia, while several left-leaning nationalist groups previously allied with the KPRF, such as the ROS, ran independently. The list of the KPRF, as assembled by Ziuganov and his comrades in arms, included mostly party members, but also several prominent nonparty members such as Glaz'ev and a small group of Agrarians who refused to follow the line of their leadership. As in 1995, the RKRP ran a joint list with several small communist sects, not with the KPRF.

As a result of the elections (see Table 2.3), the KPRF retained its position of the leading party in the electorate, as well as of the largest single party in the Duma, but the size of its delegation decreased because it was less successful in the single-member districts and especially because the rate of vote-to-seat conversion in the proportional tier of elections became less favorable for the largest parties. Unity placed a close second, distantly followed by Fatherland–All Russia. The SPS, the LDPR, and Yabloko were not very successful but still able to cross the 5 percent threshold. The results of the elections effectively crossed the candidacies of Primakov and Luzhkov out of the 2000 presidential race. None of them ran. This placed Putin, in December 1999 appointed as the acting president of Russia, in quite a favorable position. Of those ten candidates who ran against him,

Table 2.3   Results of the 1999 Elections to the State Duma of Russia

Party	Share of Party-List Vote (%)	Number of Party-List Seats	Number of District Seats	Overall Number of Seats	Overall Share of Seats (%)
KPRF	24.3	67	46	113	25.6
Unity	23.3	64	9	73	16.6
Fatherland–All Russia (including APR)	13.3	37	29	66	15.0
SPS	8.5	24	5	29	6.6
LDPR (in bloc)	6.0	17	—	17	3.9
Yabloko	5.9	16	4	20	4.5
RKRP (in bloc)	2.2	—	—	—	—
Women of Russia	2.0	—	—	—	—
Pensioners Party	2.0	—	1	1	0.2
NDR	1.2	—	7	7	1.6
16 other parties	6.0	—	8	8	1.8
Independents	—	—	107	107	24.3
Against all	3.3	—	—	—	—
Invalid votes	1.9	—	—	—	—
Total	99.9[a]	225	216	441	100.1[a]

Note: a. Does not sum to 100.0 percent because of rounding.

three, Ziuganov, Yavlinsky, and Zhirinovsky, had already lost the 1996 elections to unpopular Yeltsin, while others were secondary figures apparently seeking publicity rather than success. Putin won in the first round with 52.9 percent of the vote. Ziuganov was able to gain a share of the vote only slightly larger than that of his party in the Duma elections, 29.2 percent, while Yavlinsky received an even smaller share, 5.8 percent. Zhirinovsky, who was actually the only party-nominated candidate in the 2000 elections, fared especially poorly with 2.7 percent of the vote.

    The results of the legislative and presidential elections naturally urged Fatherland to reconsider its initial goals, but they could not eliminate it from the political arena if only because Fatherland–All Russia still controlled quite a substantial share of seats in the Duma. The choice made under these conditions by the leaders of Fatherland was quite consistent with the movement's backgrounds: they opted for becoming a part of the new party of power. The leadership of Unity could only welcome such a turn of events. At the time of the 1999 elections, Unity remained an electoral bloc without its own membership; moreover, the memberships of its "founding organizations" were largely symbolic.[62] It was only after the elections, on December 28, that Unity was officially transformed into a movement of the same name.[63] In turn, the leaders of the movement encouraged their local supporters to create regional Unity movements, though they had to remain organizationally independent. The rationale for this strategy became apparent when the national movement was transformed into a political party in May 2000. Some of the regional movements were invited to form its regional branches, but some others were not. This practically enabled the national leadership of Unity to place the process of party formation under its control by incorporating only loyal and efficient local groups. In general, however, the regional network of Unity remained to be formed. One way to achieve it was to take over the already existing and relatively well-developed network of Fatherland. The process of unification started in April 2001 when the factions of Unity and Fatherland, and their subsidiary deputy groups, People's Deputy and the Regions of Russia, created a joint council to coordinate their activities in the national legislature.[64] On April 12, 2001, Shoigu and Luzhkov announced that Unity and Fatherland were going to create a new party on the basis of their previously existing organizations. The process of unification involved several steps. First, in July 2001 the two parties created an organization named the Union of Unity and Fatherland. At that moment, however, neither the national leaderships nor the regional branches of the constituent members of the union merged. In October 2001, at the second congress of the union, it was formally joined by All Russia, even though the movement not only remained inactive since early 2000 but also announced its self-dissolution more than a year before the event. The participation of All Russia, however, was considered to be important for incorporating nonpartisan regional elites into the new party of power.[65] Thus on December 1, 2001, Unity, Fatherland, and All Russia officially merged under a clumsy label, the All-Russian Party of Unity and Fatherland–Unitary Russia, with "Unitary Russia" being designated as the official abbreviated name of the party.

The second party of power, the People's Party of the Russian Federation (NPRF), was formed in 2001 on the basis of a recently founded political movement, People's Deputy. The movement, in turn, grew out of a national legislative deputy group of the same name. The group, consisting mostly of those deputies who ran as independents in the 1999 campaign, remained thoroughly supportive of Putin and his administration throughout the term of the Duma. Why did they not join Unity or Unitary Russia instead of forming the NPRF? One part of the answer is that some of the members of the group, local notables, simply could not be incorporated into the regional structures of Unity without causing tensions within its regional branches. The second part of the answer is that the NPRF was ideologically different from Unity. The ideological standing of Unity, as expressed in its December 2001 program, combined a commitment to the strong Russian statehood with rather well-defined right positions on socioeconomic issues.[66] The leader of the NPRF, a Soviet-style manager from Tiumen province named Gennadii Raikov, defined his party as "center to the left," with social welfare and employment being its primary concerns.[67] Given the new party's unlimited support for Putin, in which it did not differ from Unitary Russia, its leftist inclinations were readily interpreted by many observers as a sign that the NPRF was conceived as a vote-splitting device that would allow for channeling votes from the KPRF to the progovernment camp without compromising Unity's free-market credentials.[68] Almost in parallel to the parties of power, the right-wing parties also underwent a complex process of unification. In May 2000 the SPS officially ceased to be an electoral bloc as it was transformed into a political movement of the same name. The founders of the movement were nine organizations, including the DVR, Democratic Russia, and New Force, and five individuals, including Sergei Kirienko, Yegor Gaidar, and two persons who were to become the movement's official front figures, Boris Nemtsov and Irina Khakamada.[69] The movement was transformed into a political party in December 2001. Some of the old-guard democrats, apparently disappointed with the new party's pro-Putin stance, left it and formed a new political movement, Liberal Russia.[70]

Russia's Party System: A Comparative Assessment

The level of development attained by a national party system can be measured by addressing two of its properties: first, whether political parties play an important role in the electorate, and second, whether they are important as agencies of democratic government (Key 1964). To start with the former aspect, political parties in the electorate are important if they coordinate voters—that is, if they are useful tools for minimizing time and effort needed to make a meaningful choice at the polls. A party system's ability to perform this function declines if it is excessively fragmented, because numerous policy alternatives become too difficult to assess and translate into voting behavior, or excessively volatile, because this naturally requires voters to process more information than when they have to deal with a stable set of policy alternatives, or both. Party system fragmentation and volatility can be measured by analyzing electoral returns. The conventional measure of party system fragmentation belongs to the family of indicators based on the Herfindahl-Hirschman index (HH), the value of which can be established by squaring the shares of the components, such as vote shares, and summing them (Taagepera and Grofman 1981). HH is easily transformable into two indices that have been employed for measuring party system fragmentation, the Rae index, $1 - HH$ (Rae 1967), and the effective number of parties, $1 / HH$ (Laakso and Taagepera 1979). Of them, it stands to reason to use the latter, for it has gained wider recognition among political scientists.[71]

The effective numbers of parties in the proportional tiers of the 1993,

1995, and 1999 elections were 7.6, 10.7, and 6.8, respectively (Moser 2001: 37, 153). If compared with well-established democracies of the West, this level of fragmentation can be estimated as very high (Lijphart 1994: 96, 160–161). Latin American party systems also tend to be less fragmented (Coppedge 1997), even though some of the elections did produce very large effective numbers of parties, such as 10.3 in the 1984 elections in Ecuador, and 9.7 in the 1990 elections in Brazil (Amorim-Neto and Cox 1997). By the standards of the postcommunist world, the level of party system fragmentation in Russia is not unusually high. For instance, Moser (2001: 45) reports that the average effective number of parties in seven elections held in Lithuania, Hungary, Poland, and Ukraine in 1991–1997 was 7.3. An even more telling example is Latvia, where elections held in 1993, 1995, and 1998 produced effective numbers of parties of 6.1, 15.0, and 13.0, respectively.[72] However, it is quite conventional to view excessive fragmentation as one of the major deficiencies of postcommunist party systems (Jasiewicz 1993). The crucial question in this respect is, of course, what level of fragmentation can be realistically assessed as excessive. Arguably, a fragmented multiparty system can be desirable under conditions when each of the parties represents a clear-cut ideological alternative that appeals to a limited yet loyal societal constituency. If this is the case, parties' ideological standings do not take much effort to decipher, while the plenitude of ideological options offered in the electoral marketplace provides the voter with a capacity to choose among a wide range of options, which is good from a normative standpoint. Do Russia's political parties fit into this model?

It seems that they do not. As follows from the analysis above, the spectrum of Russia's political ideologies that appear to be appealing to the voters comprises only three components, the left, the right, and nationalism. In Russia's parliamentary elections, however, each of these components tended to be represented, on average, by more than two important parties, and in 1995 by more than three. In 1993, only a very sophisticated voter, if anybody at all, could distinguish among the ideological stances of Russia's Choice, Yabloko, the RDDR, and the DPR. In 1995, a similarly challenging task was choosing among the policy platforms of the LDPR, the KRO, and Derzhava. By investing a lot of effort, one could figure out that the LDPR was less ethnocentric than Derzhava, but a much more efficient way of processing relevant information was to take into account that the former was Zhirinovsky's party, while the latter was Rutskoi's party. Much the same applies to one of the most persistent divisions among the right, that between VR/DVR/SPS on the one hand, and Yabloko on the other hand. True, the lack of actual ideological differentiation continuously urged party leaders to emphasize minor divisions or even to invent them, as happened with Sviatoslav Fedorov's project to make his PST a left-leaning right-wing party, or Boris Fedorov's right-wing nationalist project. Such conscious engineering of electoral cleavages did not bring any significant payoffs to the engineers themselves but made it even more difficult for voters to understand the spectrum of party options instead.[73] At the same time, those large parties that already occupied their own ideological niches continuously tried to redefine their ideologies in order to widen their electoral appeal. Thus the KPRF emerged not only as a left-wing party but also as a nationalist party (Flikke 1999). To further complicate the picture, Russia's party scene was densely inhabited with formations that did not base their electoral messages on specific ideological stances. For instance, the ideological differences between the KPRF and the APR are negligible. What makes the APR distinctive is its role as an interest advocacy group for Soviet-style agricultural managers. Even more clear-cut instances of interest advocacy electoral politics are Women of Russia and the Pensioners Party. Finally, the persistent existence of the parties of power crucially contributed to increasing the level of party system fragmentation in Russia. In 1993 the major difference between the ideologically identical VR and Yabloko was not even that the former was the party of Gaidar and the latter the party of Yavlinsky, but rather that the former was the party of power while the latter was in opposition. As I have already mentioned, other parties of power were not ideologically defined at all, and increasingly so. If the NDR could be viewed as a center-to-the-right party, neither Fatherland nor Unity could be plausibly assigned to any ideological segment. As put by one of Unity's chief campaign organizers, "the ideology of Unity is the lack of ideology."[74] This combination of factors makes it less than surprising that a recent empirical study found Russia's political parties to lack ideological cohesion to a greater extent than their east-central European counterparts (Kitschelt and Smyth 2002).

Thus it would be fair to conclude that Russia's party system is not just fragmented but rather that it is excessively fragmented. Instead of clear-cut ideological options, Russia's political parties tend to appeal to voters with a set of attractors within which ideologies are amply supplemented and sometimes substituted with personality-based electioneering and interest advocacy. This brings us to the second party system property, electoral volatility. Like fragmentation—with which it is empirically interrelated (Golosov and Ponarin 1999)—volatility can be easily expressed in a compact numerical form. The conventional index of volatility refers to the aggregate change in the vote from one party to others from one election to the next (Przeworski 1975; Pedersen 1979). The index is computed by adding the net change in the percentage shares of the vote gained or lost by each party from one election to the next, and dividing the sum by 2. A seminal study of electoral volatility in established party systems has revealed a striking bias toward continuity and persistence (Bartolini and Mair 1990).

Indeed, average electoral volatility in 131 elections held in western European countries between 1960 and 1989 was 8.4 (Mair 1997: 182). In new democracies electoral volatility tends to be higher. On this parameter, most postcommunist countries stay in the middle ground between well-established democracies and some of the Latin American countries. As reported by Mair (1997: 182), electoral volatility between the founding and second elections in the Czech Republic, Hungary, and Poland was 19.9, 25.0, and 27.6 respectively. At the same time, average volatility in elections held in 1979–1995 in Brazil, Bolivia, Ecuador, and Peru was 33.0, 34.5, 38.6, and 58.5 respectively (Mainwaring 1999: 29). In Russia, electoral volatility was 56.4 in 1993–1995 and became only slightly smaller, 45.4, in 1995–1999.[75] Thus Russia's party system is unusually volatile by international standards.

One way to explain this property is to relate it to the characteristics of the electorate. Indeed, a study focused primarily on the 1995 elections concludes that "more than three quarters of the electorate lack any party identification" (White, Rose, and McAllister 1997: 135). More recent studies, however, tend to present evidence that antiparty sentiment within the electorate has decreased (Pammett and DeBardeleben, 2000). At the same time, party identifications tend to rapidly consolidate; indeed, they are not significantly weaker than in those east-central European countries where relatively stable party systems have already emerged (Miller et al. 2000; Brader and Tucker 2001). Miller and Klobucar (2000: 668) suggest that "emerging party identification is now beginning to flourish and will play an increasingly important role in shaping citizens' political decision making." Indeed, Colton (2000) found that party identification was one of the most significant predictors of voting behavior in the 1996 presidential election. These empirical findings run in apparent contradiction with the high level of volatility in the 1999 elections, as if party identifications consolidate but, for some reasons external to the voters themselves, they fail to translate these identifications into actual electoral behavior. In a rather speculative fashion, for more survey research is obviously needed to substantiate this point, I would argue that this is the case. Consider a voter who in 1995 developed identification with the NDR. It is highly unlikely that the basis for this identification was provided by the vague center-right ideological stance of the movement. Rather, it was identification with a party of power. In 1999 the name of the NDR was still on the ballot paper, but even the least-informed voters knew that it was not a party of power anymore. Thus party identification notwithstanding, the previous identifier with the NDR had to switch his sympathies either to Unity or to Fatherland. This line of reasoning can be in part empirically justified by disaggregating the values of electoral volatility reported above into two components, the aggregate change in the vote for continuous parties and the aggregate change in the vote that occurs as a result of changes in the available set of parties. For lack of better terminology, I dub these components "voter volatility" and "party volatility" respectively. For example, a 10.2 percent decline of the share of the vote cast for the LDPR between the 1993 and 1995 elections adds 5.1 to voter volatility, while 23.3 percent of the vote received in 1999 by Unity, which did not previously contest elections, adds 11.7 to party volatility. As it turns out, the primary kind of electoral volatility in Russia is party volatility. Indeed, for the 1993–1995 period, voter volatility of only 19.1 sums up with party volatility of 37.3 to produce the overall figure of 56.4. For the 1995–1999 period, voter volatility is 18.0, and party volatility 27.4. It seems that political parties themselves, not voters, are accountable for the excessive levels of electoral volatility in Russia.[76]

Thus political parties in Russia's electorate suffer from deficiencies that cannot be attributed to the electorate itself but rather stem from the parties' own properties. It is only logical to relate these properties to an insufficient role played by parties in Russia's government. Throughout the 1993–2003 period, the executive branch of power in the country remained thoroughly nonpartisan. The presidents, Yeltsin and Putin, did not belong to any political parties. Speaking of the federal government, the waves of party penetration took place concurrently with national legislative elections, when many senior officials joined the parties of power. The parties of power, however, did not rule; nor were they accountable for their representatives in the government. For example, Chernomyrdin did perform as the leader of the NDR during the 1995 campaign, yet he did not resign after the NDR lost the elections to the KPRF and the LDPR. There was also no indication that other party leaders and activists informed Chernomyrdin's policies. Quite the reverse, the function of the NDR was to support whatever policies were pursued by Chernomyrdin. As for other senior officials who joined the NDR, the example of Putin may be quite illuminating. In 1995, when working as a vice governor in the city administration of St. Petersburg, Putin was appointed as the head of the regional branch of the movement, and he remained a member of its national political council at the beginning of the 1999 campaign, of which the leaders of the NDR were naturally well aware.[77] Putin himself, however, easily discarded this circumstance when reminded about it by saying: "Well, at that time [in 1995] everybody was in the NDR."[78] In fact, Egor Gaidar and Boris Fedorov were the only leaders of a party of power who ever resigned from their government posts after their party, the VR, was defeated at the polls. Of the other ten ministers who were on the list of the VR before the elections, only one, Anatolii Chubais, joined the newly formed DVR in 1994. Occasionally, other DVR members took ministerial positions too. The leader of the DVR, Gaidar, developed an interesting philosophical justification for their participation in the government. According to Gaidar, Russia's "democrats" were not able to take power in full because of the intrinsic weakness of the country's democratic movement. Under these conditions, it was not logical to reject government positions. Only by taking them, according to Gaidar, could the "democrats" effectively influence government policies by providing their expertise or even guidance to the powerful yet ignorant Soviet-style bureaucrats.[79] For all its similarity with the Trotskyite "entrism tactics," this philosophy allowed Chubais and others to join the executive without compromising their loyalty to the DVR. Paradoxically enough, a very similar course of action was taken by the APR. Some of Russia's ministers in charge of agriculture were APR members.

On different occasions, members of opposition parties also received invitations to join the government, and sometimes they did. In January 1995, Yeltsin appointed an influential member of the KPRF faction in the national legislature, Valentin Kovalev, as Russia's minister of justice. Soon after the appointment, however, the new minister was expelled from the party because he accepted the post without the party's preliminary approval; as put by Ziuganov, "there must be some kind of discipline."[80] When another high-standing communist Yurii Masliukov received an invitation to join the government in July 1998, the party recommended that he reject the offer.[81] However, the KPRF withdrew its recommendation after Primakov replaced Kirienko as prime minister. Masliukov's appointment, however, did not last longer than Primakov's leadership. Similarly, several members of Yabloko received government appointments in 1996–1999, but none of them received official party endorsement. The attitude of Russia's politicians toward the compatibility of party affiliation with cabinet membership was most clearly expressed by an activist of the LDPR, Sergei Kalashnikov, who joined Primakov's government as the minister of labor: "You just can't be a government member and a party member [simultaneously], I mean, in Russia. Maybe it is possible in the west. . . . All in all, I am not a member of the LDPR."[82] McFaul (2001: 1163) promptly generalizes in the following way: "When party members did join the government, their allegiances usually transferred to the prime minister and drifted away from their party leaders and organizations."

The upper chamber of the national legislature, the Federation Council, also remained nonpartisan irrespective of its makeup: popularly elected representatives (1993–1995), heads of regional administrations and legislatures (1995–2000), or their appointed representatives (2000 and henceforth). The nonpartisanship of regional elites will be discussed at length in the subsequent chapters of this analysis. What is important to mention here is that constitutionally, the powers of the Federation Council are very limited. The primary legislative body in Russia is the State Duma. In 1993–2003, it emerged as the primary source of party influence in Russia. In the immediate aftermath of the 1993 elections, it was not entirely clear whether political parties would play an important role in the Duma (Haspel 1998). In particular, the standing committees of the Duma emerged as an alternative organizational axis of legislative activities. Before long, however, it became apparent that the "dual-channel" model of legislative decisionmaking was less than efficient (Ostrow 1998). Thus already in the 1993–1995 Duma, political parties started to establish themselves as primary players on the floor (Haspel, Remington, and Smith 1998), while committees became quite susceptible to the influence of legislative parties (Remington and Smith 1995). This trend further consolidated after the 1995 elections when the left-wing opposition took a near majority of Duma seats. Indeed, the opposition profile of the legislature greatly contributed to its capacity to enact legislation independently from the executive, while interbranch relations involved not only political conflict but also a good deal of cooperation. More than anticipated, Yeltsin had to accept the legislature, and thereby the parties that played the lead in it, as legitimate participants in the decisionmaking process. In particular, the president often refrained from exercising his constitutionally granted decree authority in favor of reaching compromises on legislation passed by the Duma (Remington 2001b). After the 1999 elections, and especially after the propresidential forces in the Duma succeeded in manufacturing a stable majority that approved virtually any move of the executive, the political significance of the legislature naturally declined (Remington 2001a). By that time, however, the party-centered structure of the legislature became firmly and perhaps irreversibly established. Indeed, the factions of Unity and Fatherland–All Russia formed the core of the propresidential majority.

Arguably, this course of events would be unthinkable without the proportional tier of Russia's electoral system. With half of the deputies elected by party lists, political parties were able to secure sufficient parliamentary representation. On the Duma floor, due to the natural organizational superiority of political parties over the independent deputies, this level of representation was successfully converted into the outright domination of political parties. This, in turn, created incentives for nonpartisan Duma deputies to align either with party factions or with their "subsidiary" deputy groups such as the Agrarians and People's Power in the 1995–1999 Duma. True, the number of independent single-member district deputies in the Duma continuously remained quite substantial, and as it can be inferred from Tables 2.1–2.3, even increased after the 1999 elections. Yet even more than in 1993–1999, those deputies who were independents by their electoral origins effectively subjected themselves to party control. Indeed, one of the deputy groups, People's Deputy, served as a basis for forming a new propresidential party, the NPRF. On the other extreme of Russia's political spectrum, the Agro-Industrial Group is not only closely politically allied with the KPRF but also consists mostly of KPRF list and single-member district nominees. True, one of the deputy groups, the Regions of Russia, not only consisted mostly of independents, even though it also included a large number of nominees of Fatherland–All Russia, but also claimed to retain relative political autonomy in 2000. In 2001, after being absorbed by the propresidential majority, it effectively abandoned such claims.[83]

Thus Russia's party system did manage to take root in the national legislature. By implication, success in Duma elections emerged as a principal precondition for the survival of individual parties. This, in turn, produces strong incentives for the territorial penetration of political parties. First, local membership may be useful for completing the task of party list registration; second, local members may be nominated as the party's candidates in single-member districts, thus creating a potential for increasing its Duma delegation; third, presence in the region increases the party's visibility, thus enhancing the chances of its list in the given locality; and finally, as an extension of the previous argument, running a candidate in a single-member district may improve the party's chances in the list competition even if the candidate has no chances to win whatsoever (Golosov and Yargomskaya 1999). Of course, the deficiencies of Russia's party system described above suppress these incentives. Yet none of the counterincentives for territorial penetration induced by national party system properties can be viewed as an insurmountable obstacle. Speaking of excessive party system fragmentation, it would be simply unrealistic to assume that all of Russia's political parties are too small in terms of voter support to penetrate the localities. Electoral volatility is a stronger counterincentive, for it means that after each national legislative election, some of the parties become extinct while others have to start their penetration efforts from scratch. Of the important parties, however, rapid extinction has so far plagued only the parties of power. Yet these parties never really had to start from scratch. On the one hand, the labels of the parties of power did change, and it would be fair to assume that the electoral constituency of Russia's Choice was quite different from that of Unity. On the other hand, the administrative component of the parties of power remained intact throughout the 1993–2003 period, and their activists often switched their loyalties from the VR to the NDR to Unity or Fatherland, and finally to Unitary Russia without having any problem. Several other important parties, such as the KPRF, Yabloko, and the LDPR, remained continuous throughout the period. The same applies to the DVR after it separated itself from the party power, with the SPS emerging largely as its direct organizational continuation. The lack of political influence over the national executive, while decreasing the value of party affiliation for top regional power-holders, does not actually prevent parties from emerging on the grassroots level.

*   *   *

In 1993–2003 the institutional and political conditions of Russia remained unfavorable for party formation. The set of factors that in one way or another suppressed party formation included presidentialism (Moser 1998a; see, however, Ishiyama and Kennedy 2001), the lack of party-structured "founding" elections (McFaul 2001: 1173), and certain characteristics of the electorate jointly referred to as "fuzziness" in one of the studies (Rose and Tikhomirov 1997). A factor that is often omitted from this fairly standard list of obstacles to party development in Russia is the ban on Communist Party activities imposed by Yeltsin in 1991. In nearly all post-communist countries, communist successor parties, after experiencing painful processes of ideological and organizational transformation, emerged as pivotal elements of emerging party systems (Evans and Whitefield 1995; Ishiyama 1999). In Russia, the ban on Communist Party activities not only undermined the organizational basis of the major successor party but also severely diminished its capacity for ideological moderation by restricting its membership to the circle of hard-core "true believers" (Golosov 2000; Ishiyama 2001). Russia's national party system is excessively fragmented and excessively volatile, while the influence of national political parties over the national executive seems to be negligible. At the same time, political parties seem to be rapidly developing in the electorate, and they did manage to emerge as principal agencies of democratic decisionmaking in the national legislature. In both capacities, they have strong incentives for territorial penetration. As mentioned in Chapter 1, these incentives largely lack practical materialization. In the light of the analysis above, this suggests the existence of region-level factors that effectively resist party penetration. Moreover, it can be speculated that some of the deficiencies of Russia's national party system, especially excessive electoral volatility, are directly related to the individual parties' inability to take root in the regions. Thus region-level resistance to party development emerges as an additional factor of party underdevelopment in Russia.

Notes

1. Manifest o provozglashenii Sotsial-demokraticheskoi partii Rossiiskoi Federatsii, *Al'ternativa,* May 30, 1990.
2. For an insightful analysis of Yeltsin's political career, see Colton 1995.
3. Vystuplenie N. Travkina na I s"ezde Demokraticheskoi partii Rossii, *Demokraticheskaia gazeta,* December 22, 1990.
4. VLKSM zaregistrirovan, KPSS gotovitsia, *Kommersant,* March 18, 1991.
5. Demokraty naznachili den traura na 7 noiabria, *Kommersant,* October 22, 1990.
6. S priznannym liderom "DS" Valeriei Novodvorskoi... *Kuranty,* December 31, 1993.

7. Tsentristskii blok: Pri vvedenii chrezvychainogo polozhenia mozhete rasschityvat, *Kommersant,* January 28, 1991.

8. Demokraticheskaia partia kommunistov Rossii opredeliaetsia, *Moskovskii komsomolets,* August 27, 1991.

9. Dvizhenie za demokraticheskie reformy, *Kommersant,* July 8, 1991.

10. 22 iiulia 1992 goda sostoialas press-konferentsia... *Delovoi mir,* July 24, 1992.

11. On menial partii kak perchatki, *Komsomol'skaia pravda,* April 5, 2000.

12. Patrioty sozdali novuiu strukturu, *Kommersant,* December 30, 1991.

13. Sozdana kommunistichesko-antikommunisticheskaia koalitsia, *Kommersant,* August 31, 1992.

14. Lomanaia linia, *Moskovski komsomolets,* February 21, 1992.

15. Kak zaiavil byvshii pervyi sekretar TsK RKP V. Kuptsov... *Vechernii klub,* January 21, 1993.

16. Interv'iu s liderom Agrarnoi partii Rossii, *Izvestia,* November 27, 1993.

17. KPRF i ee fraktsia v gosudarstvennoi dume, *Molodoi kommunist,* October 1, 1996.

18. Later in 1993, Yeltsin issued another decree that stipulated for direct elections of Federation Council members by plurality in two-member districts.

19. Cited in White, Rose, and McAllister 1997: 109.

20. See *Spravochno-informatsionnye materialy: Uchreditel'nyi s" ezd obshchestvenno-politicheskogo bloka Vybor Rossii.* Moscow, 1995.

21. Party lists for all parties appeared in *Rossiiskaia gazeta,* November 12, 1993.

22. Netraditsionnye formy predvybornoi bor'by v Rossii, *Megapolis-Ekspress,* October 27, 1993.

23. Kandidat v Gosudarstvennuiu Dumu... Sergei Shakhrai, *Segodnia,* December 2, 1993.

24. Ob"edinit'sia levym silam vse trudnee, *Nezavisimaia gazeta,* September 10, 1999.

25. *Federal'noe Sobranie: Spravochnik* (Moscow: Informatsionno-Ekspertnaia Gruppa Panorama, 1996), p. 174.

26. Rossiiskoe dvizhenie demokraticheskikh reform, *Megapolis-Ekspess,* December 8, 1993.

27. "Chemodany" Govorukhina, *Kuranty,* December 20, 1993.

28. 6 noiabria v 24.00 istek srok, *Komsomol'skaia pravda,* November 9, 1993.

29. Sushchestvuet 5 obshchestvenno-politicheskikh ob"edinenii, *Segodnia,* October 30, 1993.

30. Ministerstvo yustitsii Rossii annulirovalo registratsiiu... *Trud,* August 13, 1992.

31. Udushenie liberal'noi demokratii, *Kommersant,* August 17, 1992.

32. Deiatel'nost Kompartii Rossiiskoi Federatsii... *Izvestia,* October 19, 1993.

33. Vopros ob uchastii v vyborakh postavil na gran raskola kommunisticheskoe dvizhenie, *Segodnia,* November 13, 1993.

34. Lidery predvybornykh blokov otvechaiut na voprosy, *Moskovskie novosti,* November 21, 1993.

35. Agrarnaia partia Rossii nabrala polmilliona podpisei, *Megapolis-Ekspress,* November 17, 1993.

36. Zhenshchiny Rossii, Kedr, *Kommersant-Daily,* December 10, 1993.

37. Izbiratel'nye bloki: Kto est kto, *Rossiiskie vesti,* December 11, 1993.

38. Electoral returns reported in Table 2.1 are different from those reported in

the majority of other sources for the following reason. In 1993, amid rather vocal accusations of electoral fraud, the Central Electoral Commission of Russia published electoral results without taking account the spoiled ballots. The number of such ballots became publicly known only in 1995 (www.cityline.ru/politika/fs/gd1rezv.html). To better trace continuities between the shares of vote received by individual parties, I found it useful to recalculate the 1993 results by taking into account spoiled ballots, as a result of which the shares of the vote of individual parties became smaller than it is normally assumed.

39. S"ezd partii Gaidara, *Kommersant-Daily,* June 15, 1994.

40. Uchreditel'nye s"ezdy partii, *Kommersant-Daily,* February 21, 1995.

41. Partia samoupravlenia trudiashchiksia, *Obshchaia gazeta,* October 12, 1995.

42. Partiinaia zhizn Rossii, *Kommersant-Daily,* April 29, 1995.

43. Partiinaia zhizn Rossii, *Kommersant-Daily,* June 1, 1995.

44. Prem'er ne zametil poteri boitsa, *Moskovskii komsomolets,* September 5, 1995.

45. Aleksandr Rutskoi vybiraet soiuznikov, *Segodnia,* April 7, 1995.

46. Predvybornaia platforma Kommunisticheskoi partii, *Sovetskaia Rossia,* August 31, 1995.

47. Dva izbiratel'nykh bloka kommunistov, *Segodnia,* August 12, 1995.

48. Poslednii redut, *Sel'skaia zhizn,* September 5, 1995.

49. Nikolai Ryzhkov: Nam nuzhen plan vosstanovlenia narodnogo khoziaistva, *Izvestia,* December 15, 1995.

50. Vybirali—veselilis, podschitali—proslezilis, *Moskovskii komsomolets,* January 23, 1996.

51. Edinogo kandidata—ot oppozitsionnogo bloka, *Sovetskaia Rossia,* February 13, 1996.

52. General Lebed meniaet partprinadlezhnost, *Delo* (Samara), February 23, 1996.

53. Biznes shou supermen, *Novaia gazeta,* June 24, 1996.

54. Rezul'taty torgov otmeneny, *Obshchaia gazeta,* September 3, 1998.

55. Partiinye igry s moskovskim merom, *Moskovskie novosti,* August 12, 1998.

56. Partia vlasti: Feniks iz pepla? *Russkaia mysl* (Paris), June 24, 1999.

57. Pravyi tsentr nikak ne mozhet konsolidirovat'sia, *Nezavisimaia gazeta,* August 21, 1999.

58. Troe v lodke, *Vedomosti,* September 27, 1999.

59. 29 linii politicheskogo spektra, *Russkaia mysl* (Paris), November 25, 1999.

60. "Gapon" na pansione, *Sovetskaia Rossia,* November 11, 1999.

61. S"ezd NPSR, *Kommersant,* November 24, 1998.

62. It seems that only one of them, the Popular Patriotic Party of Russia, was something of a real organization.

63. V Moskve otkrylsia s"ezd pobeditelei, *Nezavisimaia gazeta,* December 28, 2000.

64. Sozdan koordinatsionnyi sovet chetyrekh, *Nezavisimaia gazeta,* April 17, 2001.

65. "Edinstvo" i "Otechestvo" daviat na massu, *Vremia MN,* December 1, 2001.

66. Ot "Edinstva" k "Edinoi Rossii": Evoliutsia ideologicheskikh ustanovok, *Vlast,* May 25, 2002.

67. Novaia partia na politnebosklone Rossii, *Slovo,* May 25, 2002.

68. "Nardep": Mezhdu dvizheniem i partiei, *Volgogradskaia pravda* (Volgograd), July 20, 2001.
69. Pravye budut spasat Rossiiu v novom kachestve, *Kommersant,* August 17, 2000.
70. "Soiuz pravykh sil," *Novye izvestia,* December 14, 2001.
71. Other measures with similar conceptual loading are more difficult to calculate, and they have substantive shortcomings of their own (Lijphart 1994). See, however, Molinar 1991; and Dunleavy and Boucek 2003.
72. I calculated these figures on the basis of the official electoral returns as reported at www.cspp.strath.ac.uk. Due to the lack of information, electoral returns for very small parties summed up as if for one party in each of the elections.
73. For a similar argument in application to east-central European countries, see Kostelecký 2002: 175.
74. Ideologia "Edinstva" v otsutstvii ideologii, *Nezavisimaia gazeta,* September 29, 1999.
75. The values of volatility may be different from those reported by other scholars for two reasons. First, I considered several parties as continuous if they were pivotal in electoral blocs or changed their names without significant leadership changes. Second, unlike many researchers, I did not consider the VR of 1993 and the DVR–United Democrats of 1995 as continuous parties.
76. For a similar argument, see Rose, Munro, and White 2001.
77. Lider fraktsii NDR v Gosdume... *Nevskoe vremia* (St. Petersburg), August 14, 1999.
78. 7 mgnovenii iz zhizni "preemnika," *Moskovskii komsomolets,* August 18, 1999.
79. Nashi raznoglasia—eto nashi dostizhenia, *Obshchaia gazeta,* June 19, 1997.
80. Ministr yustitsii iskliuchen iz fraktsii, *Kommersant-Daily,* January 11, 1995.
81. Mesto v "etom pravitel'stve," *Sovetskaia Rossia,* August 4, 1998.
82. Glava Mintruda Sergei Kalashnikov... *Vechernii Peterburg* (St. Petersburg), July 2, 1999.
83. Oleg Morozov... *Parlamentskaia gazeta,* November 29, 2001.

3

Political Parties in the Regions of Russia: An Empirical Overview

In the previous chapter, I suggested that while, due to a constellation of political and institutional factors, Russia's political parties are relatively underdeveloped at the national level, they cannot be said to be entirely insignificant in a number of policymaking domains, and they have important incentives to penetrate the periphery of the country. This chapter demonstrates that these incentives largely lack practical materialization, and presents much of the empirical evidence to substantiate this claim. The first section presents essential background information on regional elections in Russia within the context of the evolution of Russia's federalism. The second section lays out aggregate evidence on the participation of political parties in regional executive and legislative elections. In the third section, I present factual information about the levels of electoral activity and success of individual parties, focusing primarily on the levels of party representation in the regional legislative assemblies.

Russia's Federalism and Regional Electoral Politics

A detailed discussion of the complexities of Russia's federal constitutional design is not of primary concern for this analysis. Rather, the goal is to describe the institutional framework within which regional electoral politics take place and, on this basis, to delineate the universe of elections entered into this analysis. I understand "the regions of Russia" to mean the eighty-nine federal units, or "subjects of the federation," as identified in Article 65 of the 1993 constitution. These include twenty-one republics, six territories, forty-nine provinces, two federal cities, one autonomous province, and ten autonomous districts. Despite the multiplicity of denominations, Article 5 stipulates that all of them are "equal subjects of the Russian Federation," which provides for a symmetrical structure of the country's federalism. The word "symmetrical" in the study of federalism refers to the absence of constitutionally embedded differences between the legal status and prerogatives of different subunits within the same federation (Stepan 2000: 142). It can be noted that quite consistent with this categorization, there is no difference between the constitutional standings of territories and provinces whatsoever. The word distinction is inherited from the history of administrative divisions under the Soviet system. When initially created in the 1920s, the territories tended to be large territorial units that were normally located on the boundaries of the country and sometimes (but not necessarily) included provinces, autonomous provinces, or autonomous districts as their subunits. This distinction, however, became rudimentary by the time communist rule collapsed. The federal cities, Moscow and St. Petersburg (then Leningrad), were administratively separated from their provinces already in the Soviet era, and in 1991 they were allowed to have direct mayoral elections, which were among the earliest senior executive elections held in Russia. The cities' separation from Moscow and Leningrad provinces was legitimized by granting them rights equal to those of other regions.

Other distinctions in the complex constitutional typology of Russia's regions have had more important implications for their electoral histories. The republics, autonomous province, and autonomous districts are ethnically defined regions, once created as the principal tools of pursuing Leninist nationality politics. The names of these regions are normally based on the names of "titular nationalities"—that is, those ethnic groups for whom they were expected to be territorial homes. Throughout the 1980s the Russian Soviet Federated Socialist Republic included sixteen autonomous soviet socialist republics, five autonomous provinces, and ten autonomous districts (Jacobs 1983: 4).[1] The status of republics within this hierarchy was higher than that of other units, which was reflected in the fact that autonomous provinces and districts were legally incorporated into territories and provinces, while republics stood on their own. In 1990–1991, the word "autonomous" was dropped from the official names of the republics, while all the autonomous provinces seceded from the territories they previously belonged to, and all but one officially renamed themselves as republics. This increased the number of republics to twenty and, after Ingushetia was officially separated from Chechnya in 1992, to twenty-one. Chechnya unilaterally seceded from the Russian Federation in 1991. In 1996 the two parties signed a treaty that postponed a final decision on the republic's independence for five years. In 1999–2000, however, Russian troops took control over a large and gradually increasing portion of Chechen territory and imposed a new local administration.

The authorities of some of the autonomous districts attempted to separate themselves from territories and provinces too. In the end, however, only the autonomous district of Chukotka was able to secede from Magadan province, which practically equated its status with that of provinces and territories. The same can be said about the constitutional status of the only remaining autonomous province, Jewish, after it seceded from Khabarovsk territory. As far as the remaining nine autonomous districts are concerned, Article 66 of the 1993 constitution holds them subordinated to this or that territory or province by vaguely stating that "the relations between an autonomous district within a territory or province may be regulated by federal law or a treaty between the bodies of state authority of the autonomous district and, accordingly, the bodies of state authority of the territory or province," while Article 5 indirectly stipulates that they are equal to all other regions, including those to which they are supposed to be subordinated. A minor electoral consequence of this situation was that the authorities of the autonomous districts sometimes consented to their populations' participation in the executive or legislative elections held in larger regions, but sometimes, when involved in conflicts with larger regions' authorities, they called for abstention (Wilson 2001).

The principal difference in the electoral histories of individual regions depended on whether they succeeded in becoming republics. The very existence of the republics is sometimes considered as an indication that by its constitutional design, Russia belongs to the category of asymmetrical federations.[2] From a strictly constitutional perspective, such a categorization seems to be overstated. The only sign of asymmetry actually visible in the 1993 constitution is that the republics are entitled to have their own constitutions, while all other regions have statutes as their basic laws, but the legal difference between so-understood constitutions and statutes is not spelled out, which renders the distinction void.[3] Yet the contemporary political history of Russia, including its electoral history, does not start with December 1993, and in the previous period the republics enjoyed quite an apparent constitutional supremacy over other regions. In 1990–1991, many of them issued declarations of sovereignty that stipulated the supremacy of their laws over those issued by federal bodies of power, Soviet and Russian alike, and included similar provisions in their constitutions (Roeder 1991; Kahn 2000; Suny 1993). While in many respects the consequences of the "parade of sovereignties" were of symbolic significance, Russian federal authorities did treat republics very differently from other regions. The "legal separatism" of the republics, assisted by some of their leaders' careful use of ethnic sentiment among the populace (Gorenburg 2001), started to be taken seriously in Moscow (Shlapentokh, Levita, and Liberg 1997; Treisman 1997; Lapidus 1999). One of the manifestations of such a distinctive attitude was the fact that while the heads of administration of territories, provinces, the remaining autonomous province, and autonomous districts were appointed by the federal executive in 1991 through early 1992, the republics, in accordance with their constitutions, were allowed either to elect their chief executives by popular vote or to retain Soviet-type quasi-parliamentary systems, which meant that their constitutional heads were the chairpersons of the Supreme Soviets of the republics. The Federal Treaty, signed on March 31, 1992, and then incorporated into the amended version of the 1978 constitution, further consolidated the special status of the republics within the Russian Federation by providing them with several rights not attributed to other regions (Kirkow 1998: 47).[4] While the Federal Treaty was not included in the 1993 constitution, the special status of several republics was reflected in bilateral treaties signed by them with the federal executive in 1994 and later (Kempton 1996; Treisman 1999). In the course of time, however, bilateral treaties were signed with some of the other regions as well, while the contents of such treaties became increasingly less permissive in terms of granting benefits to the signatories than they used to be in 1994–1995.[5] Starting in 2000, the federal executive exerted increasing pressure upon the republics, urging them to amend their constitutions and other legislation in accordance with federal law, and gradually depriving them of fiscal and other benefits that were previously associated with their status (Brown 2001). The May 2000 establishment of seven federal districts headed by presidential representatives played an important role in implementing these goals (Hyde 2001). Indeed, one of the representatives' explicitly stated goals was to ensure the conformity of the regional legislation with the federal legislation. Overall, then, the evolution of Russia's federalism, when viewed from the angle of the federal executive's relations with the republics, can be described as a complex process that included three phases: (1) the aconstitutionally and, to an extent, anticonstitutionally embedded asymmetrical federalism of 1991–1993; (2) the aconstitutionally embedded asymmetric federalism of 1994–1999; and (3) the constitutionally and, partly due to the establishment of the federal districts, aconstitutionally embedded symmetric federalism of 2000 to the present, which remains burdened with the legacies of the previous period's asymmetries.

It will be noticed that the second and third phases correspond to the electoral cycles as identified in Chapter 1. While the reasons for this are quite apparent, given that the first Duma elections were held concurrently with the referendum that endorsed the 1993 constitution, while the third Duma elections can be viewed as the earliest political endorsement of Vladimir Putin and his centralizing effort, such a correspondence is of great analytical value. Specifically, it allows for categorizing elections in the regions of Russia on a basis that takes into account both the evolution of the federal framework and the major thresholds in national party system development. The types of contested offices can provide another basis for such a categorization. It is possible to divide all the offices into two broad types, single-person executive positions on the one hand, and seats in multimember assemblies with primarily legislative powers on the other hand. For the sake of smoother narration, I will occasionally refer to these events as "executive" and "legislative" elections respectively, even though these two words might mean very different things in different regional contexts.

As mentioned in the previous chapter, the earliest relatively free regional elections that can be viewed as legislative elections in the broad meaning introduced above were the regional soviet elections of March 1990 (Helf and Hahn 1992). Three of the four former autonomous provinces that transformed themselves into republics elected their soviets in the end of 1991 (the second rounds of these elections took place in early 1992). These elections, due to the absence of candidates' meaningful party affiliation and the essentially predemocratic context within which they were held, are not of much interest for this study. The soviets, multimember bodies with vast but not strictly delineated powers, survived as the principal agencies of the regions' legislative power up to at least the autumn of 1993, when Boris Yeltsin decreed, either directly or by charging the regional executives, their dissolution in all regions but republics. In three regions the soviets became extinct even earlier: in Chechnya, where the Supreme Soviet was forcefully dissolved in September 1991 to be replaced with a new parliament elected in the next month; in Ingushetia, which did not have its own legislature up to 1994, even though the Ingush deputies of the Supreme Soviet of Checheno-Ingushetia were instrumental in performing certain representative functions; and in Kalmykia, where its Supreme Soviet dissolved itself under pressure from the republic's president in May 1993. The majority of soviets in regions other than republics were indeed dissolved by the executives in late 1993. Five republics also elected new legislatures as early as December 1993, as did six others in the course of 1994. As many as nine, however, allowed their soviets or the provisional parliaments elected by them to serve their full terms up to March 1995, December 1995 (Adygeia), and even December 1996 (Khakasia). In Chechnya, the parliament elected in 1991 was dissolved by the republic's executive as early as June 1993. In 1996 and 1997 the republic witnessed two legislative elections: the "collaborationist" People's Assembly was elected in June 1996, only to wither away after the Russian troops left the republic several months later, while the proindependence parliament was elected in early 1997, only to wither away when Chechnya again was occupied by Russian troops in 1999. Other regions elected their new legislatures either in December 1993 or in the early months of 1994, especially in March. There were several cases when legislative elections in regions other then republics were delayed, principally due to the executives' reluctance to convoke them, to the end of 1994, and in one case, Ul'ianovsk province, to December 1995.

One of Yeltsin's decrees that dissolved the soviets in regions other than republics stipulated that the new legislatures, like the 1993 national Duma, could be elected for only two year terms, which meant that fresh elections had to be held on a massive scale from December 1995 to March 1996 (Slider 1996). In the course of time, however, the majority of regional legislatures attempted to unilaterally extend their terms in office. After a series of complex maneuvers involving the federal executive and the judiciary, almost all of them succeeded in achieving this goal by extending their terms to 1996 or 1997, most often to the end of the respective year. Thus a typical legislature elected in March 1994 was in session for about two and a half to three and a half years. Their successors had longer lives and normally served for four or five full years. In general, it can be said that starting with 1996–1997, regional legislative elections were being held on a fairly regular basis. At the same time, it is worth mentioning that federal law allows for extending the terms of regional bodies of power, executive and legislative alike, in order to make them concurrent with other regional or federal elections, even though extensions for more than one year are not permissible. This provision allowed the parliament of Kabardino-Balkaria that was elected in December 1997 to extend its term to December 2003, which makes it the longest-living legislature in the contemporary history of Russia. Table 3.1 reports aggregate evidence on regional legislative elections in Russia. Note that the ways of aggregating data by electoral cycle and year are different.

In none of the electoral cycles did the number of legislative elections coincide with the number of regions that held them. Relevant information is provided in Table 3.2. Regions in the second column of the table are mostly republics. The reasons why they did not hold legislative elections in the course of the given electoral cycles, as well as why Chechnya held two elections in less than one year, have been addressed above. With the exceptions of Chechnya and Kemerovo province, whose 1996 legislature was elected for a two-year term only, regions in the third column are those that used the systems of staggered elections, locally referred to as deputy rotation. This means that they reelected parts of their legislatures on a biannual basis. The rotation elections were held in whole regions, not in selected districts, which allows for considering them as separate events. The statistics presented in Tables 3.1 and 3.2 and elsewhere in this chapter do not however take into account either second-round elections in those regions that use majority systems (which, in particular, means that if the first round took place in 2000 and the second in 2001, then the given elections are counted as being held in 2000), or by-elections held in individual districts, even though the numbers of districts simultaneously holding by-elections were at times quite substantial. I also excluded the 1994 elections in Taimyr autonomous district because a court ruling invalidated the results.

Regional executive elections started earlier than legislative elections yet took more time to assume regularity. It has already been mentioned that

Table 3.1   Regional Legislative Elections in Russia, 1991–2003, by Electoral Cycle and Year

Electoral Cycle/Year	Number of Legislative Elections Held in Republics	Number of Legislative Elections Held in Other Regions	Total
By Electoral Cycle			
1991 to November 1993	4	0	4
1st electoral cycle	18	67	85
2nd electoral cycle	19	71	90
3rd electoral cycle	17	69	86
Total	58	207	265
By Year			
1991	4	0	4
1992	0	0	0
1993	5	5	10
1994	6	61	67
1995	8	2	10
1996	3	27	30
1997	4	30	34
1998	5	12	17
1999	9	4	13
2000	2	21	23
2001	2	30	32
2002	5	13	18
2003 (January–July)	5	2	7
Total	58	207	265

Table 3.2   Regional Legislative Elections in Russia, 1993–2003, by Region

	Regions That Did Not Hold Legislative Elections	Regions That Held Two Legislative Elections	Total Number of Regions That Held Legislative Elections
1st electoral cycle	Adygeia, Chechnya, Khakasia, Ul'ianovsk	None	85
2nd electoral cycle	Karachaevo-Cherkesia, Mordovia, Taimyr, Tatarstan	Chechnya, Kemerovo, Sverdlovsk, Volgograd, Vologda	85
3rd electoral cycle	Chechnya, Ingushetia, Kabardino-Balkaria, Kalmykia, Volgograd	Sverdlovsk, Vologda	84

among the first regions to hold them were Moscow and St. Petersburg, which elected their mayors concurrently with the first Russian presidential elections in June 1991. The same applies to Tatarstan, which was the first among Russia's republics to introduce its own presidency. By December 1991–March 1992, nine other republics followed Tatarstan's example, despite the fact that by that time, the federal authorities introduced a one-year moratorium on holding elections. This became possible because when the moratorium was introduced, election dates in these republics had already been officially determined. In seven of them, Adygeia, Kabardino-Balkaria, Marii El, Mordovia, Sakha, Tyva, and Chechnya, the presidents were indeed elected and took office. In two, Kalmykia and Chuvashia, election results were invalidated due to technical reasons, while the Mordovian presidency was abolished by the republic's Supreme Soviet in 1993. Effective presidential elections in Kalmykia and Chuvashia, as well as in Bashkortostan and Ingushetia, were held in 1993. Four republics, Buriatia, Karelia, Komi, and North Ossetia, shifted to presidentialism and held their executive elections in 1994, Khakasia in 1996, Altai Republic in 1997, Mordovia in 1998, Karachaevo-Cherkesia in 1999, and Udmurtia in 2000. As of 2003 the only region that has not ever had a directly elected chief executive is Dagestan. Instead, it has a collective presidency named the State Council, composed of the representatives of the republic's ethnic groups and elected by the Constitutional Assembly, which in turn consists of the members of the republic's legislature and the delegates of municipal assemblies. It is the chairman of the State Council who can be viewed as the holder of the chief executive office in Dagestan. Of course, the special case is Chechnya, which passed through two executive elections in December 1995 and in January–February 1997, the former resulting in the election of a pro-Russian leader who was however ousted in less than a year, and the latter resulting in the election of a secessionist president who also later lost his power. The federal authorities appointed a new pro-Russian head of the administration of Chechnya in 2000.

In contrast to the republics, other regions had the heads of their administrations appointed by Boris Yeltsin, normally but not necessarily by consent with the regional soviets, in late 1991 to early 1992. It was only in April 1993 that elections in eight regions other than republics were convoked by the regional soviets, normally in situations when Yeltsin's appointees were involved in political struggles with them, which resulted in a no-confidence vote. In one of these regions, Cheliabinsk province, Yeltsin's appointee did not participate in the elections and did not recognize their results, which resulted in a period of dual power that lasted for several months. In the end, the elected head of administration had to give up. In two other regions, Amur and Briansk provinces, the elected chief executives were later dismissed by Yeltsin for the positions they took during the constitutional crisis of 1993. Overall, then, only five of the eight chief executives elected in 1993, those of Krasnoiarsk territory and Lipetsk, Orel, Penza, and Smolensk provinces, managed to maintain their positions. Only one of the regions other than republics, Irkutsk province, held executive elections in 1994, and none of them held such elections in the first half of 1995.[6]

Hence the history of regular chief executive elections in the majority of Russia's regions starts with the beginning of the second electoral cycle, when as many as sixteen chief executives were elected in the second half of 1995, most of them concurrently with the national legislative elections, and as many as forty-seven in the course of the following year. The chief executives of Russia's regions are normally elected for terms of four or five years. In Ingushetia, Ruslan Aushev convoked fresh presidential elections in 1994, a year after he was initially elected in 1993. The president of Kalmykia, Kirsan Iliumzhinov, also served for less than three years in his first term, which started in 1993; in this case, however, the second term was constitutionally extended to seven years, which made Iliumzhinov's 1995–2002 term the longest in post-Soviet Russia. Since that time, however, federal law has limited to five years the term for which a Russian official can be elected. Table 3.3 presents aggregate evidence on the chronology of regional executive elections in Russia by year and electoral cycle. The table aggregates information only about effective elections—that is, those for which the results were officially recognized as valid and binding. Information about ineffective elections is omitted. Those elections that were held in two rounds, one of them in December and another in January, are dated and counted according to the timing of their first rounds. Table 3.4 contains information about the numbers of regions that held executive elections in the course of those two electoral cycles when such elections took place on a regular basis. Belgorod and Nizhnii Novgorod provinces held premature elections in the second electoral cycle for different reasons: the former because of the political maneuvering of the incumbent governor, who apparently wanted to be reelected before Russia entered the expectedly turbulent period of Yeltsin's departure from power, and the latter because its elected chief executive was appointed as a minister to the federal government. The same applies to Primorskii territory in the 1999–2003 electoral cycle. The incumbent governor of Magadan province died in 2002, while the incumbent governor of Taimyr autonomous district resigned because he was elected governor of another region, which is why Magadan and Taimyr held premature elections in early 2003. The presence of many republics in the second column of the table is only logical given the complexities of their electoral histories.

As follows from the discussion above, the role of the federal authorities in the apparent stabilization of regional election patterns was not

Table 3.3   Regional Executive Elections in Russia, 1991–2003, by Electoral Cycle and Year

Electoral Cycle/Year	Number of Executive Elections Held in Republics	Number of Executive Elections Held in Other Regions	Total
By Electoral Cycle			
1991 to July 1995	17	11	28
2nd electoral cycle	20	70	90
3rd electoral cycle	17	71	88
Total	54	152	206
By Year			
1991	7	2	9
1992	1	0	1
1993	4	8	12
1994	5	1	6
1995	2	14	16
1996	4	43	47
1997	7	8	15
1998	6	4	10
1999	1	15	16
2000	3	38	41
2001	5	12	17
2002	8	4	12
2003 (January–July)	1	3	4
Total	54	152	206

Table 3.4   Regional Executive Elections in Russia, 1995–2003, by Region

	Regions That Did Not Hold Executive Elections	Regions That Held Two Executive Elections	Total Number of Regions That Held Legislative Elections
2nd electoral cycle	Dagestan, Udmurtia	Belgorod, Chechnya, Nizhnii Novgorod	87
3rd electoral cycle	Bashkortostan, Chechnya, Dagestan, Karachaevo-Cherkesia	Magadan, Primorskii, Taimyr	85

entirely unambiguous. In particular, the 1991 and 1994 moratoria on holding elections deeply affected the political lives of the regions. Even after the adoption of the 1993 constitution, the federal authorities remained instrumental in postponing executive elections in the majority of regions to 1995, 1996, and sometimes to 1997. This, in combination with the fact that a large number of republics retained nonpresidential forms of government well after the 1993 constitution was adopted, arguably contributed to maintaining aconstitutional asymmetries inherited from the previous period of Russia's political development. At the same time, it is clear that starting with 1993 Russia entered a period of gradual stabilization and unification of regional electoral practices. These processes were strongly stimulated by the lawmaking and law-enforcing activities of the federal executive. The pattern of holding regular regional legislative elections was established already in the first electoral cycle and remained stable after that, while regional executive elections were being held on a relatively regular basis throughout the second and third electoral cycles. Thus regional elections became a pivotal component of political life at the regional level.

Political Parties in Regional Elections: Aggregate Evidence

The purpose of this section is to present general information about the levels and dynamics of party activities in the regional electoral arenas. It is only natural to divide these arenas into two categories, executive and legislative. Judging from the theoretical arguments and evidence from Russia's national politics presented in the previous chapter, one would logically expect that political parties were more active and important in legislative elections. This, indeed, seems to be the case. Yet given that executive elections are of primary importance in the vast majority of regions, I will start with them.

A conventional way to look at regional executive elections in 1996–1997 has been to place them in the context of national politics (Hahn 1997). Such an approach is strongly assisted by the fact that many important candidates in regional executive elections were supported by conflicting national political entities, either by the All-Russian Coordination Council (OKS) or by the Popular Patriotic Union of Russia (NPSR). The latter entity was an "all-Russian public movement" founded in August 1996 on the basis of a coalition that supported Gennadii Ziuganov's unsuccessful bid for the Russian presidency. The programmatic declaration of the NPSR stated "the rejection of the current regime's policies, which are disastrous for Russia, and the reversal of this anti-people's course by constitutional means" as its primary political goals.[7] In this vein, the declaration contained a good deal of nationalist and social protectionist rhetoric, but it did not state anything specifically communist or socialist (Flikke 1999). The formal leaders of the NPSR were Ziuganov and Nikolai Ryzhkov, the former Soviet prime minister and the head of the People's Power deputy group in the Duma. The coordination council of the movement also included the leaders of two parties that allied themselves with the Communist Party of the Russian Federation (KPRF) during Ziuganov's presidential campaign, the Agrarian Party of Russia (APR), and Derzhava.[8] In an interview given prior to the opening of the constituent congress of the movement, Ryzhkov mentioned that the NPSR was joined by as many as forty-four organizations, including fourteen all-Russian, thirteen interregional, and seventeen regional.[9] In general, however, the participation of political parties in the NPSR was not very pronounced. Formally speaking, it was not a coalition but rather a new political movement with its own political agenda, which is apparent by the fact that the majority of its leaders were prominent opposition figures who were not, however, affiliated with the KPRF, such as filmmaker Stanislav Govorukhin or writer Valentin Rasputin. The same pattern was observable at the regional level, as the local branches of the NPSR started to be formed in the regions and registered with the local departments of justice as separate organizational entities. Also, neither when it was formed nor afterward did the NPSR restrict its goals to the electoral arena.

In contrast, the OKS emphasized its coalition nature and its electoral goals. Like the NPSR, it was founded in August 1996. Its leader, Sergei Filatov, who was officially designated the "commissioner in charge of the elections of the heads of subjects of the Russian Federation," claimed that nineteen parties and movements formed the OKS, including Our Home Is Russia (NDR), Democratic Russia's Choice (DVR), and the Russian Socialist Party, in order to coordinate their activities during the regional executive campaigns. The structure of the OKS included a central body led by Filatov and local bodies, which were regional coordination councils that also functioned on a coalition basis. As of September 1996, twenty-six such councils were said to be already formed and twenty-six more in the process of formation.[10] Neither compositions of these coalitions nor even their positions on individual candidacies were necessarily identical to those of the national coalition.[11] The OKS worked hand-in-hand with the federal executive and was often considered as its "political arm." At the same time, the presidential administration was directly and sometimes very actively involved in regional executive campaigns. An influential aide to Yeltsin, Georgii Satarov, stated that "holding gubernatorial elections as a means of strengthening regional power and consolidating the president's vertical of power is our priority goal," adding that in order to achieve this goal, the presidential administration was launching a new task force, the Council for Political Planning.[12] While the existing evidence on the federal executive's involvement in regional executive elections is mostly anecdotal, which is not surprising given the secretive nature of its involvement, it is reasonable to believe that it was quite substantial. Apparently, the role of the OKS in promoting individual candidacies was at best secondary.

The candidates actually endorsed by the OKS and supported by the presidential administration were most often Yeltsin-appointed incumbents. There were instances when the OKS endorsed alternative candidates (in Khakasia, Krasnodar territory, and Ul'ianovsk province), instances when no candidate was endorsed (in Astrakhan province), and instances when more than one candidate was endorsed (in Volgograd, Ivanovo, and Riazan provinces), but this does not change the overall picture of support to Yeltsin's appointees, their actual relationships with those parties that participated in the OKS notwithstanding. At the same time, the Yeltsin-appointed incumbents tended not to emphasize the OKS endorsement in their campaign rhetoric. In fact, many of them did not invite the OKS to endorse them. What mattered was the practical support of the presidential administration. In a way, this logic applies to the NPSR as well: in the vast majority of cases, it supported viable challengers who were not necessarily in ideological or political affinity to the left-wing opposition. This trend became stronger over time. In September 1996, the NPSR published its "list of support" for eleven regions.[13] Even this list included not only committed communists such as Aleksandr Chernogorov in Stavropol territory and noncommunist long-standing oppositionists with national reputations such as Nikolai Kondratenko in Krasnodar territory, but also relatively politically disengaged people like Vadim Gustov in Leningrad province. Later, the NPSR terminated the practice of publishing lists in favor of a more pragmatic approach, picking up its preferred candidates in the midst of the campaigns and sometimes even in the interims between their first and second rounds (which was the case with Evgenii Mikhailov in Pskov province, Leonid Gorbenko in Kaliningrad province, and Yurii Evdokimov in Murmansk province). In Khabarovsk territory and some of the autonomous districts, the NPSR supported incumbent governors whose candidacies were also endorsed by the OKS.

Hence the principal problem with assessing the results of the second-cycle regional executive elections in terms of ideologically loaded contests between the two nationwide entities, the OKS and the NPSR: it was simply impossible to say which of them won. In December 1996 both sides claimed victory (Belin 1997a). The deputy head of the presidential administration, Aleksandr Kazakov, stated that of forty-five heads of administration elected by the end of 1996, thirty-seven were "acceptable" for the federal executive, while only eight could be viewed as oppositionists. Assessing the same election results, the NPSR spokesman counted as the opposite side's victories only those twenty incumbents who were actually elected, which stood for the impressive score of 25:20 in favor of opposition.[14] Political analyst Grigorii Belonuchkin invested quite an impressive and penetrating effort into interpreting the 1996–1997 election results in fifty-five regions in terms of bipolar contestation. He ended up with three different "scores": OKS to NPSR, 22:28; the party of power to the opposition, 27:20; and the "acceptable" heads of administration to the "unacceptable" ones, 46:9.[15] Beyond this comic situation lies a substantive problem. Can candidate endorsements by the OKS or the NPSR in the 1996–1997 elections be viewed as a meaningful form of party support? It seems that the answer to this question has to be negative. The notion of party support cannot be applied to situations when candidates themselves do not choose under what label to run (and if they did, they preferred to portray themselves as independents), when the same label can be attached to several candidates in the given contest, and when the decision to support this or that candidate is being made in the course of the election campaign by assessing his or her chances to win, not on the basis of programmatic proximities. Besides, both OKS and NPSR endorsements were anything but binding. Consider those nine heads of administration who, on the basis of their stances during their campaigns, were assigned by Belonuchkin to the category of "unacceptable" for the presidential administration. In the course of the 1999 Duma campaign, only five of them could be listed as active supporters of the opposition, while four others joined rival political camps (Orttung 2000: xviii), which indeed stood for an almost random distribution. At the same time, of the sixteen regional heads who were elected in 1996–1997 and listed by Orttung as firm supporters of Unity, only eight were Yeltsin's appointees. Others were successful challengers, often explicitly supported by the NPSR during their campaigns, such as Kursk governor Aleksandr Rutskoi or Kostroma governor Viktor Shershunov. In fact, Belonuchkin placed both of them into the category of "unacceptable."[16]

In addition, the activities of the OKS were chronologically limited to the period when Yeltsin's appointees were in office and subject to direct elections. In 1997 this period came to its end. Since that time, there has not been any national political coalition with goals similar to those of the OKS. The NPSR, for its part, was practically incapacitated by the political maneuvering of the KPRF leadership in 1998–1999 (March 2001: 276–277). Few relatively observable organizations on the national political scene, such as the APR, left it, while newly formed left-wing groups did not join it. The regional branches of the NPSR did participate in several regional elections, mostly legislative, but they did so on their own initiative or, more likely, on the initiative of local KPRF organizations that sometimes preferred to use the label of the NPSR. In this analysis, I will proceed on the assumption that candidate affiliations with the OKS and the NPSR did not constitute party affiliation. This naturally leads me to turn to party nomination, an institutional form that, as I have argued in Chapter 1, is binding and therefore significant. Equally important is that, in contrast to support from national coalitions, party nomination can be established quite unambiguously: a candidate either runs as a party nominee throughout the campaign up to the election date, with the form of nomination being a piece of information available to the voter on the ballot paper, or does not, which makes it possible to consider the candidate as independent.[17]

In the following presentation of empirical evidence, only the data on elections held in the second and third electoral cycles are included. Overall, I aggregated information on 175 regional executive elections, 88 in the second electoral cycle, and 87 in the third electoral cycle.[18] The first question that empirically points to the scope of party activities in regional executive elections is how many of them were actually contested by party nominees. In the second electoral cycle, party nominees were present in a majority of elections, 48, but just 32 in the third, which suggests a drastically decreasing pattern. The actual extent of party presence, however, is better addressed by a series of empirical indicators that take into account individual candidacies. Overall, the second- and third-cycle regional executive elections were contested by 459 and 562 candidates respectively (only those whose candidacies were not withdrawn by the election date and who therefore received votes are taken into account). Political parties nominated only 74 and 46 of them respectively. An even more telling picture arises when we look at the electoral results. Of the elections held in the second cycle, only 13 brought party nominees to senior executive offices, while in the third electoral cycle only six victories of party nominees were registered. Table 3.5 summarizes some of these indicators as percentage shares. One of the possible reasons for this pattern of decay becomes apparent on first look at the data. It seems that those relatively few party candidates who ran in the executive elections were less successful than independent candidates. In the second electoral cycle, indeed, the share of winners among party nominees was 17.6 percent, while among independents it was 19.5 percent; in the third electoral cycle, these figures were 15.7 percent and 13.0 percent respectively. The difference is statistically insignificant. Yet it is clear that in the third cycle the level of party activities in regional executive elections became so low that the level of their success did not really matter. The vast majority of candidates were independents.

In individual regions, the overall shares of the vote received by party candidates could be quite substantial. Table 3.6 reports information about those regions that, on this parameter, can be rated as leading in each of the

Table 3.5 Political Parties in Regional Executive Elections, 1995–2003

	2nd Electoral Cycle	3rd Electoral Cycle
Percentage share of elections contested by party-nominated candidates	54.5	36.8
Percentage share of elections in which party nominees won offices	14.8	6.9

Table 3.6   Regions in Which Party Nominees Won the Largest Shares of the Vote in Regional Executive Elections, 1995–2003

	2nd Electoral Cycle		3rd Electoral Cycle	
No.	Region	Share of the Vote (%)	Region	Share of the Vote (%)
1	Tyva (1997)*	79.5	Mordovia (2003)*	94.3
2	Khabarovsk (1996)*	78.2	Khabarovsk (2000)*	87.8
3	Jewish autonomous province (1995)*	70.1	Altai territory (2000)*	77.4
4	Orenburg (1995)*	68.2	Ivanovo (2000)*	48.5
5	Vladimir (1996)*	64.0	Altai republic (2001)*	34.9
6	Briansk (1996)*	55.1	Tambov (1999)	29.5
7	Tver (1995)*	50.5	Omsk (1999)	26.4
8	Altai territory (1996)*	46.9	Irkutsk (2001)	25.0
9	Smolensk (1998)*	46.5	Kamchatka (2000)*	20.0
10	Khakasia (1996)*	42.1	St. Petersburg (2000)	18.5

Note: Asterisks indicate cases of party-nominated candidate victories. Party-nominated candidates also won second-cycle elections in Sverdlovsk (1995), Riazan (1996), and Pskov (1996) provinces. The shares of the vote jointly gained by all party-nominated candidates in the first rounds of these elections were 39.2, 38.3, and 22.7 respectively.

two electoral cycles. Numbers reported in the table are shares of the vote cast for all party-nominated candidates either in the single or in the first round of the given elections. The most interesting piece of evidence reported in this table is not the scope of party decay, for this aspect is already evident from the previously reported data, but rather the striking lack of correspondence between the two lists. Only two regions, Khabarovsk and Altai territories, can be found on both of them. This suggests a great degree of instability in the regional patterns of party candidate nomination. In order to test this suggestion with a greater precision, I calculated a Pearson's r correlation coefficient between the overall percentage shares of the vote received by party-nominated candidates in the second and third electoral cycles (I took average shares for those regions that held two elections in the course of the given electoral cycle). The coefficient is 0.24, significant at 0.05.

Let us now turn to the electoral arena that is presumably more hospitable for political parties, regional legislative elections. In contrast to executive elections, races for regional legislative seats were never considered important events within the national political context. Exceptions, such as the 1998 elections to the legislatures of Volgograd province and St. Petersburg, are few. Correspondingly, there were no national political entities comparable to the OKS and the NPSR in terms of their involvement in this segment of regional political life. This being said, it is logical to jump directly to the performance of party nominees in regional legislative elections. Three major aggregate empirical indicators are available for 258 elections held in the regions of Russia in 1993–2003:[19] (1) the number of elections contested by party candidates, (2) the number of elections in which at least one seat was won by a party candidate, and (3) the average percentage shares of seats won by party candidates. The number of contested elections increased from 56 in the first electoral cycle to 78 in the second and decreased slightly, to 73, in the third. A more curvilinear pattern emerges from the comparison of numbers of elections with one or more seats won by party candidates, 49 in the first electoral cycle, 69 in the second, and 57 in the third. Since the numbers of elections held in each of the electoral cycles are different, Table 3.7 reports the same data as percentages, as well as average percentage shares of party deputies in regional legislatures. It is this third indicator that points to the curvilinear pattern most tellingly.

In contrast to executive elections, political parties are not inactive in their search for legislative seats. In all three electoral cycles, party candidates were present in the majorities of elections. At the same time, it is clear that they have not been very successful in their quest. While the level of party representation in the second-cycle legislatures can be viewed as more than symbolic, this cannot be said about the first and third electoral cycles, even though the role of political parties in legislative elections was never as negligible as it was in executive elections: in each of the corresponding electoral cycles, party nominees won almost twice as large a share of legislative seats as of executive offices. Does a greater level of activity correspond with a greater level of stability in candidate nomination patterns? The lists of top regions in terms of party representation in legislatures reported in Table 3.8 suggests that there is indeed more stability.[20]

Table 3.7   Political Parties in Regional Legislative Elections, 1993–2003

	1st Electoral Cycle	2nd Electoral Cycle	3rd Electoral Cycle
Percentage share of elections contested by party-nominated candidates	65.9	88.6	85.9
Percentage share of elections in which party nominees won seats	57.6	78.4	67.1
Average percentage shares of seats won by party nominees	12.5	21.8	14.3

Table 3.8   Regions in Which Party Nominees Won the Largest Shares of Seats in Regional Legislative Elections, 1993–2003

	1st Electoral Cycle		2nd Electoral Cycle		3rd Electoral Cycle	
No.	Region	Share of Seats (%)	Region	Share of Seats (%)	Region	Share of Seats (%)
1	Krasnodar (1994)	80.0	Krasnoiarsk (1997)	80.5	Kemerovo (2003)	97.1
2	Moscow (1993)	72.3	Krasnodar (1998)	78.0	Krasnoiarsk (2001)	83.3
3	Kaluga (1994)	63.2	Kemerovo (1996, 1999)	72.1	Sverdlovsk (2000, 2002)	80.6
4	St. Petersburg (1994)	56.0	Volgograd (1997, 1998)	68.8	Bashkortostan (2003)	79.8
5	Saratov (1994)	52.9	Sverdlovsk (1996, 1998)	67.3	Pskov (2002)	51.7
6	Amur (1994)	46.7	Koriak (1996)	60.0	Udmurtia (2003)	47.0
7	Vologda (1994)	41.7	Novosibirsk (1997)	55.1	Novosibirsk (2001)	45.8
8	Udmurtia (1995)	38.0	Adygeia (1995)	54.5	Briansk (2000)	43.2
9	Sverdlovsk (1994)	35.7	Riazan (1997)	50.0	Kamchatka (2001)	41.0
10	Briansk (1994) and Kamchatka (1994)	33.3	Briansk (1996)	47.9	Riazan (2001)	38.2

While there is little similarity between the lists of regions with high party representation in the first and second electoral cycles, more than half of the regions on the third-cycle list are also on second-cycle list. Bivariate correlation analysis confirms this conclusion. While the Pearson's r coefficient between the percentage shares of party representatives in the first and second electoral cycles is 0.33 (significant at 0.05), the level of correlation between the second and third cycles is much higher, 0.58 (significant at 0.001). Yet it is also clear that there was a downward trend in this continuity. When regressing the third-cycle variable on the second-cycle variable, I found the unstandardized beta-coefficient to be as low as 0.56 (significant at 0.001). The value of intercept is positive, though.

So far, this analysis has fully confirmed my expectation that political parties find their niche in legislative rather than in executive elections. The level of party activity in executive elections seems to be too low, and regions where such activity is important are too few. This has an important implication for the strategy of data presentation in this study. In the rest of this chapter, I will deal exclusively with the activity and performance of political parties in the regional legislative elections. This does not mean that executive elections will be ignored in the further analysis. Quite the reverse, a large part of Chapter 4 will focus on the complex interplay of the two principal electoral arenas of Russia's regions. Then it will be only logical to pay attention to those few regions where party-nominated candidates won or came close to winning in executive elections. But for characterizing the levels of activity of individual parties, which is the primary goal of the following section, legislative elections will suffice.

Political Parties in Regional Legislative Elections: Individual-Level Evidence

This section is mostly descriptive. On the basis of the empirical evidence at my disposal, I will identify those parties that were active in the regional electoral arenas and specify the levels of their activity by introducing several relevant empirical indicators. The majority of parties in this analysis are local branches of national political organizations whose origins and programmatic standings have been analyzed in the previous chapter. However, there were certain differences between the compositions of actors on the national and regional party scenes.

First, regional party scenes tend to be less populated than the national scene. As is already clear from the previous section of this chapter, there are many regions where political parties simply do not contest elections. Even if they do, the overall number of participating parties tends to be relatively small in comparison with national elections. Unfortunately, the data at my disposal do not allow for making this claim empirically testable for the time span of the first electoral cycle. For the second and third electoral cycles, however, I was able to establish the numbers of parties that contested each of the regional legislative elections except those in Chechnya. If "party" is understood as any entity that contests elections under its own label—that is, if electoral blocs are counted as individual parties—then the average numbers of parties in the second- and third-cycle regional legislative elections were 7.3 and 4.0 respectively. If each of the entities within the electoral blocs is counted separately, the numbers grow to 8.8 and 4.7 respectively. The diversity of the regions on this parameter is quite striking. While elections with only one or two parties on the ballot were by no means unusual, in several regions the numbers of participating electoral associations and blocs seemed to be unreasonably large. For instance, 41 seats in the legislature of Krasnoiarsk territory (1997) were contested by as many as 40 parties that formed 25 electoral blocs; similarly, 29 parties belonging to 20 blocs contested 35 seats in the legislature of Moscow (1997). The existence of such outliers partly explains why the average numbers for the second electoral cycle are so large. But they are still smaller than the numbers of parties that contested the 1995 and 1999 national legislative elections.

Turning to a more substantive point, it is important to establish whether the parties in regional legislative elections were actually the same as those in the national electoral arena. Below I will demonstrate that by and large they were. There are, however, several important differences that have to be described before I turn to the systematic exposition of the empirical evidence. To start with, the left-wing segment of the national political spectrum is absolutely dominated by the KPRF. This is not necessarily the case—or at least this was not necessarily the case—in the regions. In the previous chapter I briefly mentioned that before the Constitutional Court of Russia allowed the communists to start rebuilding their central party organization, some of the regional left-wing activists had already created locally based organizations. In Kamchatka province the local left-wing movement Comrade was registered as early as January 1992.[21] The leader of the movement, Mikhail Mashkovtsev, was later elected as the first secretary of the provincial committee of the KPRF, but by that time the name recognition and the local popularity of the movement were such that it survived in its capacity as the principal left-wing organization of Kamchatka and later, when Mashkovtsev won executive elections, as its ruling party. From the very moment when it was established, the Comrade movement was unambiguously communist—that is, it was not a coalition (even though its initial membership was partly recruited from the Russian Communist Workers Party [RKRP]). In contrast, some of the left-wing movements in the regions were more than just communist. For instance, a movement under the lengthy name "For Genuine People's Power, Civil Peace, and the Interests of the Man of Toil," locally often referred to as "ZPN" based on the Russian abbreviation of the first three words, was created and sustained as a coalition that included the KPRF and another left-wing party important in Altai territory, the APR.[22] Yet another left-wing movement, Fatherland, in Krasnodar territory, was founded in 1993 to embrace, in the words of one of its leaders, "more than 30 patriotic organizations of the territory, including the territory's branch of the KPRF, the Agro-Industrial Union, the kazaks', women's, and youth organizations."[23]

The left-wing movements mentioned above proved to be sustainable over time, and they survived well through the third electoral cycle. This cannot be said about all such organizations that proliferated on the eve of Russia's regional electoral politics. Some of them participated in the first-cycle elections simultaneously with the KPRF by running their candidates in different districts; others entered electoral coalitions with the KPRF and the APR. There were also cases when such movements were deliberately used as umbrellas for KPRF candidates and their allies, which in contrast to the cases described above limited their activities to individual electoral campaigns. All in all, the existence of the local left-wing movements used to be a characteristic feature of regional electoral arenas, even though few such movements survived into the third electoral cycle. Yet another local peculiarity of a similar kind is the participation of the Popular Patriotic

Union of Russia in regional legislative elections. As I have already mentioned, the NPSR was founded not as a coalition but rather as a separate movement that was entitled to establish regional branches and indeed established them. Sometimes they were used for running communist and left-leaning candidates in regional legislative elections.

It is also important to mention that some of the communist parties of the ethnic republics remained independent from the KPRF in the first and second electoral cycles. For instance, the Communist Organization of the Republic of Tatarstan, later renamed the Communist Party of the Republic of Tatarstan (KPRT), was registered in February 1992, well before the KPRF was formed. In 1993 and later, the party pursued a policy of "equal distances" from the KPRF and the RKRP, but this started to cause increased tensions within the KPRT after Ziuganov's party ultimately established itself as the major party of Russia's left. In March 1997 these tensions resulted in a party split on the question of whether the party should join the KPRF as its regional branch. For a certain period of time, both factions fought for the right to retain the KPRT party label. In the end, however, the proindependence faction, led by Vladimir Mashkov, had to give up and create its own party, the Communist (Bolshevik) Party of the Republic of Tatarstan, while their opponents kept the label and ultimately joined the KPRF.[24] It is worth mentioning that this situation was not inflamed by nationalist sentiment. The "Bolsheviks" were more ideologically radical than the proponents of joining the KPRF. In other republics, this was not necessarily the case. In Sakha, the local communist party, named the Communist Party of the Republic of Sakha–Yakutia (KPRSYa) and consisting primarily of ethnic Yakuts, remained independent from the KPRF for more than ten years. As an alternative, the ethnic Russian activists in the south of Sakha created an entity called "the regional branch" of the KPRF and fought an ideological war against the leaders of the KPRSYa, accusing them, in particular, of "Yakut nationalism and the lack of working place influence."[25] In this case too, the national leadership of the KPRF eventually succeeded in transforming a larger formation into its branch, but this process was finalized only in February 2002.[26] Hence the third category of distinctly regional left-wing organizations, in addition to the previously described categories of local left-wing movements and, in the second electoral cycle, NPSR branches, is that of independent communist parties in the ethnic republics, further occasionally referred to as republican communist parties.

To what extent can such entities be viewed as independent from the KPRF? It can be assumed that the NPSR branches were least independent among them, even though sometimes they had to take into account policy preferences of the KPRF's allies, such as the APR. Local left-wing movements and republican communist parties, in contrast, did not necessarily support the KPRF in all its endeavors, including those in the national electoral arena. For instance, the Fatherland movement in Krasnodar territory and the KPRSYa cooperated with the Power to the People bloc rather than with the KPRF in the 1995 Duma elections. Even for such organizations, however, ties with the KPRF are essential means of survival. First, their grassroots organizations largely coincide with those of the KPRF. Should the KPRF withdraw, these organizations become depopulated overnight. The second and perhaps more important aspect is that these organizations' candidates would be in trouble if forced into electoral competition with KPRF-nominated candidates. To avoid such a turn of events, these organizations have to be very careful about setting their policy agendas in coordination with the KPRF. Of course, the question remains as to why the KPRF itself tolerates the existence of the local left outside of its organizational framework. A simple answer to this question would be that it does not. Indeed, since 1993 most of the local left-wing movements have become extinct, while all republican communist parties have eventually joined the KPRF. A more complex answer taking into account the regional patterns of politics, as well as a couple of exceptional cases, will be provided in the subsequent chapters. Here, it is sufficient to say that for all their independence, the organizations discussed above remain within reach of the KPRF, both organizationally and politically. This fact will be used as a basis for categorization that, while not being employed in the rest of this chapter, will play an important role in the subsequent analysis. Namely, the KPRF itself, electoral blocs including the KPRF, the NPSR, local left-wing movements, and republican communist parties will be in certain cognitive contexts viewed and analyzed jointly as a single entity dubbed the "KPRF conglomerate."

The right-wing camp always lacked a dominant party that would play a role distantly comparable to that of the KPRF among the left-wingers. Throughout all three electoral cycles there were several national political parties that adhered to the right and were represented in regional legislative elections. One peculiarity of the regional electoral arenas that has to be mentioned in this connection is that sometimes, and rather often in the first electoral cycle, the coalitions of right-wing parties did not formally establish electoral blocs but rather merged to establish local "democratic movements." In contrast to the left-wing movements discussed above, the right-wing movements were normally created solely for the purpose of contesting the given elections and disappeared after them. What is similar is that the circle of founders of such movements was not strictly delineated, even though it was widely assumed that the local branches of Democratic Russia, Russia's Choice (VR), and sometimes the RPRF were instrumental in forming them. By the beginning of the second electoral cycle, such movements became extinct in the majority of the regions, partly because the electoral legislation formalized the rules according to which electoral blocs could be formed. Exceptions to this rule are few. One of them is the Equal Rights and Legality (RiZ) movement in Tatarstan. Formed in 1992 by several deputy groups in the republic's Supreme Soviet, as well as by the regional branch of the Democratic Party of Russia (DPR),[27] later it embraced or perhaps even spanned Tatarstan's branches of several right-wing parties, such as Yabloko and the VR, yet continued to exist on its own as a "nested doll" conglomerate of many right-wing groups.[28] One apparent reason for such longevity is that from the very beginning, the RiZ advocated a very distinctive policy agenda that combined an antisecessionist stance with a right-wing position on socioeconomic issues. The majority of local democratic coalitions formed in the first electoral cycle apparently lacked such region-specific policy agendas.

Yet another feature of the regional electoral arenas that made them to an extent different from the national arena was a very wide presence of interest groups as candidate-nominating entities. True, national legislative elections were invariably contested by parties more or less directly linked to interest groups too, and one such party, Women of Russia, even managed to cross the 5 percent barrier in the 1993 party-list elections. What makes the situation in the regional elections specific is that they were often contested not by political parties linked to interest groups but by interest groups as such. Trade unions (that is, the local federations of former official trade unions, their branch divisions, and newly formed independent trade unions), veterans/invalids organizations, women's and youth associations, and business associations were among common participants in regional legislative elections. In the second electoral cycle, however, their activities in the electoral arenas slowed to become almost unobservable in the third electoral cycle. Partly this happened because in 1999 federal law explicitly restricted the circle of possible participants in elections to "political public associations," which entailed the withdrawal of most trade unions and some of the veterans associations from the electoral arenas.

The widespread presence of interest groups in regional legislative elections poses a methodological problem. Figures reported in Tables 3.6–3.8 are calculated in a way that takes into account interest groups. Formally, I have justified such an approach by defining a party as any group that contests elections under its own label. Yet it remains possible to challenge it on substantive grounds. To take a somehow extreme example, does it make sense to treat a candidate nominated by the Trade Union of the Air Crew of Astrakhan as a party nominee? I would argue that it does. Within the context of electoral competition, any label matters. By skipping party affiliation altogether, a candidate voices out his or her nonpartisanship more vocally than a candidate who explicitly states his or her affinity with a societal group, even if this group is just a unionized air crew; by stating such an affinity, at the same time, a candidate distances him- or herself from more ideologically loaded political affiliations. Some observations suggest that this logic was well available to the participants in the regional legislative elections. For instance, the 1997 elections in Astrakhan province were contested by an electoral bloc called the Defense of Taxpayer Rights, which was formed by two apparently apolitical entities, the Housing Initiative and the Union of Local Self-Government. Was it an interest group? Not exactly, because beyond the formation, there was the regional branch of Yabloko, which wanted its candidates to be coordinated and labeled but feared to run them under the party's own name because of its unpopularity in the region.[29] The 1997 and 2001 elections in Krasnoiarsk territory were contested by a regional movement called the Women of Beloved Krasnoiarsk Land. Despite its harmless name, this was an organization of the extreme left.[30] Hence interest groups can be fairly political.

In one way or another, all the peculiarities described above can be viewed as specific extensions of national political institutions. What about specifically regional political organizations? Throughout the period, there were no legal restrictions on their formation or electoral participation, and it would be tempting to suggest that they did not miss these opportunities. Overall, the empirical evidence at my disposal suggests that they did. There are few instances when purely regional political organizations achieved high levels of representation in the legislative assemblies. One such instance is the republic of Tyva, where the 1998 elections were successfully contested by an electoral bloc named Solidarity and based upon the People's Front Free Tyva, an ethnic organization that in the early 1990s advanced secessionist claims.[31] Overall, Solidarity won three of the twenty-one seats in the regional legislature. Other ethnic parties in the republics were even less successful. For instance, the 1993 elections in Marii El brought one of the thirty seats to the ethnic movement Marii Ushem; the Tatar Party of National Independence Ittifak won one seat in the legislature of Tatarstan in 1995; and the 1995 elections in Udmurtia were lost by all ethnic groups that participated in them. In the regions other than republics, local political parties were even more rare and unusual. There was only one region that had developed a system of locally based parties, Sverdlovsk province. There were also several cases of successful electoral participation by interest advocacy groups that were not linked or analogous to the national organizations and thus qualified as regional parties, but there was nothing specifically regional in their preelection rhetoric. Such was a movement called the Medical Doctors of Kaluga Province, which took two of the twenty-one seats in the 1996 regional legislative elections. All in all, politically active regional parties are few, and even fewer of them are important. This is not to say that regional sentiment or regional concerns are not salient in the arena of legislative elections. But what is clear is that such sentiment is more often expressed by nonpartisans or by the nominees of national parties than by the nominees of regional parties. For instance, in the 2001 elections in Krasnoiarsk territory the electoral bloc Ours, whose rhetoric was explicitly based upon the idea of fighting the "occupants" who took over the territory after Aleksandr Lebed was elected as its governor,[32] was formed by the local branch of the national Fatherland movement and by a local interest advocacy group, the Movement in Support of the Countryside.

For the reasons cited above, I will organize the following exposition of the empirical evidence without paying much attention to local parties. For each of the electoral cycles, I report information on those organizations that, on their own or by joining electoral blocs, participated in more than five regional legislative elections. I use the following empirical indicators. First is the percentage share of elections contested by a given party in a given electoral cycle. Second is the percentage share of elections in which the given party won seats, further referred to as the "percentage share of successful elections." Finally is the average percentage share of seats won by a given party in the legislative assemblies, further referred to as the "average seat share." It is important to mention that the values of average seat shares were calculated in a way that took into account only those assemblies where seats were actually gained. That is, if a party contested ten elections but won seats in only one, the average seat share of 10 percent means that it won 10 percent of seats, not 100 percent of them, in the only successful election. As previously, all by-elections, elections in Chechnya, and the 2003 elections in North Ossetia are excluded. Most parties in this analysis are the regional branches of national parties. There were several cases when I ascribed to this category formally independent regional parties that used the same label as the national parties and were effectively included in their national organization networks, such as the Regional Party Yabloko in Moscow. Indeed, the actual extent of such parties' independence was by no means larger than that of regional branches. On the contrary, I treated as separate entities those organizations that, while using the same label as a national party, were organizationally and politically detached from them. For instance, the regional branch of the NPSR was registered with the help of the authorities of Saratov province in order to split the communist vote, and its candidates were actually in competition with those of the KPRF. In addition to national parties, I provide information about the electoral participation of local left-wing movements and republican communist parties, and of local democratic coalitions as described above. Integrating basic information about interest groups into this framework seemed to be especially difficult because of the miscellaneous composition of these groups. I sought to solve this problem by identifying the two most widespread categories of interest groups active in the electoral arenas, trade unions and veterans/invalids organizations, and providing aggregate information about them. For instance, I understood "veterans organizations" to include both the regional branches of their national unions and purely regional associations, both the remnants of the Soviet-era "Councils of Veterans of the Great Patriotic War, Labor, Armed Forces, and Law Enforcement Agencies" and the relatively new organizations such as the Union of Veterans of Afghanistan. The data in the tables below apply to the whole set of such vastly different organizations, not to any specific group.

The problem of electoral blocs deserves special treatment. As is already clear from the data reported at the beginning of this section, blocs are quite characteristic of regional legislative elections, which makes it imperative to report aggregate evidence on the extent to which these activities spread and succeed. The problem is, of course, that if an electoral bloc consisting of four parties gains 20 percent of the seats in regional legislative assemblies, it is difficult to say with precision what share of success comes from each of its participants. Estimating it at 5 percent for each of the contributors does not work. This problem could be easier to solve with the left-wing parties simply because, among them, the major contributor is easily identifiable, but even among the left there were cases when the Agrarians were quite important. Among the right, identifying the major contributor is too often an insurmountable task. Yet it is also clear that the individual influence of political parties cannot be equated with their influence exerted through coalition politics. The less than perfect solution to the problem was to calculate the values of two sets of indicators for each of the parties. First, I report the values that take into account all cases of the given party's electoral participation, in coalitions or on its own. Then, in parentheses, I report values that apply only to the independent electoral participation of the given party. Of course, the values coincide if the party did not participate in blocs (but not if it ran only in blocs, which is only a theoretical possibility in my data set). As any aggregates, both kinds of values have their disadvantages in the sense that they either overstate or understate the levels of activity of any given party. That is why they have to be juxtaposed for analytical purposes.

The data on party activities in the first-cycle elections are reported in Table 3.9. As follows from the table, none of the parties were able to contest a majority of elections, and only the KPRF, with thirty-six elections contested, came close to this target. Overall, the KPRF was also a lot more successful than other parties. It won seats in twenty-two legislatures. The average seat share held by the KPRF was, however, only 10.2 percent, or even 7.3 percent if blocs are discounted. On this parameter, a more successful party was the APR, which however contested much fewer elections. Local left-wing movements and republican communist parties also did relatively well. It is worth mentioning that in this category, the ratio of contest-

Table 3.9   Empirical Indicators of Party Activity and Success in the First-Cycle Regional Legislative Elections, 1993–1995

Parties	Percentage Share of Elections Contested	Percentage Share of Successful Elections	Average Percentage Share of Seats
The Left			
KPRF	42.4 (37.6)	25.9 (22.4)	10.2 (7.3)
Local left-wing movements and republican communist parties	23.5 (23.5)	16.5 (16.5)	13.0 (13.0)
RKRP	12.9 (7.1)	4.7 (2.4)	7.5 (3.9)
APR	17.6 (15.3)	11.8 (10.6)	14.6 (14.0)
Nationalists			
LDPR	23.5 (23.5)	2.4 (2.4)	12.0 (12.0)
The Right			
Democratic Russia	18.8 (14.1)	3.5 (0)	5.6 (0)
Local democratic coalitions	12.9 (12.9)	7.1 (7.1)	7.9 (7.9)
DPR	16.5 (14.1)	3.5 (1.2)	8.8 (3.6)
RDDR	8.2 (5.9)	1.2 (1.2)	5.7 (5.7)
RPRF	11.8 (8.2)	2.4 (1.2)	3.1 (3.3)
PES	8.2 (5.9)	2.4 (0)	5.5 (0)
Parties of Power			
VR/DVR	22.4 (20.0)	11.8 (10.6)	10.6 (11.1)
PRES	8.2 (7.1)	3.5 (3.5)	6.5 (6.5)
Interest Groups			
Trade unions	27.1 (24.7)	14.1 (11.8)	6.8 (5.3)
Veterans/invalids	35.3 (32.9)	10.6 (8.2)	5.7 (2.8)

Note: Values in parentheses apply only to the independent electoral participation of the given party; bloc participation is discounted.

ed elections to those elections in which seats had been won was the highest in the first electoral cycle. The least active and successful among the left-wing parties was the RKRP. The only nationalist party of the first electoral cycle was the Liberal Democratic Party of Russia (LDPR). But while it took part in as many as twenty elections, it won seats in only two; the relatively large average seat share results largely from the party's successful performance in a single region, Krasnodar territory. Of the right-wing parties, the most active were Democratic Russia and the DPR, which contested only sixteen and fourteen elections respectively. They desperately lost almost all these elections. Three other right-wing parties, as well as local democratic coalitions, were less active and similarly unsuccessful. One may be tempted to suggest that this happened because the major party of power of the first electoral cycle, Russia's Choice/Democratic Russia's Choice, was also to a large extent a programmatic right-wing party. Such an expectation holds to a limited degree only. In fact, the VR/DVR was able to contest about every fifth election. While it won seats in slightly more than half of them, the average seat share is similar to that of the KPRF, which suggests that at the regional level, the VR/DVR was not a party of power at all. Another political formation of this category, the Party of Russian Unity and Accord (PRES), was neither active nor successful. The selected types of interest groups, trade unions and veterans associations, seem to be quite widespread in the first-cycle elections. They also won seats in relatively large numbers of regions. However, it seems that the sizes of their assembly delegations were negligible. As follows from the table, electoral blocs were not very characteristic of the first electoral cycle. The average ratio of all elections contested by a given party in blocs as a percentage of all contested elections is 16.9. The largest of these ratios (45.0) is that of the RKRP, whose most common coalition partner was, of course, the KPRF; then follow the RPRF (30.5), the Party of Economic Freedom (28.0), and the Russian Movement for Democratic Reforms (28.0), which often ran its candidates jointly with Democratic Russia, and then Democratic Russia itself (25.0).

As becomes clear from Table 3.10, in the second electoral cycle the KPRF decisively established itself as the major party at the regional level. While it contested as many as fifty-two elections on its own or within electoral blocs, the true extent of its electoral presence can be revealed by complementing this figure with elections contested by the NPSR, local left-wing movements, and republican communist parties. True, there were instances when they overlapped—when, for tactical reasons, some districts were contested by KPRF nominees and others by NPSR nominees, as happened in the 1997 elections in Nizhnii Novgorod province. Yet such instances did not abound. By and large, it would be fair to assume that the KPRF and its substitutes participated in about 80 percent of the second-cycle regional legislative elections, and won seats in more than 50 percent. Average seat shares held by them were also quite impressive, more than one-fifth for the KPRF and local left-wing movements. The two remaining left-wing parties, the RKRP and the APR, also became more active than in the first electoral cycle, but they did not become more successful. The percentage shares of successful elections remained almost unchanged, slightly larger for the RKRP and slightly smaller for the APR; the average seat shares won by the parties on their own were also stable. In this respect, blocs with the participation of both parties were much more successful, but it is hardly doubtful that the principal reason for these blocs' success was that they contained the KPRF too. The second electoral cycle also witnessed a tremendous expansion of the electoral activities of the LDPR. It

Table 3.10   Empirical Indicators of Party Activity and Success in the Second-
Cycle Regional Legislative Elections, 1995–1999

Parties	Percentage Share of Elections Contested		Percentage Share of Successful Elections		Average Percentage Share of Seats	
The Left						
KPRF	59.1	(50.0)	46.6	(38.6)	21.2	(22.1)
Local left-wing movements and republican communist parties	17.0	(15.9)	11.4	(11.4)	22.8	(22.8)
NPSR	10.2	(9.1)	4.5	(3.4)	15.7	(14.9)
RKRP	19.3	(13.6)	5.7	(2.3)	11.9	(3.7)
APR	21.6	(14.8)	10.2	(6.8)	18.0	(14.3)
Nationalists						
LDPR	73.9	(72.7)	4.5	(4.5)	6.9	(6.9)
ChR	33.0	(25.0)	6.8	(3.4)	5.7	(2.6)
RNRP	6.8	(6.8)	1.1	(1.1)	2.0	(2.0)
KRO	15.9	(6.8)	3.4	(0)	4.5	(0)
ROS	9.1	(4.5)	1.1	(0)	12.5	(0)
The Right						
Democratic Russia	6.8	(2.3)	1.1	(0)	4.1	(0)
Yabloko	37.5	(31.8)	14.8	(11.4)	8.5	(8.3)
DPR	10.2	(4.5)	3.4	(0)	4.5	(0)
DVR	13.6	(10.2)	3.4	(1.1)	8.7	(5.7)
PST	9.1	(2.3)	5.7	(1.1)	4.8	(1.9)
Parties of Power						
NDR	27.3	(22.7)	13.6	(11.4)	7.1	(4.2)
Interest Groups						
Trade unions	20.5	(18.2)	3.4	(1.1)	22.9	(3.6)
Veterans/invalids	11.4	(9.1)	4.5	(2.3)	14.1	(3.1)

Note: Values in parentheses apply only to the independent electoral participation of the given party; bloc participation is discounted

contested as many as sixty-five of eighty-eight elections, which gave it almost universal presence in the regions of Russia. The party's performance, however, was remarkably unsuccessful. LDPR nominees won seats in only four regional assemblies, and even in these assemblies the LDPR's average seat share was only 6.9 percent. A similar pattern was displayed by a conglomerate of newly formed nationalist organizations that were linked to the charismatic personality of Aleksandr Lebed: his movement, Honor and Motherland (ChR), his party, the RNRP, and to a lesser extent, what remained of the Congress of Russian Communities (KRO) after its 1995 electoral demise. As follows from the table, the ChR was especially active in regional legislative elections, as it was able to contest each third of them.

The level of its success was, however, negligibly small. Other Lebed-oriented organizations fared even worse. A left-wing nationalist group, the Russian All-People's Union (ROS), was also noticeable in the regional electoral arenas, but its only success was achieved in tandem with the KPRF. Among the right-wing organizations, Yabloko demonstrated the largest degree of activity in the second electoral cycle. It was also second only to the KPRF in terms of the overall number of successful elections; the average share of seats it won was small but not negligible. Other right-wing parties fared much worse. All of them, including the DVR, performed about as poorly as the minor right-wing parties of the first electoral cycle. The performance of the only party of power, the NDR, was quite comparable to that of its predecessor, the VR/DVR: it contested slightly more elections and won seats in slightly more elections, but the average share of gained seats was even smaller. If electoral blocs are discounted, the value of the indicator for Yabloko is twice as large. The levels of activity and success of interest groups significantly decreased in comparison with the first electoral cycle. Coalition building in the 1995–1999 period became more active than previously, as indicated by the fact that the average ratio of elections contested by a given party in blocs as a percentage of all contested elections grew from 16.9 to 30.1. Four parties, the Party of Workers Self-Government (PST), Democratic Russia, the DPR, and the KRO, were more likely to contest elections in blocs than on their own.

Finally, Table 3.11 provides information about the third electoral cycle. It seems, however, that the emerging picture largely replicates that of the first electoral cycle. The KPRF remained the most widespread party, and the overall share of elections it contested was only slightly smaller than in 1995–1999. The share of successful elections, however, noticeably decreased, and the quality of success, as measured by the average seat share, drastically deteriorated. The RKRP and the APR performed systematically worse than in the second-cycle elections. Local left-wing movements and republican communist parties became rare participants in regional legislative elections, even though they continued to win seats in the majority of elections they contested and their seat shares remained quite substantial. This suggests that only the strongest of them managed to survive. The only nationalist party that remained active in the regional electoral arenas was the LDPR, like in the first electoral cycle. Its level of activity, however, decreased, while the level of success decreased even further by all accounts. The same can be said about the party that was still most active among the right, Yabloko. The Union of Right Forces (SPS), the successor to the DVR and a plethora of other right-wing groups, entered the regional electoral arenas too, but this can be hardly characterized as a very successful entry. The DPR continued to be marginally present in regional legislative elections, this time accompanied by Sergei Kirienko's

Table 3.11   **Empirical Indicators of Party Activity and Success in the Third-Cycle Regional Legislative Elections, 1999–2003**

Parties	Percentage Share of Elections Contested		Percentage Share of Successful Elections		Average Percentage Share of Seats	
The Left						
KPRF	57.6	(56.5)	38.8	(38.8)	10.4	(10.4)
Local left-wing movements and republican communist parties	8.2	(5.9)	5.9	(3.5)	38.1	(22.5)
RKRP	16.5	(14.1)	1.2	(1.2)	4.0	(4.0)
APR	17.6	(15.3)	8.2	(7.1)	8.9	(9.0)
Nationalists						
LDPR	42.4	(41.2)	2.4	(2.4)	2.8	(2.8)
The Right						
SPS	22.4	(20.0)	4.7	(2.4)	8.2	(1.9)
Yabloko	23.5	(20.0)	7.1	(3.5)	7.5	(4.2)
DPR	9.4	(4.7)	2.4	(0)	4.1	(0)
New Force	7.1	(2.4)	1.2	(0)	3.8	(0)
Parties of Power						
Unity / Unitary Russia	21.2	(17.6)	18.8	(15.3)	21.6	(16.7)
Fatherland	25.9	(18.8)	10.6	(5.9)	9.2	(4.0)
NPRF	12.9	(11.8)	4.7	(3.5)	26.0	(2.3)
Interest Groups						
Pensioners Party	11.8	(10.6)	1.2	(1.2)	7.1	(7.1)

Note: Values in parentheses apply only to the independent electoral participation of the given party; bloc participation is discounted

party, New Force. As described in the previous chapter, several entities could claim the role of the party of power in the course of the third electoral cycle. Two of them were Unity and Fatherland, which had undergone a complex process of unification that as late as 2002 resulted in the formation of a new party, Unitary Russia. The data suggest that in the course of the third electoral cycle, Fatherland was generally more active than Unity. The overall pattern of its performance was, however, strikingly similar to that of the NDR in the second electoral cycle: relatively many elections contested—with few of them bringing legislative seats to the party—with the number of these seats too small to make the words "party of power" applicable. Unity, in contrast, participated in a relatively small number of elections, but it won seats in almost all of them. Unitary Russia generally followed this pattern, which explains why in my data presentation it is shown as a successor to Unity, not to Fatherland. The shares of seats won by Unity/Unitary Russia were larger than those gained by any of the previous "parties of power." The NPRF did not perform any better than minor right-wing parties. Its relatively large average seat share stems exclusively from the 2003 elections in Kemerovo province, where it entered a bloc with Unitary Russia and a local left-wing movement. Note, however, what happens if bloc participation is not taken into account. The electoral participation of interest groups in the third-cycle elections became reduced to an absolute minimum. The Pensioners Party, entered into Table 3.11 under this rubric, was not an interest group but rather a political formation that appealed to a specific societal constituency—without any particular success, as follows from the table. The number of blocs in the third electoral cycle became smaller than previously. This time, the most active participants in blocs were the DPR and New Force, distantly trailed by Fatherland.

In certain respects, the individual-level evidence reported above does not add much to what could be already inferred from the aggregate-level evidence reported in the previous section. The already familiar pattern of upsurge in the second electoral cycle and decay in the third electoral cycle is quite visible in the dynamics of electoral participation displayed by the KPRF and other left-wing parties, the LDPR, and Yabloko—that is, continuous parties. Yet continuous parties are very few. Of the twenty-five national political organizations about which information is included in the previous tables, only five, the KPRF, the APR, the RKRP, the LDPR, and the DPR, were active in all three electoral cycles, and only three, Democratic Russia, the VR/DVR, and Yabloko, were active in two consequent electoral cycles each. Of course, this is not surprising given the tremendous level of volatility in the national political arena. If national parties come and go, it is only logical to expect that the same will happen with their regional branches, even though the data reported above suggest that this rule is not as universal as it may seem (consider the case of the DPR). Yet this is surprising given a relatively high degree of continuity between the levels of overall party representation in the regional legislatures reported in the previous section. It seems that overall party representation is a phenomenon that exists independently from the representation of individual parties.

*   *   *

The regularity of Russia's regional elections, both executive and legislative, was established in parallel with the country's slow drift toward symmetrical federalism in 1993–2003. The pattern of holding regular regional legislative elections was evident already in the first electoral cycle and remained stable after that, while regional executive elections were held on a relatively regular basis throughout the second and third electoral cycles. Thus elections became a pivotal component of political life at the regional level. At the same time, the role of political parties in regional executive elections remained small throughout the whole period and became reduced to complete insignificance in the third electoral cycle; their role in the regional legislative elections was systematically greater yet remained small in comparison with well-established democracies, and tended to decrease in the third electoral cycle. The overall pattern of party activity in the regions seems to gradually stabilize, but is supplemented with a high degree of changeability in the compositions of individual political parties present in the regions.

Notes

1. On the origins and the political meaning of Soviet "federalism," see Bunce 1999.
2. For a useful discussion of symmetrical and asymmetrical models of federalism and their applicability to contemporary Russia, see Stepan 2000. See also DeBardeleben 1997; Lynn and Novikov 1997; and Hughes 2002.
3. Article 66 of the constitution stipulates that statutes are to be adopted by the regional legislature—that is, not by referendum, which remains a possibility in republics.
4. Tatarstan and Chechnya, as well as Ingushetia, which did not exist at that time as a separate entity, did not sign the treaty. See Khrushchev 1994.
5. On the fiscal privileges enjoyed by the republics, see Smith 1996, and Mitchneck, Solnick, and Stoner-Weiss 2001.
6. In October 1994, Yeltsin issued a decree in which he delayed the elections of heads of administration until 1996.
7. Deklaratsia dvizhenia NPSR, *Sovetskaia Rossia,* August 10, 1996.
8. Vo glave dvizhenia NPSR, *Sovetskaia Rossia,* August 10, 1996.
9. 7 avgusta otkryvaetsia uchreditel'nyi s"ezd dvizhenia Narodno-patrioticheskii soiuz Rossii, *Sovetskaia Rossia,* August 6, 1996.
10. Demokraty ob"ediniaiutsia, *Birobidzhaner Shtern* (Birobidzhan), September 25, 1996.
11. Gospoda demokraty, k vam edet revizor, *Rossiiskaia gazeta,* September 28, 1996.
12. Vybory gubernatorov proidut pod zhestkim kontrolem Kremlia, *Izvestia,* August 20, 1996.
13. Oppozitsia na starte, *Moskovskie novosti,* September 24, 1996.
14. Vybory zakonchilis—pobedu prazdnuiut vse, *Segodnia,* December 12, 1996.
15. Gubernatorskie vybory—1997, www.cityline.ru/politika/vybory/ rre97t.html.
16. See also Belin 1997b; Tolz and Busygina 1997; and Solnick 1998.
17. In several regions, candidates in gubernatorial elections were allowed to be nominated by several entities simultaneously, which made it theoretically possible to be a party nominee and an independent at the same time. Such instances, which were quite rare and unusual, are counted as cases of party nomination in the data presentation that follows.

18. Two elections held in Chechnya are excluded because of the lack of reliable information on candidate nomination. I also had to exclude the 2003 elections in Belgorod province because they took place after the manuscript was completed.

19. Here and later, the May–June 2003 elections in North Ossetia are excluded because they took place after the manuscript was completed. As previously, I exclude elections held in Chechnya.

20. Table 3.8 shows average percentage shares for those regions that held two elections in the course of a given electoral cycle.

21. Kamchatka krai nashenskii, *Pravda Rossii,* November 2, 1995.

22. Kto stanet osnovnym pretendentom? *Svobodnyi kurs* (Barnaul), August 1, 1996.

23. Partia vlasti na Kubani—eto soiuz patriotov, *Pravda,* April 4, 2002.

24. Politicheskie partii i obshchestvenno-politicheskie dvizhenia v Respublike Tatarstan, www.tatar.ru/party_1.html.

25. Politicheskie partii—respublika Sakha (Yakutia), socarchive.narod.ru/bibl/polros/Sakha_r/partii-sak.html.

26. KPRS(Ya) preobrazovana v regional'noe otdelenie KPRF, *Yakutia* (Yakutsk), February 5, 2002.

27. V Tatarstane sformirovan izbiratel'nyi blok, *Rossiiskaia gazeta,* June 17, 1992.

28. Vybory v Tatarii i Bashkirii, *Segodnia,* February 23, 1995.

29. Novosti, *Yabloko Rossii,* March 1997.

30. Kak vybirat budem? *Rabochii* (Krasnoiarsk), November 11, 1997; Esli by zhenshchiny vsei zemli... *Segodniashniaia gazeta* (Krasnoiarsk), July 19, 2001.

31. V poiskakh vykhoda... iz Rossii? *Russkaia mysl* (Paris), December 12, 1998.

32. Pobednye reliatsii, *Segodniashniaia gazeta* (Krasnoiarsk), December 27, 2001.

4

The Supply Side: Party Labels and Party Resources

The empirical evidence presented in the previous chapter suggests that in the majority of Russia's regions, the services offered by political parties remain out of demand. Of course, an alternative interpretation of the data is that services are unavailable. After all, political parties may simply be absent in the regions. The first section of this chapter presents the available empirical evidence on their presence. In the second section, I demonstrate that despite the apparent oversupply of party labels in the regions of Russia, even the strongest parties are actually constrained in their capacity for electoral participation. In the third section, I briefly review services offered by political parties to candidates in regional elections. I will demonstrate that while party affiliations may be useful for the majority of candidates, there are numerous and easily available alternatives to the services parties can offer.

The Oversupply of Party Labels

As argued in Chapter 1, the simplest commodity a party may provide to its candidate is a party label. Party labels are important because they are primary means of voter coordination in any electoral campaign, and they are also useful for providing coordination among candidates themselves. Yet if no right-wing party is available, a right-wing candidate has no choice but to run as an independent. From the prehistory of national political parties in Russia as described in Chapter 2, one may infer that there were simply no parties at the regional level. This would explain why party candidates were so few in the first electoral cycle and afterward. The available empirical evidence on regional party penetration in 1991–1993 is scarce and fragmented. Yet the overall impression made by putting the fragments together is that at least the most important of those parties that were spawned by the 1989–1991 political mobilization managed to maintain certain levels of territorial penetration throughout the period, even though their membership drastically declined, while the Communist Party, once it was reconstituted in 1993, did not take long to became almost universally present in the localities (Golosov 1995; Brown 1998).

Among the right-wing parties, the most common survivors seemed to be Democratic Russia and its major constituent members, the Democratic Party of Russia (DPR), the Republican Party of the Russian Federation (RPRF), and the Social Democratic Party of Russia (SDPR). The data from party congresses may be revealing in this respect. In May 1993 the SDPR still had as many as sixty regional branches.[1] The October 1993 RPRF congress brought together the representatives of fifty-three regional branches.[2] In December 1992 an informed observer at the DPR congress characterized it as "the most distinctly mass organization currently in existence in the country."[3] Indeed, as of 1992 the DPR was estimated to be "the only Russian opposition party with chapters in all centers of the republics, as well as in many district centers and villages," and to comprise 543 organizations throughout Russia (Pribylovskii 1992: 22). Of course, such estimations should be treated with a grain of salt. Theoretically, a local or even regional organization could consist of just one person. Yet this still fits into a very narrow notion of party presence. Indeed, what is under discussion now is a party's ability to keep its label, which does not depend on the size of its membership. A more substantive argument in this context would be that not every branch or organization that sent its representative to a party congress was necessarily a legal entity that was registered locally and thus entitled to nominate its candidates. In this respect, an illuminating piece of evidence, in the form of an officially published list of parties that were registered by October 1993, comes from Kaluga province.[4] The list is also interesting because it reports membership figures at the time of registration. These figures are not realistic for political movements, because if they did not have registered, card-carrying members, they could report to have as many members as they wanted. For instance, the regional branch of Democratic Russia was said to have 120,000 members. Parties with registered memberships, however, were more constrained in their wishful thinking. Overall, the list includes twenty-seven entities. Eleven of them are economic interest groups. The remaining sixteen, in addition to Democratic Russia, include the Communist Party of the Russian Federation (KPRF, 4,820 members), the DPR (324), the Agrarian Party of Russia (APR, 192 members), the Russian Communist Workers Party (RKRP, 57 members), the People's Party Free Russia (30 members), the RPRF (30 members), and the Party of Economic Freedom (PES, 22 members). Hence both the principal left-wing organizations and the most important "democratic" leftovers from the late perestroika period were in place.

Another piece of relevant information comes from an analytical report prepared for the regional administration of Omsk province by an anonymous observer in August 1993.[5] The report makes clear that the largest party active in the province was the KPRF, with 7,800 members. Among other opposition parties, the RKRP and Workers Omsk are mentioned as losing their memberships to the KPRF. Moreover, the report suggests that the memberships of Workers Omsk and the KPRF largely overlapped in the sense that the majority of the participants in the former were also KPRF members, even though the personal compositions of their leaderships were different. This resulted in the KPRF's ability to control the actions of Workers Omsk. In this connection, the report mentions a conflict at one of the meetings of the movement when the members of the KPRF, apparently dissatisfied with the movement leaders' proposals, suggested that if the communists went away, there would be not much of Workers Omsk to remain. According to the report, there was also a branch of the Russian All-People's Union (ROS) in the region. Indeed, the national leader of the ROS, Sergei Baburin, originated from Omsk and continued to be engaged in local politics long thereafter (Melvin 1998). The membership of the ROS, however, was estimated at sixty people at most; about a half of them were Baburin's personal supporters, who did not participate in the activities of the ROS. Of the other half, about fifteen were KPRF members. The report also mentions the People's Party Free Russia as an organization with about ten active members, the RPRF with about thirty active members, and the SDPR with fourteen members, only four of whom continued to be interested in politics. No estimated membership of Democratic Russia is provided, but it is mentioned as being able to hold meetings of its supporters.

A typical picture of parties in existence at the regional level in 1993 that can be derived from a variety of sources is thus. First, invariably there was a branch of the KPRF with a membership rarely smaller than 2,000 people. Most of them did not join the party but rather reestablished their KPSS membership. For instance, the Volgograd branch of the KPRF, one of the largest in Russia, included more than 10,000 members, but only 62 of them joined the party for the first time.[6] The branches of the RKRP and the APR were also typically present, but they tended to be much smaller. Small local groups normally represented the nationalist camp. Of the right-wing parties, most observers mentioned Democratic Russia, the RPRF, the DPR, and the SDPR. Their memberships are invariably estimated as very small and overlapping, since the three parties were also collective members of the movement. It seems that the 1993 campaign gave a strong impetus for revitalizing old and creating new party organizations in the localities. The absence of the Liberal Democratic Party of Russia (LDPR) in the above-cited cases of Kaluga and Omsk, then, is not surprising. Apparently, before the 1993 elections the level of the LDPR's territorial penetration was quite low. Even those few regional branches that survived through the 1991–1993 period gradually lost their connections with the central leadership and pursued their own strategies, sometimes as minor parties in com-

munist-led coalitions, as happened in Mordovia.[7] The 1993 success in
party-list competition—or even anticipation of this success as a result of
Vladimir Zhirinovsky's skillful campaigning—entailed a massive wave of
LDPR penetration into the localities. For instance, it was reported that the
Smolensk province branch of the LDPR, registered on December 9, 1993,
had seventy-five members on the day of elections, and the membership
continued to grow rapidly.[8] The parties of power, the Party of Russian
Unity and Accord (PRES) and especially Russia's Choice, also invested
their efforts in territorial penetration. The membership of Russia's Choice
partly overlapped with the memberships of previously existing right-wing
organizations, but there was also an influx of new members. For instance,
the elected cochairmen of the Mordovian branch of Russia's Choice were
the mayor of the republic's capital, the editor of the republic's most popular
newspaper, and a member of the presidium of its Supreme Soviet. None of
them were previously in Democratic Russia or in any of its constituent parties.[9]

As a result of the October–December 1993 upsurge, the numbers of
parties registered in the regions increased. For instance, the former chairman of the Central Electoral Commission, Alesandr Ivanchenko, reported
that by the 1994 regional legislative elections, there were 163 entities that
were entitled to nominate their candidates in the republic of Chuvashia, and
more than 200 in Tula province (Ivanchenko 1996: 230). Characteristically,
Ivanchenko mentioned this in connection with the fact that none of these
entities actually nominated a single candidate. Of course, it must be
remembered that at that time, the notion of a "public organization entitled
to nominate its candidates in elections" embraced many interest groups
that, for one reason or another, included such provisions in their bylaws.
But, as has been demonstrated in the previous chapter, some of them did
not abstain from exercising this right.

Much more comprehensive evidence on the levels of party penetration
is available for the period of 1995–2003. Throughout the period, the
Central Electoral Commission published data on the numbers of organizations eligible for electoral participation in the regions quite systematically,
after almost each of the regional elections was held.[10] Only information
about the regionwide organizations, not those in smaller administrative
units, was included. I aggregated these data as average numbers of parties
registered in the regions by year. The result is presented in Table 4.1. Note
that this mode of presentation has two major disadvantages: first, the averages are calculated not for the whole set of regions but only for those that
held elections in the given year, and second, the lists of regions for individual years are not the same. That is why I report the numbers of regions
entered into my calculations as a separate column in the table. This being
said, it appears that the levels of party presence in the regions were quite

Table 4.1   **Average Numbers of Organizations Entitled to Nominate Their Candidates and Registered Regionally, 1995–2001**

	Number of Regions	Average Number of Organizations
1995	24	68.5
1996	51	51.9
1997	36	82.6
1998	22	70.0
1999	19	56.0
2000	43	43.3
2001	41	44.4

impressive throughout the period, even though they did have their ups and downs. These ups and downs, however, are difficult to relate to the dynamics of Russia's party system development. Instead, they have a lot to do with the legal definition of a candidate-nominating entity. In particular, the rather sharp decrease in the number of parties in 1998–1999 can be related to the enactment of the amended Law on the Basic Guarantees of Electoral Rights, which eliminated most interest groups from the electoral arena. However, the consequences of this institutional reform ceased to be felt by 2001, when the average number of candidate-nominating entities slightly increased in comparison with the previous year. Candidate-nominating entities, even after they were redefined as "public political associations" and thus legally obliged to pursue political goals, continued to be in quite ample supply in the regions.

Of course, one may be tempted to ask what individual organizations are beyond the impressive numbers in the table. Unfortunately, the lists of registered parties are available neither for the whole time span covered in the table nor for the majority of regions included. In fact, I was able to investigate such lists, dated circa December 2001, for only ten regions.[11] Generally, the information I derived from analysis of these lists turned out to be quite consistent with the data reported above. There are indeed huge numbers of political parties in the regions of Russia. The overall number of national parties that had branches in the selected regions was 114. True, as many as 59 of them were represented in only one or two regions, and 26 others could be found in three to five regions. There were also 60 regional parties. All those parties that had branches in more than five regions are listed in Table 4.2. Also, the table lists several parties that had branches in smaller numbers of regions but, at a given moment of time, used to be active in regional legislative elections, as reflected in Tables 3.9–3.11.

Of course, the omnipresence of the KPRF and the LDPR is not surprising, given the levels of their electoral activity as described in the previous chapter. The Union of Right Forces (SPS), which also appears to be quite a

Table 4.2   Branches of National Political Parties in Ten Selected Regions, ca. December 2001

Parties	Numbers of Regional Branches
Fatherland, KPRF, LDPR, RNRP, SPS, Unity	10
APR, Union for People's Power and Labor, Women of Russia	9
ChR, Lebed Young People's Movement, New Force, Russian Party of Social Democracy, Russian Party of the Future, Russian Socialist Party, Union of Labor, Yabloko	8
Cedar, Derzhava, DVR, Pensioners Party, Regions of Russia, Spiritual Heritage	7
DPR, For Equal Rights and Justice, NDR, Orthodox Party of Russia, Russian United Social Democratic Party, Union Party	6
NPRF	5
KRO, PST	4
Democratic Russia, PRES	3
PES, RKRP	2
NPSR, RPRF	1

widespread party, is the major successor to the perestroika-era democratic movement. One could also logically expect the parties of power to penetrate the localities. At the same time, information reported in Table 4.2 is puzzling in several respects, and some of this information does not seem to match the realities of Russia's regional electoral politics as described in the previous chapter. Yet puzzles tend to be cognitively useful, which is why it is expedient not to ignore them. Three of them deserve special treatment. First, why are parties that have never been active in the regional electoral arenas present on the regional registrars quite widely? Second, why are parties that can be reasonably believed to have become extinct several years prior still there? And third, why do parties that merged continue to be registered as separate entities? All three questions are unrelated to the most important parties. In the remaining part of this section, I will deal mostly with rather insignificant formations. The reason for treating them seriously is that for all their individual insignificance, jointly they form the largest section of the market of party labels available to regional politicians.

Turning to the first question, let us look at an entity whose presence in Table 4.2 is perhaps most unexpected, the Orthodox Party of Russia (PPR). Russia's Ministry of Justice registered the party in May 1998. Its regional branches were registered in the localities soon after that event.[12] The word "Orthodox" in the party's name refers to Orthodox Christianity, and judging from this name, one would logically expect it to be clerical. It is not. In fact, as stated by the chairman of the PPR at the party's congress in 2002, "the Orthodox Party of Russia always was and still is a secular, lay organization that equally respects any religious choice including agnosticism."[13]

The key to the puzzle of the PPR apparently lies neither in its ideology (indeed, an organization that describes itself as "a party of all normal, commonsense people" does not seem to have much of the sort) nor in its societal constituency (which could have been provided by church attendees but seemingly was not), but rather in its origins. Several former officials in the central apparatus of the Soviet-era young people's organization, the Komsomol, formed the PPR after being solicited by a long-standing nationalist politician, German Sterligov, to do the job.[14] Sterligov himself was not among the official leaders of the new formation, and it is only possible to speculate about why he sponsored the PPR, especially given that he headed his own movement, Word and Action. A quite plausible explanation is that he intended to register a list of the PPR in the 1999 Duma elections if his own movement were to be disqualified.[15] Sterligov's unclear motivation notwithstanding, at some moment of time he needed a party, and it was delivered to him. But delivery had a condition attached: the party's founders had to take care about registering its regional branches. As I argued in Chapter 2, the branches could be useful if the PPR indeed were to venture to participate in the Duma elections. Registering regional branches was not difficult, though. While I do not possess information on how it was achieved in the case of the PPR, the mechanics, as they emerge from the Law on Public Associations, which regulated them (Article 21), involved the following easy steps: (1) provide the regional department of the Ministry of Justice with certain documentary evidence on the organization, such as its statute, its official address, and the official application signed by the members of the "permanent ruling body of the organization"; (2) pay a small fee; and (3) present the minutes of a congress, conference, or meeting at which the branch was established. Of these three clauses, perhaps the most difficult to fulfill was to recruit the members of the permanent ruling body, those people—two or three of them would suffice—who would be in charge of the whole affair. Here is where the Komsomol backgrounds of the founders of the PPR could have become an important asset. With a couple of people ready to do the paperwork, and perhaps with a small amount of money subsidized to them, assembling a founding conference, producing its minutes, or both, would not be a tremendously difficult task.

The case of the PPR is comic in many respects. Sterligov was not a very well-known national politician at the time the PPR was formed, and for reasons not to be discussed here, he did not participate in the 1999 elections. Thus it is not surprising that the local branches of the PPR became inactive immediately after they were formed.[16] This was not necessarily the case with other little-known parties in Table 4.2. Consider the Union for People's Power and Labor, a political organization formed in 1998 by Andrei Nikolaev. At that time, Nikolaev was considered as a close political ally of Yurii Luzhkov, while his organization, in the perception of many, was nothing less than a nucleus of Luzhkov's party.[17] This project never materialized, but Nikolaev also had a reputation of his own. This, at least initially, brought rather important regional politicians under his banners, the most prominent example being perhaps a long-standing opponent of the Primorskii territory authorities and once a mayor of Vladivostok, Viktor Cherepkov, and the governor of Yaroslavl province, Anatolii Lisitsin.[18] In other regions, the branches of the union were formed under the auspices of less prominent but still quite respectable public figures, such as a chief engineer of a local power plant in Buriatia.[19] After its unsuccessful participation in the 1999 Duma elections within the Electoral Bloc of General Andrei Nikolaev and Academician Sviatoslav Fedorov, the entity disappeared from the Russian political arena. Yet its regional branches did not disappear from the regional registrars of political parties. Hence my solution to the puzzle is indeed simple. Since the regional branches of political parties emerge largely as a product of the activities of national party elites who are interested in territorial penetration, and since it is technically easy to have a branch of a national political party registered, the natural result is the proliferation of party branches. Therefore, even those parties that are small and impotent at the national level are still capable of building their territorial networks.

Do their labels remain effectively, not only formally, in supply? One would be tempted to suggest that irrelevant parties remained registered simply because nobody cared about removing them after they effectively ceased to exist. This might be the case with the Union for People's Power and Labor, a formation of relatively recent origin. However, an attempt to reduce the number of parties by means of their obligatory reregistration undertaken by the Ministry of Justice and its regional departments in 1998–1999 did not result in the disappearance of several parties that, by all accounts, became irrelevant long before this happened with Nikolaev's group.[20] This brings us to the second puzzle posed by the empirical evidence, why such parties continuously renewed their existence in the regions. Consider such a remarkable survivor as the DPR, still present in six regions of the selected ten by the end of 2001. In all its history, the DPR managed to win seats in only one national Duma election, in 1993. It did not participate in the 1995 and 1999 elections. After the departure of its founder, Nikolai Travkin, and after a brief period of experimentation with Sergei Glaz'ev, then a second-rank figure in the left-wing opposition, it did not have prominent national leaders either. By all accounts, it was dead as a national party. Yet as demonstrated in the previous chapter, it continued not just to exist but also to play a certain part in regional electoral politics. The mechanics of the DPR's survival become apparent from the analysis of its electoral participation in the 1995–2003 regional elections. In the second electoral cycle, it participated on its own—that is, without entering blocs—in only two regional legislative elections, in Altai territory and in Samara province. It nominated one candidate in each of the elections. In five regions, the DPR participated in electoral blocs. In three of these blocs, the DPR allied itself with the Congress of Russian Communites (KRO), which is not surprising given the DPR strategy in the 1995 national Duma elections. In two blocs, the DPR's partner was the Party of Workers Self-Government (PST), while two other blocs joined the DPR with Yabloko and Honor and the Motherland (ChR). Generally, this circle of coalition partners fits well into the pattern of the "third force" coalition that was envisioned but never materialized in the 1996 national presidential elections. Two other blocs in which the DPR participated are entirely different. In Novosibirsk province, it allied itself with Our Home Is Russia (NDR) and a local group called Novosibirsk Democratic Front to form a bloc called Union, which was regarded as an invention of local authorities who, in anticipation of an ideologically polarized election, pursued two goals: first, to prevent the KPRF and the LDPR from taking a majority of seats in the regional legislature, and second, to achieve that by bringing in loyal right-wing politicians, not those at odds with the authorities.[21] In Moscow, quite in contrast to Novosibirsk, the DPR allied itself with several local groups to form a bloc led by, and even named after, the most vocal opponent of Moscow city authorities, Nikolai Gonchar.[22] Hence the label of the DPR was still in use, but the modes of its utility were quite specific. First, local DPR leaders who actually possessed the label did not refrain from using it for nominating themselves in regional elections. Second, the label of the DPR was employed for forming electoral blocs that sought to win seats for the leaders of participating organizations by rhetorically affiliating them with nationally prominent politicians. Indeed, the names of such blocs in Arkhangel'sk and Kaliningrad provinces were "Yavlinsky–Fedorov–Lebed" and "The Supporters of Aleksandr Lebed, Sviatoslav Fedorov, and Sergei Glaz'ev for Regional Development," respectively. Third, the label of the DPR was used for forming electoral blocs by nonparty affiliated political actors who, for one reason or another, found increased coordination among their supporters desirable. A modest payoff in the form of endorsing the local DPR leader's candidacy seemed to be a price quite acceptable for both partners in such transactions.

The example of the DPR demonstrates that its label did not lose its utility long after the party effectively withdrew itself from the national political arena. Of course, the level of utility was rather low. Of the seven instances of the DPR's electoral participation in the second electoral cycle, there were only three elections that can be counted as minimally successful for blocs that involved the party. Overall, they won four seats in regional legislative assemblies. But this was still a benefit. As for costs, keeping a party label once obtained was obviously a low-cost procedure. Even if requested by the authorities to renew it by means of reregistration, the holder of the label could easily afford that by meeting the requirements described above. That is, the ratio of benefits provided by keeping the label to the costs associated with maintaining it remained larger than one for local party leaders. For local party members, however, the situation was different. In brief, they simply could not use the label as they wished. The simplest good that can be delivered by a party—party nomination—comes with a string attached. It involves getting authorization from the local party leadership, which is already costly. More complex services, such as presence on candidate lists endorsed by electoral blocs, are even more difficult to solicit. The logical corollary is that under conditions when party labels are easy to obtain and easy to keep, a rational strategy for a politician who for whatever reason seeks party affiliation would be not to join an existing party but rather to form a party of his own. This leads us to the third puzzle posed by the data reported in Table 4.2, why parties that merged at the national level continued to exist as separate entities regionally.

Consider the case of the SPS. When it was formed as an electoral bloc on the eve of the 1999 national Duma elections, it officially included four cofounding organizations: New Force, Democratic Russia's Choice (DVR), Young Russia, and Lawyers for Human Rights and the Life of Dignity. On a less formal basis, the bloc embraced ten more groups such as, among others, Democratic Russia, the PES, the Russian Party of Social Democracy, and the Free Democrats of Russia. Soon after the elections, the bloc was transformed into a new political organization bearing the label of the SPS. By July 2000 it had as many as nineteen regional branches, only one of which was created anew—that is, without the participation of preexisting parties. Most often, the regional branches of the SPS involved the local branches of the DVR and other initial participants in the bloc, particularly New Force but sometimes also Yabloko, the RPRF, and other right-wing organizations.[23] By the end of 2000, such branches had reportedly been created in about sixty regions.[24] One could logically expect this process to sweep away the majority of right-wing parties, or at least those of them that joined the SPS. It did not. Most of these parties' regional branches not only continued to be officially registered, but also continued to function as if nothing had happened. For instance, in May 2001 the majority of regional branches of the DVR were in existence, and they defied the efforts of the national leaders of the SPS, who urged their self-dissolution.[25] It was only a year later that the regional branches of the DVR and New Force ceased to exist in the majority of regions (Young Russia never had a regional network). Smaller organizations that once participated in the SPS preferred to continue their shadowy existence both nationally and in the regions. Such were, for example, the local branches of the Russia's Choice movement,

Forward, Russia! and Free Democrats of Russia in Tver province.[26] The reason for their survival was not that they were politically important. It seems that a party label, irrespective of whether the given party became extinct or merged with other parties at the national level, remains a valuable commodity for its holder. This, in combination with the low costs of keeping the label, creates incentives for preserving it. Yet as I have already argued, the label can be effectively held by one or, at best, several individuals. Hence the paradoxical situation when parties abound yet there are no party members. In general, however, this analysis leaves little ground to believe that party labels are not used because they are not in supply. They appear to be in oversupply, but not in demand.

Candidate-Nominating Capacities of Political Parties

Party labels are important. They provide voters with vital information about candidates' policy preferences, thus bridging the gap between the politician and the voter and allowing the latter to minimize the costs of electoral choice. However, the informational utility of party labels for candidates critically depends on two circumstances. First, to be useful, a party label has to be recognizable. Second, it also has to be attractive to a portion of voters that is significantly large to allow for the candidate's election, or at least for enhancing his electoral resources obtained by different means, such as personal reputation. It seems that the majority of party labels available in the regions of Russia do not meet the first requirement, and even fewer satisfy the second. But there are exceptions. In some of the regions, such as Moscow, St. Petersburg, and Sverdlovsk province, quite significant portions of electors are inclined to support right-wing policies at the polls, and they are quite aware of what parties can be realistically associated with advancing such policies, even though such perceptions can vary across regions. In other regions, the parties of power, with their programmatic commitment to stability, or nationalists, with their foreign policy concerns, gain momentum. The national electoral results of 1995 and 1999 clearly demonstrate that at the national level of Russia's electoral politics, political parties and their labels are useful informational shortcuts. Perhaps the clearest manifestation of the persistent linkage between policy preferences and party choice is the continuously successful performance of the KPRF in national elections. As demonstrated in the previous chapter, the KPRF is also more successful than other parties at the regional level. Yet here, its success does not match its gains in the national electoral arena. Table 4.3 provides a statistical proof. For each of the electoral cycles, I regressed the percentage shares of regional assembly seats held by the KPRF conglomerate, as defined in the previous chapter, on a single independent variable, the

Table 4.3   KPRF Performance in National and Regional Legislative Elections, 1993–2003

Electoral Cycle	Number of Observations	B		Intercept	R-squared
1993–1995	85	0.28*	(0.11)	1.16	0.07
1995–1999	84	0.78***	(0.17)	−3.82	0.20
1999–2003	83	0.38***	(0.12)	−3.25	0.10

Notes: The dependent variable is the percentage share of regional assembly seats held by the KPRF conglomerate; the independent variable is the percentage share of the vote cast for the KPRF in national Duma party-list elections. Parentheses indicate standard errors.
* Significant at 0.05.
** Significant at 0.01.
*** Significant at 0.001.

percentage shares of the vote cast for the KPRF in national Duma party-list elections.[27] The lack of association, as it emerges from the table, is quite striking. But perhaps more important is how much better the KPRF performed in national elections than it did in the regional ones. As follows from the equations, in a region with the level of KPRF list support as high as 30 percent, the party itself or its local reincarnations could count on obtaining 9.6 percent of legislative seats in the first electoral cycle, 19.6 percent in the second electoral cycle, and 8.2 percent in the third electoral cycle.

Possible explanations to this phenomenon include, first, the voters' inclination to behave differently in different elections, and second, electoral system effects. Both theories will be addressed further. But for them to be true, an important condition has to be fulfilled: to match in performance in national party-list elections, where obviously each seat is contested by the party, the KPRF has to run its candidates for the majority of seats in regional legislatures. This does not appear to be the case. While complete information about party candidate nomination is available for none of the electoral cycles, the data sets for the second and third cycles are fairly comprehensive. The data are available for seventy-five and eighty-two elections respectively. Using this data set, I established that the average percentage shares of plurality/majority seats contested by the candidates of the KPRF conglomerate were 40.3 and 26.7 percent respectively. Table 4.4 contains information about the number of regional legislative elections in which the candidates of the KPRF conglomerate contested the specified percentage shares of plurality/majority seats. As becomes clear from the table, regional elections in which the communists contested at least half of seats were relatively rare already in the second electoral cycle (thirty-three of seventy-five elections); in the third cycle they became unusual indeed

Table 4.4   **Numbers of Regional Legislative Elections in Which Candidates of the KPRF Conglomerate Contested the Specified Percentage Shares of Plurality/Majority Seats, by Electoral Cycle, 1995–2003**

Percentage Shares of Seats Contested	Numbers of Elections, 2nd Electoral Cycle	Numbers of Elections, 3rd Electoral Cycle
90.0–100.0	5	2
70.0–89.9	12	2
50.0–69.9	16	16
30.0–49.9	10	16
10.0–29.9	11	11
0.1– 9.9	6	4
0	15	31
0–100.0 (total)	75	82

(twenty of eighty-two elections). The KPRF conglomerate simply abstained from running its candidates. Why so?

The primary reason why a party with a strong electoral appeal may abstain from electoral participation is, of course, a lack of committed activists. At the first glance, such an explanation does not apply to the case of the KPRF. True, there are several very small regions with territorially dispersed populations that tend to vote for noncommunist parties in national elections. In such regions, exemplified by Nenets and Taimyr autonomous districts, it would be difficult to expect vibrant communist activities, and indeed the KPRF conglomerate did not take part in elections there. In the majority of regions, however, the organizations of the KPRF seemed to be quite alive throughout the second and third electoral cycles.[28] Consider the case of Novgorod province. It is a small region with a population of only 738,000; the voters are less likely to support the KPRF here than in many other localities, as testified to by the fact that only 18.2 percent of them voted for the party in the 1995 national Duma elections. Despite these relatively unfavorable backgrounds, as of March 1997 the regional branch of KPRF had as many as 1,164 people in twenty-two towns and districts of the province. While the vast majority of them reestablished their former KPSS memberships in the same way as in Volgograd province, 210 people were neophytes who joined the party in 1995–1996.[29] True, slightly more than 1,000 members is not a formidable political force, but it must be enough for recruiting a candidate for each of the twenty-six electoral districts in the province. In fact, however, the local branch of the KPRF nominated only nine candidates in 1997, and it abstained from participation in the 2001 regional legislative elections. An even more puzzling example comes from Nizhnii Novgorod province. The regional branch of the KPRF, with more than 5,000 members, is quite large by Russian standards, and it is politically active.[30] In 2000 the KPRF-supported candidate was elected as a governor of the province. Yet the party did not nominate a single candidate in the 2002 regional legislative elections.

Hence the explanation that relates the lack of electoral activities on the part of the KPRF to its organizational absence in the regions does not hold, even though it may be well applicable to many other parties. However, in plurality/majority elections, which are the most widespread in Russia's regions, the availability of loyal party members is not the only thing that matters. Personal reputations of the available candidates are important too. Running candidates who are unable to win is costly, and it scarcely helps to enhance the party's own reputation. A detailed analysis of the occupational structure of candidates in regional legislative elections will be provided in Chapter 5. Here, it is important to make two very general points regarding the personal backgrounds of the KPRF activists. First, as demonstrated by the main body of research on the KPRF organization, approximately 60 percent of the KPRF membership is over sixty years old (Makarkin 1996; Urban and Solovei 1997). This is not surprising, given that membership recruitment tends to be low and that the majority of the current members are former members of the KPSS. In postcommunist Russia, elderly persons whose major income derives from pensions are not a highly reputable category of the population. In fact, in those elections where there is a legal requirement of more than one candidate on the ballot, and where a certain candidate is generally believed to be unbeatable, such that nobody wants to run against him or her, it is usual to hire a pensioner as a voluntary second-runner.[31]

The second major category of KPRF activists, comprising individuals often younger than sixty, includes those people who joined the party because of their ideological commitment. In the Soviet era, they were often troublemakers well outside of the establishment. A middle-aged woman from Khakasia explained her motivation in the following way: "I wanted to join the party in the Soviet time, but apparently my straightforwardness prevented it. Not every boss likes to hear the truth. Now, as I see the people's deteriorating conditions, I decided to join the communist party together with my sister."[32] Such potential candidates also have little if anything to add to their party's reputation. These categories of activists only partially overlap, and both are important for the party. The pensioners are indispensable for holding party meetings and demonstrations, thus maintaining the image of the KPRF as the only mass party of contemporary Russia. In low-turnout elections such as regional legislative contests, they also form a visible and sometimes decisive section of the electorate. Without the "true believers," the KPRF would not be able to perform such activities as door-to-door canvassing, picketing, distribution of party newspapers and leaflets, and so on.[33] But for all their importance, they are not good enough as candidates. First, their social standings are too low, which corresponds to fairly low-profile personal reputations. Second, their incentives for communist party membership, as described above, do not necessarily presuppose desire to run for public offices. Third, many of them lack the political skills or political flexibility that would allow them to do the job.

Candidate recruitment is a persistent topic in comparative literature on political parties and elections.[34] In particular, it has been argued that while parties as organizations require a certain minimum of "true believers" to be viable (Panebianco 1988: 10), the overall pattern of candidate recruitment necessarily has to involve office-seeking motivation, which makes it imperative to identify and bring under the party's banners candidates with greater personal appeal (Schlesinger 1984). It has been demonstrated that the strategy of candidate recruitment pursued by the KPRF in national legislative elections gradually shifts in the direction of nominating more candidates belonging to the administrative and economic elites (Ishiyama 2000). The regional branches of the KPRF can pursue a similar strategy. But arguably, they are more constrained to do so than the party as a whole in national elections. First, regional branches are close to the party's radical rank-and-file. The most immediate consequence is that regional party leaders often refuse to accept the programmatic and tactical innovations induced by the national leadership (March 2001). A related consequence is that wealthy businesspeople are less likely to make it onto the lists of candidates nominated by the KPRF in regional legislative elections than to make it onto national party lists. Moreover, if they do, the party activists and the core communist electorate may reject them, which makes the whole enterprise senseless. Since 1997 the branch of the KPRF in Novosibirsk province has been continuously strong enough to maintain massive presence in the regional legislative assembly. An influential businessman and owner of one of the province's largest enterprises, Mikhail Titov, sought to enter the assembly on the communist ticket, for which end he even joined the party.[35] He lost the election to another businessman. Novosibirsk province is rather unusual in the sense that its administrative and economic elite is rather segmented and politically engaged, which allows for such political alliances. In many other regions, an enterprise manager would think twice before allying himself with the communists. This applies even to those regions where governors won with KPRF support. In Stavropol territory, for example, the KPRF is the ruling party in this (admittedly, very limited) sense, and quite influential businesspeople have joined it.[36] Yet none of them ran for regional legislative elections as a KPRF nominee.

Hence, despite the KPRF's organizational superiority, and related to its basic organizational properties, there are serious constraints on the party's candidate-nominating capacity. The basic dilemma is that its activists are not likely to win, while those candidates who are probable winners may be unacceptable for its activists. Under such conditions, abstention from candidate nomination may be not the worst strategy available. However, there are additional reasons for such a strategy. The second major reason is coalition building. In plurality/majority elections, there are two ways in which coalitions may be forged. One of them is when the interested parties create an electoral bloc. This, as we have seen, was indeed the choice of the KPRF in many second-cycle elections and in some of the third-cycle elections as well. However, there are several conditions under which blocs are useful electoral vehicles rather than unnecessary twists in parties' preelection strategies. First, the balance of resources among the potential participants in the bloc must be transparent enough to allow for avoiding conflicts among them when it comes to the most important question, how many candidates preferred by each of the individual parties should be jointly nominated. Second, the informational value of the selected joint label must be greater than that of the strongest individual participants' labels. Third, if elected, the bloc nominees belonging to individual parties must be expected to retain a certain level of loyalty to other participating groups.

This, in fact, is a rather demanding combination of requirements. Speaking of the political realities of Russia's regions, their fulfillment was most probable under conditions when the KPRF was undeniably stronger than its partners, and when the principal reason for creating a bloc was its expectation that under a joint label, its candidates would fare better than otherwise. Consider the 1997 regional legislative elections in Novosibirsk and Riazan provinces. In both regions, the KPRF was not the monopolistic party of the left. The local branches of the APR were quite vibrant in the countrysides of the provinces, and they pursued their own policy agendas, sometimes departing from the KPRF as far as to endorse noncommunist candidates in gubernatorial elections, as had happened in Riazan.[37] The KPRF, on the other hand, could rely upon the left-wing vote of the urban electorate. Both organizations were successful in the national party-list elections in the regions, which means that their labels were valuable for their electorate. At the same time, it was clear that when engaged in face-to-face races in single-member districts, they confronted a real danger of losing to a third party. In Novosibirsk province, it was the regional branch of the LDPR that, after quite an impressive success in Novosibirsk city council elections, ran its candidates in all districts.[38] The solutions to the problem found by the left-wingers in Novosibirsk and Riazan provinces were similar: to divide the electoral districts in a way that would allow them to avoid face-to-face races. In Novosibirsk province, this solution was formalized by creating a preelectoral alliance, even though both parties proceeded to nominate their own candidates.[39] In Riazan province, the coalition was thoroughly informal. Overall, the KPRF nominated thirty-two and twenty-three candidates, and the APR four and seven candidates, in

Novosibirsk and Riazan provinces respectively. The elections returned seventeen Communists and three Agrarians in Novosibirsk, and eight Communists and four Agrarians in Riazan, which means that the selected strategy paid off quite generously by Russian standards. But of course, its side effect was that the number of KPRF-nominated candidates was smaller than it could have been otherwise.

Regional legislative elections in Novosibirsk and Riazan provinces were clear-cut cases of interparty electoral cooperation among the left. Such cases, however, are relatively rare. More often, the KPRF entered into similar yet even less formal alliances with local nonpartisan elites by supporting independent candidates. One of the major aspects of regional politics in Samara province was the persistent conflict between the regional governor, Konstantin Titov, and the mayor of the city of Samara, Georgii Limanskii. On the eve of the 2001 fresh mayoral elections, the regional branch of the KPRF unexpectedly endorsed Limanskii, who was not previously noticed as a left-winger.[40] Soon after the mayoral elections, the province proceeded to elect its regional legislature. In these elections, the alliance between Limanskii, who sought to create a strong anti-Titov opposition in the legislature, and the Communists, who sought to increase their legislative representation, consolidated to an extent that allowed Limanskii to speak of his own "team" of candidates, which included several KPRF nominees.[41] In the end, the KPRF nominated as few as six candidates for twenty-five seats in the legislature, but two of them won. As a result, Samara province turned out to be one of very few regions where communist representation in regional legislative assemblies did not decline in the third electoral cycle. Besides, the elections returned five deputies who were neither nominated by the KPRF nor even publicly sympathetic to the communist rhetoric, but who as the members of the "team of Limanskii" received the party's wholehearted support.[42] For both parties, therefore, their alliance was quite profitable. For the Communists, the profit arrived with a string attached: some of the districts had to remain uncontested by them. The Samara example is very illuminative in the sense that the "team of Limanskii" publicized its activities. In many other regions, the KPRF delivered its support to individual candidates who, while not bound by any obligations either mutually or with the party, could be expected to be useful if elected, and had good chances to win. Like Samara, Tver province does not display strong procommunist inclinations. There, the Communists nominated nine candidates in the 2001 regional legislative elections. None of them won. At the same time, the party abstained from candidate nomination in four districts in favor of incumbent legislators who were generally considered front-runners.[43] While only two of them regained their seats, this provided the Communists with a minimum of influence on the legislative floor, something that they would not have achieved otherwise.

Thus the second reason why the KPRF may abstain from nominating its candidates is coalition politics, if understood broadly as to embrace informal coalitions with individual resourceful politicians. The third possible reason is a political climate induced by a strong anticommunist attitude of the regional executive, sometimes with elements of overt political repression. Such occurrences seem to be rather rare and unusual, but they do take place. Consider the 1996 elections to the legislature of Saratov province. There, the Communists did not nominate their candidates at all and ran as independents, but this did not prevent massive violations of their rights. In clear contradiction to the law, the state-controlled media did not provide space for publishing their preelection documents and announcements, while the regional electoral commission simply refused to register several candidates known as KPRF members.[44] Even an external observer who was anything but a KPRF sympathizer estimated that the campaign was held "on the wave of the regional administration's fight against the ghost of communism."[45] Under conditions in which the costs of party affiliation are high while the level of ideological polarization is such that the party-mobilized electorate learns about the programmatic standings of candidates anyway, a party label may be of no value. The 2002 regional legislative elections in Saratov province are illustrative in this respect. This time, the KPRF nominated twenty-one candidates. Only fifteen of them were on the ballot on the day of elections: five were denied registration; one, Ol'ga Alimova, who managed to get registration and who was generally considered an unbeatable candidate in this district, witnessed the withdrawal of all other candidates, which according to the Russian law made the election void.[46] Of the remaining KPRF candidates, none gained a seat, even though fourteen of them were second-runners in their districts.

The association between ideological polarization and the KPRF's unwillingness to nominate its own candidates in regional legislative elections is particularly observable in concurrently held campaigns for different-level offices, such as the 2002 executive and legislative elections in Penza province. The gubernatorial incumbent, Vasilii Bochkarev, was in a close contest with a high-profile left-wing politician of a national reputation, Viktor Iliukhin, who had a "team" of candidates supported by him in the legislative elections. Naturally, many of them were KPRF members, but they ran as independents. Iliukhin was generally considered a very likely winner, which theoretically could have increased the value of the KPRF label in legislative elections quite in the same manner that happens with presidential favorites' parties in many concurrent elections worldwide (Samuels 2002). In fact, however, even Iliukhin himself did not make much use of his high KPRF standing in the course of the campaign. Rather, his strategy was built upon creating an image of an experienced, responsible politician committed to overcoming corruption, mismanagement, and the resulting underdevelopment in the province.[47] Combining such an image with supporting KPRF-nominated legislative candidates was costly enough. As a result, the communist label was skipped in both elections.

Hence for a variety of reasons discussed above, the label of the KPRF is available to far fewer legislative candidates than there are legislative seats to be contested. Yet while it is true that throughout the whole period under observation the label of the KPRF remained most valuable in Russia's political marketplace, there were occasions when other party labels acquired comparable value. This applies primarily to the parties of power, and especially to Unity, which in its first national legislative election captured a portion of the vote quite comparable to that of the KPRF. A comparison between the KPRF and Unity can be especially instructive given the ideological distance between the two entities, and their different relations with the executive, at both the national and regional levels. The most visible obstacle to such a comparison is, of course, Unity's late arrival to regional electoral arenas. Due to its complex organizational history, discussed in Chapter 2, Unity had an excuse for ignoring regional elections in 2000–2001, which it actually did. In fact, this excuse was not as good as it could seem. First, Unity regional movements obtained eligibility as early as the second half of 2000. Second, nothing prevented the original founders of the national Unity bloc from replicating this experience in the regions. They just did not. Let us assume, however, that the true era of Unity's electoral participation in the regions of Russia started in December 2001. At that time, Unity was not only fully eligible; judging by appearance, it was also a full-fledged party in organizational terms. For instance, of the ten regions for which I have complete lists of registered parties as of the period late 2001–early 2002, Unity had district-level organizations in six. In this respect, it was matched neither by the KPRF nor by the LDPR. The available self-estimates of party membership, sometimes at as high as 1 million, do not seem to be very realistic, but it seems to be plausible that by 2002, Unity did succeed in recruiting hundreds of people in each of the eighty-eight regions where it had registered branches.[48] From this perspective, it is interesting to look at the pattern of candidate nomination accepted by Unity and its successor, Unitary Russia.

Table 4.5 reports information about the participation of Unity in the plurality/majority tiers of eleven regional legislative elections held from December 2001 to September 2002.[49] Unity did not participate in the remaining thirty-two elections. Yet as is clear from the table, even when it did run its candidates, many districts remained uncontested by them. In fact, there were no elections in which Unity was able to contest a majority of seats. On average, the KPRF tended to nominate more candidates. In the analysis above, one of the reasons identified for the KPRF's abstention from candidate nomination was the low availability of high-profile office-

Table 4.5   Participation of Unity in Regional Legislative Elections, December 2001–September 2002

Region	Number of Plurality/ Majority Seats	Number of Unity-Nominated Candidates	Number of Winners Among Unity Candidates
Krasnoiarsk	22	9	2
Primorskii	39	8	1
Khabarovsk	25	3	0
Kamchatka	39	6	1
Moscow province	50	8	2
Novosibirsk	49	8	1
Pskov	22	6	2
Tver	33	13	8
Saratov[a]	35	4	3
Tambov[b]	50	3	1
Tiumen	25	2	1

Notes: Proportional tiers excluded.
a. Unitary Russia.
b. Electoral bloc Motherland (Unity, Fatherland, and regional movement Rebirth of Tambov Land).

seeking candidates. At the first glance, this explanation is very unlikely to be applicable to Unity. Even though little is known about the sociological profile of Unity members in the regions, it can be rather safely assumed that they are neither aged pensioners out of touch with regions' political lives nor "true believers" of primarily ideological concerns. Are they office-seeking careerists? An illuminating piece of evidence on this matter can be derived from the 2001–2002 political developments in Pskov province. By October 2001 it became clear that the governor of Pskov and a defector from the LDPR, Evgenii Mikhailov, was going to use the regional branch of Unity as a principal vehicle in his struggle for control over the regional legislature. Practically, this constituted a valuable bargaining point for those Pskov businesspeople who could establish their control over the branch. And this could be achieved quite easily, by filling the branch with their clients. As a result, in two weeks in late October the number of applications for party membership exceeded the number of already recruited members. Most of the applicants were employees of two industrial enterprises and one bank. When describing this situation, a local observer mentioned that in private, some of the employees disclosed that they joined Unity under the threat of losing their jobs.[50] Clearly the businesspeople themselves could count on being nominated as Unity candidates, if they wished so and if Mikhailov did not mind. But most of the party recruits were not expected to run in elections. They were there for a different reason.

The Pskov model seemed to be quite widespread in the regions of Russia. Yet there were other models. The membership of the regional branches of Unity was often formed by one of the founding organizations of the original Unity bloc of 1999, the Popular Patriotic Party of Russia, a political extension of the network of Afghan war veterans that had become active in Russia's electoral politics already in 1993. Its leader, Frants Klintsevich, joined the top leadership of Unity and its parliamentary faction, and he reportedly invested his efforts into promoting the Afghan war veterans to leadership positions in regional branches, as happened in one of the most important of them, the Moscow city branch.[51] Virtually all Unity branches have experienced the influx of politically engaged individuals who viewed the new "party of power" as a possible remedy for the lack of personal reputations and resources.[52] In contrast to the Pskov employees, these categories of members were quite well noticed in regional electoral politics years before Unity was formed, and the results of their previous experimentation were not very encouraging. Meanwhile, Unity's persistent claim for the role of the party of the noncommunist majority made it quite sensitive to the electoral returns it could expect from its members. A defeat in regional elections could have harmed its national reputation. A minor party of power of the 2001–2003 period, the People's Party of the Russian Federation (NPRF), tried the strategy of massive candidate nomination in one region, Nizhnii Novgorod province, where its nominees ran in thirty-eight of forty-five districts. Thirty-seven of them lost, which was justly regarded as a humiliating defeat. The regional branches of Unity could hardly afford this strategy. Their candidates had to win. Yet potential winners were not necessarily in supply.

This situation was further aggravated by the fact that while Unity was a party of power at the national level, it did not perform in this capacity in many of the regions. Some of the regional executives, such as Khabarovsk territory strongman Viktor Ishaev, could afford to ignore it. It is not surprising that, thus reduced to the role of one among the plethora of small right-wing groups, Unity nominated only three candidates in the December 2001 Khabarovsk regional legislative elections, and none of them won. In regions with left-wing executives, such as in Kamchatka province, the local branches of Unity were in opposition to them. And the same was sometimes the case in regions where the executives, while engaged in political struggles with the left, made different political bets, such as in Samara province. The branch of Unity in the region was said to be in opposition to the local authorities to an extent that made its activities "almost clandestine."[53] Under such conditions, Unity was bound to confront difficulties similar to those experienced by the KPRF in some localities, and indeed Unity candidates did not contest the 2001 Samara regional legislative elections.

Hence the lack of credible candidates is a problem that is not alien to

Unity. Its major problem, however, can be related to coalition building much in the same way as with the KPRF. There were quite a few regions where local Unity branches were fully endorsed by the executives and successfully recruited local elites, administrative and business alike, under their banners. For example, the branch of Unity in Tambov province, headed by the governor himself, also included the mayor of Tambov, the directors of the largest industrial enterprises, the rectors of the region's higher-education institutions, many local legislators, and a national Duma deputy.[54] This was a party of power by any account. Yet slightly more than a year after such a formidable political machine was assembled, the Motherland bloc created by Unity, Fatherland, and the local movement Rebirth of Tambov Land, was able to nominate only three candidates in regional legislative elections, and to win one seat. How was that possible? As it appears from local observers' accounts, the real goal of creating the bloc was not to nominate candidates but rather to support those who were likely not only to win but also, upon winning, to retain loyalty to the regional administration. Such people were to be met not only in Unity. In fact, some of the KPRF-supported candidates fully met the requirements.[55] Thus Unity did help to forge a coalition, but this was a coalition of personalities, not parties, and its basis was loyalty to the regional administration, not programmatic affinities. The three candidates officially nominated by the Motherland bloc were Afghan war veterans who were to be rewarded for their activism during the formative phase of Unity in Tambov, and for their continuous work for the party. For them, the Unity label was an important addition to their otherwise bleak public reputations. For the purposes of coalition building, however, a more extensive use of the label could be harmful. As euphemistically put by the head of the Unity regional branch in Tomsk province briefly before legislative elections in which his party did not nominate candidates, lawmaking "is a difficult job of not everybody's liking. It is a lot more pleasant to talk on TV. But lawmaking is not for all. . . . The Tomsk Unity formed its list of support in the December elections on the basis of individuals' ability to work in the legislature. That is, is the candidate ready to work in the [regional] Duma or not. And not at all on the basis of whether he is a brilliant politician or tribune."[56] Lists of support endorsed by Unity are nothing new in Russia's regional politics. A similar strategy was once pursued by the NDR and by the local movements controlled by the regional executives.[57]

Hence, paradoxically enough, the holders of the most valuable party labels of the third electoral cycle, the KPRF and Unity, were constrained in their candidate-nominating capacities. Despite the vast differences between the two parties, the constraints were similar: first, the low availability of credible candidates, and second, the side effects of coalition building in largely nonpartisan environments. Of course, other parties occasionally become important at the regional level too. The analysis above helps to explain why, for most parties, the rise to situational political prominence does not entail running more candidates in regional elections. The low availability of credible candidates partly explains why the regional branches of Democratic Russia and the DVR in Tver province, after being quite instrumental in securing victory for a committed right-winger in the 1995 gubernatorial election, were unable to nominate a single candidate in the 1997 regional legislative elections. The sophisticated coalition-building strategy of the Moscow mayor explains why his own party, Fatherland, which won a landslide in the 1999 national legislative elections in the city, abstained from candidate nomination in the 2001 races for the regional legislature.

Alternatives to Party-Related Resources

For all the importance of party labels, it would be unrealistic to assume that they are the only good an aspiring politician can obtain by joining a party. Other party resources matter too. In a mutually profitable relationship, a party gives its resources to a candidate, who pays off with loyalty. In this section, it will be demonstrated that while this aspect of party utility cannot be discarded as something insignificant in Russia's electoral context, party resources are not of decisive importance either, which happens partly because there are important and easily available alternatives to them. In general, a party can be useful to its candidate for the following three reasons. First, it can nominate him or her. Second, it can help him or her to secure registration. Invariably in the first and second electoral cycles, and optionally in the third electoral cycle, this involved collecting certain amounts of signatures on a petition to support a nomination. Alternatively in the third electoral cycle, a party could provide funds for making a candidate deposit. The third and perhaps most important reason is, of course, a party's direct engagement in a candidate's campaign. This may involve a wide variety of activities, from door-to-door canvassing by party activists to financial sponsorship.

Of these three, party nomination remained as easily obtainable as it was easily replaceable throughout the three electoral cycles. The vast majority of regional electoral laws allowed it. In the first electoral cycle, there was only one case in which political parties were banned from participation in regional legislative elections (at the time of the 1994 elections in Ingushetia, all parties were banned by an executive decree), and several cases in which regional laws did not explicitly mention them as candidate-nominating entities,[58] which prevented political parties from participation in regional legislative elections in Rostov province. The latter legal obstacle, however, was not insurmountable. In Sakha, where it formally existed, political parties were allowed to attach their labels to candidate-nominating groups, so that a candidate could be nominated by "a group of voters of the Social Democratic Party of Yakutia." In the 1999 elections in Komi republic, political parties were excluded because none of them was quick enough to change its bylaws in accordance with the amended version of the federal law guaranteeing citizens' electoral rights. In all other elections, political parties were fully eligible. To nominate candidates, they normally had to convoke a regional party conference, which was not a formidably difficult logistical task, especially given the fact that memberships of the majority of parties were very small. It is important to mention that none of the regional electoral laws obliged parties to nominate their members only. Anybody could obtain party nomination. Yet to be nominated in other ways was even easier, including nomination by a group of voters, self-nomination, and less often, nomination by a workplace group or by a single voter. Self-nomination and nomination by a single voter, who could be a candidate's relative, were obviously easy to obtain. Obtaining nomination from a group of coworkers could be difficult only for the unemployed. As far as a less strictly defined group of voters is concerned, few of the executive election laws, and almost none of the legislative election laws, specified what was the minimum size of a group, which meant that coworkers and relatives would suffice. An electoral official in Sakha added such a plausible extension of the list of nominators as "a group of old ladies sitting on the bench near the doorway."[59]

That is, in technical terms, party nomination was neither difficult to obtain nor difficult to skip. Exceptions to this rule were rare. The most important of them can be related to mixed electoral systems involving party lists or other provisions that made party nomination imperative, a topic addressed in Chapter 7. Here, it is sufficient to say that few such systems were ever used in regional legislative elections, and even if they were, the sizes of proportional tiers were invariably smaller than those of plurality/majority tiers. Thus even though some of the seats became unavailable to a candidate who, for whatever reason, preferred to run as an independent, he or she could contest other seats. At the same time, in the majority of regions local election laws made party nomination potentially risky, because in comparison with the alternative ways of nomination, holding a party conference was a rather complex procedure with several formal requirements attached. Most of the parties were able to fulfill these requirements for one or more of the following reasons: first, because they were relatively well organized, which applies primarily to the KPRF; second, because they were too small to have any difficulty assembling their entire membership in a conference hall (it seems that many of them could hold conferences in taxis); and third, because the local electoral commissions tended not to inspect the candidate nomination process very closely. However, there were several instances when entire groups of party-nominated candidates were disqualified by regional electoral commissions for formal reasons. In the 2001 legislative elections in Novosibirsk province, the candidates of an electoral bloc tellingly labeled Stalin Bloc–Communists were first registered but then, after a court appeal, denied registration because one of the founding groups, Women's Movement Kindness, had not obtained the approval of its conference for creation of the bloc, and because the leaders of the bloc had not obtained written permission from Joseph Stalin's relatives to use his name in its label.[60] In this case, the founding groups were not especially well organized, they had small but not symbolic memberships, and perhaps most important, the political outlook of the bloc invited some scrutiny. Retrospectively, it can be said that the Stalinists would have fared better in running as independents, which illustrates a relative disadvantage that can be entailed by party nomination. From the same example, however, it can be inferred that conditions under which such a disadvantage materializes are rather rare and unusual.

Signature collection entails a more demanding threshold in Russia's electoral campaigns. Many parties and individual candidates in national elections were unable to collect the required numbers of signatures. The same applies to regional executive elections. The reason is clear: in both national and regional executive elections, the numbers of signatures to be collected tend to be quite substantial. Yet in executive elections, which are normally contested by the prominent representatives of regional elites, methods of signature collection tend to be related to the resources at these elites' disposal, not to their political affiliations. This problem will be treated at some length in Chapter 5. Here, it is sufficient to cite an observer in Tatarstan who describes the routine of signature collection in the republic as follows: "Forms for signature collection are being distributed among the working place activists with an explicit reminder, 'If you don't collect enough signatures, you get fired.' . . . There are also softer ways: in the railway construction department, where there were no such threats, [the managers] simply asked several women who were not very burdened with their work to sign [the petition] for all workers. After signatures were there, it was a technical problem to write in the signers' personal data, because they were all on file."[61] Of course, counterfeiting signatures is illegal, and there were few cases when "softer ways" of signature collection backfired, but in principle, overtly illegal practices, including explicit threats, are not necessary. The costs of signing a petition are so small that, if a collector turns out on behalf of a locally authoritative "boss," signatures can be delivered without any coercion.

The resources at the disposal of regional legislative candidates are incomparably smaller than those of major executive candidates. Yet the amount of signatures to be collected is smaller too. Normally these amounts are legally set as 1 or 2 percent of the voters registered in the electoral district. In 1995–1998 the average number of registered voters per district in regional legislative elections was approximately 32,270. This means that, by and large, a candidate had to collect 300 to 700 signatures in order to be nominated. Needless to argue at length, such a petition can be easily delivered by employees of a single middle-size industrial enterprise. Yet it is also clear that, if only for the reason that not every candidate in Russia's regional legislative is an enterprise manager (even though a lot of them are), party activists can be instrumental too. Of course, this applies only to parties with certain amounts of active members—that is, primarily to the KPRF and, in certain localities, to various right-wing groups such as Yabloko, the DVR, and the SPS, as well as to the parties of power. To those candidates who, in contrast to administrative and economic elites, do not have compliant employees at hand, political parties can provide valuable support. But similar to what happens with party nomination, there are easily available alternatives. Since 1993, signature collection has become popular in Russia as a seasonal job, especially among university students. In 1997–1998, one signature could be sold to an aspiring candidate for approximately one to one and a half rubles.[62] Admittedly, this was not a very profitable business, but it did provide sizable additions to the students' scarce incomes. Note that there were no limitations on how many petitions a single citizen could sign. In the 1995 national Duma elections, there was a case when two candidates in the same district in Moscow were successfully registered after presenting their petitions signed by absolutely identical sets of persons.[63] Apparently, they used the services of the same signature collectors. As far as candidates themselves are concerned, the price of 1,400 rubles (in the first half of 1998, equivalent to about U.S.$280) was not symbolic but quite affordable for an average, fully employed person. Thus party services could be useful, yet almost anybody could afford to hire signature collectors instead, and personal effort as a way of signature collection was feasible too. In fact, in a small region a candidate could be required to collect several dozen signatures, which could be delivered for free by friends, relatives, and coworkers. True, in the first electoral cycle there were several instances when regional laws placed party-nominated candidates in a relatively privileged position. This was achieved by allowing a party to collect a certain amount of signatures that were jointly considered as valid for all candidates nominated by the given party (Sungurov 1996). In the 1994 legislative elections in St. Petersburg, such a provision resulted in a proliferation of party nominees. Later, however, such provisions were eliminated from regional electoral laws as contradicting the principle of all candidates' equality.

Therefore, neither nomination nor signature collection made the involvement of a party imperative, even though in both cases it could be useful. The third and most important step to the desired outcome was of course the campaign itself. Electoral campaigns in Russia, as elsewhere, involve such standard components as door-to-door canvassing, public rallies, the distribution of campaign leaflets and posters, and media campaigning. As elsewhere again, and increasingly so, the first three components are less important than the fourth. The potential utility of political parties, however, is largely restricted to the three less important components. Only one party, the KPRF, practices grassroots electioneering in the form of door-to-door activities on a wide scale. The activities of "communist agitators" have been noticed in many regional electoral campaigns.[64] As put by a Russian politician who was never sympathetic to the KPRF, the party's agitators in Kaluga province "work smoothly, they know how to make people listen, they reach virtually everybody by exploiting people's dissatisfaction with the authorities."[65] The problem with door-to-door electioneering is that while it may be useful in the countryside and in small towns, it tends to reach restricted audiences in large cities. Moreover, the audiences it reaches already consist of KPRF voters. Yet in general, it cannot be denied that in a majority of regions, a candidate supported by the KPRF is best equipped for door-to-door outreach. Almost the same can be said about public rallies, even though the circle of parties that are capable of organizing them is wider: in addition to the KPRF, it includes Yabloko, some other right-wing parties, the LDPR, various groups of the extreme left, and occasionally parties of power and interest advocacy groups such as the Union of Labor. In this respect, the Communists are at advantage too because they can assemble relatively large numbers of their activists and committed supporters, but other parties can occasionally afford levels of spending and logistical support that are unavailable to the KPRF. For instance, the regional movement Fatherland in Krasnodar territory was able to stage quite massive rallies partly because it could provide buses for transporting people from the countryside to Krasnodar, where rallies took place.[66] The role of political parties in distributing campaign leaflets and posters is about the same as in signature collection: they can do the job, but others can do it too. The same students who collect signatures tend to migrate into the next phase of the campaign as paid workers whose specialization is defined quite unambiguously: "those who post leaflets" *(raskleishchiki listovok).*

In terms of media outreach, Russia's political parties are not very useful. The KPRF has its own print media, both in Moscow and in some of the regions, but circulations are so small that these newspapers can be made available to a restricted number of activists only. There are also two independent national newspapers that are quite sympathetic to the KPRF, a daily, *Sovetskaia Rossia,* and a weekly, *Zavtra.* The circulation of both papers is larger, but it is quite limited too.[67] Small-circulation newspapers available only to party activists are also continuously published by Yabloko and the LDPR. Since approximately 1998, Russia's political parties have established quite a firm presence on the Internet. The Internet sites of some are quite impressive.[68] Yet given the limited availability of the Internet in Russia, it is highly doubtful that a party site makes any significant difference for electoral outcomes, especially at the regional level. The principal medium of Russia's electoral campaigns is television. Television, however, is not controlled by any of the political parties, nor is it easily accessible by the majority of them. The vast majority of electronic media in the regions are controlled by the regional administrations, either directly, which is the case with the so-called state television and radio corporations, or indirectly, because independent broadcasters are licensed by the regional authorities. Hence to obtain media access in the regions of Russia, good relations with the heads of administration are essential, money is very helpful, while political parties do not help to obtain media access.

Of course, a good election campaign is more than a sum of the components listed above. Political parties can be employed as campaign organizers, helping their candidates from the first to the last step and coordinating several individual campaigns simultaneously, which is what they do in Russia. Yet they are not the only, and perhaps not even the most important, providers of such services in Russia. An interested candidate, provided he or she has enough funds, can turn to a variety of private businesses that organize election campaigns on a professional basis. The local denominations of such businesses and of the profession itself vary. They are called "political technologists," "public relations people" *(piarshchiki),* "politologists," "image makers," and sometimes even "political psychologists." In this study, to avoid confusion, I will refer to all such denominations of the profession as "political consultants." Indeed, what they do is fairly close to the already widespread and increasingly demanded vocation of political consultants in the Western democracies (Luntz 1988; Petracca 1989). Professional political consultants were rather widely employed already in the 1995 national Duma campaign.[69] The major political consulting firms of that time, such as Nikkolo-M, referring to Niccolo Machiavelli, and Image-Contact, originated from Moscow. After making their startup capital in the national elections, they turned to the peripheries of the country and managed to penetrate them quite deeply. Consider the 1998 presidential elections in Buriatia, a relatively small and not very rich republic in East Siberia. Of the two major candidates, including the incumbent president, Leonid Potapov, one hired Nikkolo-M, the other Image-Contact. As described by a local observer, "they completely assumed the roles of candidates' headquarters, which made the locals absolutely unnecessary in the campaign. This, by the way, becomes trendy: elections in the periphery have become an arena of professional contests among Moscow image making firms."[70] It seems that since that time, Nikkolo-M and Image-Contact have remained the major providers of political consulting services in Russia.[71] In the third electoral cycle, however, they started to be increasingly challenged by local firms. As put by a political consultant in Krasnoiarsk territory, "regional politicians and businesses have already had an opportunity to work with Moscow [political consulting] specialists while local [specialists] were growing and developing. Now here we are, and we have one advantage, knowledge. We know better about our territories, provinces, cities, enterprises, and structures. That is why local public relations agencies and consulting groups will be in demand."[72] In part, the market conditions for local political consultants in the regions improved because Moscow firms moved some of their operations to the former Soviet republics, especially to Ukraine.[73]

The major job of political consultants is to organize individual politicians' campaigns. In general, electoral coordination cannot be expected to be of their concern, and one might argue that they are not able to deliver a commodity held exclusively by political parties, their labels as information shortcuts to policy preferences. Not necessarily. In Novosibirsk province, the label of the KPRF is quite important and valuable. For a candidate who runs in a plurality district with a strong KPRF-nominated candidate, then, it is very important to split the communist vote. In 2000 a group of Novosibirsk individuals obtained registration for a regional political movement, Communists for People's Power. The individuals were long noticed as being connected with a local political consulting firm, Sibir-Forum.[74] Four people affiliated with Communists for People's Power ran in the 2001 regional legislative elections, two of them in the districts contested by the leaders of the regional KPRF branch and the legislative faction of the party. Both Communist leaders lost, even though it does not seem that the movement forged by the political consultants contributed much to their defeat. Yet another invention of political consultants that gained nationwide notoriety in 2000–2001 was a commercial firm, Patriots KPR, with the acronym obviously referring to the KPRF and the word "patriots" to one of its most commonly used campaign slogans. People affiliated with the Patriots KPR ran in the executive elections in Briansk province[75] and Altai Republic,[76] and in mayoral elections in the important city of Sochi.[77] None of them, of course, had any relation to the KPRF. They were hired vote-splitters.

Thus in terms of campaign organization, political consulting can achieve almost everything a political party can achieve, and sometimes even more. Since 1999, Russia's electoral authorities have become increasingly attentive to the activities of political consultants, which resulted not only in a number of meetings held by the chairman of the Central Electoral Commission, Aleksandr Veshniakov, with the representatives of leading political consulting firms, but also in proposals to make their services a subject of legal regulation by incorporating such provisions into the country's electoral law.[78] Yet for many candidates, there is one problem with political consulting firms: their services are quite costly. Unfortunately, they do not publish price lists. When the problem of costs was discussed by a group of prominent journalists and political consultants in St. Petersburg on the eve of the 2002 regional legislative elections, the figure of U.S.$120,000 was cited as a reasonable price for a well-organized campaign.[79] While it is obvious that political consultants themselves can provide inflated figures because they are interested in having their services overvalued, and while the 2002 elections in St. Petersburg were unusual in that the city itself is richer than many other localities, and stakes in its elections were higher even than in comparably rich regions, the price was not estimated as unrealistic by the participants in the discussion (in fact, they concluded that another figure cited in the press, $777,000, was unrealistic indeed).

    This brings us to another question. As demonstrated above, money can buy a lot in Russia's regional elections. One might argue that for a political party to be instrumental, it has to perform just one but decisive function, solicit money for its candidates. Evidence on this matter is scarce, and the primary fact to be taken into account is that, unlike in the majority of western European democracies (Gunlicks 1993; Alexander and Shiratori 1994), there are no regular state subsidies for political parties in Russia, even though they do receive subsidies in election time. Political parties are legally entitled to have property, even though they cannot use this property for profit-making activities,[80] to establish membership dues, and to create their electoral funds during campaigns in which they nominate candidates. Individual candidates create their own electoral funds. According to the majority of regional electoral laws, these funds may include transfers from political parties alongside candidates' own funds, state funds, and donations from organizations and individuals. In all types of elections, there are legally established limitations on the overall sizes of such funds. For instance, in the 1999 national legislative elections the electoral fund of an individual candidate could not exceed U.S.$62,223, and of a party or electoral bloc, $1,605,576. Observers tend to allege that legally allowed funds are too small, which makes most of the campaign spending and related fundraising illegal.[81] Hence by definition, the question of how much money a political party can provide to its candidate can render only a highly speculative answer. A useful roundabout approach to the problem may be related to the question of sources for such funds. Membership dues can be discarded as a possible source of funds for all parties including the KPRF, which appears to collect them on a fairly regular basis.[82] As of August 2001, the size of membership dues in one of the KPRF's regional branches was established at 1 percent of a member's income, with a 0.5 percent discount for pensioners.[83] Assuming that an average employee salary in Russia at that time was about $70 per month, that about 60 percent of KPRF members were pensioners with incomes of about $20 per month, and that half of the estimated 500,000 members paid their dues, the last assumption being admittedly too optimistic, we can calculate that the annual KPRF income from dues was $1,200,000—that is, $13,630 for each of the eighty-eight regional branches. This could be a useful contribution for renting party offices and, occasionally, for transporting party members to public rallies, but definitely not for conducting full-scale electoral campaigns. Little has been ever heard about other parties' membership dues. It seems that most of them are happier with having members than with charging them, which theoretically means that outside of the electoral arenas, Russian political parties simply do not have money of their own. True, at different times it was widely alleged that the KPRF and the LDPR received significant portions of their incomes from their factions in the national legislature,[84] but such allegations have never been proven.

What can be considered as generally supported by factual evidence is that in the course of national electoral campaigns, Russia's political parties receive funding from private businesses. Influential industrialists, such as Viktor Vid'manov of Rosagropromstroi group, are members of the national leadership of the KPRF, and there are wealthy businesspeople in its national legislative faction. They subsidize the party legally, by contributing to its official electoral funds, and it is hardly doubtful that they make other donations too.[85] The circle of businesses that financially support the KPRF has been reported to include not only those based in Moscow but also those in the periphery, especially in those regions where executive power was held by left-leaning politicians. The LDPR also secured funds by offering safe places on its national party list to businesspeople, such as Mikhail Gutseriev, and by converting its political power in the only region where its representative won a governorship, Pskov province, into financial support from Pskov-based businesses, such as a large alcohol-producing plant, Pskovalko.[86] Many observers also noticed ties between businesses and several other parties, such as between Gazprom and the NDR in 1995, or between RAO Energia and the SPS in 1999. The mechanism of channeling funds from businesses to regional campaign organizers has been described as involving the following steps. First, it is necessary to register a charitable foundation with officially stated goals such as the development of civil society or the enhancement of civic activity. Second, interested businesses donate funds to the foundation. Third, the foundation contracts several firms, also registered for this special occasion, to provide services such as research. The firms' services invariably involve massive research-related expenses, which is not surprising given that, in fact, funds flow out in cash for campaign-related expenditures. The foundation occasionally makes symbolic contributions to official electoral funds too.[87]

Thus political parties, or at least the most important of them, can be viewed as efficient fundraisers, which means that candidates who lack their own funds cannot view the prospect of receiving them from their party as entirely unrealistic. Yet it is also clear that such a possibility can materialize for very few people. Party-funded candidates can be expected to be either very loyal activists or high-profile personalities whose affiliation with the party can enhance their own electoral chances. While candidates belonging to the latter category are in short supply by definition, it seems that credible candidates in the former category turn out in insufficient numbers too. For all others, there are many available alternatives to party-related resources.

*   *   *

When writing this chapter, I recalled a food store of the late Soviet era, approximately 1989–1990. The shelves were not actually empty. Rather, they were filled with commodities that were out of demand, such as canned sea kale. If you were desperately hungry, you could buy enough food to eat. If you wanted something better than canned sea kale, such as meat, you could buy it too, but only on rare occasions and only in frozen form, and the quality of that frozen meat was not very inspiring indeed. That is why people with some extra money in their pockets tended to ignore food stores. They went to the market, where they could buy fresh meat or whatever they wanted for prices that, in least in retrospect, seemed quite reasonable. Getting back to the regions of Russia, party labels are quite in supply but not in demand; those party resources that are actually demanded are in scarce supply; and there are viable alternatives to almost anything a party can offer in the political marketplace.

Notes

1. S"ezd sotsial-demokratov, *Kommersant-Daily,* May 12, 1993.
2. IV s"ezd Respublikanskoi partii, *Moskovskii komsomolets,* October 17, 1993.
3. S"ezd Demokraticheskoi partii Rossii, *Kommersant-Daily,* December 19, 1992.
4. *Znamia* (Kaluga), October 9, 1993.
5. Obzornyi analiz omskogo partiino-politicheskogo protsessa, www.univer. omsk.su/omsk/politics/parties93.txt.
6. Na nedavno proshedshei 28-i oblastnoi konferentsii kommunistov, *Volgogradskaia Pravda* (Volgograd), April 1, 1994.
7. Respublika Mordovia, *Rossiiskii sbornik,* 1995, p. 218.

8. V Smolenske v partiiu Zhirinivskogo uzhe ochered, *Rabochii put* (Smolensk), December 22, 1993.

9. 11 oktiabria v Saranske proshlo uchreditel'noe sobranie, *Vechernii Saransk,* October 15, 1993.

10. In relatively few regional cases, the figures were said to be unavailable.

11. Altai Republic, Irkutsk, Kaluga, Karelia, Kemerovo, Khabarovsk, Novosibirsk, Orel, Riazan, and Sakha.

12. See, for instance, I pravye, i levye, i tsentr, *Lipetskaia gazeta* (Lipetsk), January 26, 2002.

13. Doklad predsedatelia TsK Pravoslavnoi partii Rossii, *Trud,* January 29, 2002.

14. Naslednitsa komsomola: Otvetrabotniki VLKSM stroiat pravoslavnuiu partiiu, *Moskovskie novosti,* May 18, 1999.

15. Pervyi otkaz, *Vremia MN,* October 5, 1999; Okolotserkovnye radikaly v izbiratel'nykh blokakh, *Russkaia mysl* (Paris), November 4, 1999.

16. Karmannykh partii bol'she ne budet, *Novoe delo* (Makhachkala), January 25, 2002.

17. Patrioty smeshchaiutsia v tsentr, *Izvestia,* November 18, 1998.

18. Levotsentristskii blok formiruetsia v zdanii merii Moskvy, *Vremia MN,* November 12, 1998.

19. Eshche odna partia, *Buriatia* (Ulan-Ude), November 13, 1998.

20. Miniust propalyvaet partiinye griadki, *Novye izbestia,* July 2, 1999.

21. Soiuzniki vysadilis v oblsovete, *Novaia Sibir—Molodaia Sibir* (Novosibirsk), August 4, 1997.

22. Veselaia kompania iz "Nashego goroda," *Moskovskaia Pravda,* November 25, 1997.

23. I Gaidar vperedi, *Prizyv* (Vladimir), August 3, 2000.

24. Raz yacheika, dva yacheika—budet partia, *Nizhegorodskie novosti* (Nizhnii Novgorod), November 18, 2000.

25. Kreml tolkaet DVR v ob"iatia Yavlinskogo, *Novye izvestia,* May 18, 2001.

26. Tverskie demokraty ob"ediniaiutsia, *Veche Tveri* (Tver), February 9, 2001.

27. As suggested in the previous chapter, making a distinction between the KPRF conglomerate and noncommunist parties is normally unproblematic. The only exception is the 2003 legislative elections in Kemerovo province, which were contested by a bloc consisting of a local left-wing movement and Unitary Russia. When treating these elections here and later in this book, I estimate the KPRF conglomerate's share of seats to be half of those won by the bloc overall.

28. For an impressive description of the scope of KPRF activities in one of the administrative districts of Volgograd province, see Kurilla 2002.

29. Politicheskii prognoz—97, *Novgorodskie vedomosti* (Novgorod), March 5, 1997.

30. I opyt, i molodost, *Pravda KPRF,* August 7, 2001.

31. Vybory v Novgorode pobili rekordy neiavki izbiratelei, *Segodnia,* October 10, 2000.

32. I pod lezhashchii pamiatnik zhivaia voda bezhit, *Khakasia* (Abakan), December 22, 2001. For a similar story, see O, Marat! *Molodoi dal'nevostochnik* (Khabarovsk), October 4, 2000.

33. Est takaia partia, *Vesti* (Petropavlovsk-Kamchatskii), November 15, 2001.

34. See Gallagher and Marsh 1998.

35. Po kommunistam proshelsia Mamai, *Novosti v Novosibirske* (Novosibirsk), January 11, 2002.

36. Umnye sudiat po delam, *Stavropol'skaia Pravda* (Stavropol), December 8, 2001.

37. Glavnyi agrarii oblasti, *Trud,* December 3, 1996.

38. Spisok kandidatov: Taina za sem'iu pechatiami, *Novaia Sibir—Molodaia Sibir* (Novosibirsk), December 1, 1997.

39. Vybory deputatov Novosibirskogo oblastnogo soveta vtorogo sozyva, *Politicheskii monitoring* no. 3, 1998.

40. Samarskie politologi sovetuiut, *Delo* (Samara), March 9, 2001.

41. Georgii Limanskii, *Samarskaia gazeta* (Samara), December 7, 2001.

42. Levye v Dume, barin v Parizhe, *Sovetskaia Rossia,* December 18, 2001.

43. Politicheskii peizazh, *Karavan* (Tver), October 24, 2001.

44. Dva Aiaksa, *Sovetskaia Rossia,* August 26, 1997.

45. Saratovskii gubernator v bor'be s prizrakom, *Segodnia,* September 2, 1997.

46. Aiatskov ubedil elektorat, *Nezavisimaia gazeta,* September 17, 2002.

47. Masshtab oblastnoi—tsena gosudarstvennaia, *Pravda KPRF,* April 5, 2002.

48. Partbilet na vse sluchai zhizni, *Vedomosti,* August 13, 2002. As of October 2001, in such a relatively typical middle-size region as Tomsk province, there were 625 Unity members. See Legko li byt partiei vlasti? *Tomskii vestnik* (Tomsk), October 13, 2001.

49. The April 2002 elections in Sverdlovsk province are excluded because they were held by the proportional system.

50. "Medvedi" optom, ili komu nuzhen rost riadov pskovskogo "Edinstva," *Pskovskaia gubernia* (Pskov), November 29, 2001.

51. Novoe vremia—novye partii—novye liudi, *Vecherniaia Moskva,* November 1, 2001.

52. Otnoshenia dolzhny byt chestnymi, *Nashe vremia* (Rostov-na-Donu), November 24, 2000.

53. Maska, kto ty? *Soiuz* (Moscow and Minsk), November 15, 2001.

54. Osobennosti medvezh'ei zhizni, *Tambovskii kur'er* (Tambov), September 18, 2000.

55. Liubit po-russki, a golosovat s umom, *Tambovskaia zhizn* (Tambov), January 4, 2002.

56. Legko li byt partiei vlasti? *Tomskii vestnik* (Tomsk), October 13, 2001.

57. See Kto tam shagaet pravoi? *Izvestia Yug* (Rostov-na-Donu), December 12, 1998.

58. See Ob obespechenii izbiratel'nykh prav grazhdan pri vyborakh v zakono-datel'nye (predstavitel'nye) organy gosudarstvennoi vlasti sub"ektov Rossiiskoi Federatsii i organov mestnogo samoupravlenia, 68-I GD.

59. Pervye 500 kandidatov uzhe na podkhode, *Nashe vremia* (Yakutsk), October 11, 2002.

60. Anpilov pal zhertvoi Stalina i ego potomkov, *Novaia Sibir—Molodaia Sibir* (Novosibirsk), October 26, 2001.

61. Muzhik i partii, *Vecherniaia Kazan,* January 30, 1996.

62. Vybory—sposob zarabotat, *MK—Tula,* July 29, 1997; Vybory—98, *Birzha + Avto* (Nizhnii Novgorod), August 27, 1998.

63. V kakikh detaliakh priachetsia d'iavol, *Izvestia,* February 1, 1996.

64. See, for instance, Kto "svalil" na vyborakh kommunistov, *Birobidzhaner Shtern* (Birobidzhan), November 15, 2001; and Vlast, k schast'iu, u naroda, *Sovetskaia Chuvashia* (Cheboksary), May 12, 2000.

65. Prizrak otsidelsia i snova zabrodil, *Obshchaia gazeta,* March 14, 1996.

66. Krasnodarskii krai, *Kommersant-Vlast,* November 28, 2000.

67. As of 1999, the circulation of *Sovetskaia Rossia* was 300,000 copies. See Tsena golosa—kusok kolbasy, *Sovetskaia Rossia,* February 6, 1999.

68. See www.edin.ru, www.kprf.ru, www.ldpr.ru, www.sps.ru, and www.yabloko.ru.

69. V kakikh detaliakh priachetsia d'iavol, *Izvestia,* February 1, 1996.

70. Imidzhmeiker Baikal pereekhal, *Obshchaia gazeta,* June 11, 1998.

71. Prishlo vremay dlia novoi uslugi, *Sovetnik,* July 30, 2001.

72. Tri dnia, kotorye potriasli Krasnoiarsk, *Sovetnik,* May 28, 2001.

73. Byl o polittekhnologakh, *Novyi vek* (Kiiv), November 17, 2001.

74. A tainoe stanovitsia yavnym, *Vedomosti Novosibirskogo oblastnogo soveta deputatov* (Novosibirsk), November 16, 2001.

75. Dvoiniki kandidatov v deputaty razmnozhaiutsia kak kroliki, *Brianskoe vremia* (Briansk), October 25, 2000.

76. Na post glavy Respubliki Altai budut pretendovat 11 chelovek, *Altai Weekly Review* (Barnaul), December 17, 2001.

77. Kandidaty-bliznetsy ("dvoiniki" v izbiratel'nykh kampaniiakh), www.roiip.ru/public/brothers.htm.

78. Khartia ne pomogla, *Izvestia,* July 3, 2001.

79. Skol'ko stoit stat deputatom zakonodatel'nogo sobrania Sankt-Peterburga? *Monitoring teleefira/Politika (VPS),* October 14, 2002.

80. This provision tends to be ignored by parties anyway. For example, most of the real estate and means of transportation acquired by the LDPR were registered as private properties of Vladimir Zhirinovsky, which is why the size of the property can be established with some precision. As of 1998 it included 122 apartments in different regions of Russia, not too much for a major national party with a relatively well-developed regional network. See Korol chlenskikh vznosov, *Novaia gazeta,* October 5, 1998.

81. Skol'ko stoiat parlamentskie vybory? *Kommersant-Vlast,* January 19, 1999.

82. Uchredit partiiu neslozhno, *Izvestia,* November 20, 2001. It seems that in the period of late 2001–early 2002 the regional branches of Unity also started to collect dues. See "Edinstvo" Rossii prirastaet okrugom, *Vostochno-Sibirskaia pravda* (Irkutsk), November 28, 2001.

83. Reporter poluchil zadanie... *Priamurskie vedomosti* (Khabarovsk), August 30, 2001.

84. Kurs molodogo lobbista v Okhotnom riadu, *Novye izvestia,* January 16, 1999.

85. Zoloto KPSS—desiat let spustia, *Moskovskie novosti,* May 1, 2001.

86. Den'gi partii, *Vedomosti,* September 13, 1999.

87. O nekotorykh osobennostiakh organizatsii i provedenia izbiratel'nykh kampanii v Rossiiskoi Federatsii, *Vremia* (Omsk), June 9, 1999. Compare to evidence from Italy (Rhodes 1997).

5

The Demand Side:
Candidates Seeking Office

Politicians do not value party affiliations for themselves. Rather, political parties are valued as a means of achieving electoral success—that is, if they help politicians gain the offices they seek or maintain those they already hold. In this chapter, I examine the utility of political parties in Russia from this specific standpoint. Political parties cannot be expected to be very useful under conditions when electoral outcomes are predetermined. For parties to exist, a certain level of uncertainty is a necessary condition. And in politics, uncertainty stems from conflict within the elite. Intraelite conflict as a factor of party formation is dealt with in the first section below. Two subsequent sections discuss incentives for party affiliation that, within this conceptual framework, can be attributed to the principal categories of office-seekers: executive candidates and legislative candidates. I will demonstrate that regional political realities severely constrain these incentives.

Political Conflicts and Party
Formation in the Regions of Russia

Conflict lies at the heart of politics. Under conditions of authoritarianism, conflict within the power elite may manifest itself in bureaucratic intrigue, ideological purges, or sometimes in overt violence. Democracy legitimizes conflict by providing those involved with a powerful tool of conflict resolution—elections. Once all factions of the elite agree that the principal problem around which their conflicts arise—who governs—can be effectively and bindingly resolved at the polls, democracy, or at least the potential for democracy, is in place (Przeworski 1988). This in turn stimulates the formation and subsequent institutionalization of political parties (Panebianco 1988: 33–67). Building on a rather common metaphor, if democracy replaces bullets with ballots, then it needs to replace weapons too, and that is what political parties can be expected to do: they deliver votes. Hence political parties emerge from the continuous presence of conflict waged in the electoral arena. The presence or absence of such conflict can be established empirically, by studying electoral outcomes.

As demonstrated in Chapter 3, postcommunist transitions in the regions of Russia were accompanied by a massive shift of power to the holders of senior executive offices, who were gradually subjected to direct elections. Thus the question of who governs became largely, even though not entirely, reduced to the question of who wins in the electoral arena. In order to develop hypotheses that can be tested statistically using the available data set, I will analyze in depth a case of the successful formation of a regional party system in Sverdlovsk province. Admittedly, this case deviates from what we observe in the universe of available cases of party development in Russia's regions. Precisely for this reason it can be viewed as cognitively important. Deviant case studies constitute a category of comparatively oriented case studies that, rather than being purely descriptive, can contribute to building theory (Lijphart 1971). Thus my strategy is built on the expectation that the specific mode of party formation in Sverdlovsk province, if reconstructed as a contingency of "points of departure" from the paths of other regions, will result in a model of systemic explanatory power, and this model will in turn allow for building testable hypotheses. The role of "path contingency" in comparative social research can be justified with reference to the fact that theory building with a comparative method necessarily involves identifying complex patterns of causation that vary according to the path taken by a given system (Ragin 1987). For instance, a path-contingent approach seeking to base cross-national explanations on models derived from in-depth studies of national political experiences has been developed for the study of democratization in Latin America (Karl 1990).

The formation of those parties that later came to play important roles in the political arena of Sverdlovsk province can be traced to 1993,[1] when the region's Yeltsin-appointed governor, Eduard Rossel, along with many other of the regions's leading decisionmakers, started to advocate the idea of creating a "Urals republic" on the territory of the province (Moser 1998b). Rossel insisted that the legal status of the province had to be equalized with that of the ethnic-based republics, which was justified primarily with reference to the claimed necessity of transferring "real control" over the region's economy from Moscow to Ekaterinburg, the province's capital.[2] On October 27, 1993, the provincial soviet adopted the constitution of the republic. Elections of the republic's chief executive and legislature were scheduled for December 1993, to be held concurrently with national elections. On November 9, however, Boris Yeltsin dissolved the soviet and dismissed Rossel.[3] The vacant position of the region's chief executive was filled by Aleksei Strakhov, then deputy head of the Ekaterinburg city administration. Rossel's sudden demotion forced him to exploit his personal popularity in the electoral arena. From this perspective, the December 1993 elections to the Federation Council provided the ousted governor with an opportunity to make a political comeback. But now devoid of any advantages of the governor's office, Rossel had to find a replacement. To this end, he initiated the formation of a political movement, Transformation of the Urals. Several small right-wing groups previously active in the region joined the movement, but they did not constitute its organizational basis (Privalov 1995: 36). Apparently, Rossel's personal appeal mattered more. The movement was quite visible in the political arena of Ekaterinburg in the course of the Federation Council campaign, which proved to be successful.

Rossel's success in the Federation Council elections allowed him to regain legitimacy but not power. Due to the national moratorium on holding executive elections, this entry was closed. Under such circumstances, regional legislative elections that were to be held in March 1994 assumed primary importance. Transformation of the Urals participated in these elections in a loose coalition with a group of local politicians who ran under the label of the Party of Russian Unity and Accord (PRES). Jointly, the two parties received five seats in the twenty-eight-member legislature. It may seem that such a result was far from being overwhelmingly successful, but it must be taken into account that only five of the remaining deputies were party nominees, while eighteen of them were independents. This effectively made Transformation of the Urals the dominant force in the legislature and allowed Rossel, with support of many independents, to win election as the chairman of the legislature.[4] In 1994–1995 the region witnessed a series of acute political struggles between the executive, headed by Strakhov, and the Duma. These struggles were focused not only on the problems of economic policy but also on two major political issues: adopting the statute of the province and holding a fresh gubernatorial election. Rossel easily won the first of the struggles. In the fall of 1994 the statute, based on the draft of the constitution of the Urals republic, had been adopted by the legislature.[5] In 1995, Rossel succeeded not only in making the legislature call for fresh elections, which was not very difficult indeed, but also in making Moscow accept this idea, thus lifting the moratorium (Gorfinkel and Rusakova 1995). Strakhov, whose previously pursued strategy did not involve any significant activities in public political arenas, attempted to mimic Rossel's efforts by creating his own political vehicle, a regional branch of Our Home Is Russia (NDR).[6] Quite unexpectedly for many observers, another prominent official, the deputy head of regional administration, Valerii Trushnikov, had joined the gubernatorial race. In the August 1998 election, Rossel, with 26.0 percent of the vote, emerged as the leader in the race, even though this was hardly a landslide. Strakhov, whose campaign was largely built on his association with the NDR,[7] placed a close second with

23.4 percent, while Trushnikov received as much as 20.3 percent of the vote. Aleksandr Lebed, then a rising star in Russia's national politics, endorsed the candidacy of Trushnikov. In the course of the runoff campaign, he came out in support of Rossel.[8] This turned out to be a reasonable strategy, for Rossel won the election with 59.9 percent of the vote against 32.1 percent for Strakhov. Such a result helped Trushnikov to gain appointment as the prime minister of the province. As for Strakhov, his high place on the national list of the NDR in the December 1995 national Duma elections secured him a seat, which made him practically retreat from the front line of Sverdlovsk regional politics.

Before long, however, the political elite of the province became involved in a new conflict. In the December 1995 mayoral elections in Ekaterinburg, Rossel supported the candidacy of his longtime political ally and former leader of the local branch of PRES, Anton Bakov. His victory would have strongly consolidated Rossel's control over the major city of the province (Kiselev 1996). After an aggressive campaign waged by Bakov against the incumbent mayor, Arkadii Chernetskii, the latter won the election with 70.8 percent of the vote against 16.0 percent for Bakov. As a result the regional legislative elections held in April 1996 witnessed a pattern of competition quite reminiscent of that of the gubernatorial elections, with Strakhov effectively replaced by Chernetskii. The statute of the province provided for the election of the two chambers of the assembly by different formulas, single-member plurality for the upper chamber and proportional representation for the lower chamber. Elections were to be held biannually. The upper chamber had a two-year term, while the deputies to the lower chamber served for four years, but each of the elections returned half of its members. In order to implement this routine in 1996, the remaining half of the seats were filled by those elected in 1994.[9] The 1996 campaign strongly encouraged the development of Transformation of the Urals. Its previously ill-defined structure was improved by creating the movement's local branches in practically every town of the province and even in the countryside. At the same time, Strakhov's political legacy in the form of the NDR became easily available to Chernetskii. His political bloc, Our Home Is Our City (NDNG), was formally established by two insignificant right-wing groups, but the bulk of the membership was provided by the NDR.[10] In this enterprise mayors of several smaller cities of the province joined Chernetskii to resist what they called an "unjust system of budget allocation that ignores the programs of city and district development."[11] Moreover, Trushnikov, who owed his post to electoral success more than to personal loyalties, decided to repeat the once successful move and created a bloc of his own, Mining Industrial Urals.

Rossel's movement won the legislative elections by a rather wide margin, with 35.4 percent of the party-list vote against 15.6 percent for the

NDNG. The Communists received 15.6 percent of the vote too. Mining Industrial Urals gained 12.3 percent, which was apparently not enough to secure Trushnikov's job. Rossel fired him almost immediately after the results of the elections were announced.[12] Trushnikov, however, remained quite an influential politician, and his bloc not only survived but also transformed itself into a political movement of the same name. Unfortunately for Rossel, he could neither fire Chernetskii nor get rid of the NDNG. Quite the reverse, during the interlude between the 1996 and 1998 regional legislative elections, Chernetskii transformed the NDNG into a movement with a robust and widespread organizational structure.[13] The political standing of the movement vis-à-vis Transformation of the Urals in the 1998 campaign can be best characterized in Chernetskii's own words: "As of now, our positions are antagonistic."[14] Chernetskii's inability to keep the regional branch of the NDR within his orbit was a serious setback for his organizational efforts. A wealthy businessman, Valerii Yazov, was elected as its chairman and thus effectively appropriated the label.[15] Given that in early 1998 the political influence of Viktor Chernomyrdin was great, and that nobody expected Yeltsin to fire him in several months, this was a valuable label. Two newcomers, the Industrial Union and Social Help and Support (SPP), also joined the campaign. The former was an electoral bloc. One of its founders was PRES, still headed by Bakov, who by that time had become wealthy enough to start his own political game outside of Rossel's circle.[16] The bloc's electoral rhetoric was aggressively populist, strongly focused on the issues of social protection.[17] Much the same, of course, can be said about the SPP with its self-explanatory label.[18] Both groups apparently sought to steal the left-wing vote from the Communists, in which they succeeded only in part. The Industrial Union and the SPP received 6.1 and 5.1 percent respectively of the party-list vote in the 1998 elections, while the joint list of the Communist Party of the Russian Federation (KPRF) and the Agrarian Party of Russia (APR) received 11.8 percent, only 3.1 percent less than the share of the vote gained by the joint list of the KPRF and the Russian Communist Workers Party (RKRP) in 1996. The winner of the 1998 elections was the NDNG with 20.6 percent of the vote. Yazov's NDR also fared quite well, as 8.2 percent of the voters supported its list. Mining Industrial Urals, with 7.6 percent of the vote, managed to retain a good portion of its 1996 electorate. As for Transformation of the Urals, it received only 9.3 percent of the vote, which was a disastrous result. Rossel's capacity to control the regional legislature drastically decreased. This was especially bad news in light of the fact that Rossel's second direct gubernatorial election was to take place in 1999. In the end, however, the emergence of the regional "new left" turned out to be beneficial for Rossel.

On the eve of the 1999 campaign, the most widespread expectation was that it would be a close race with Rossel and Chernetskii as the most probable front-runners.[19] However, this expectation did not take into account the emergence of a new actor in the political arena of Sverdlovsk province. One of the leaders of the Industrial Union, Aleksandr Burkov, proved to be a very talented politician who successfully complemented populist zeal in his public rhetoric with practical activities, which gained him national media acclaim if not notoriety. The major issues of Burkov's own political movement, May, were wage and pension arrears.[20] The activists of the movements violently occupied the offices of municipal officials and enterprise directors and refused to leave until the office-holders consented, or at least promised, to pay wages, a tactic referred to as "forced dialog between society and the authorities."[21] More important, May was instrumental in replacing directors' "pocket" trade unions with militant unions in as many as twenty-seven industrial enterprises of the province.[22] Ironically enough, Burkov was quite an influential businessman himself, and even more so was his close political ally, Anton Bakov. This provided Burkov's campaign with all necessary funding. In the first round of the gubernatorial election, Rossel received 38.8 percent of the vote, Chernetskii placed third with 15.5 percent, while Burkov, with 18.4 percent, entered the second round. Such a turn of events was extremely advantageous for Rossel. Burkov's populist rhetoric appealed to a significant portion of the electorate, but for the majority of voters he remained an unpredictable and potentially dangerous political outsider. The runoff was won by Rossel, with 63.1 percent of the vote, by a margin of more than 30 percent. Building on this success, Rossel's bloc, based on Transformation of the Urals, placed first in the 2000 regional legislative elections by party lists. It received 21.7 percent of the vote against 14.7 percent for the NDNG and 12.2 percent for May. This signified the start of May's decline. Some of its voters readdressed their hopes for greater social protection to the regional branch of the Pensioners Party. Chernetskii retained his role as an important actor in the political arena of the region, and he even tried to consolidate this role by allying himself with a prominent national political force, Fatherland.[23] The members and organizational resources of the NDNG were transferred to the regional branch of the movement. Judging from the results of the 2002 regional legislative elections, this investment did not pay off. The Unity and Fatherland bloc received 18.4 percent of the vote, distantly tracing Rossel's bloc, which gained its best share of the vote since 1996, 29.4 percent. This allowed the governor to reestablish his political control over the legislature.

The results of the 1996–2002 regional legislative elections by party lists in Sverdlovsk province are reported in Table 5.1. As becomes apparent from a comparison with national electoral returns, discussed in Chapter 2, Sverdlovsk province did indeed develop its own party system. The two major parties, Transformation of the Urals and the NDNG, remained sus-

Table 5.1   Results of Regional Legislative Elections by Party Lists in Sverdlovsk Province, 1996–2002

Party	Percentage Share of the Vote in Regional Legislative Elections by Party Lists			
	1996	1998	2000	2002
Transformation of the Urals (in blocs in 2000–2002)	35.4	9.3	21.7	29.4
Our Home Is Our City (1996–2000)–Unity and Fatherland bloc (2002)	15.6	20.6	14.7	18.4
NDR	—	8.2	—	—
Mining Industrial Urals	12.3	7.6	3.3	—
SPP	—	5.1	4.6	4.9
Industrial Union (1998)–May (2000, 2002)	—	6.1	12.2	4.7
Pensioners Party	—	—	—	6.1
KPRF (in blocs in 1996–1998)	15.6	11.8	9.9	7.3
LDPR	3.1	4.6	—	—
Yabloko	4.0	—	4.9	3.8
Other parties, invalid votes, and votes against all parties	14.0	26.7	28.7	25.4

tainable throughout the period, even though in the end the latter traded its own label for a label of a major national political party. The SPP and May developed their national political organizations, which occasionally participated in elections outside of Sverdlovsk province, but the region remained their principal base. At the same time, truly national political parties, such as the KPRF, the Liberal Democratic Party of Russia (LDPR), and Yabloko, always fared worse in Sverdlovsk province than they did in the majority of other regions. One might plausibly suggest that this happened because local groups captured large portions of their vote. The development of a locally based party system is in fact a unique property of Sverdlovsk province. True, the levels of party representation in regional legislative assemblies were higher in several regions, such as Krasnoiarsk, Krasnodar, Kemerovo, and Volgograd in the second electoral cycle, and Krasnoiarsk and Kemerovo in the third electoral cycle. In Krasnoiarsk territory, however, the electoral arena was filled primarily with the local branches of national political parties. In each of the remaining three regions, single dominant parties swept legislative seats, which does not fit into the notion of party system development. Once the uniqueness of Sverdlovsk province is empirically established, it becomes possible to proceed with the explanatory part of deviant case analysis. What are the "points of departure"?

One might suggest that an important factor accounting for the observed deviation was Rossel's conflict with Moscow on the issues of federalism and regional autonomy. However, similar outcomes were not brought about in every region where similar possibilities existed. Whereas the elites of several resource-rich regions had at one time or another been involved in conflicts with Moscow, most of them preferred to settle these conflicts by means of bargaining (Solnick 1995; Umnova 1996). Even very acute conflicts of this kind did not necessarily exert any impact on party formation, with available alternatives ranging from elite consolidation on a nonparty basis in Tatarstan (Ishiyama 1996) to the situation in Primorskii territory that could be described in terms of "warlordism" much more adequately than "multipartyism" (Kirkow 1995). An examination of the case of Sverdlovsk province allows for identifying a different point of departure that has played a crucial role in the formation of political parties. Insofar as Rossel remained an undisputed leader of the region's political elite, no need for political parties had been felt. But as soon as he was dismissed and started to fight to restore his authority, Transformation of the Urals was launched. Rossel's immediate political rivals were those members of the regional political elite who capitalized on his dismissal, not the federal authorities. What happened in the province in the autumn of 1993 and subsequently was therefore a conflict within the regional elite, even though it was complicated by the direct involvement of federal authorities.

True, intraelite conflict, especially in the course of the second electoral cycle, was by no means unusual in the regions of Russia. The reasons for such conflicts are very interesting in themselves, but they are of little concern for this particular analysis. From the existing small body of literature on the subject, it would seem that many such conflicts concerned issues of economic policy and privatization (Slider 1994; Hughes 1994; McAuley 1997; Kirkow 1998; Gel'man, Ryzhenkov, and Brie 2000). Yet irrespective of the causes for which these conflicts were waged, many of them did not contribute to party formation, or at least did not contribute to the same extent as happened in Sverdlovsk province. Hence a qualification is needed, and indeed it is quite obvious that we can hardly expect intraelite struggles to assist party development if none of the conflicting factions choose to use party labels or party-related resources to achieve their goals. Rossel created a party in order to win gubernatorial elections. From the statistics presented in Chapter 3, it would seem that few regional politicians followed his example. I would hypothesize that this is the second point of departure. Yet to create a party does not necessarily mean to make it sustainable. A theoretically possible outcome of intraelite conflict in Sverdlovsk province was that Rossel could have abandoned Transformation of the Urals after his return to power. But to afford this, Rossel would have had to reestablish his full control over the region, which he did not. His power remained continuously challenged by different elite factions. This leads us to the third point of departure: even when and where political parties prove to be instrumental in electoral arenas, a decisive victory by one of the participants in the conflict, resulting in this actor's monopolistic control over the decisionmaking process in the region, impedes the process of party formation.

The resulting path-contingent model of regional party system formation can be explained as a diachronic projection of the identified pattern of causality with all the stated qualifications: (1) intraelite conflict waged in electoral arenas, (2) the use of political parties by at least some of the participants in the conflict, and (3) the indecisive result of the conflict. Each of the points of departure constitutes a hypothesis that requires empirical verification. But is it possible to measure the intensity of political conflict by analyzing electoral outcomes? The most straightforward measure of electoral competitiveness is of course power change by electoral means. If elections result in the transfer of power from an incumbent to a challenger, then it can be safely assumed that the elections were competitive.[24] Of the eighty-eight executive elections that were held in the regions of Russia in the second electoral cycle, Chechnya excluded, incumbents won in forty-five.[25] By this criterion, therefore, the second-cycle elections were highly competitive. In the third electoral cycle, however, the level of competitiveness apparently decreased: incumbents won fifty-five of eighty-seven elections.[26] When comparing the figures for the second and third electoral cycles, it must be taken into account that while in the former, open races were extremely rare occasions, as only four of the elections were not contested by incumbents, the number of such elections increased to thirteen in the latter; that is, of the elections that they actually contested, incumbents won with 53.6 percent in the second electoral cycle, and with as much as 74.3 percent in the third. Still, by comparative standards, the rate of incumbent executives' survival in Russia does not seem to be unusually high.[27] The measure used for statistical analysis is an interactive variable that is intended to reflect two principal aspects of the phenomenon under observation, the electoral success of the incumbents and their vulnerability as expressed in electoral returns. To construct the variable, I start by introducing a dummy, with a value of 1 being attributed to those cases when incumbents lost executive elections, and a value of 0 to the cases when incumbents won or abstained from running. Then I multiply the value by the percentage shares of the vote received by the most successful challengers in the second or single rounds of voting. Thus the variable discounts the levels of challenger success in those elections that were won or uncontested by the incumbents, but brings them in to measure the vulnerability of those incumbents who actually lost. In this capacity, the variable can be related to electoral marginality as a difference between the percentage shares of the vote gained by the incumbent and challenger in the given election (Garand and Wink 1993). I dub this variable "CHELS," referring to its major function, to measure challengers' electoral success.

The second measure is the effective number of candidates (ENC), a standard indicator introduced in Chapter 2. Being generally accepted as a measure of political fragmentation, the effective number does not empirically overlap with CHELS. Indeed, there is no logical association between an incumbent's ability to hold on to his office and the level of fragmentation. Say a challenger won the 1996 gubernatorial elections in Krasnodar territory by an 82 percent margin (CHELS = 75.0), with the effective number of candidates at 1.4. Almost the same effective number of candidates were registered in the 1996 elections in Vologda province, but these were decisively won by the incumbent (CHELS = 0). For the purpose of data homogenization, when calculating the values of ENC, I used the shares of the valid vote jointly cast for all candidates in the single or first rounds of regional executive elections. In particular, this means that I have recalculated the officially published election results to discount the shares of invalid votes and votes cast against all candidates. The average effective numbers of candidates in the elections held in the second and third electoral cycles were 2.4 and 2.6 respectively. This could indicate that the average level of elite fragmentation increased, which is a finding that is not quite consistent with the previously reported increase in incumbency advantage. The reason for this apparent inconsistency is as follows. In the second electoral cycle, the average ENC in twenty regions with the lowest levels of fragmentation was 1.3; in the third cycle, it was 1.2. At the same time, the levels of fragmentation in the twenty top regions on this parameter were 3.9 in the second electoral cycle and 4.7 in the third. That is, the average ENC for the whole period increased because of the emergence of a small group of regions with extremely high levels of fragmentation. Indeed, standard deviations for my data sets skyrocketed from 0.99 in the second electoral cycle to 1.32 in the third. In general, the levels of fragmentation in regional executive elections are high enough to indicate the rather widespread presence of intraelite conflict.

The remaining two variables used in the analysis below pertain to the role played by parties in regional executive elections, which corresponds to the second clause of the model. Both of them, party-nominated incumbent (PNI) and party-nominated challenger (PNC), assume the values of the percentage shares of the vote received by the respective categories of candidates in the regional executive elections, with PNC referring to the joint shares of the vote in those cases when more than one party-nominated challenger was present. Quite consistently with what was reported in Chapter 3, the role of parties in regional executive elections was found to be not very important, and it drastically decreased over time. In particular, party-nominated incumbents were present in eight and four elections in the second and third electoral cycles respectively. Party-nominated challengers were more widespread, but the level of their success was low. By juxtaposing this finding with the model reported above, one could infer that the major reason for party underdevelopment in the regions of Russia is not the lack of intraelite conflict but rather the lack of party involvement in these conflicts. To make such an inference, however, it is important to empirically verify the model itself.

As a dependent variable, I use one indicator that in Chapter 3 was introduced as the principal measure of party development in the regions, the percentage share of seats held by party nominees in legislative assemblies. The data set includes all regions that have held both executive and legislative elections in the given electoral cycle.[28] If a region had two elections of either type, I used averages as the values of all variables. Independent variables are CHELS, ENC, PNI, and PNC. Using ordinary least squares (OLS) estimation, I ran separate regressions for the second and third electoral cycles. The results are reported in Table 5.2. It is only in the second electoral cycle that CHELS works as expected, so that turnover by electoral means appears to be conducive to party development. In fact, in the second-cycle regression it is the only variable that fully justifies my theoretical expectations. ENC, PNI, and PNC are all positively associated with party development, but the associations are not statistically significant. In the second electoral cycle, therefore, political parties formed primarily in those regions where incumbent governors lost elections on a wide margin. The picture for the third electoral cycle is different. This time, ENC emerges as strong predictor of party formation, while CHELS not only loses all significance but also changes its direction. Party nomination vari-

Table 5.2 Intraelite Conflicts and Party Formation in the Regions of Russia, by Electoral Cycle, 1995–2003

Variables	2nd Electoral Cycle			3rd Electoral Cycle		
	Parameter Estimate		T-value	Parameter Estimate		T-value
Intercept	7.72	(6.04)	1.28	−2.01	(4.94)	−0.41
CHELS	0.27***	(0.07)	3.74	−0.14	(0.10)	−1.35
ENC	1.10	(2.32)	0.48	6.03***	(1.85)	3.26
PNI	0.24*	(0.14)	1.72	0.11	(0.14)	0.74
PNC	0.14	(0.14)	1.03	0.25	(0.26)	0.99
Number of observations	83			79		
R-squared	0.20			0.15		
Adj. R-squared	0.16			0.10		

Notes: The dependent variable is the share of seats won by party nominees in regional legislative assemblies. Parentheses indicate standard errors.
  * Significant at 0.1.
  ** Significant at 0.05.
  *** Significant at 0.01.

ables do not work better than previously, even though they are still positively associated with the dependent variable. In the third electoral cycle, therefore, political parties formed primarily in regions with high levels of fragmentation in executive elections.

What explains the observed difference between the two electoral cycles? Two of the variables, CHELS and ENC, are both empirical indicators of intraelite conflicts waged in electoral arenas, but they perform this role in different ways. In the second electoral cycle the most favorable context for party development was set by power change by electoral means. It was the presence of strong challengers who were capable of defeating the incumbents that induced party formation. Yet if the challenger is strong, the level of fragmentation will decrease unless the incumbent is extremely weak, which in the majority of cases was not the case. In a close race between a strong challenger and a strong incumbent the effective number of candidates is close to 2. In the third electoral cycle, as it appears from the data reported above, not only were there fewer strong challengers, but more important, their presence became unrelated to party development. Instead, political parties were at an advantage in the environments of extreme political fragmentation, in which both incumbents and challengers were unable to rally large portions of the vote. I would assume that both a face-to-face struggle between strong rivals and a war of all against all (as happens under the conditions of extreme fragmentation) are conflict-ridden conditions, even though the modalities of conflict are different.

Thus my hypothesis that intraelite conflict is conducive to party formation holds for both electoral cycles. My hypothesis regarding the instrumental use of political parties as an incentive for their formation holds to a very limited extent. True, the use of political parties by both incumbents and challengers seems to be positively associated with party formation. Few incumbents have ever chosen to be party-nominated though. Even when they have, it did not contribute much to party formation, which would logically suggest that incumbents did not find political parties very useful to furthering their careers, whether because they lost or for other reasons.

Regional Executives:
Institutional Alternatives to Party Affiliations

The case of Sverdlovsk province is deviant in the sense that—unlike all the remaining regions—it managed to develop a system of sustainable, locally based parties. In many other respects, the course of events in the province's intraelite conflict is fairly typical. Consider the composition of the major participants in the region's turbulent political developments. After being removed by Yeltsin, Rossel almost immediately assumed control over the regional legislature. It was in his capacity as chairman of the legislative assembly that he won gubernatorial elections. His major rivals in this undertaking were, in addition to the incumbent governor, another high-standing official in the regional executive, Trushnikov, and the mayor of the region's capital city, Chernetskii. It is quite logical to associate Trushnikov's subsequent disappearance from the electoral arena with the fact that he lost his standing within the structures of power, as well as Chernetskii's survival with the fact that he did not. Despite the uniquely important role that was played by political parties, intraelite conflict in Sverdlovsk was waged not so much by party politicians but rather by politicians with certain institutional affiliations. Does such a categorization hold in cross-regional perspective?

As mentioned above, incumbents won in forty-five of the eighty-eight executive elections in the second electoral cycle. Only four elections were uncontested by incumbents, which means that overall, as many as thirty-nine challengers won gubernatorial offices. Among them, the largest group consisted of the chairpersons and deputy chairpersons of regional legislative assemblies. They won in Altai territory and Amur, Kaluga, Kurgan, Lipetsk, Tambov, Vladimir, Voronezh, and Sverdlovsk provinces. With the only exception of Rossel, all these challengers were the preferred candidates of the Popular Patriotic Union of Russia. Unlike Rossel, the majority of them, six, were not party nominees. Local political movements with quite self-explanatory labels nominated the remaining two candidates. Aleksandr Surikov's movement in Altai territory, For Genuine People's Power, Civil Peace, and the Interests of the Man of Toil, was a loose coalition of the Communists and the Agrarians. Much the same can be said about Nikolai Vinogradov's movement in Vladimir province, Justice and People's Power. The KPRF and the APR were indeed the most important political parties that joined the movements. However, they also included trade unions, women's and youth organizations, and a plethora of others.[29] In Vladimir province, for instance, an association of the handicapped was also a collective member.[30] Hence the movements embraced whatever civic activism could be found in the regions.

At the same time, both Surikov in Altai and Vinogradov in Vladimir managed to rally around themselves the majorities of regional elites, especially the heads of local administrations and directors of the most important industrial and agricultural enterprises,[31] thus unifying regional elites against the Yeltsin-appointed incumbents. Yet to achieve that, their movements were insufficient. Even though they could be instrumental for mobilizing civic activism and societal support, the anti-incumbent mobilization of the elites required more solid power bases. Regional legislative assemblies provided such bases. A detailed analysis of the models of separation of power employed in the regions of Russia will be presented in Chapter 6.

Here, it is sufficient to identify four major ways in which assembly leadership could be instrumental for waging intraelite conflicts. First, the regional legislative process itself, especially the budgetary process, could be employed for providing benefits to subregional elites, thus luring them into anti-incumbent coalitions.[32] Second, the legislative assembly itself included many important elite members and thus was capable of performing as an organizational network for the anti-incumbent opposition. Third, the assembly, even in political contexts strongly dominated by incumbent governors, was still capable of effective oversight, which could be of crucial importance for waging political warfare.[33] Finally, much in the same way as happened in the national Duma, the assembly leadership provided its holders with certain financial and logistic resources that would have been unavailable otherwise. In their entirety, these advantages were arguably greater than those provided by political organization. Thus it is not surprising that the majority of the chairpersons of legislative assemblies, who quite similar to Surikov and Vinogradov challenged incumbent governors from the left and won, were not party nominees. In the second gubernatorial elections, Surikov's movement nominated him again, but Vinogradov chose to run as an independent, even though his movement apparently remained quite alive and well.[34]

The mayors and deputy mayors of regional capital cities were the second category of important challengers in the second-cycle executive elections. An analysis of municipal self-government in postcommunist Russia cannot be undertaken here at any length. Suffice it to say, municipal offices, including those of city mayors, experienced an evolution similar to that of the regional executives, from appointment by senior executives to direct elections (Ryzhenkov and Vinnik 1999), even though many mayors in the course of the second and even third electoral cycles remained appointed or elected by municipal assemblies.[35] In the process, mayors acquired electoral experience and political resources of their own. Yet perhaps more important, a city hall as such is a potentially powerful political tool in contemporary Russia (Friedgut and Hahn 1994; Evans 2000). In the majority of regions, capital cities concentrate large portions of industrial enterprises, commerce, and population. They also have specific interests to fight for. It was not unusual that regional administrations pursued economic policies that favored rural peripheries rather than the urban centers (Gel'man, Ryzhenkov, and Brie 2000). In the second electoral cycle, chief capital city officials won over incumbents in two regions, Karelia and Smolensk province, and they emerged victorious in two open races, in Irkutsk and Nizhii Novgorod provinces. Only one of these challengers was party-nominated, Aleksandr Prokhorov in Smolensk province, whose candidacy was endorsed by the KPRF. This was a useful endorsement in a region where the party used to do remarkably well in all national elections.

At the same time, Prokhorov turned out to be one of only two candidates nominated by the KPRF itself, not by local left-wing organizations, who ever won gubernatorial elections in Russia. Yet his relations with the party were quite ambiguous from the very start.

Judging from the reports of political observers, the Communists nominated Prokhorov, a nonparty politician previously unnoticed in close connections with the KPRF, not to emphasize his ties with the party. In fact, the first preference of the regional branch of the KPRF was Anatolii Luk'ianov, one of the national leaders of the party, who however refused to run. Rather, the Communists' goal was to vocally distance themselves from the incumbent governor, Anatolii Glushenkov, who won the 1993 gubernatorial elections as the party's preferred candidate but defected when in office.[36] Prokhorov claimed, not entirely implausibly, that he was surprised when he learned about the party's decision to support him.[37] An even more amusing fact was that in the course of the campaign, the federal executive shifted to support Prokhorov too, as his unsuccessful rival bitterly admitted.[38] To conduct the campaign, Prokhorov hired a team of political consultants, which was not a great burden given that some of the city's industrialists were alleged to have heavily sponsored him.[39] In the end, Prokhorov won by a 20 percent margin, but his relations with the KPRF remained quite ambiguous throughout his term and the party did not nominate him for the 2002 election, which he lost. The case of Prokhorov reveals not so much why mayors need party support but rather why they do not. Mayoral offices are supplied with resources, interests, and societal bases of support of their own.

Of course, mayors and deputy mayors of regional capital cities are not the only category of public servants who have tried their luck in regional executive elections. In the second electoral cycle, as many as seven elections were won by state and municipal officials who occupied second- and third-rank positions in state and municipal administrations. This category is quite miscellaneous due to the fact that the offices held by the challengers came with a wide variety of interests and resources attached. In the 1996 elections in St. Petersburg, the city's deputy mayor, Vladimir Yakovlev, challenged his boss, the incumbent mayor and a prominent "first-wave democrat" Anatolii Sobchak. The candidacy of Yakovlev, who claimed to be an experienced manager who would run the city in a businesslike fashion, was endorsed by a wide spectrum of political forces in the city: in the second round, he was supported both by the KPRF and Yabloko.[40] That is why he did not need a single-party nomination for the purposes of voter mobilization. At the same time, the resources associated with the position of the deputy mayor were quite comparable with those associated with the chief regional executive position. A different situation occurred in the 1995 elections in Tver province. There, the incumbent governor, Vladimir

Suslov, was supported by the presidential administration on the one hand, and by the local branch of the KPRF on the other.[41] The challenger, Vladimir Platov, was the head of administration of the small Bezhetsk district. This was not an adequate resource base for gubernatorial races. To complement his otherwise scarce resources, however, Platov could rely on his reputation as a committed reformer. He waged an ideological campaign, complete with rhetoric full of references to the values of democratic self-government, "people's power."[42] "People's Power" was also the label of a regional movement that nominated him. The movement was created by the local branches of Democratic Russia, Democratic Russia's Choice (DVR), and a bunch of smaller right-wing groups specifically for the purpose of supporting Platov's candidacy. Given the lack of Platov's own resources, and the heavily ideological overtones of his campaign, this was a reasonable strategy that probably contributed to the challenger's eventual success. When comparing the cases of St. Petersburg and Tver province, it becomes apparent that for those state officials who ran in executive elections, party resources could be useful only as complements to the insufficient resources attached to their offices.

One more office membership that has to be entered into this analysis is that of the national parliament. National Duma deputies won as many as ten executive elections in the second electoral cycle. Eight of the successful challengers were elected to the Duma in single-member districts, not by party lists. This immediately reveals the nature of resources they could rely upon in their gubernatorial bids. Winning a national Duma seat in a single-member district is an undertaking that is in many respects similar to winning a senior executive office. For one thing, the number of single-member districts per region is small. In the ten regions where Duma deputies actually won executive elections, the average number of districts per region was 2.3; six of them territorially coincided with districts. Thus Duma elections are good rehearsals for executive elections. Given that in the second electoral cycle almost all regional governors were appointees, this even placed the Duma deputies in an advantageous position, for they had experience lacked by many of their opponents. In the process of Duma campaigning they accumulated electoral resources that could be reinvested in gubernatorial bids. In the majority of cases, these resources were unrelated to political parties. Indeed, of those eight district deputies who won executive elections, only one, Aleksei Lebed in Khakasia, was party-nominated. The nominating entity was the Honor and Motherland movement led by his brother, Aleksandr Lebed.

In contrast to the district deputies, the two party-list deputies who won executive elections were both party-nominated. A local left-wing movement, Patriotic Briansk Land, nominated Yurii Lodkin in Briansk province. Lodkin, a long-standing leader of the Briansk left, created the movement in

1993 as his personal political vehicle[43] in a situation that was quite reminiscent of that in Sverdlovsk province: like Rossel, Lodkin was demoted by Yeltsin in the fall of that year.[44] He was then elected to the national legislature and eventually won gubernatorial elections too. Throughout the period, the movement was undoubtedly instrumental in his political warfare against the Yeltsin-appointed governors, and he remained politically dependent on the KPRF as a national political figure.[45] Then the fact that he chose to run as a party nominee was not surprising. An even more revealing case is that of Evgenii Mikhailov in Pskov province. In contrast to Lodkin, who after all had quite solid political credentials in his region, Mikhailov was largely a creation of the party that nominated him, the LDPR (Slider 1999). He lost the 1995 district elections and was brought to the national legislature only because he was on the LDPR list too, and the party's performance in the region was quite impressive. Even during the gubernatorial campaign, the major electioneer for Mikhailov was not the candidate himself but rather Vladimir Zhirinovsky.[46] Of course, party nomination was essential for Mikhailov's success. Yet it is clear that the case of Mikhailov was very unusual. For the majority of Duma deputies who tried their luck in the arenas of regional executive elections, party affiliation was not an important resource.

In the second electoral cycle, challengers belonging to the four categories identified above won in 34.1 percent of the executive elections, incumbents in 51.1 percent, and other challengers in 14.8 percent. In the third electoral cycle, the picture was different in the sense that a larger share of elections, 63.2 percent, resulted in incumbent victories. Correspondingly, the share of elections won by assembly leaders, city leaders, state and municipal officials, and Duma deputies declined. As mentioned in Chapter 3, only six winners were party nominees. Among them were three incumbents and two national Duma deputies. Hence the value of party nomination in the third electoral cycle became negligible. The analysis above suggests that this happened largely because institutional affiliations, rather than party affiliations, were of primary importance for winning executive elections. Is this inference testable in a way more robust than descriptive statistics may offer? My attempt to achieve that, presented below, is based on the hypothesis that incumbents fare well in executive elections if they are not seriously challenged. This is a strong assumption given that the flourishing literature on economic voting by and large assumes that incumbents win elections if they perform well in terms of economic policy (Fiorina 1981; Lewis-Beck 1988). Yet only poor statistical models tend to explain all the variations in the observed phenomena. My less ambitious purpose here is to establish the relative weight of institutional affiliations and party affiliations as factors of incumbent success. The dependent variable could be a dummy distinguishing between the situations when the incumbents win and the situations when they lose. Yet given the modest size of my sample and the multiplicity of factors that have to be incorporated into the model, I found it more expedient to use a ratio-dependent variable, the percentage share of the vote received by the incumbent in the first or single round of regional executive elections. For certain cognitive purposes this could be a less than perfect measure. Theoretically, candidates who receive 49.9 percent of the vote may lose elections, while the threshold for winning elections may be extremely low, without any minimum limits but zero. Yet despite the oft-cited proverb "nothing succeeds like success," the notion of faring well in elections is not reducible to the notion of winning them. An incumbent may be vulnerable even if winning in the end, or he or she may win elections by a huge margin. Thus the share of the vote, in contrast to the victory or defeat dummy, allows for distinguishing situations that are substantively different.

The independent variables employed in my analysis are the raw numbers of challengers belonging to the following categories (shorter denominations occasionally used further in this analysis are given in parentheses): heads or deputy heads of legislative assemblies or their chambers (legislative leaders), heads or deputy heads of administration of regions' capital cities (city leaders), state and municipal officials of different standings (officials), and national Duma deputies (deputies). Of the other challengers, I single out a category of businesspeople. This category embraces quite a number of occupational statuses, from the chairpersons of Soviet-style collective farms, renamed as "cooperatives" though unchanged otherwise, to the private entrepreneurs of recent origins, and from the mighty tycoons in control of whole sectors of the economy to modest self-employed traders. In fact, the data at my disposal often do not allow for making subtler distinctions. Yet given the role played by financial resources in Russia's elections as described in the previous chapter, placing businesspeople at large into a separate category seems to be justifiable. Then there is the category of "others." It is quite possible to speculate that the mere presence of many candidates reduces the share of an incumbent's vote, thus accounting for the lion's share of variations in the dependent variable. Indeed, the raw numbers of candidates in Russia's regional executive elections were quite impressive: on average, 5.2 in the second electoral cycle and 6.5 in the third. It is therefore important to test whether the proliferation of candidates as such makes incumbents more vulnerable. Two variables pertain to party activities in regional executive elections. One of them, "party incumbent," is a dummy that assumes a value of 0 if incumbents were not nominated by political parties, and a value of 1 if they were. The other, "party challengers," is the raw number of party-nominated challengers in a given election. The sample for my analysis does not cover the whole universe of executive elections held since 1995. For an obvious reason, I had to exclude seventeen elections uncontested by incumbents. In addition, I excluded three of the second-cycle elections, in Kabardino-Balkaria, Kalmykia, and Tatarstan, because they were uncontested in the sense that only incumbents' names appeared on the ballot papers. There were no such instances in the third electoral cycle. The 2003 elections in Belgorod province are excluded because of lack of data. Thus the sample includes eighty-one and seventy-four executive elections held in the second and third electoral cycles respectively.

The results of multiple regression analysis (OLS model) are reported in Table 5.3. These results can be viewed as strongly confirming my previously stated expectations regarding the role of institutional affiliations in determining electoral outcomes. There is some difference between the second and third electoral cycles, though. Most obvious, the legislative leaders' capacity to challenge the incumbents drastically declined over time, while city leaders, in contrast, seemed to reinforce their positions. The presence of state and municipal officials in the electoral arenas consistently depressed the incumbents' prospects for superior electoral performance throughout the period. The role of national legislators, very pronounced in the second electoral cycle, declined in the third, while the reverse is true

Table 5.3   Factors of Incumbents' Electoral Success in the Second- and Third-Cycle Regional Executive Elections, 1995–2003

Variables	2nd Electoral Cycle		3rd Electoral Cycle		All Elections	
	Parameter Estimate	T-value	Parameter Estimate	T-value	Parameter Estimate	T-value
Intercept	65.48***(4.74)	13.82	76.82***(4.81)	15.97	69.34***(3.32)	20.88
Legislative leaders	−18.08***(6.44)	−2.81	−6.82 (7.86)	−0.87	−15.75***(4.93)	−3.20
City leaders	−17.91** (8.06)	−2.22	−22.26***(6.17)	−3.61	−18.95***(4.83)	−3.93
Officials	−5.60** (2.45)	−2.28	−6.66** (2.52)	−2.65	−5.59***(1.69)	−3.30
Deputies	−6.64** (3.17)	−2.10	−5.69* (3.11)	−1.83	−6.41***(2.17)	2.96
Businesspeople	−3.62* (1.84)	−1.97	−4.23** (1.78)	−2.38	−3.37***(1.27)	−2.65
Others	−0.98 (1.59)	−0.62	−2.35 (1.83)	−1.29	−0.84 (1.13)	−0.74
Party incumbent	3.33 (7.51)	0.44	9.90 (10.15)	0.98	3.96 (5.87)	0.67
Party challengers	−3.46 (2.54)	−1.37	0.68 (3.63)	0.19	−3.65* (2.01)	−1.81
Number of observations	81		74		155	
R-squared	0.32		0.42		0.32	
Adj. R-squared	0.25		0.34		0.28	

Notes: The dependent variable is the share of the vote received by the incumbent. Parentheses indicate standard errors.
* Significant at 0.1.
** Significant at 0.05.
*** Significant at 0.01.

regarding businesspeople. The hypothesis according to which a mere prolif-eration of candidates negatively affects incumbents' performance does not hold, because parameter estimates for the "other candidates" variable are always insignificant, even though the directions are as predicted. Thus in general, institutional affiliations do matter. As follows from the statistical analysis, party affiliations do not. True, the number of party-nominated challengers does become marginally important in the third electoral cycle, and for all its insignificance the variable exerts a theoretically expectable impact. Both the "party challenger" and the "party incumbent" variables are consistently insignificant, even though the latter has the expected signs in all regression models. This is puzzling. After all, the upper lines in Table 3.6, which lists the cases of most successful party performance in regional executive elections, are occupied by cases of incumbents' success, Tyva, Khabarovsk territory, the Jewish autonomous province, and Orenburg province in the second electoral cycle, and Mordovia, Khabarovsk, and Altai in the third electoral cycle. In order to solve this puzzle, it stands to reason to take a closer look at these cases, as well as at the cases when party-nominated incumbents actually lost (the case of Mordovia will be discussed in Chapter 8).

Khabarovsk territory and the Jewish autonomous province are adjacent regions; moreover, in the Soviet era the latter was a part of the former. Perhaps this accounts, at least in part, for similarities in the patterns of regional politics.[47] In both regions, the incumbent governors—Viktor Ishaev and Nikolai Volkov respectively—are Yeltsin appointees who have ruled their regions since 1991 without confronting any serious political challenges. Both were among those very few governors whose candidacies in the second-cycle elections were simultaneously supported by the presidential administration and the NPSR. Correspondingly, the KPRF did not nominate or even support any alternative candidates in these elections.[48] Nor were there signs of intraelite conflict, as neither capital city mayors nor assembly leaders were among the challengers. Under such conditions, few observers could doubt that both Ishaev and Volkov would win by wide margins, irrespective of who would nominate them. In fact, four "initiative groups of voters" and the regional federation of trade unions simultaneously nominated Ishaev.[49] The powerful incumbent chose to run as a trade union candidate. Even though by all appearances this was by far not a critical choice, Ishaev's affiliation with the trade unions could be of certain symbolic value as an additional manifestation of his social protectionist policy agenda. In his second direct elections Ishaev replicated this strategy, this time running as a candidate of the trade unions' political organization, the Union of Labor.

In a similar vein, Nikolai Volkov, whose managerial credo was perhaps best expressed in his categorization of the region's population as "one large family,"[50] was nominated by an entity that was straightforwardly dubbed "Electoral Bloc in Support of Nikolai Mikhailovich Volkov" and comprised of as many as seven entities, including the trade unions, the Union of Labor, the regional women's union, the council of veterans, and the regional branches of three political parties both of the left and right, the NDR, the APR, and the PRES. The Communists did not officially join the bloc, and local observers even expected them to nominate their own candidate, but they did not.[51] By comprising nearly all of the remaining political and societal groups in the region, Volkov's bloc served as a manifestation of unanimous support to the incumbent. When running in the second elections, Volkov received support from many political groups, again including the KPRF, but this time he ran as an independent.[52] Clearly, party nomination of the incumbents in both regions was not very important, and one might speculate that many other governors could easily have arranged such nominations if they had wished. In general, I would not agree. It seems that the model described above was available only under the conditions of the complete lack of contestation in the executive elections—that is, when the incumbents were challenged neither by ideological opponents nor by institutionally affiliated rivals. Such conditions could be found in several other regions, but by and large they were unusual.

Two other regions at the top of Table 3.6 fall into a different category, much more representative of the conditions under which incumbents chose party nomination. The Yeltsin-appointed governor of Orenburg province, Vladimir Elagin, was involved in a protracted political struggle with the opposition that included the local branches of the KPRF and the APR. Both parties were quite influential in the region, as shown by the fact that the Communists managed to make a political deal with the mayor of Orenburg, Gennadii Donkovtsev, while one of the region's representatives in the national legislature was a prominent Agrarian, Aleksei Chernyshev. Briefly before the 1995 gubernatorial elections, Elagin initiated the formation of his own political movement, which was named Rebirth of Orenburg Land.[53] In contrast to the entities that nominated Ishaev and Volkov, Elagin's movement was quite firmly located in the right-wing segment of the region's political spectrum, as demonstrated by the fact that it was conceived as a regional branch of the NDR.[54] Hence Elagin's strategy was aimed at increasing political polarization in the campaign and, by this means, rallying the noncommunist vote. In one instance, this strategy proved to be successful, as Elagin won against Donkovtsev by a 37 percent margin, even though it may be speculated that Donkovtsev was not a credible left-wing candidate after all.[55] It is also important to take into account that Russia's prime minister at the time and leader of the NDR, Viktor Chernomyrdin, originated from Orenburg province, which is why the region's authorities enjoyed an especially cozy relationship with the national executive. After Elagin's victory, Rebirth of Orenburg Land remained inactive for several years, only to be revitalized on the eve of the 1999 gubernatorial campaign.[56] This time, both Donkovtsev and Chernyshev challenged the incumbent, while Moscow's support to him became less pronounced with the demotion of Chernomyrdin in 1998. Not only Chernyshev's own party, the APR, but also the Communists endorsed his candidacy, while Donkovtsev emerged as a splitter of the noncommunist vote. As a logical conclusion to this story, Elagin lost to Chernyshev in the second round of the elections.

In the 1997 elections in Tyva, the incumbent president, Sherig-ool Oorzhak, ran as a nominee of the electoral bloc Leader, comprising the regional branch of the NDR and the Union of Women of Tyva. The incumbent's situation was quite complicated, as he was involved in an acute struggle with the chairman of the republic's legislature, Kaadyr-ool Bicheldei, once a founder of the region's major perestroika-era anticommunist and ethnonationalist group People's Front Free Tyva.[57] Not surprisingly, Bicheldei's candidacy was endorsed by the remnants of the republic's "democratic movement."[58] Another important challenger was Aleksandr Kashin, leader of the regional branch of the LDPR and later mayor of the republic's capital, who vocalized the dissatisfactions of the ethnic Russian minority. Under these conditions, Oorzhak's association with the NDR verified his right-wing credentials on the one hand, and indicated his commitment to the territorial integrity of Russia on the other. Both aspects were quite salient in the campaign. Even though Oorzhak won the 1997 elections by a wide margin and replicated this success in 2002, the republic continued to be torn by extremely intensive intraelite struggles throughout his rule. It was widely alleged that Oorzhak's victory in 2002 largely resulted from the massive use of electoral fraud and coercion.[59]

Despite the vast differences between the political contexts in which their second-cycle executive campaigns took place, Orenburg province and Tyva had one important thing in common. In both, chief executives were vulnerable, which made them employ all available resources including party nomination. They managed to win. For the majority of party-nominated incumbents in regional executive elections, their experimentation with political parties went in vain. Yurii Matochkin, the Yeltsin-appointed governor of Kaliningrad province, ran an ideological campaign against the local Communist leader, Yurii Semenov.[60] To this end, Matochkin assembled an electoral bloc, Amber Territory of Russia, comprising the local branches of the NDR, the DVR, Yabloko, Forward, Russia! and a number of other right-wing groups. The bloc was quite a useful device in the sense that Matochkin managed to defeat Semenov in the first round, blocking his participation in the second. However, Matochkin's rival in the second round, a manifestly apolitical economic manager, Leonid Gorbenko, defeated the incumbent by a 10 percent margin after receiving support from the local branch of the KPRF as well as the NPSR at the national level.[61] One could speculate that a campaign emphasizing Matochkin's managerial skills rather than his ideological commitments would have brought better results. Petr Marchenko was nominated by the NDR to wage a similarly ideological and equally unsuccessful campaign against the Communist challenger in Stavropol territory.[62] Marchenko and Matochkin received, respectively, 37.6 and 31.3 percent of the vote in the first round elections. Two other party-nominated incumbents, Askharbek Galazov in North Ossetia and Vadim Solov'ev in Cheliabinsk province, fared even worse, with respective vote shares of 9.7 percent and 16.0 percent. Thus overall, of the eight incumbents who were nominated by political parties in the second-cycle elections, two won by wide margins, two won by narrow margins, two lost by narrow margins, and two lost by wide margins. This explains the results of the statistical analysis reported above.

Therefore, political parties become insignificant because the participants in regional executive elections have an important alternative to rely upon. As we have seen, challengers' institutional affiliations, rather than their party affiliations, are important for undermining incumbents' hold on power. However, one could argue that institutional affiliations identified above are only important within the context of executive elections. In the elections of multimember bodies such as legislative assemblies, the advantages of assembly or city leadership could be very pronounced, but they were unlikely to make much difference for the composition of elected bodies. Meanwhile, regional assemblies, not the executive, are the primary institutional sites of party activities in Russia. Thus it is important to test whether the argument according to which institutional affiliations contribute to the decline of party affiliations holds if applied to legislative elections too.

Regional Legislators: Occupational Alternatives to Party Nomination

One of the most important findings in previous research on regional legislative elections in Russia is the superior level of electoral success enjoyed by administrative and economic managerial elites. Slider (1996) used data on a majority of the 1994 elections published by the analytical department of Russia's presidential administration (Smirniagin 1995) to examine the occupational backgrounds of the elected deputies. Following the taxonomy of occupational backgrounds introduced by Smirniagin, Slider found that 29.1 percent of the deputies were from "executive posts in local administrations," 23.5 percent were "managers of enterprises," 15.1 percent were from the "intelligentsia," 6.3 percent were from "commercial structures," and 2.9 percent were "lawyers." The same study broadly related the electoral prominence of administrative and economic elites to the underdevelopment of political parties at the regional level. Relying upon less comprehensive data sets from the first electoral cycle, Golosov (1997) and Hughes (1997) arrived at very similar conclusions regarding the role of the "bosses" in suppressing party development. It has been also empirically demonstrated that in the single-member plurality tier of national legislative elections, the utility of personal political resources of nonelectoral origins is greater than that of party support (Golosov 2002). In this study, I will analyze the occupational backgrounds of the regional legislators elected in the second electoral cycle not so much to establish whether the "elite colonization" of the assemblies persisted, but rather to examine its consequences for party development more closely than has been done in previous research. As a result of setting this specific research agenda, I had to redefine previously used occupational categories in accordance with the pivotal concept of this study, party utility. Overall, I analyzed the occupational backgrounds of 3,420 deputies elected to the regional assemblies in eighty-four regions that held legislative elections in the course of the second electoral cycle. For technical reasons related to data availability, I had to exclude the two elections held in Chechnya, the 1996 elections in Sverdlovsk province, and the 1998 elections in Vologda province.[63] At the same time, I included information on some of the deputies who gained their seats in by-elections, a category that was omitted from my analysis in Chapter 3. The overall number of party nominees in the data set is 636; 427 of them were nominated by the KPRF or other organizations in the KPRF conglomerate, and 209 by other parties. The percentage share of party nominees among all deputies, 18.6, is smaller than the average percentage share reported in Table 3.7. The principal reason for this discrepancy is related not to the above-mentioned differences in the data sets but rather to the difference between the modes of data aggregation. In particular, some of the assemblies with unusually large numbers of deputies, such as in Bashkortostan and Dagestan, did not score high on party representation.

Deputies' occupational statuses were established on the basis of their self-stated professional backgrounds, which alongside some other essential data such as the date of birth, the form of nomination, and occasionally party membership, were legally required to be identified on the ballot paper. The regional electoral commissions or the Central Electoral Commission of Russia officially published these data. One serious limitation that stems from this method of data collection is that, being free to state any professional backgrounds they found more appealing to the electorate, the incumbent legislators often preferred to describe themselves by their professional statuses outside of the legislature. Thus the category of

legislators below includes only the minority of legislative incumbents—
that is, those who chose to be described in this way on the ballot papers. Of
course, making such a choice was indicative in itself, which defines the category not only in formal but also in substantive terms. Specifically, individuals who identified themselves as incumbent legislators either did not hold
jobs outside of the assemblies, or found these jobs not very important for
the purpose of appealing to the electorate. Both their actual occupations
and electoral prospects were related to the fact of legislative incumbency.
Other incumbents apparently had different resources to rely upon. Thus,
while the aggregate data reported below do not allow for estimating the
advantage of incumbency in Russia's regional legislative elections, they are
quite suitable from the standpoint of the principal goal of my analysis: estimating the varying levels of party utility for the different occupational categories of regional legislators.

What kinds of candidates are most likely to fare well in regional legislative elections without relying upon party affiliations? The previous section of this chapter suggests several categories that are worth examining
from this perspective. Of course, legislative leaders are too few to make a
significant difference, even though it can be plausibly suggested that their
reelection bids are normally successful. Naturally, national Duma deputies
participate in regional legislative elections on very rare occasions, such as
if they have in mind winning not only assembly seats but also assembly
chairmanships.[64] The three remaining categories, however, are large
enough to make a significant difference in legislative elections. These are
city leaders, officials, and businesspeople. The first of these categories,
however, has to be broadened in order to fit into the new empirical field.
Within the context of executive elections, there is only one kind of city that
provides its leaders with superior resources, the capital city of a region.
Within the context of legislative elections, however, leadership in much
smaller cities, rural districts, and even villages may matter a lot. There is no
need to argue at length that the head of a local administration is an important figure in a given locality. As put by a Russian observer, the head of
administration in a district is "the tsar, God, and military leader."[65] His or
her prominence does not depend on the specific way of acquiring leadership, by appointment, by indirect elections, or by direct elections.

While all three ways could be found in the regions of Russia throughout the period 1993–2003, the importance of the office stemmed not only
from its political weight but also from its holder's ability to deliver certain
social services to the population. Local administrations and municipal self-
government bodies are in charge of heating, water supply, and other matters
of primary importance (Young 1997). It seems likely that since 1993, local
administrations have been taking over social services faster than they have
been able to privatize the housing and the retail sales enterprises they used

to own (J. Hahn 1994). That is why the holders of such positions can be expected to be at an advantage if they choose to contest regional legislative elections. In the empirical analysis below, the category of municipal leaders embraces not only the heads of local administrations and self-government bodies but also their deputies. The category of officials is different because it includes administrative managers of different standings in the federal, regional, and municipal bodies of government. Advantages associated with holding such offices vary depending on the available resources. At one extreme, the category includes vice governors, ministers, and heads of departments in the regional governments or administrations whose positions are quite powerful by any account. The same applies to the heads of the regional and subregional offices of certain federal agencies, such as the Pension Fund of the Russian Federation. At the other extreme, the category embraces rather modest state employees such as police officers and clerks.

When analyzing the electoral advantages of businesspeople in the previous section of this study, I tended to concentrate on the superior financial resources available to them. It appears that money is indeed a very salient factor of their success in regional executive elections, and it cannot be denied that matters of finance are important in smaller electoral arenas too. But there is more. The economic infrastructure inherited by Russia from the Soviet era is such that an industrial enterprise often provides jobs and occasionally benefits such as housing, childcare, and even healthcare to the vast majority of the population in the given locality. After communism, the value of "caring for the collective" remains deeply imbedded in the business ethic of Russia's industrial managers (Kharkhordin and Gerber 1994; Brown 1996). True, after communism, enterprise directors surrendered some of their functions related to social services to local administrations; at the same time they acquired a previously unknown tool of personal reputation building, the ability to pay wage arrears (Lehmann, Wadsworth, and Acquisti 1999). The role of economic managers in delivering social services tends to be even greater in the countryside. In the past the chairperson of a collective farm, alongside the party and soviet bodies, was instrumental in providing social benefits to the peasants (Stuart 1983). This situation, as well as the general structure of agricultural management in the country, remained largely unchanged throughout the period 1993–2003 (Barnes 1998). As used further in this study, the category of businesspeople is rather encompassing. First, I do not make any distinction among the forms of property that are attached to managerial positions in the economy. The senior managers in private enterprises, state enterprises, and agricultural cooperatives are all counted as businesspeople. Second, senior managerial positions taken into account include not only directors, chairpersons of the councils of directors, and other standings that can be unequivocally located at the top of managerial hierarchies, but also deputy directors and, in the case of industrial enterprises, heads of engineering departments. I also included all members of the governing bodies *(pravlenia)* of commercial firms. However, middle- and low-level industrial and commercial managers are included in the "social sector" category, introduced below.

For all three occupational categories identified above, party affiliation is not likely to be an important electoral resource. For municipal leaders and officials, the probable formula of electoral success is "power + social services." But for the businesspeople, it is not just money. Rather, it is "money + social services." Both formulas nicely fit into the analytical framework centered on the concept of patron-client relationships.[66] It seems that the clientelist networks currently in operation in the regions of Russia are rooted in the late Soviet period, and that their persistence has been reinforced by the continuity of subnational elite structures at the regional level (Matsuzato 1999). A concept that may provide an additional insight into this inquiry is the "multifaceted" notion of social capital.[67] Not going into the theoretical discussion of what actually constitutes social capital, for the largely empirical purposes of this analysis it is sufficient to say that the notion is normally used to refer to the advantages associated with belonging to the social networks of trust and sympathy. If municipal leaders or businesspeople win a legislative seat because of the superior financial and organizational resources available to them, then something else than social capital is in operation. Yet if they win because their positions in local social networks provide them with reputations that are sufficient for evoking trust and sympathy in the electorate, then it is likely that their social capital pays off. The problem with the occupational categories identified above is that the two aspects cannot be distinguished empirically. That is why I introduce an occupational category that, by and large, lacks the political and financial advantages, yet whose members are likely to be endowed with significant amounts of social capital, the category of medical doctors. While it is clear that medical doctors are not important political figures, their financial standing, as a result of the collapse of the Soviet healthcare system (Cassileth and Vlassov 1995), is rather disappointing. They are scarcely able to invest large personal funds into their campaigns. At the same time, they actively contest regional legislative elections and, as will be shown, win in quite significant numbers. One of the possible reasons is that the profession of medical doctors not only places them, so to say, at the interweaving of social networks, but also naturally invites trust and sympathy. This is especially so in the countryside, where the profession has been held in high respect since the nineteenth century (Pirumova 1986). If the social capital hypothesis holds, then medical doctors will skip party affiliation. If it does not, then they will be as likely to be party-nominated as several other categories identified below. It must be noted that this category, as used here, includes medical doctors in different status positions, from rank-and-file physicians to clinic directors and also a small number of paramedics.

Three categories are introduced to embrace those deputies for whom (due to the lack of political, financial, or social capital) party affiliation could be of more importance. One of them, the "social sector," includes low- and middle-level state and private firm employees plus those few pensioners and even fewer unemployed who managed to gain seats in regional legislative elections. The reason why this category is analytically central is precisely the complete lack of nonparty resources that can be attributed to the category as a whole, even though it is beyond any doubt that many individuals did possess such resources of one kind or another on a selective basis. Two additional categories occupy quite adjacent points on the scale of expected party utility, but they can be located on the opposite sides from the point hypothetically attributed to the "social sector." On the one hand, there is the category "professionals," embracing those deputies whose professional backgrounds can be hypothetically viewed as endowed with certain amounts of social capital. The most prominent groups within this category are university professors, researchers at academic institutions, journalists, and lawyers. On the other hand, there is the category "political sector," embracing those deputies whose professional backgrounds, as stated on the ballot papers, are primarily political. This category embraces employees of regional legislative assemblies, aides to national and regional legislators, activists of political and public organizations (trade unions included), and members of municipal assemblies. For this category, as is only natural to expect, party nomination is of primary value.

Table 5.4 reports the results of the empirical inquiry that utilized the analytical framework introduced above. Quite in line with previous research on the occupational structures of regional legislative assemblies, the data confirm the prominence of power and business elites. Overall, the three politically and/or financially resourceful categories of deputies (businesspeople, municipal leaders, and officials) held more than 60 percent of seats in the second-cycle legislatures. In the context of this analysis, however, it is more important to look at the shares of party nominees within each of the categories. In this respect, the data fully confirm the expectations stated above. The most politically resourceful category, municipal leaders, scores lower than any other on this parameter. Then follow officials, with their more limited yet sizable power resources, and businesspeople, with their combination of financial and social capital. Perhaps the most interesting finding is that among medical doctors, the share of party nominees is only marginally larger than among businesspeople, which indicates that social capital is quite an efficient substitute for party-related resources. The shares of party nominees among legislators and professionals are

Table 5.4   Occupational Backgrounds of Regional Legislators and Party Representation by Occupational Categories, 1995–1999

Occupational Category	Percentage Share of Deputies Belonging to This Category	Percentage Share of Party Nominees Within This Category
Businesspeople	41.6	13.2
Municipal leaders	10.7	6.0
Social sector	9.4	37.1
Officials	8.9	12.4
Legislators	8.8	27.0
Medical doctors	7.3	13.7
Professionals	7.2	27.8
Political sector	6.1	41.0
Total/Average for all categories	100.0	18.6

Note: 3,420 individual observations.

almost identical, which places both categories somewhere in the middle of my scale. This is fully consistent with my expectations regarding the latter category, but looks puzzling in respect to the former. This puzzle, however, will be addressed in Chapter 6. Finally, and as expected again, the largest shares of party nominees can be found among the social and political sectors of the regional legislators. In fact, the prominence of power and business elites in the regional legislative assemblies of Russia is by no means unusual in comparative perspective. Similar groups are overrepresented in the legislatures of the well-established democracies too, both at the national level (Loewenberg and Patterson 1979; Norris 1997) and at the subnational level (Jewell 1982). What is different about Russia is that exactly those categories of people who possess superior electoral resources use them to skip party affiliation.

In order to clarify this finding, I introduced an additional distinction into the category of party-nominated deputies. I analyzed the occupational backgrounds of the deputies elected as nominees of the KPRF and related groups, as nominees of other parties, and as independents. The results, reported in Table 5.5, suggest not only that the recruitment patterns are different but also that there is a clear opposition between the KPRF conglomerate and independents, with other parties representing an intermediate case. True, the largest single category is invariably that of businesspeople. However, they constitute a far smaller share among the KPRF conglomerate deputies than among independents. Overall, businesspeople, municipal leaders, and officials constitute 66.4 percent of independents but only 43.0 and 37.0 percent of the non-KPRF and KPRF deputies respectively. At the same time, the joint share of social and political sectors rises from 11.8 per-

Table 5.5   Occupational Backgrounds of Regional Legislators by Political Affiliations, 1995–1999

Occupational Category	KPRF Conglomerate	Other Parties	Independents
Businesspeople	28.1	32.5	44.4
Municipal leaders	3.3	3.8	12.4
Social sector	21.8	12.4	7.3
Officials	5.6	6.7	9.6
Legislators	13.6	11.0	7.9
Medical doctors	3.7	8.6	7.7
Professionals	11.0	10.0	6.4
Political sector	12.9	14.8	4.5
Total	100.0	99.8[a]	100.2[a]
Number of observations	427	209	2,784

Note: a. Does not sum to 100.0 percent because of rounding.

cent among independents to 27.2 percent among the noncommunists, and to 34.7 percent among the KPRF conglomerate nominees. Here again, the very fact that the KPRF advances nonelite candidates is scarcely surprising. That is what left-wing parties are expected to do. What is important and quite unusual about Russia is that elite candidates choose to run as independents. Given the superior electoral chances of these candidates, this alone explains why the gains of party nominees in regional legislative elections are so modest. Thus high statuses in key political hierarchies and/or superior financial resources substitute for party affiliations. But perhaps even more important, other substitutes are available too. In particular, it has been demonstrated that candidates in possession of social capital are also unlikely to run as party nominees.

*   *   *

In Chapter 4, I arrived at the conclusion that while party labels in the regions of Russia are not in short supply, credible party candidates are, and that those candidates who choose to run as independents can count on finding an alternative to almost any service a party can offer—provided, of course, that they can afford it, for each of these alternatives comes with a certain price. Hence the primary question addressed in this chapter: What allows them to get along without parties? I have demonstrated that while political parties may assume utility and thus start to form within the context of intraelite conflicts, the principal participants in the majority of such conflicts tend to rely upon superior resources provided by their institutional affiliations. In executive elections, these resources substitute for party affiliations in two senses. First, by ensuring the organizational and financial superiority of their holders, they allow them to conduct electoral campaigns without party assistance. Second, information conveyed to the voters by the labels attached to institutions and businesses is at least as valuable as information conveyed by party labels. The same applies to regional legislative elections, where party affiliation is most likely to be skipped precisely by those categories of candidates who have something else to rely upon. In fact, in these smaller and less important electoral arenas, available substitutes for party affiliation tend to proliferate, as the advantages of administrative and economic power become complemented by the advantages of social capital.

Notes

1. For an overview of the early phase of party formation in Sverdlovsk province, see Fish 1995: 139–142, 148–156. See also Gel'man and Golosov 1998; and Startsev 1999.

2. V Rossii sozdana novaia respublika, *Kommersant-Daily,* October 28, 1993. For Rossel's exposition of the concept of the republic, see Ural'skaia respublika—put k territorial'nomu ustroistvu i upravleniiu Rossiiskim gosudarstvom, *Ural'skaia respublika i problemy stanovlenia rossiiskoi gosudarstvennosti* Ekaterinburg: n.p., 1993, pp. 6–16.

3. Eduard Rossel zaiavil o gotovnosti otstaivat v parlamente ideiu "Ural'skoi respubliki," *Kommersant-Daily,* December 21, 1993.

4. V Ekaterinburge sostoialos pervoe zasedanie Sverdlovskoi oblastnoi dumy, *Rossiiskaia gazeta,* April 30, 1994.

5. Vozvrashchenie v politiku, *Kommersant,* June 29, 1994.

6. Zvonok v Amsterdam, *Ural'skii rabochii* (Ekaterinburg), May 17, 1995.

7. "Partia nachal'stva" vybory ne proigrala, *Moskovskii komsomolets,* August 23, 1995.

8. V Ekaterinburge k vlasti prikhodit novaia komanda, *Izvestia,* November 9, 1995.

9. Sverdlovskaia oblast v fevrale 1996 goda, *Politicheskii monitoring,* February 1996.

10. Ekaterinburg—bastion edinstva demokratov, *Vek,* April 5, 1996.

11. Eduard Rossel, *Kommersant-Daily,* May 18, 1996.

12. Politicheskaia zhizn regionov: Ekaterinburg, *Kommersant-Daily,* April 23, 1996.

13. Vzgliad so starta, *Vechernii Ekaterinburg,* March 4, 1998.

14. Gubernator i mer nachali predvybornuiu voinu, *Kommersant,* February 12, 1998.

15. Vertikali NDR, *Oblastnaia gazeta* (Ekaterinburg), February 13, 1998.

16. Situatsia izmenilas do neuznavaemosti, *Delovoi ekspress,* April 22, 1998.

17. Ta zavodskaia prokhodnaia, *Ural'skii rabochii* (Ekaterinburg), May 20, 1998.

18. Gosudarstvennuiu vlast chestnym liudiam, *Ural'skii rabochii* (Ekaterinburg), April 3, 1998.

19. Stepashina zhdut v Sverdlovskoi oblasti, *Nezavisimaia gazeta,* July 21, 1999.

20. Opasnaia igra, *Oblastnaia gazeta* (Ekaterinburg), September 7, 1999.

21. Vybory gubernatora Sverdlovskoi oblasti, *Novaia Sibir—Molodaia Sibir* (Novosibirsk), September 17, 1999.

22. Kogda spiashchii prosnetsia, *Moskovskie novosti,* September 6, 1999.

23. Komu dostanetsia vlast v votchine prezidenta? *Liudi kak oni est,* August 23, 1999.

24. For an extensive theoretical treatment of what constitutes electoral competitiveness, see Bartolini 1995.

25. When calculating these figures, I assumed that in those cases when ethnic republics shifted from parliamentary systems to presidentialism, incumbents were heads of parliament. This, however, does not apply to those republics where, by the time of holding first direct executive elections, the positions of heads of republic had been established and the holders of such offices had been already elected by the parliaments, such as in Komi and Mordovia.

26. In the second electoral cycle, I counted Aman Tuleev, a long-standing oppositionist who was appointed as a governor three months before the elections, as a challenger. In the third electoral cycle, I assigned to the category of incumbents Konstantin Titov, who allegedly for tactical reasons resigned briefly before the elections. After that, the federal law prohibited those officials who resigned prematurely from participating in fresh elections. The 2003 elections in Belgorod province are excluded.

27. Compare with the United States (Beyle 1995).

28. Because of a lack of data, I had to exclude Chechnya from the second-cycle data set, and North Ossetia and Belgorod province from the third-cycle data set.

29. Pryzhki v meshke, *Trud,* August 11, 1995. See also 1000-letie Vladimira, *Kommersant-Daily,* September 12, 1995. For a complete list of collective members as of 2002, see Dvizhenie "Spravedlivost i narodovlastie," *Vladimirskie vedomosti* (Vladimir), March 5, 2002.

30. Avtomarafon kak oruzhie invalidov v bor'be za svoi prava, *Sovetskaia Rossia,* December 4, 1999.

31. Gennadii Churkin, *Pravda—5,* October 22, 1996.

32. Altaiskim gaidarovtsam ponravilos reshenie konstitutsionnogo suda, *Svobodnyi kurs* (Barnaul), February 15, 1996.

33. Skandal na Altae, *Kommersant-Daily,* December 26, 1995.

34. Podderzhat na vyborakh, *Vladimirskie vedomosti* (Vladimir), January 24, 2001.

35. See, for instance, Mnogo li u vas naznachentsev? *AiF—Severnyi Kavkaz* (Stavropol), October 24, 2002.

36. Gubernatorskie vybory v Smolenske, *Kommersant,* May 16, 1998.

37. Prokhorovskoe pole na Smolenshchine, *Sovetskaia Rossia,* May 12, 1998.

38. Anatolii Glushenkov: ia ochen blagodaren Yuriiu Luzhkovu, *Kommersant,* May 16, 1998.

39. Smolenshchina do, vo vremia i posle vyborov, *Interfaks AiF,* May 25, 1998.

40. "Yabloko" podderzhivaet Yakovleva na vyborakh, *Nezavisimaia gazeta,* June 1, 1996.

41. S moroznykh stupenei—v kreslo gubernatora, *Trud,* December 21, 1995.

42. Deviatyi krug po semi kholmam, *Rossiiskaia gazeta,* June 27, 1995.

43. Sostoialos zasedanie rukovoditelei, *Pravda,* November 11, 1993.

44. Lodkin was elected as a governor in April 1993.

45. Vybory—96, *Rossiiskie vesti,* November 28, 1996.

46. Poslednii brosok na zapad, *Izvestia,* September 9, 1997.

47. The Jewish autonomous province owes both its name and its status as a separate federal unit to the Soviet leadership's attempt to create a Jewish homeland in the Far East, undertaken in 1928 (Weinberg 1998). The attempt was unsuccessful. As of today, Jews constitute about 4 percent of the region's population.

48. On KPRF's support to Ishaev, see Bol'shoi tur, *Sovetskaia Rossia,* December 7, 1996.

49. Vsekh zhdut urny, *AiF—Dal'info* (Vladivostok), August 7, 1996.

50. "Chelovek slova" ne byl vstrechen molchaniem, *AiF—Dal'info* (Vladivostok), December 21, 1995.

51. Biulleten bol'shoi—vsem mesta khvatit, *Birobidzhaner shtern* (Birobidzhan), August 10, 1996.

52. Kommunisty s kandidatom opredelilis, *Birobidzhaner shtern* (Birobidzhan), March 10, 2000.

53. Politicheskaia pogoda Orenburzh'ia, *Rossiiskie vesti,* August 25, 1995.

54. Serp ostalsia, a molot slomalsia, *Rossiiskie vesti,* July 21, 1995.

55. Naprasno ob"iavili mera krasnym, *Rossiiskie vesti,* November 1, 1996.

56. Blagie namerenia ot vyborov do vyborov, *Vechernii Orenburg,* August 12, 1999.

57. O zolotom zapase i dyriavom karmane, *Izvestia,* March 13, 1998.

58. Vsem vlastiam nazlo, *Itogi,* April 1, 1997.

59. Dina Oiun ozadachivaet Vladimira Putina, *Tsentr Azii* (Kyzyl), June 28, 2002.

60. Gubernskie igry v zapadnom anklave, *Izvestia,* October 3, 1996.

61. Ot Sakhalina do Kaliningrada, *Sovetskaia Rossia,* October 22, 1996.

62. Marchenko's candidacy was also endorsed by Yabloko, but not by the DVR and Democratic Russia, which supported his deputy, Aleksandr Korobeinikov. See Pripisali sebe status demokratov, *Rossiiskaia gazeta,* October 12, 1996.

63. However, the data from the 1998 elections in Sverdlovsk province and from the 1996 elections in Vologda province are included.

64. Those three national Duma deputies who actually won regional assembly seats are included in the category of legislators.

65. Cited in Evans 2000.

66. See Roniger and Gunes-Ayata 1994. For an application to contemporary Russian politics, see Afanas'ev 1997.

67. For a variety of perspectives and empirical applications, see Putnam 1993; Portes 1998; and Dasgupta and Serageldin 2000.

6

The Demand Side: Executive Control and Legislative Autonomy

While some of the functions of political parties are performed in the electoral arenas, politicians seek votes not because they have intrinsic value of their own, but rather because in democratic contexts, votes are necessary for obtaining power, which is exercised within institutional constraints. The first section of this chapter focuses on the formal, parchment institutions that exist in the regions of Russia. I empirically demonstrate that while clear manifestations of presidentialism can be found in some of the regions, this is not the case in many others, and it would be fair to say that the most widespread constitutional model on the regional level of Russia's politics is semipresidentialism. It is the constitutionally stipulated importance of the regional legislatures that makes control over them essential for maintaining the executives' political superiority. The second section examines mechanisms of control as they work in the regions of Russia. The analysis demonstrates that contexts within which political parties have been successfully used for this end are rare and unusual, while regularly employed mechanisms of control do not involve political parties. The third section provides a different perspective on the same phenomenon by investigating the role of political parties in achieving and maintaining legislative autonomy.

Political Institutions in the Regions of Russia

As demonstrated in Chapter 3, the evolution of Russia's federalism generated two principal types of regions, republics and the rest. Throughout the history of postcommunist Russia, and especially in the early years of postcommunism, the republics were largely free to set their own institutional designs, while the remaining regions stepped onto the track of institution building not only later but also under stronger constraints imposed by the federal authorities. An important peculiarity inherited by the republics from the Soviet past was the fact that by the time the old order collapsed, they already had their own constitutions. These constitutions were adopted in

1978 as part of a reform that was launched with the adoption of the 1977 constitution of the Soviet Union and the 1978 constitution of Russia. In the same way that the Russian constitution was virtually identical to the Soviet one, the constitutions of the republics (then autonomous republics) copied the Russian constitution and thereby each other. All of them, while stipulating the leading role of the communist party, established political systems that were formally based upon the notion of omnipotent assemblies, the soviets. From a constitutional standpoint, the governments of the republics were executive committees not only appointed by the soviets but also subject to unlimited censure at any time. In 1988 the republics entered the stage of constitutional amendment, which in its early phase simply followed constitutional reforms implemented at the upper levels of the Soviet quasi-federation, the Soviet Union and the union republic of Russia. It was only in the second half of 1990 that each of the republics assumed a specific pace of constitutional reform. By that time, the articles stipulating the leading role of the communist party were, as a rule, already removed from their constitutions.

The first series of independent constitutional amendments undertaken by the republics are of little interest for this analysis because they concerned mostly declarations of sovereignty, elevating their status by dropping the word "autonomous" from their official names and stipulating the supremacy of their laws over those of the Soviet Union and Russia. The second series of amendments can be related to the establishment of directly elected presidencies in some of the republics, a process briefly reviewed in Chapter 3. It is important to mention here that shifts toward systems with directly elected presidents were accompanied with the enactment of new constitutions in relatively few republics, such as in Bashkortostan, where the two events occurred simultaneously, and in Altai Republic, Buriatia, and Komi, where presidential elections took place to enact the rules set by recently adopted new constitutions. In the vast majority of cases, directly elected presidencies arrived as a result of amending the 1978 constitutions. In fact, these constitutions survived for a long time in quite a number of the republics, and one of them, Karelia, was still using a thoroughly amended and reamended version of its 1978 constitution in 2003. Only three republics, Sakha, Tatarstan, and Tyva, adopted new constitutions before December 1993. It seems that the major event that urged many of the republics to abandon their old constitutions was the national political crisis of 1993. In 1994, new constitutions were adopted in as many as seven republics, and four more joined them in 1995. The late switchers were Karachaevo-Cherkesia, Altai Republic, Kabardino-Balkaria, and Chuvashia, which kept their 1978 constitutions up to March 1996, June 1997, September 1997, and November 2000 respectively.

The level of continuity between the 1978 constitutions and their amended versions should not be overestimated. There is indeed little in common between the Karelian constitution still in effect in 2003 and its predecessor. Yet this continuity should not be underestimated either. The very fact that the republics were so slow to adopt new constitutions reflects one of the most salient characteristics of regime transition in this category of Russia's constituent units, an unusually high level of old elites' survival. This in turn can be related to the high rate of survival of those individuals who effectively headed the republics throughout the latest phase of the Soviet system. In accordance with the 1978 constitutions, these individuals were institutionally located in the soviets, not in the executives, because the constitutionally defined senior officials in the republics were the chairpersons of the Supreme Soviets. By virtue of holding these positions, they acquired political resources that enabled them to remain in control of local power hierarchies after the communist party and its mechanisms of political integration collapsed. A shift to directly elected presidencies, which occurred in the majority of the republics, did not elevate new elites to power either. Rather, they institutionally redefined the incumbent heads of republics and the existing power hierarchies. The chairpersons of the Supreme Soviets or new legislatures that replaced them won the first presidential elections in as many as thirteen republics. Cases when legislative leaders did not win the first executive elections are few, and their miscellaneous nature is quite in keeping with their exceptionality. These are Ingushetia, where there was no chairperson of the Supreme Soviet because the Supreme Soviet as such did not exist; Karachaevo-Cherkesia, the only republic with an appointed head of administration; and three republics where unusually intensive intraelite conflict enhanced the electoral strength of relative outsiders, Kalmykia, Chuvashia, and Khakasia. The head of the executive won presidential elections in only one republic, Tyva. Thus the soviet hierarchies, as impersonated by their heads, survived in almost the two-thirds of the republics. The migration of legislative leaders to directly elected executive positions had an important consequence for institution building in the republics. The causal logic generating this consequence can be formally explicated in the following way.

Consider the chairperson of a republic's Supreme Soviet who is contemplating a switch to a directly elected presidency. The reasons for such switches varied. In most cases, they could be related either to the enhancement of the symbolic capital in possession of the given politician by conferring on the chairperson an additional portion of legitimacy, as happened in Tatarstan, or to political pressure from the federal authorities, at times quite explicit in their will to get rid of the "Soviet legacies" in the republics. The strongest pressure of this kind was exerted in the aftermath of the October 1993 events in Moscow, which explains why so many republics adopted new constitutions in December 1993 through 1994. What is important here is that the heads of the Supreme Soviets had no reason to consider a switch to a directly elected presidency as an effective way of enhancing their own power. In fact, they were already in control. Thus the primary consideration that had to be entered into a legislative leader's calculus was how to avoid risks associated with constitutional reform, not how to maximize power for the newly established office. As I have already mentioned, in three regions such risks materialized in full, with people from outside the existing elites taking power. In such cases, legislatures remained the outgoing elites' last resort, as epitomized by the fact that the elected president of Kalmykia started his activities in office with pressing the Supreme Soviet into self-dissolution. Thus for a head of a Supreme Soviet, a rational risk-aversion strategy could be to go on with establishing a directly elected presidency, to invest all efforts into winning the position, but at the same time to constitutionally ensure the legislature's significant powers. There was a secondary consideration that, upon entering the calculus of the legislative leader, could entail the same conclusion. Political resources already in his possession were all related to legislative leadership. Not only was he already in control of the assembly, but he could also ensure that his allies, not his opponents, would take over the legislature upon his departure. As a result, a slow reform involving constitutional amendment rather than profound change emerged as an acceptable option. The logic explicated above allows for making a prediction that strong presidencies are not likely to be found in the republics. The empirical proof will be provided further in this section. Already at this point, however, it becomes possible to suggest that the legacies of the Soviet-era quasi-parliamentarism are not to be discarded in the analyses of the republics' institutional design.

This logic does not necessarily apply to regions other than republics. It is possible only to speculate about what would have happened had the regions been allowed to undertake executive elections as early as in 1991. I suggest that, had this been the case, the legislative leaders would have won many senior executive positions outright, with all the consequences observed in the republics coming as a logical attachment. In fact, however, the national legislature delegated the authority to appoint regional executives to the president of Russia. Thus the two principal actors in the regional political arenas—the appointed executives and the soviets, most of which were elected in March 1990—were defined by federal law, not by the regions' own institution-building efforts. The power to define their own institutional design was first vested into the regions other than republics by a law passed by the Supreme Soviet of Russia on March 5, 1992, "The Law on Territorial, Provincial Soviet of People's Deputies and on the Territorial, Provincial Administration." As follows from the title, the law applied to territories and provinces, and it was extended to Moscow, St. Petersburg, and the Jewish autonomous province, but not to the autonomous districts. Article 4 of the law stipulated that "a territory or a province has its statute that, on the basis of the Constitution of the RSFSR and of the laws of the RSFSR, establishes the outline *(skhemu)* of territorial/provincial government, specifies the structure, functions, and powers of the soviet and administrative bodies, the rights and responsibilities of their heads, the forms of citizens' involvement in the activities of the territorial, provincial soviets and of the territorial, provincial administrations." The statutes were to be adopted by the acting soviets and, in the course of no more than one month, registered by the presidium of the Supreme Soviet of Russia. This body was entitled to deny registration to those statutes that were not in accordance with the federal law, which could be overruled only by the Constitutional Court of Russia.

The law was both drafted and adopted by a legislative body that was increasingly involved in political conflict with the national executive. This explains the legislature's desire to constrain the powers of the executive-appointed governors. The law identified the soviets as "the holders of all rights of property" in the regions, even though this right was not to be extended to the federally owned objects. This established the soviets as primary movers in the process of privatization. They were also vested with vast powers in such critical domains as budgetary policy, subnational taxation, and financial policy. The second section of the law regulated the appointment powers of the soviets. First, the soviets were entitled to a vote of no confidence in the executive by a two-thirds majority, which entailed their demotion in the course of two weeks. Second, the soviets had the power to establish the outline of the administration—that is, to determine its internal organization including the number of deputy heads and the structure of departments. Third, the soviets confirmed the appointment of the first deputy head of administration. Fourth, they confirmed the appointment of the heads of the following crucial departments: finance, social protection of the population, internal affairs, justice, and state property management. Fifth, the holders of two of these positions, the heads of the departments of finance and social protection, could be dismissed only with the consent of the soviets. Finally, the law stipulated that any of the officials in the executive could be subjected to a vote of no confidence by the soviet. Thus the powers of the soviets were quite comprehensive. The law thoroughly ignored the fact that by the time it was passed, nearly all the chief executives in the regions to which it applied were the president's appointees. Instead, it stipulated for the elective executive. This did not remove Yeltsin's appointees but was not absolutely inconsequential either, for the law implied that once a governor received a vote of no confidence and was thus demoted, his successor had to be determined by popular vote. At the same time, the law legitimized the office of the governor as the principal executive office at the regional level by stipulating that "the head of the territorial or provincial administration directs the activities of the territorial or provincial administration in accordance with the principles of undivided authority *(edinonachalie)* and is responsible for its due performance" (Article 36). This was a major departure from the 1978 constitution of Russia, which vested executive powers in the soviet's executive committees rather than in individual senior executives.

Once the law came into effect, regions were free to adopt statutes of their own, and some of them started to draft such statutes. For instance, the Cheliabinsk province soviet, jointly with the representatives of the regional executive, drafted a statute that was discussed at the soviet's meeting in November 1992. As it seems from an observer's account of the meeting, the executive was not very satisfied with the preliminary result, alleging that the draft cited at length the constitution of Russia and many federal laws, but did not "say anything specific about the functions of local authorities."[1] This is a statement that points directly to the major problem with drafting regional statutes as occurred in 1992–1993. The statutes were to be adopted by the soviets. However, the amount of power vested in the soviets by the 1992 law was such that they hardly had any incentive to adopt local basic laws that would change the status quo, while adopting statutes simply reproducing the norms of the federal law did not make much sense, on the one hand, and could have been objected to by the executives who wanted to enhance their powers, on the other hand. Stoner-Weiss (1997: 79) mentions that in all four of the regions she visited in the course of field research in Russia, the local officials cited the 1992 law as the authority for their governments' operations. The only region that actually passed its own basic law before December 1993 was Sverdlovsk province. Its basic law—that is, the ill-fated constitution of the Urals republic mentioned in the previous chapter—was not enacted due to the intervention of federal authorities. Yet another region that moved in the same direction was Vologda province. After holding a referendum on transforming the province into a republic, which was overwhelmingly supported by the voters on April 25, 1993,[2] its legislature drafted and was fully prepared to adopt the constitution of the Vologda republic.[3] While not so well articulated, similar considerations of deriving more autonomy from Moscow apparently drove the statute drafting process in Irkutsk province, where it was reported that the draft "was at variance with the center on the issues of property on local natural resources and the region's right to engage independently in foreign trade."[4] Such considerations became largely irrelevant in the aftermath of the October 1993 crisis, when even the republics became quite cautious in expressing their dissatisfaction with federal authorities. By the end of 1993, therefore, none of the regions actually succeeded in adopting its statute. At the same time, the 1993 crisis and the constitutional reform that followed jointly produced new, apparently more powerful incentives for institution building in the regions.

In the process of the constitutional reform, the federal executive dissolved or charged the regional executives with the dissolution of soviets. According to a executive decree titled "On the Bases of Organization of State Power in the Subjects of the Russian Federation," issued on October 22, 1993, the soviets were to be replaced with new representative bodies that were to be elected from December 1993 through March 1994. While the decree did not directly apply to the republics, it "recommended" them to proceed with constitutional reform along the same guidelines. The decree contained several specific regulations regarding the new legislative bodies. Their size could not exceed fifty members, and their terms were set for two years. Clearly, these provisions degraded the political standing of the legislatures. While the decree said little about the powers of the legislatures, they appeared to be significantly reduced. Their budgetary powers were reconfirmed with a clarification that the budget had to be introduced by the executive, while their powers applying to subnational taxation and finance were circumscribed by indication that the related regional laws could only be adopted if introduced or preliminarily approved by the executive. Regarding the previously sweeping appointment powers of the legislatures, the decree bluntly stated that the composition of the regional administration was to be determined by the head of administration (Article 9). The decree also greatly enhanced the legislative powers of the executives by stipulating that no legislation could become law without the chief executive's signature. The executive's refusal to sign legislation could be reversed only by a two-thirds majority vote in the assembly (Article 4). According to the decree, the 1992 law remained in force insofar as it did not contradict the decree. Since, however, the 1992 law was a detailed document of sixty-eight articles, while the decree itself contained only ten, the federal executive had to determine the scope of the contradictions in a more detailed way. This was achieved by issuing another decree on December 22, 1993. The decree listed those articles of the 1992 law that the decree made ineffective. Now it became clear that the legislatures were deprived of most of their powers. These included the power to act as "the holder of all rights of property"; some other powers in the field of economic policy; the powers to confirm administrative appointments; all corresponding censure powers; and the power to remove the governor by a vote of no confidence. Thus, according to the decree, the new assemblies had to operate as purely legislative bodies, with almost no nonlegislative powers whatsoever, even though they were still entitled to determine the internal organization of the executive by establishing its "outline." At the same time, their powers in the fields of regional legislation, budgetary processes, and subnational taxation were circumscribed to a much lesser degree.

The 1993 federal constitution stipulated that the republics had their constitutions, while all other regions, including the autonomous districts, were entitled to adopt their statutes. According to the constitution, there was only one way of adopting the statutes, by legislatures. Apparently, this disappointing circumstance was not fully understood by many of the regional executives during the initial phase of constitutional reform, when new legislative assemblies were not in existence. Several regional administrations were quick enough to draft the statutes and schedule referenda on their adoption to be held concurrently with the March 1994 regional legislative elections.[5] These attempts went in vain. The executives had to accept the unavoidability of the newly elected legislatures' participation in statute drafting and adoption. After the legislatures were indeed elected, the process slowly moved on. Only twelve regions adopted their statutes by the end of 1994. The most productive years in terms of regional institution building were 1995 and 1996, when twenty-eight and seventeen statutes were adopted respectively. The remaining eleven regions adopted their statutes later. The latest among them was Vladimir province, which lived without its own statute up to August 2001. In fact, quite similar to what happened in 1992–1993, the regions were not required to move fast. Up to October 1999, they could use the 1992 law, as amended by the 1993 decree. Their willingness to adopt statutes was caused not by pressures from the federal authorities but rather by incentives of their own.

Clearly the 1993 amendments to the 1992 law were expedient for the regional executives but not for legislatures. Thus the process of statute drafting and adoption emerged as a natural frontline in the legislatures' fight to regain some of their previously held powers, and at the same time as a bastion of the executives' resistance. That is why the process of regional institution building was so protracted. The group of those regions that adopted their statutes by the end of 1994 included two basic types: those where the new legislatures were thoroughly controlled by the executives (such as Novgorod province), and those where the new legislatures were overwhelmingly controlled by antiexecutive majorities (such as Tambov province). In correspondence with this division, from the very start the process of institution building in the regions produced two types of statutes, those that were quite in keeping with the 1993 decrees and those that generally ignored the decrees by introducing norms similar to those of the nonamended version of the 1992 law. But as follows from the chronological outline above, in the majority of regions power balances were more complicated, which resulted in protracted struggles and stalemates. For instance, in Kemerovo province, a struggle between the Yeltsin-appointed governor and the opposition-controlled legislature postponed the adoption of the statute for more than a year.[6] In several regions, the legislatures simply refused to subject the adopted statutes to the chief executive's signature, while in other regions the governors refused to sign them.[7] While intraelite conflicts at the regional level definitely added to the intensity of these struggles, there were instances when even consensual elites became divided on the issues of institution building. Consider the case of the region that was the latest to adopt its statute, Vladimir province. The region's legislature, while hostile to the Yeltsin appointee, was continuously composed of the supporters of its left-wing governor elected in 1996. However, when it came to statute drafting, the drafts produced by the executive and by the legislature were incompatibly different. The legislature's draft provided for its powers to confirm senior administrative appointments, to vote no confidence in the governor and all other members of the administration, and to make rulings on all issues not resolved by federal or regional law. The executive's draft denied the legislature of the first two of these powers, granted the third of them to the executive itself, and in addition entitled the executive to dissolve the legislature.[8] Thus even in the absence of significant political conflicts, the institutionally embedded interests of the political actors ignited controversies among them.

A weapon actively employed in these struggles, often but not necessarily to the benefit of the executives, was the Constitutional Court of Russia. In January and February 1996, respectively, it issued rulings on the recently adopted statutes of Altai territory and Chita province. The Altai legislators went especially far in their effort to undermine the Yeltsin-appointed executive by adopting a statute that literally left no place for him. This was the only statute in the whole history of Russia's regional institution building that stipulated for an indirect election of the chief executive by the legislature itself. The ruling of the court stated that this norm was unconstitutional. In addition, the ruling denied the legislature the power to remove the head of administration and several high-standing executive officials, the list of whom coincided with the list provided in the 1992 law, by voting no confidence in them. It also reconfirmed the legislative powers of the executive by stipulating that the regional laws had to be signed by the head of administration, not only by the chairperson of the assembly. At the same time, the ruling agreed with the Altai legislators rather than with the executive regarding some of the legislature's powers in the field of economic policy. The ruling on the statute of Chita province stipulated that the legislature's right to confirm the appointments of the executive officials contradicted the principle of separation of powers. Thus in general the Constitutional Court constrained the legislatures in their attempts to recover the vast powers granted to the soviets by the 1992 law. Note, however, that unlike laws, these rulings were not likely to be considered as binding decisions regarding the statutes of those regions to which they did not directly apply. In a situation when the legislature assumed powers already denied to it by the rulings, the executive had the option of going to the

Constitutional Court with good chances of winning the case. Yet if the executive restrained, the statute remained in effect. For instance, the statute of Amur province, as adopted in December 1995, supplied its legislature with some of the rights explicitly denied to it by the Constitutional Court. According to an observer's report, the legislators reacted to this in cold blood: "That is not our problem. . . . Let the constitutional court repeal our statute, and then we'll see."[9]

While institution building in the regions proceeded on its own, the national legislature was involved in a prolonged struggle with the executive on the legislation that was to replace the 1992 law and the 1993 decrees. In April 1995, the Duma, or rather the left-wing majority of its deputies, passed the document. It is not surprising that the document granted comprehensive powers to the regional legislatures. In particular, the draft preferred by the Duma majority stipulated that the heads of administration could be elected either directly or by regional legislatures or, finally, by specially convened assemblies.[10] It is also not surprising that the Federation Council and then the president declined to accept it. An amended draft was passed by the Duma in May 1998, only to be vetoed by the Federation Council. It was only in October 1999 that the new law, "On the General Principles of Organization of the Legislative (Representative) and Executive Organs of State Power of the Subjects of the Russian Federation," came into effect. In contrast to its predecessors, the law equally applied to the republics and other regions of Russia. It established that the regions had to have directly elected senior officials or heads of executive bodies of power. They also had to elect legislatures that retained all previously held powers in the fields of budgetary policy and subnational taxation. Speaking of the appointment powers of the legislatures, they were expected not only to "determine the structure of the highest body of the executive power of the region" but also to issue resolutions that would "appoint and dismiss individual officeholders or confirm their appointments if such an order of appointment is stipulated by the Constitution of the Russian Federation, the federal law, or the statute (constitution) of the subject of the Russian Federation" (Article 5). In fact, this ambiguous formulation ultimately legitimized much of the appointment powers taken by the legislatures in 1994–1998. The legislatures were also entitled to vote no confidence in those officials whose appointment needed their confirmation. Yet another power provided to the legislatures was to vote no confidence in the elected chief executives. In Article 19, however, the law circumscribed this right by stating that the grounds for a vote of no confidence could be sufficient only in two cases: first, if the executive issued acts violating Russia's constitution, the region's statute, or other laws, provided that the fact of violation was established by court and that the acts were not amended in the course of one month after the court's decision; and second, if the executive grossly violated federal or regional law, federal presidential decrees, or federal resolutions in a way that "entailed massive violation of citizen rights and freedoms." Thus the law effectively provided for the possibility of an impeachment procedure, while ruling out the possibility of a vote of no confidence for political reasons. The executives, in turn, were entitled to dissolve the legislatures on the same grounds.

In 2000–2002, the 1999 law was amended several times. However, these amendments were unrelated to the models of separation of power in the regions. Therefore, the 1999 law provided the legal framework within which the regional branches of power were expected to operate throughout the third electoral cycle. The law established a two-year transition period in the course of which the regions were obliged to amend their legislation in correspondence with it, to which the regions responded at different paces and in different ways. Twelve regions went as far as to adopt entirely new constitutions or statutes. Other regions amended their already existing legislation. One of the two republics where there was no directly elected chief executive, Udmurtia, established a presidential system in accordance with the 1999 law, even though the second such republic, Dagestan, did not. A provision of the 1999 law almost universally adopted in the regions was the above-cited clause on impeachment, always in parallel with the executives' assembly dissolution powers. As far as assembly appointment powers were concerned, regional political contexts, rather than the provisions of the federal law (which were indeed quite ambiguous in this respect), determined the scope of constitutional amendment. Unfortunately, literally no systematic empirical research has been conducted on this crucial phase of institution building in Russia's regions,[11] and even fragmented evidence is quite scarce. From this evidence, however, it appears that the general trend was a shift toward enhancing the executives' powers at the expense of the legislatures, which logically corresponds to the process of the political reinforcement of the executive as described in the previous chapter. What is empirically observable is the general result of this process.

For my analysis of the regional models of separation of powers, I used a comprehensive collection of the regional constitutions and statutes published on the Internet by the Foundation for the Development of Parliamentarism in Russia.[12] When accessed in April 2002, the collection contained the documents as they were amended or adopted anew by June–July 2001, that is, by the time the deadline for amending the regional legislation set by the 1999 law was within sight. As a methodological foundation of my analysis, I employed, even though in a significantly modified way, a comparative framework developed and applied for a cross-national study of the powers of the presidency (Shugart and Carey 1992), which makes it imperative to briefly address the underlying theory. In their study, Shugart and Carey identify four "regimes," or constitutional models, on the basis of such parameters as separation of assembly and cabinet survival, and president's authority over cabinet.[13] Two of these regimes are characterized by near-zero values of the latter parameter. One of them, premier-presidential, exists if the government is subject to assembly confidence and can be removed by it, which signifies a full-fledged governmental responsibility to the assembly, even though the elected president not only exists but also possesses considerable powers. The second regime, assembly-independent, bears some semblance to what can be found in contemporary Dagestan, a single case that will not be analyzed at any length. It is therefore of little interest for this study. In contrast, the third regime, presidential, can be found in regions of Russia in quite significant numbers. In its pure form, it can be attributed to all those regions where assemblies have almost no say regarding the composition of the executive, leaving aside their right to determine the administrations' and governments' "general outlines." In those cases when assemblies are endowed with powers to appoint, dismiss, and censure the executive, president-parliamentary regimes are in place. Sartori (1997) rejects the idea of classifying constitutional regimes according to the differences in who controls the origin and survival of the executive and assembly, relying instead on induction from the individual cases that he considers prototypical. This leaves him with the concept of semipresidentialism as introduced by Duverger (1980). The two concepts, while being built on different theoretical premises, partially overlap on their empirical referents, which is why Russia as a whole has been characterized in both ways (Shugart 1996; Elgie 1999). However, the concepts suggested by Shugart and Carey better fit into those comparative perspectives that make differentiation between premier-presidential and president-parliamentary regimes empirically relevant.

The basis for identifying different regime types is the scope of separation of assembly and the executive survival, not the scope of legislative powers at the disposal of the executive.[14] Thus later in the analysis I will concentrate on the former aspect at the expense of the latter. Of course, assemblies survive separately if the executives cannot dissolve them. On this parameter, however, the 1999 law left little space for cross-regional variation and, as I have already mentioned, this provision of the law was most thoroughly reproduced in the regional statutes and constitutions. Speaking of other aspects of separate survival as identified by Shugart and Carey, there is cross-regional variation on cabinet formation, cabinet dismissal, and censure. Each of these aspects can be expressed as a continuum of assembly powers by using an interval scoring method. When devising such a method, I departed from the methodology used by Shugart and Carey in order to better address the constitutional realities of Russia's regions. On the aspect of the assembly's involvement in determining the composition of the executive, I score a 6 to those cases when assembly confirmation is needed for all senior executive positions (that is, for every single minister in a republic's government or for every single member of a regional administration); I score a 5 to those cases when assemblies confirm the appointment of prime ministers and important ministers and members of administrations as defined in the 1992 law; if in the above formulation, prime ministers are replaced with deputy heads of administrations, this produces a score of 4; I score a 3 to those cases when the assembly confirms the appointment of prime ministers but not any other executive officials; if, in a similar way, it confirms the appointment of deputy heads of administrations, the score is 2; and I score a 1 to those cases when the assemblies confirm the appointment of certain executive officials who stay lower on the administrative ladder.[15] A score of 0 means that an assembly has no appointment powers whatsoever. In addition, I introduce the score of 3.5 to reflect those relatively rare situations when constitutions or statutes did not list the executive officials whose appointments had to be confirmed by legislatures.[16] The scores for the assembly's powers to influence executive dismissals are built in exactly the same way as the previous scale—that is, I score a 6 for situations when the chief executives may dismiss any of the government ministers or members of administration only upon the assembly's consent, and down to the score of 0 when the chief executive may dismiss all of them without any assembly involvement. The scoring method for the censure powers of the assembly is based on the combination of the same scale with a number of coefficients by which the appointment/dismissal scores have to be multiplied. These coefficients are 1 if the assembly's censure powers are unrestricted; 0.5 if a vote of no confidence by the assembly leads to the official's dismissal on certain conditions, such as if only the repeatedly expressed lack of confidence in a given official within a specified period of time results in his removal; and 0.25 if the legal consequence of a vote of no confidence is not specified, which could allow for interpreting the event as inconsequential. The coefficient 0 is used if the basic law does not mention the vote of no confidence whatsoever. To illustrate the method of scoring with a hypothetical example, consider a region where the assembly's approval is needed to appoint the first deputy head of administration and important members of administration and to dismiss them, and where the assembly can vote no confidence in them on certain conditions. This combination yields the score of 4 on the first parameter, the same score on the second parameter, and $4 \times 0.5 = 2$ on the third parameter, which sum to 10.

The aggregate results of my analysis are presented in Table 6.1. I excluded from my calculations only two regions, Chechnya and Dagestan. When assessing the results, it is worth taking into account that by these scales, Russia as a whole scores 4.5 (= 3 + 0 + 1.5). This means that on the average, the regions of Russia stay further from the presidential pole of the continuum than the federal constitution provides. It is important to note that the difference between the republics and other regions is quite well articulated. On the average, the scope of legislative appointment powers in the republics is so comprehensive that most of them fall into the category of premier-presidential, rather than presidential-parliamentary, regimes. The reasons why the republics were likely to retain strong assemblies have been discussed at the beginning of this section. Now, with the proper means of measurement at hand, it becomes possible to test the model empirically. Unfortunately, the small number of republics does not allow for calculating meaningful correlation coefficients. It is feasible, however, to examine bivariate relationships in a less demanding way. To achieve that, I divide the republics into two groups, those with the aggregate scores of assembly appointment powers from 4.5 to 18, which I consider strong powers, and those with these scores below 4.5, which I do not consider strong powers. The threshold has been set arbitrarily on the level of Russia as a whole. The second variable entered into this analysis is whether the legislative leader won the first direct executive elections in the given region (1) or not (0). As it follows from Table 6.2, there is a rather strong bivariate relationship

Table 6.1   Legislative Appointment Powers in the Regions of Russia, Average Scores, ca. 2001

	Republics	Other Regions	All Regions
Executive appointment	3.7	2.2	2.6
Executive dismissal	1.2	0.6	0.7
No confidence	2.8	1.3	1.6
Total	7.7	4.1	4.9

Table 6.2   Legislative Appointment Powers and Legislative Leaders' Success in the First Direct Executive Elections in the Republics of Russia, 1991–2000

		Legislative Leader Won in First Direct Executive Elections	
		1	0
Strong Legislative Appointment Powers	1	Sakha, Tatarstan, North Ossetia, Karelia, Komi, Adygeia, Bashkortostan, Udmurtia, Mordovia, Kabardino-Balkaria, Buriatia, Altai Republic	Tyva, Karachaevo-Cherkesia
	0	Marii El	Khakasia, Ingushetia, Kalmykia, Chuvashia

between the two variables. Thus the hypothetical model explicated at the beginning of this chapter generally holds.

While on average the regions other than republics are much closer to presidentialism, their institutional designs are by no means homogeneous. Table 6.3 reports information about the scores of assembly appointment powers in different regions. In fact, in as many as thirty regions other than republics, the scores are higher than 4.5, while in only twenty-six of them are they lower than 2, which allows them to be characterized as presidential regimes. The majority of regions, like Russia as a whole, have president-parliamentary regimes. Moreover, in some of them, the scope of assembly appointment powers is such that a proper categorization would be premier-presidentialism. Setting the threshold score for this category at 9, which corresponds to a system where an assembly confirms the appointment of prime minister, can remove him by a vote of no confidence, and is entitled to confirm his removal by the chief executive, we can establish that as many as fifteen regions, six republics, and nine others are premier-presidential regimes.

Executive Control over Legislatures and Political Parties

The formal models of separation of powers are generally assumed to bear heavily on the functioning and properties of political parties. As put by Samuels (2002: 462), "presidentialism imposes an institutional configura-

Table 6.3   Numbers of Regions with the Identified Scores of Legislative Appointment Powers, ca. 2001

Scores	Number of Republics	Number of Other Regions	Number of Regions
18	2	0	2
14	0	2	2
12	1	3	4
10	2	1	3
9	1	3	4
8	3	10	13
7	0	1	1
6, 6.25	3	2	5
5	2	8	10
4, 4.25, 4.75	2	5	7
3	2	2	4
2, 2.5	0	5	5
1, 1.5	1	4	5
0	0	22	22
Total	19	68	87

tion on political parties that generates different organizational imperatives and electoral behavior." It is widely recognized that the introduction of direct presidential elections exerted the most important impact upon party formation in the United States (Beck 2000), thus determining a very specific shape of the party system that emerged in the country. Presidentialism is likely to generate nonideological vote-seeking parties instead of ideologically rooted policy-seeking parties (Strom 1990; Samuels 2002). At the same time, the need to support the government serves as an incentive to party discipline in parliamentary systems (Epstein 1964; Bowler, Farrell, and Katz 1999). Such an incentive is absent in presidential systems. When applied to several cases of presidentialism in Latin America, this line of reasoning led Linz (1990, 1994) to conclude that presidential regimes act as major obstacles to party development. Indeed, the presidents of Brazil have continuously tried to govern in an autonomous fashion above parties (Mainwaring 1993), which accounts for the low level of party discipline in Brazil (Amorim-Neto 2002). Hence there is "inverse relationship between party strength and executive strength" (Shugart 1998). By and large, the ongoing debate on the relationship between institutional design and party systems suggests that strong constitutional powers of the executive promise no good for party development, while powerful assemblies are associated with well-developed political parties. Given the observed variation of institutional designs in Russia's regions, this provides me with a hypothesis that can be easily tested empirically. To do that, I calculated a correlation coefficient between party strength, as expressed by the share of party nominees in regional legislative assemblies elected in the third cycle, and assembly strength, as expressed by the scores reported above. In keeping with theoretical expectations, there is a positive association between the two variables. Yet the association is extremely weak (the Pearson's r correlation coefficient = 0.18, insignificant). Thus it seems that institutional design in the regions of Russia is simply unrelated to political parties.

In order to explain this finding, it is worth having a second look at the political incentives that generated the observed cross-regional variation on institutional design. As we have seen, the republics were most likely to deviate from presidential forms of government under conditions when political power was concentrated in the hands of legislative leaders. In their pursuit of risk-averse institution-building strategies, legislative leaders opted for systems that allowed them to capture newly established presidencies without sacrificing their already acquired assets in the legislatures. Now it can be argued that in the long run, such a strategy could backfire. By endowing an assembly with significant appointment powers, a short-sighted institutional engineer could, at a given moment of time, confront a situation with a disobedient assembly that would form a government at its own political will, thus depriving the institutionally weak chief executive of any effective powers. The logic of such a situation can be assumed to be beneficial for party development. In order to form a responsible government on the basis of the legislative majority's expressed political preferences, the assembly would need to become politically structured. It can be argued that a certain level of intraparliamentary party organization is a necessary prerequisite for such a course of events. This scenario, if it had materialized in the republics, would have revealed a fundamental flaw in the strategy of institution building pursued by their leaders. In fact, however, nothing like this has ever happened. Apparently, the perils posed by uncontrollable assemblies under the conditions of constitutionally weak presidential powers were well understood by the republics' executives, which provided them with incentives to confront and neutralize the threat. This implies the following causal sequence: the smaller the constitutional powers of the presidency, the greater the interest of its holder in political control over the assembly, and the greater the obstacles to party development. The constitutionally weak presidents of the republics, in contrast to those of them who assumed vast constitutional powers precisely because they lacked political resources of their own, were normally well-entrenched insiders. In general, this explains why none of them failed to prevent party formation, even though some of them did fail to preserve power. Specific mechanisms, however, have to be discussed at more length. The political dimensions of these mechanisms will be addressed later in this analysis. Here, I will concentrate on the institutional devices employed to make assemblies controllable.

Consider electoral districting. In the first electoral cycle, several regions—mostly but not exclusively republics—determined the boundaries of electoral districts, or some of the electoral districts, according to the existing intraregional administrative divisions. Electoral units drawn in this way are referred to locally as administrative-territorial districts (ATDs). This practice did not go unnoticed by public opinion and the national legislature. On the one hand, there were instances when the legality of administrative-territorial districts was questioned in courts. For instance, regional legislative elections in Ul'ianovsk province were disrupted and did not take place until December 1995 because of a court decision regarding electoral districting. On the other hand, as early as 1994 a federal law established the "average norm of representation," defined as voting population size divided by the number of districts, as a standard from which the sizes of individual districts could deviate by no more than 10 percent, and by no more than 15 percent in scarcely populated or distant areas that were difficult to access *(trudnodostupnye)*. This provision was applied to all regional legislative elections, and indeed the majority of regions abolished ATDs by the beginning of the second electoral cycle. At the same time, the "one person, one vote" principle remained unimplemented in many republics. This was

achieved in two ways. Three republics, Adygeia, Komi, and Marii El, conducted their second-cycle elections by using what may be viewed as an
innovative development of the idea of a mixed electoral system. Each voter
was endowed with two votes, one of them being cast in a district drawn on
the basis of the "average norm of representation," and the other in an
administrative-territorial district. This system was also employed in the
third-cycle elections in Tatarstan. The second way to maintain ATDs was
bicameralism, with administrative-territorial districts being employed for
electing upper chambers. This system was used in the second-cycle elections in Bashkortostan, Karelia, and Sakha. Adygeia introduced an upper
chamber based on administrative-territorial districts in the third electoral
cycle. While the legality of using administrative-territorial districts for
electing single chambers remained questionable, upper chambers involving
such districts were ultimately legitimized by the Constitutional Court of
Russia when, in its ruling of June 1998, it established that the law "did not
impede the right of the subjects of the Russian Federation to . . . create a
two-chamber structure of legislative (representative) bodies, within which
one of the chambers consists of the representatives of administrative-territorial units or municipal formations." Information about the use of ATDs
for electing the legislatures of Russia's republics is provided in Table 6.4.

Consider the political consequences of using administrative-territorial
districts for regional legislative elections. Invariably this resulted in huge
overrepresentation of rural areas at the expense of urban population. Yet
another result that was observable in several republics was the overrepresentation of "titular nationalities" at the expense of ethnic Russians and

**Table 6.4   Administrative-Territorial Districts and Bicameralism in the Republics
of Russia, 1993–2001**

Region	Electoral Cycle	Share of Seats Filled from ATDs in the Single or Lower Chamber (%)	Share of Seats Filled from ATDs in the Upper Chamber (%)
Adygeia	2	40.0	N/A
Adygeia	3	0.0	100.0
Bashkortostan	1, 2	0.0	100.0
Kabardino-Balkaria	1, 2	0.0	100.0
Karelia	1, 2	0.0	100.0
Komi	1, 2	40.0	N/A
Marii El	1	73.3	N/A
Marii El	2	25.4	N/A
Sakha	1, 2	0.0	100.0
Tatarstan	1	46.9	N/A
Tatarstan	3	48.5	N/A
Chuvashia	1	59.6	N/A

certain ethnic minorities who reside primarily in urban areas, such as Jews. A more important consequence, however, can be related to the structure of electoral opportunities created by this kind of districting. When assessing this structure, it is worth taking into account that throughout most of the period under observation, federal law did not constrain local administrative elites in their pursuit of legislative seats. As demonstrated in the previous chapter, this allowed the local administrative "bosses" to become an important category of regional legislators. However, it can be argued that conditions for their success varied depending on districting. In regularly drawn districts of large size, heads of local administrations could confront each other, thus possibly clearing the way for alternative candidates; in regularly drawn districts of small size, the "bosses" could not contest every district in urban areas, where administrative units often comprise large masses of population. On the contrary, in administrative-territorial districts, the heads of local administrations emerge as natural claimants for success. If the function of such an electoral district is to provide representation to an administrative unit, then the head of that unit is an ideal representative. Consider the occupational composition of the chambers of the legislature of Bashkortostan elected in 1995 and 1999, as reported in Table 6.5. In the 1995 assembly, heads of local administrations had a near majority in the upper chamber, and in 1999 they were in an outright majority. When assessing these data, it is worth taking into account that in 1995–1999 there were no direct elections of the heads of local administrations in Bashkortostan. They were all presidential appointees, and they continued to perform their administrative functions while seated in the legislature. This means that in practice, the president exerted complete control over the upper chamber of the assembly. The constitution of Bashkortostan endows

Table 6.5   Occupational Composition of the Legislative Chambers of Bashkortostan, 1995 and 1999, Percentage Shares

	1995		1999	
Occupational Categories	Lower Chamber	Upper Chamber	Lower Chamber	Upper Chamber
Heads/deputy heads of local administrations	18.4	49.3	0.0	50.7
Businesspeople	10.5	26.7	6.7	29.2
Officials	23.7	11.6	13.3	11.8
Others	47.4	12.3	80.0	8.3
Total	100.0	99.9[a]	100.0	100.0

Note: a. Does not sum to 100.0 percent because of rounding.

its legislature with comprehensive appointment powers, with a joint score as high as 8, which places the republic somewhere on the borderline between presidential-parliamentary and premier-presidential regimes. However, the two chambers of the legislature can only exercise these appointment powers jointly. Given that one of the chambers was, in effect, constitutionally subjected to the control of the executive, its vast appointment powers were void.

The same model was applied for legislative elections in another republic with vast assembly appointment powers, Tatarstan. Constitutionally, Tatarstan is a clear-cut case of a premier-presidential regime, with an aggregate score of assembly appointment powers of 18. Unlike in Bashkortostan, its legislature is unicameral, but about half of the deputies are elected in ATDs. Like in Bashkortostan, the heads of local administrations are presidential appointees. The republic's executive seems to consider their participation in regional legislative elections as a kind of career aptitude test. Indeed, on the eve of the 1995 campaign, President Mintimer Shaimiev made it clear that he would "hardly wish to continue working with those of them who would not secure the trust of the people."[17] During the 1999 regional legislative campaign, administrative-territorial districts became a major political issue. The leaders of Tatarstan's opposition parties launched a hunger strike pressing the authorities for redistricting.[18] They also attempted to act in courts, but in the end the Supreme Court of Tatarstan ruled that ATDs were not in contradiction to the law.[19] As a result of the elections, only one of sixty-two heads of administration on the ballot lost. Shaimiev immediately dismissed him.[20]

Perhaps the most conflict-ridden elections involving the issue of districting took place in Adygeia in 2001. ATDs have been employed for electing the republic's legislature since 1995, initially along the same lines as in Tatarstan. Sensing that the system's lack of correspondence with federal legislation could backfire in the future, the president of Adygeia, Aslan Dzharimov, launched a constitutional reform that introduced bicameralism instead, with the upper chamber being elected in ATDs. The political rationale for the reform was quite transparent: without unequal districting, the republic's capital with its largely Russian and anti-Dzharimov population would have taken the upper hand in the legislature at the expense of the predominantly Adygean, pro-Dzharimov countryside and small towns.[21] Losing control over the powerful assembly would have severely reduced the scope of Dzharimov's powers. However, the Supreme Court of Adygeia, and then the Supreme Court of Russia, ruled that ATDs violated the law,[22] as a result of which the elections were postponed twice. In the end, the presiding body of the Supreme Court of Russia overruled the previous decisions, and the bicameral legislature came into existence.[23] Thus administrative-territorial districts, often in combination with bicameralism, serve as an institutional counterbalance built into constitutionally strong legislatures. This generalization can be proven statistically. I regressed the aggregate appointment power scores of the assemblies on two dummy variables, bicameralism (0 unicameral, 1 bicameral) and the use of administrative-territorial districts in unicameral assembly elections (0 no, 1 yes). Multiple regression results (ordinary least squares estimation) are reported in Table 6.6. As it follows from the results, administrative-territorial districts, in both bicameral and unicameral systems, are rather strongly associated with the forms of regional government that vest assemblies with significant appointment powers.

The institutional devices described above are not, however, available in the majority of regions. In fact, they have never been used even in many republics. This brings us to the political mechanisms of control over assemblies. Theoretically, these mechanisms need not be necessarily averse to party development. First, the executive can put an assembly under its political control by being affiliated with a manageable party of legislative majority—that is, with a party of power. Second, the executive can control an assembly by inducing an influential minority faction that, by means of bargaining on the assembly floor, would serve as an axis of a proexecutive majority coalition. Both mechanisms have actually been employed in the regions of Russia, but both are rare and unusual. In order to understand why, it stands to reason to subject such cases to deeper examination. Speaking of the first of the mechanisms identified above, there were few regions where, at a given moment of time, legislative elections resulted in the outright victories of proexecutive parties.[24] In the second electoral cycle, the winning parties were invariably either local left-wing movements or the Communist Party of the Russian Federation (KPRF).[25] The movements Fatherland in Krasnodar territory and the Bloc of Aman Tuleev in

Table 6.6   Institutional Design and Districting in the Regions of Russia, ca. 2001

Variables	Parameter Estimate		T-value
Intercept	4.26***	(0.45)	9.52
Bicameralism	6.40***	(1.68)	3.82
Administrative-territorial districts in unicameral assembly elections	6.32***	(2.33)	2.72
Number of observations	87		
R-squared	0.20		
Adj. R-squared	0.18		

Notes: The dependent variable is the aggregate score of assembly appointment powers. Parentheses indicate standard errors.
   *** Significant at 0.01

Kemerovo province have already been mentioned in the previous chapters. Fatherland won the 1998 regional legislative elections as a personal political vehicle of the governor of Krasnodar territory, Nikolai Kondratenko. In fact, soon after the event the name of Kondratenko was inserted into the official label of the movement, so that it came to be called Fatherland–Kondratenko. In Kemerovo province the label of the party of power contained no information but the governor's name on the day of the 1999 elections. Both governors were indeed extremely popular in their regions. Suffice it to say, Kondratenko won the 1996 gubernatorial elections with 82.0 percent of the vote, while Tuleev received 94.5 percent of the vote in 1997. They were obviously among the most politically resourceful governors that ever took office in the regions of Russia. On the one hand, this explains why their endorsement was so important within the context of legislative elections. On the other hand, this does not answer the question of why group endorsement of candidates was necessary at all. Both Kondratenko and Tuleev could have endorsed individual independent candidates instead, which was a strategy successfully pursued by no less popular governors in a variety of regions.

The answer to this question can be related to the peculiarities of the paths to power taken by Kondratenko and Tuleev. Both governors won in protracted struggles against Yeltsin-appointed incumbents. In these struggles, both struck political alliances with the KPRF without being party members, or indeed without being ideologically committed communists. Kondratenko was a Russian ethnonationalist with strong anti-Semitic overtones continuously present in his public rhetoric,[26] while Tuleev's personal ideology could be better characterized as nostalgic for a strong, unitary, multiethnic empire.[27] At the same time, the Krasnodar and Kemerovo branches of the KPRF were quite massive in membership and well organized,[28] and their participation in protracted wars against Yeltsin appointees further enhanced both their organizational resources and their electoral appeal. Practically, this meant that with or without the popular governors' support, the regional branches of the KPRF could claim large portions of legislative seats for themselves. At the same time, it was clear that such support could substantially contribute to the communist candidates' success. From a strictly electoral perspective, therefore, the KPRF and the governors were mutually interested in creating coalitions. The terms of contract, however, had to be defined in accordance with the amount of political resources at the disposal of the contracting sides. Hence the different shapes of proexecutive coalitions in Krasnodar territory and Kemerovo province, and hence the similarity of electoral outcomes. In Krasnodar, the regional branch of the KPRF authorized some of its members to run as nominees of Kondratenko's Fatherland and served as the principal organizational weapon of Fatherland's campaign.[29] As a reward for loyalty, the majority of Fatherland nominees were KPRF members, and Fatherland indeed won in a landslide: it gained thirty-eight of fifty contested seats, twenty-six of which were allocated to KPRF members. Formally, this provided the KPRF with a comfortable legislative majority. In fact, however, the party did not take over the assembly. When it convened for its first session, the communists tried to elect the head of the regional branch of the party as the assembly's speaker. However, Kondratenko, while not participating in the session's deliberations, made it clear that his preferred candidate was the incumbent speaker. He won by a margin of two votes, which means that Kondratenko's endorsement was imperative not only for noncommunist Fatherland nominees, but also for independents and even for some of the KPRF members.[30] Thus the KPRF won elections but Kondratenko took over the assembly.

The case of Kemerovo province is even more illuminating. In his bid for executive power, Aman Tuleev extensively relied on the support of the KPRF. In the spring of 1995, his cooperation with the party was formalized under the auspices of a new movement, People's Power, that brought under Tuleev's banners not only the KPRF itself but also a variety of trade unions, organizations of women, veterans, and youth, and the like. Under the label People's Power–The Bloc of Aman Tuleev, the movement was successful in the December 1996 elections to the legislative assembly of the region, with eight of the seventeen elected deputies being members of the movement. Soon after that, Tuleev won gubernatorial elections by a huge margin, but his relations with People's Power and its principal component, the KPRF, started to deteriorate. Indeed, the faction of the movement in the regional legislature behaved quite independently from Tuleev, and it was clear that the legislative agenda was set by the KPRF, not by the governor. On the eve of the 1999 elections Tuleev announced that he had left the movement.[31] Then he authorized the formation of a new bloc, this time called simply the Bloc of Aman Tuleev. Formally, none of the previous participants in People's Power were among the parties that formally established the bloc. These were two political nonentities, the Russian Zemstvo (Local Self-Rule) Union and the Association of Employees of the Law Enforcement Organs of Russia. In fact, however, the strategy of Tuleev aimed at causing a split in People's Power by luring some of its members into the new bloc. What a defector received in exchange was Tuleev's endorsement and thus a sizable supplement to his electoral chances. In this case, of course, party loyalty had to be replaced with personal loyalty to Tuleev. The deal seemed to be quite attractive for many of the left-wing activists, who were swift to change tables. In the 1999 elections, neither the old People's Power nor the KPRF nominated their candidates, but party members ran against the nominees of the Bloc of Aman Tuleev in almost every district.[32] As a result of the elections, the bloc took thirty-four of thirty-five seats in the assembly, thus achieving the highest level of party representation at the regional level ever witnessed in Russia. The scope of executive control over the legislature was quite impressive too.

These cases demonstrate that while the local parties of power were indeed instrumental from the standpoint of executive control over legislatures, the purpose of creating the parties of power themselves was different. Both Kondratenko and Tuleev were authoritative enough to create manageable legislative majorities. However, they had to deal with the residuals of the intraelite conflicts that brought them to power. These conflicts empowered local KPRF branches to an extent that posed a danger to the governors' otherwise unchallenged grasp on the regions. Thus they had to be placed under control too, and the best pretexts for doing so were provided by regional legislative elections, with the popular governors' endorsement being traded for political autonomy of the left either on a collective (Krasnodar) or selective (Kemerovo) basis. Such a strategy on the part of the executive can be dubbed "party capture," with parties, not legislatures, emerging as the strategy's primary targets.

This point can be illustrated by the example of the third region where the left-wing forces won both executive and legislative elections, Volgograd province. Unlike in the two previously discussed regions, Volgograd's communist governor, Nikolai Maksiuta, was not a local hero of overwhelming political authority. In the 1996 elections, he lost to the Yeltsin-appointed incumbent in the first round, to win only in the second by a narrow margin of less that 7 percent. Already at the time of the 1996 elections, Maksiuta was widely considered as "politically dependent" on the local branch of the KPRF, led by an influential member of the party's national leadership, Alevtina Aparina.[33] While Maksiuta himself was careful to reject these claims, at times even suggesting that he was prepared to "suspend" his KPRF membership (which in fact he did not),[34] it was clear that his personal endorsement would not be sufficient for a candidate's victory in regional legislative elections. Moreover, Aparina's threat that "under certain conditions," Maksiuta could be deprived of party support, had to be taken quite seriously by the governor.[35] This constellation of circumstances practically excluded Maksiuta from effective influence upon regional legislative campaigns. As a result of staggered elections that took place in March 1997 and December 1998, the KPRF won twenty-two of thirty-two seats in the regional legislature. Immediately after that, the legislature started to exercise its appointment powers in a way that left little doubt regarding who controlled it, the governor or the KPRF itself. Fortunately for Maksiuta, his noncommunist predecessor and the first-cycle legislature, where communists were in minority, traded off a statute that created a very clear-cut presidential regime, with the legislature being almost totally unable to influence the personal composition of the administrative bodies. In fact, it could rely only on one residual power descending to the 1992 federal law, the power to establish the outline of provincial government. In the beginning of 1999, the legislature passed a law on the new outline, according to which there had to be three vice governors instead of one. Two of the three appointees to newly established posts were nominated by the KPRF.[36] Constitutionally, Maksiuta was still able to reject the communist nominees and to appoint anybody he wanted. Yet given the prospects of fresh gubernatorial elections in 2000, such a decision could have been less than wise. In fact, the KPRF-controlled legislature paid off by passing an electoral law that replaced a two-round majority with plurality as the formula for gubernatorial elections, and was quite instrumental during Maksiuta's second campaign.[37] Indeed, Maksiuta won his second term with a modest 36.7 percent of the vote. Thus the governor's cozy relationship with the party went on. However, his control over the legislature was not a component of this relationship. Quite the reverse, the KPRF used the legislature as a means of influencing the executive policy. Admittedly, this is an ordinary situation in many presidential systems. But in Russia, where many governors are capable to avoid party control altogether, Maksiuta could hardly be considered as a showcase of strong executive powers.

The case of Volgograd points to a problem that has to be confronted by any governor who seeks to control a legislature by creating a party-based parliamentary majority. In most cases, "capturing" a party during an electoral campaign is neither easy nor necessary. It is not easy because, as we have seen, the strategy of party capture requires an unusual concentration of authority in the hands of the executive. It is not necessary because in the majority of regions, political parties do not pose a threat of taking monopolistic control over legislatures. From this perspective, the Volgograd scenario is more likely to materialize than those of Krasnodar or Kemerovo. What makes the Volgograd scenario so rare is that, for a good reason, it has to be avoided by regional executives. Consider those regions where the local left-wing movements or the KPRF emerged as major forces in gubernatorial coalitions and proceeded to win not majorities, but sizable minorities (one-third to one-half of the seats) in the second-cycle regional legislative elections, which took place concurrently with the gubernatorial elections or later. Overall, there were four such cases, Stavropol territory and Briansk, Novosibirsk, and Riazan provinces. Three of these regions, with the exception of Novosibirsk province, were listed by a KPRF intraparty publication as those where the left-wing governors permitted the KPRF organizations to control key positions in local administrations.[38] This suggests that like in Volgograd, the KPRF was able to convert its electoral assets, via substantial assembly representation, into effective control over administrative appointments. Thus it effectively emerged as something reminiscent of a ruling party. In all three regions, the left-wing governors were able to win their second elections.

In the fourth region, Novosibirsk province, there was a different turn of events. In 1995, Vitalii Mukha won gubernatorial elections with the support of the KPRF. Judging from election results, Mukha was a very weak claimant for the post. He received 18.1 percent of the vote in the first round of the elections. However, several months after he won in the second round, Mukha announced that he refused to join the KPRF and criticized it as a party "whose leaders used to deceive the people, so that the people lost their trust in them."[39] The only KPRF activist ever appointed to Mukha's administration served as his press secretary. Already in January 1996 the regional leaders of the KPRF had to recognize that their hopes for Mukha were misplaced.[40] While the party was quite successful in the 1997 regional legislative elections, in which it took more than a third of the seats, Mukha was instrumental in preventing the leader of the regional party branch, Viktor Kuznetsov, from becoming the legislature's speaker.[41] Thus the political price for KPRF support was not paid. In the 1999 gubernatorial elections Kuznetsov ran against Mukha and took 15.8 percent of the vote against just 17.9 percent cast for the latter. None of them made it into the second round, as a result of which the mayor of Novosibirsk replaced Mukha as governor. Arguably, the outcome would have been different if he had confronted Mukha in the second round.[42]

Thus the strategy of controlling the legislature by winning a legislative majority for a proexecutive party does not work because it is costly and difficult to pursue. The second theoretically conceivable party-based strategy, controlling the legislature by manufacturing a coalition of loyal parties on the assembly floor, has few empirical referents in the regions of Russia. Some of the reasons for this situation will be addressed in the next section of this chapter. However, a certain amount of factual information is available. The most clear-cut case is Sverdlovsk province, where due to the fact that the whole lower chamber of its assembly is elected by proportional representation, the governor has no choice but to deal with party-based factions, and the party of Eduard Rossel, Transformation of the Urals, has always been in minority. Of the twenty-eight seats in the lower chamber, it held eight seats in 1998–2000, seven seats in 2000–2002, and with twelve seats fell short of majority after the 2002 elections. Apparently the 2000–2002 period was especially difficult for the governor. The balance of power in the lower chamber of the assembly was thus: the major opposition party, Our Home Is Our City (NDNG), held eight seats; then followed Transformation of the Urals/Unity of the Urals with seven seats; two parties, the communists and the left-leaning populists of the May movement, held four and three seats respectively; and six seats were jointly held by four minor formations. The coalition strategy pursued by Eduard Rossel involved two major components: first, making situational deals with the communists; and second, creating a manageable faction of the right. Such a faction, named Union of Right Forces (SPS), absorbed some of the deputies elected on the tickets of minor formations, while its leader actually entered the legislature as a nominee of Rossel's party. Obviously, such a two-sided alliance was difficult to sustain, and it was not necessarily reliable, as shown by the fact that Rossel's allies were unable or unwilling to prevent one of the NDNG leaders, Evgenii Porunov, from becoming the chamber's speaker.[43] At the same time, the alliance served as a working progovernor majority in the legislature, thus permitting Rossel to pursue an independent strategy of administrative appointments. The situation blew up when it came to amending the regional statute, which required a two-thirds legislative supermajority. The statute had to be amended in accordance with the 1999 law.[44] If the legislature failed to do that, it faced the possibility of dissolution. But for Rossel, there was much more at stake, because one of the amendments that had to be introduced into the statute was the one that allowed him to run for a third term. The opposition factions were able to resist amendments by causing a legislative deadlock that lasted for eight months.[45] An even more complicated problem suddenly emerged with the SPS. The national leaders of the party urged the faction to vote against a third term for Rossel. In the end, at the price of heavy bargaining, the governor succeeded in urging twenty of twenty-eight deputies to vote for amendments. The national leadership of the SPS, in turn, proceeded to expel the members of the Sverdlovsk legislative faction from the party.[46] Thus the party structure of the legislature collapsed under the pressure of Rossel's fight for control over the legislature. If it had survived, Rossel would have lost. Similar developments were observable in Krasnoiarsk territory, where due to the use of proportional representation, party factions constituted an important element of legislative structure.[47]

Both strategies of executive control over assemblies discussed above are rare, and now it is understandable why. Quite the reverse, the third strategy, bargaining with individual deputies, is fairly common, but it has nothing to do with political parties. By their electoral origins, the candidates who are disposed for bargaining are often, but not necessarily, independents. Their party affiliations simply do not matter. Consider the 1997 regional legislative elections in Moscow. Briefly before the elections, the city administration led by Yurii Luzhkov produced several partly overlapping lists of preferred candidates. The lists, jointly or individually referred to as the "list of Luzhkov," were made available to the press.[48] Among about seventy persons on the lists, there were nominees of Democratic Russia's Choice (DVR), Yabloko, Our Home Is Russia (NDR), and also KPRF members who ran as independents. At the same time, each of these parties nominated candidates who did not receive Luzhkov's endorsement.[49] Luzhkov's list was not based on programmatic affinities. Instead, it singled out those candidates who, once elected, could provide the mayor with political support. The elections returned only eight party deputies, three of them belonging to Yabloko, two to the DVR, and one to the NDR. Twenty-seven deputies were independents. A different perspective from which to view the election results, however, was provided by the fact that twenty-seven of the deputies, independents and party nominees alike, were previously on Luzhkov's list.[50] A year later, the governor of St. Petersburg, Vladimir Yakovlev, pursued a similar strategy. The 1998 elections to St. Petersburg's legislature were held by a two-round majority system. Soon after the first round, some of the city's print and electronic media, especially those that were allegedly controlled by city government, started to propagate the "St. Petersburg list." The content of media messages left little doubt that the list actually included candidates preferred by Yakovlev. Similar to Moscow, such candidates were mostly independents but also nominees of different parties, from the right to the KPRF.[51] Similar to Moscow, the elections returned a legislature that contained thirty-six independents and fourteen nominees of six different parties, yet a more politically important result was that the "St. Petersburg list" took thirty-one seats.[52]

After the nationally publicized elections in Moscow and St. Petersburg, "governor lists" became fashionable in regional legislative elections. To cite a few examples, in the third electoral cycle such lists made their appearances in Voronezh,[53] Leningrad,[54] Moscow,[55] and Omsk provinces.[56] An interesting case is Stavropol territory with its rather weak communist governor, Aleksandr Chernogorov. One of the Chernogorov's major problems throughout his first term was the lack of legislative support. Indeed, only ten of the twenty-five members of the regional legislature elected in 1997 were KPRF nominees. At the same time, the majority of deputies were independents not only by their electoral origins but also in the more fundamental sense of being in opposition to the governor. In an attempt to place the legislature under his political control, Chernogorov not only formed his list of candidates for the 2001 elections but also, despite his otherwise undeniable loyalty to the KPRF, filled it with many noncommunist candidates. The communists, for their part, not only supported this strategy but also abstained from candidate nomination in the 2001 elections while allowing party members to run as independents. In exchange, they traded off the right to exclude several candidates from the "list of Chernogorov" and to fill it with several party loyalists instead.[57]

Throughout the third electoral cycle, "governor lists" remained the core strategy of attaining executive control over regional legislatures. This strategy had more or less explicit manifestations, though. There were several instances when the executives came fairly close to creating their own parties of power, falling short only on urging them to perform as candidate-nominating entities. Perhaps the most noteworthy case of this kind is Cheliabinsk province. In many respects, developments in the province were similar to those in Krasnodar and Kemerovo. After a protracted struggle against Yeltsin's appointee, a popular left-winger, Petr Sumin, won the 1996 gubernatorial elections. Throughout this struggle, he relied upon his own political movement, For the Rebirth of the Urals (ZVU), formed on the basis of local communist groups including the KPRF, the Russian Communist Workers Party (RKRP), and Workers Russia.[58] In the regional legislative elections, held concurrently with the gubernatorial elections, the movement supported candidates in every electoral district, but only a few of them were communists. As put by one of the leaders of the movement, Vladimir Utkin, "we are a team, and there is no place for division into different 'isms' within the team; for us, it does not make any difference whether you are a communist, a centrist, or whatever. What is important is to consolidate all political forces that want to provide the population, at this stage, with a minimum of social guarantees."[59] Later in the same interview, Utkin made it clear that the main purpose of forming the "team" was to avoid vote splitting. In general, the strategy was quite reminiscent of "party capture" as witnessed in several other regions. The difference was that unlike in Krasnodar and Kemerovo, the local branches of the left-wing parties that formed the ZVU were militant but organizationally weak and not very appealing to the region's electorate, as demonstrated by the fact that in the 1995 national legislative elections in Cheliabinsk province, the list of the KPRF received 14.7 percent of the vote. Under such conditions, the ZVU could better perform its function by endorsing candidates but not nominating them. Indeed, the latter would necessarily involve bargaining with the left-wing parties.

The less explicit manifestation of the "governor lists" strategy was to endorse or otherwise support individual candidates without actually publishing their names on lists. Factual information about this mechanism of securing control over legislatures is scarce not only because it was used on individual bases, which makes relevant information difficult to retrieve, but also because through most of the period under observation, it was barely legal. Indeed, many regional laws, in accordance with federal legislation, would allow for interpreting direct executive endorsements as pressure on voters, and organizational support to individual candidates as a violation of the principle of candidates' equality. In fact, however, such support is an important part of Russia's regional political life. The vice speaker of the 1999 Duma, Liubov Sliska, whose rich background in Saratov provincial politics undoubtedly makes her a very well-informed observer, identifies four major ways in which the regional executive can facilitate the election of its preferred candidates.[60] The first is to provide favorable media coverage. As put by Sliska, "on the one hand, because of administrative pressure the media may, under different pretexts, refuse to publish the undesirable candidates' paid [election] materials. On the other hand, the electronic and print media may be filled with indirect advertisement on behalf of the representatives of [executive] power." Second, Sliska writes that "unofficial" and "official" candidates do not receive equal opportunities for face-to-face meetings with the voters, because the latter can hold a meeting at any workplace, at any kind of public facility, and so on, while the former are often offered less convenient places for meeting voters. Third, executive power may boost the reputation of an "official" candidate by providing or improving, on the candidates behalf, basic services to the population, such as garbage removal or heating and hot water supply. Finally, Sliska identifies electoral fraud as a way of helping "official" candidates to take the desired seats.

Thus political control of the executives over legislatures can be achieved in different ways. "Party capture," while an apparently efficient strategy in itself, requires a very rare constellation of political factors as its precondition. Intralegislative bargaining is less than efficient. Moreover, this strategy necessarily involves making political concessions to the proexecutive parties and legislative factions. Such concessions may effectively place the legislature under the control of parties, not of the executive, which is all the more dangerous given that some of the legislatures are constitutionally endowed with significant appointment powers. Alternatively, the executives may either suppress political parties by means of institutional manipulation, as with administrative-territorial districts, or provide their bases of legislative support by using nonparty mechanisms in their more or less explicit manifestations. One question that remains to be answered is what sustains the loyalties of thus-elected deputies during their legislative terms. Of course, the once obtained benefits of executive support may enter the perspective reelection calculus of an incumbent deputy. At the same time, they have other institutionally defined interests that, in the most general formulation, fall under the category of legislative autonomy. In the next section, I will demonstrate that conditions under which such interests are being formed in Russia's regional legislatures are favorable for keeping loyalty directed toward executives, not toward political parties.

Legislative Autonomy and Political Parties

Autonomy is the legislature's "capacity to gather information, cultivate policy expertise, and make decisions independently from other institutions" (Carey, Formanek, and Karpowicz 1999: 571). The constitutionally strong assemblies of parliamentary regimes, despite their vast appointment powers, often lack autonomy because they are subordinate to party leaders who occupy cabinet positions (Cox 1987). While this generalization is less applicable to those countries with fragmented party systems where government composition is often defined by complex bargaining on the legislative floor than to those countries where binary party system formats leave little space for independence from cabinet pressure (Norton 1988), it would be fair to say that under parliamentarism, political parties have little to add to legislative autonomy. Under presidentialism, the relationship between party strength and legislative autonomy is less straightforward. On the one hand, the lack of party control over the legislative agenda, in combination with low party discipline, has been viewed as a major reason for policy gridlock in Brazil (Geddes and Neto 1992; Mainwaring and Pérez Linán 1997). On the other hand, in the United States, where legislative autonomy is recognizably very high, this quality is often connected not with party strength but rather with the legislature's ability to develop a system of strong, specialized committees (Polsby 1968). From this perspective, some of the Latin American legislatures failed on autonomy because they failed on effective internal coordination, which in turn can be attributed to the underdevelopment of their committee systems no less than to the underdevelopment of political parties (Morgenstern and Nacif 2002). Indeed, U.S. political parties lack the internal discipline characteristic of parties in many other well-established democracies (Epstein 1986). It is partly for this reason that committees are able to serve as hotbeds of legislative autonomy. It has been argued that in Russia's 1993 national legislature, policy gridlock was largely caused by an attempt to combine a committee system with politically strong and ideologically rigid yet undisciplined parties (Ostrow 1998). However, in the 1995 national legislature, with the antiexecutive coalition several votes short of outright majority, strong committees emerged as the principal tools of avoiding gridlock (Remington 2001b), which greatly contributed to legislative autonomy in Russia (Shevchenko and Golosov 2001).

Thus the primary question to be addressed concerns the internal organization of Russia's regional assemblies. Are they party-structured or committee-structured, or not structured at all, the last version arguably indicating a complete lack of legislative autonomy? Of course, given the lack of party representation in regional legislative assemblies as reported in Chapter 3, one would not bet on parties as principal elements of their internal organization. At this moment, however, it stands to reason to present more evidence on the matter, which is all the more important given that very little is actually known about what is happening inside Russia's regional legislatures. Before turning to scattered evidence from individual regions, a piece of relatively comprehensive information can be derived from one of the publications of Russia's Central Electoral Commission.[61] On April 14, 1999, the commission charged regional authorities with forming new regional electoral commissions along guidelines that, in particular, required granting representation to those political parties that had their factions in the State Duma of Russia and in the legislative assemblies of the regions themselves. Such electoral commissions were indeed formed in eighty-one regions in April through September 1999—that is, at the end of the second electoral cycle. None of the regions deprived the four parties then represented in the national legislature from exercising their right to nominate members of the electoral commissions. Since this right was exercised almost irrespective of whether these parties were actually in existence in the regions, this aspect is of little interest for my analysis. In contrast, political parties that had their factions in regional legislative assemblies sent their representatives to electoral commissions in only fifteen regions. The numbers of such representatives are quite illuminative because it can be plausibly assumed that each of the party-based factions nominated one electoral commission member. Proceeding from this assumption, it can be established that as many as eleven of the fifteen legislatures contained just one party-based faction each. Two such factions could be found in each of three legislatures, in Kamchatka, Sverdlovsk, and Yaroslavl provinces. The record number of party-based factions, four, was registered in Krasnoiarsk territory. Of course, a legislature that contains just one faction can be hardly characterized as faction-structured. Even though this does not fully apply to the legislatures of Krasnodar territory and Kemerovo province, where single factions absorbed the vast majorities of deputies, the overall conclusion would be that the number of faction-structured legislatures at the end of the second electoral cycle was no more than six. It must be immediately recognized that this very modest figure probably underestimates the actual spread of factions in Russia's regional legislatures. The reason is not only that eight regions remain out of the calculus. By granting representation only to parties that had factions in regional legislatures, the Central Electoral Commission discounted those factions that were not created on the basis of officially registered "electoral associations and blocs." Therefore, it remains useful to cast a less comprehensive yet closer look at individual regions.

Generally, the fragmentary evidence at my disposal suggests that figures derived from the publication are far from entirely unrealistic. In those legislatures where, according to the data, there were single-party factions, the factions were most likely those of the KPRF. Creating viable communist factions in regional legislatures was one of the strategic goals of the KPRF, as witnessed by the fact that the party even formed a special body attached to its national leadership, the Council of KPRF Faction Coordinators in Legislative Assemblies.[62] The level of representation in the assemblies attained by the KPRF in the second electoral cycle did indeed allow for creating minority factions in approximately half of the regions.

However, it appears that this target has never been achieved. For instance, the electoral bloc of the KPRF and the Agrarian Party of Russia (APR) won six of fifty seats in the 1997 elections to the Moscow Provincial Duma, and the fact that the Communists, not the Agrarians, were the leading party in the bloc was never questioned by local observers. Yet when it came to forming factions, the Agrarians created one, but the KPRF did not.[63] The reason is clear: it was easier to lure independent deputies into a more moderate agrarian faction than into a communist one. Thus to create a communist faction, a small group of communists elected to the assembly could suffice technically but not politically. The second limitation on creating KPRF factions was, paradoxically, the communists' friendliness toward noncommunist but left-leaning regional executives. In the 1997 elections to the legislature of Kirov province, the KPRF won ten of fifty-four seats, and the APR just four. The Agrarians, however, played a pivotal role in the loose alliance of the region's left with the governor, Vladimir Sergeenkov. As a result, there was no KPRF faction in the region's legislature, while the faction of the APR not only existed but comprised the majority of deputies rather than four party nominees.[64] Clearly, in this case the APR emerged as a mechanism of executive control over the legislature, while the KPRF was prepared neither for assuming this role nor for going into opposition. From the two examples above, one may infer that the factions of the APR were fairly common. It seems that in fact they were not. While it is true that the managers of agricultural enterprises, once elected to regional legislatures, sometimes joined with APR nominees to form deputy groups, the level of APR representation in the legislatures was insufficient to make this practice widespread. Other parties formed their factions in regional legislative assemblies only episodically. Sometimes such factions consisted exclusively of those deputies who ran and won as independents, as was the case with the SPS in Nizhnii Novgorod province.[65] In other cases, factions consisted mostly of party nominees, as was the case with Yabloko in St. Petersburg.[66] Both patterns, however, were fairly unusual.

One would expect the parties of power to constitute a special case. Consider the NDR. From its inception in 1995, the party strove to occupy the niche of a national ruling party with widespread regional presence, as shown by the fact that its political council included the heads, deputy heads, prime ministers, and deputy prime ministers of fifty-three regions.[67] On the one hand, like the KPRF, the NDR created a body that was charged with coordinating activities of its representatives in regional legislatures.[68] On the other hand, given that the executives were interested in taking regional legislatures under their political control, one might suggest that the factions of the NDR could be created precisely for this end. Indeed, by the end of 1997 the leaders of the movement reported that it had factions in as many as twenty regional legislatures, and that it was to form them in fifteen to sixteen regions more. The initial ways of creating NDR factions were fairly uniform across the regions: the party included those proexecutive deputies who were elected as independents.[69] The influx of NDR nominees into regional legislative assemblies could be expected to boost the formation of its factions on a more partylike basis. In the beginning of 1998, however, as many as eleven regional leaders who sat on the political council of the NDR, including such influential figures as Mikhail Prusak of Novgorod province and Vladimir Chub of Rostov province, jointly stated that they did not find the formation of NDR factions in "their" legislatures expedient, which effectively stopped the process.[70] It seems that after the movement's leader, Viktor Chernomyrdin, was dismissed as Russia's prime minister, even those factions that were formed in 1996–1997 started to disappear. This explains why there were so few party factions in regional legislatures by the spring of 1999. After the 1999 national legislative elections, Unity started to display a very similar pattern of faction formation. Thus the factions of Unity, consisting exclusively of nonparty nominees, emerged in the legislatures of Kaliningrad province, where the faction was initially labeled Unity of Independent Deputies of the Region,[71] and Murmansk province.[72] The influx of Unity nominees into regional assemblies starting in December 2001 further increased the number of such factions. For instance, in Tver province Unity formed its factions both in the regional legislature and in the administrative center's city council.[73] But, similar to what had happened with the NDR before, the overall results of these efforts were inconclusive.

Thus it may be argued that Russia's regional legislative assemblies, with the exception of those that have large portions of deputies elected by proportional representation, are by and large not faction-structured. Now it can be added that even those factions and deputy groups that actually exist are often not party-based. As I have already mentioned, agrarian deputy groups normally comprise agricultural managers who have little to do with the national policy agenda of the APR. Similarly, the "bosses" of industrial enterprises sometimes form their own deputy groups, as happened in Perm province, where the largest faction in the regional legislature was called Industrialists of Kama Region.[74] Obviously, these are cases of corporate, not political, internal structuring of the legislative bodies. Consider the legislative assembly of St. Petersburg, which due to a long history of intraelite struggles in the region and perhaps related to its comprehensive appointment powers has been continuously faction-structured despite the fact that all its members came from single-member majority districts. As of November 2000, it consisted of seven factions. Only three of them, Yabloko, the SPS, and Unity, were party-based. Four others, Legality, Union, the Districts of St. Petersburg, and the Industrial Faction, were not. The speaker of the assembly characterized them as interest advocacy clubs.[75] This is not to say that the faction structure of the St. Petersburg assembly, as described above, did not have a political dimension. In fact, Yabloko, Legality, Unity, and less consistently the SPS stood in opposition to the governor, while other factions provided him with a narrow-margin legislative majority. Yet it is clear that to sustain this majority, the governor had to bargain on the issue positions of corporate groups, not on programmatic political issues. It is ironic that when describing the "faction structure" of the third-cycle legislature of Orenburg province, consisting of two deputy groups, Commonwealth and Unitary Russia, a local observer was careful enough to mention: "It does not involve politics whatsoever."[76]

The committee structure of Russia's regional legislatures is difficult to examine because the relevant data are in very short supply. Fortunately, a Moscow-based policy analysis group, Panorama, has published on the Internet the results of its research on the lawmaking activities of eighteen regional legislatures elected in the second electoral cycle. In particular, the publication contains comprehensive and, as far my partial cross-checking with other sources could confirm, fully reliable information about the committee structures of fifteen regional legislatures.[77] It is important to mention that while information on three legislatures is less than complete, the publication leaves no doubt that they were committee-structured too. Those fifteen regions, which are fully covered in the source and therefore can be entered into this analysis, include three republics (Altai, Karelia, and Chuvashia) and twelve other regions from Pskov province in the northwest of Russia to Primorskii territory in the far southeast, which makes it possible to consider the sample as reasonably representative. As it appears from my analysis, the committees, sometimes called permanent commissions, are omnipresent in Russia's regional legislatures, but the overall number of committees tends to be relatively small. On the average, a regional legislative assembly contained 5.4 committees.[78] Since comparativists often view the strength of committee systems as dependent on the levels of individual committees' specialization (Olson and Mezey 1991), one would view the small numbers of committees as a sign of their weakness. This line of reasoning, however, has to be moderated against the fact that regional legislative assemblies are small themselves. In the selection of fifteen regions employed for this analysis, the average number of deputies elected in the second-cycle elections was 38.1, and the average number of deputies per committee, 7.1. Of course, a seven-member committee is scarcely too large to prevent its members from developing policy expertise. Moreover, it stands to reason that smaller committees would serve as personal policy vehicles of their members.

What policy domains are covered by committee activities? A technical problem with answering this question is that in different regions, committees are organized in different ways. In order to overcome this difficulty, I employed the following procedure of assessing committee specialization. First, I identified thirty-eight "small" policy domains addressed by individual committees, as expressed in their official names. Each of the policy domains received a score according, first, to the number of regions where correspondingly specialized committees were registered, and second, to the number of specializations that coexisted with the given policy domain under the auspices of the same committee. To give a hypothetical example, if a committee that dealt exclusively with toys was registered in one region, the policy domain of toys scored a 1, but if in the same single region there was a committee on toys and candies, each of these policy domains scored a 0.5. If the same situations were replicated in two regions each, then the respective scores would be 2 and 1, and so on. The maximum theoretically possible score, 15, indicates that the given policy domain was present in every region, and that in each of them, it was exclusively addressed by a separate committee. As a second step, I joined the thirty-eight "small" policy domains into four "large" ones, identified as the state, economy, society, and nature, and calculated aggregate scores for these domains by summing the scores of individual components. The maximum theoretically possible score for a "large" domain is 15 multiplied by the number of "small" domains it includes.[79] The results of my calculations are reported in Table 6.7. In order to provide fuller and perhaps simpler organized information, I also included data on the numbers of regions where the given policy domains received their expression in committee structures, irrespective of whether they had the committees that addressed the corresponding issues exclusively.

As it follows from the data, the committee structures of Russia's regional legislative assemblies were heavily focused on policy domains related to the economy. The state and society scored almost equally, while nature-related policy domains came in a distant fourth. Judging from the accounts of the assemblies' legislative activities published by the Panorama group, such a committee structure corresponds well to what the assemblies actually do. It is very illuminative that state structure, the only policy domain that directly applies to their appointment powers, scores so little. Speaking of the state, the primary issue addressed by the assemblies is local self-government. This is not surprising given that the municipal officials constitute a large part of the deputies, and that many intraelite conflicts at the regional level directly involve the problems of the "vertical" separation of powers between regional and local authorities. The assemblies also extensively deal with the issues of social protection, which partly reflects the deputies' reelection concerns. However, economic policy in general and budgetary, financial, and fiscal matters in particular absolutely dominate the agendas of Russia's regional legislatures, as reflected in their committee structures. Clearly, this bias well corresponds with the occupational structures of the assemblies—that is, with the overrepresentation of busi-

Table 6.7   Committee Structures in Fifteen Regional Legislative Assemblies Elected in the Second Electoral Cycle, 1995–1999

Policy Domain	Specialization Score	Number of Regions
Legislation	6.0	8
The state	15.2	14
Local self-government	5.2	11
Law enforcement	3.1	5
Human rights protection	1.6	4
Public associations	1.5	5
Interethnic relations	1.3	4
State structure	1.3	3
Interregional relations	1.2	3
Economy	37.9	15
Economic policy	6.5	11
Budgetary policy	5.9	15
Financial policy	4.4	13
Agriculture	4.3	9
Fiscal policy	4.1	12
Industry	1.8	6
Food supply	1.5	3
Entrepreneurship	1.3	4
Transportation	1.3	5
Communications	1.3	5
Construction	1.3	5
Foreign trade	1.0	1
State property management	0.8	2
Retail market	0.8	2
Fuel and energy	0.5	2
Economic security	0.3	1
Housing and services	0.3	1
Roads	0.3	1
Banking	0.2	1
Society	15.5	15
Social protection	10.8	15
Healthcare	1.3	3
Science	0.8	3
Education	0.7	3
Mass media	0.7	3
Culture	0.5	2
Tourism	0.3	1
Mass sports	0.2	1
Professional sports	0.2	1
Nature	6.7	11
Natural resources	3.4	9
Nature protection	3.3	9

nesspeople. But it is instructive to look at the overrepresentation of businesspeople from a different angle. In the previous chapter, I argued that they win elections because of the superior resources available to them. But one crucial decision that has to be made by any candidate, irrespective of his or her resources, is the decision to run. If the regional legislatures were not important, regional economic elites would not invest their efforts into colonizing them. As it has been demonstrated above, the assemblies could be important because of the appointment powers that they are endowed with in some of these regions, yet for these powers to be exercised, they have to be politically independent from the executive. Such a condition, however, is rare and unusual. At the same time, politically loyal deputies do not necessarily lack their own policy agendas. The opportunity to pursue these policy agendas motivates them to seek legislative seats, with political loyalty to the executive being delivered in exchange. Now it is apparent that the policy domain within which such agendas can be set and pursued is the economy. This, in turn, implies that far from being politically independent from the executive, the regional legislatures can achieve substantial autonomy as collective economic policy decisionmakers. For this to be achieved, they develop strong committees. Strong parties, however, are not only irrelevant but possibly even harmful from the point of view of defending so-understood legislative autonomy. Thus it is only logical that Russia's regional legislative assemblies are committee-structured, not party-structured. In fact, the argument that party factions are harmful for the work of regional legislative assemblies is fairly common in Russia.[80]

Legislatures where these two principles have to coexist are few, and the most likely outcome of such coexistence seems to be legislative stalemate. Consider one of such exceptional cases, the legislature of Adygeia, elected in December 1995. Due to a very specific constellation of local circumstances, such as the proximity of the conflict-ridden Krasnodar territory and the heavily procommunist attitudes of the voters, and despite the use of ATDs, the legislature of Adygeia included quite a few party deputies: of the forty-four initially elected members, fifteen were KPRF nominees, and nine were APR nominees. The Communists, by recruiting ten independents, managed to form a majority deputy group named For Professional Parliament. The Agrarians joined nine party members and seven independents to form a minority Agrarian Deputy Group. Three of the deputies did not join either of the groups. At the first plenary session of the legislature, the two groups became involved in an intense conflict over who would head the committee on budgetary, financial, fiscal, and economic policy, a Communist or an Agrarian. Being unable to win the vote, the Agrarians left the session, which resulted in a stalemate simply because there was no longer any quorum.[81] It was only at the end of February 1996, after a series of negotiations involving both the deputy groups and the executive, that the assembly was able to start its legislative activities.[82] By 1997, after by-elections in two districts, the state council included four factions and deputy groups: the KPRF, the APR, People's Power, and Accord for the Sake of Progress. The numbers of deputies in these formations were thirteen, nine, ten, and fourteen respectively.[83] Even though People's Power included left-leaning independents and often voted with the Communists, the left now lacked an outright majority in the legislature. In fact, the perfect equilibrium of political forces in the assembly made its political structure irrelevant: it could only work if structured in a different way. Thus even in the presence of the faction structure, the committee structure emerged as the basic precondition for legislative efficiency.

Thus in general the regional assemblies of Russia can be characterized as politically dominated by the executives yet enjoying a certain degree of legislative autonomy, which is institutionally supported by their committee structures. Such a configuration arguably supports nonpartisanship among those deputies who enter the assemblies as independents. How does it affect party nominees? The political domination of the executives entails an important consequence—a lack of party discipline on the assembly floor. As we have seen, party-based factions in the second-cycle assemblies were often formed by the KPRF or local left-wing movements. These factions comprised legislative majorities in very few regions, and in most cases they were in opposition to the regional executives, a combination of properties that rendered them politically irrelevant. Their individual members were not fully deprived of an opportunity to pursue their specific policy agendas by means of legislative activity, particularly via the committee system. Such an activity was essential for pursuing successful reelection strategies. But for this end, loyalty to the executive was highly desirable if not unavoidable. Consider the case of Belgorod province. The Yeltsin-appointed governor, Evgenii Savchenko, managed not only to retain a definitely noncommunist political profile in a region with sweepingly procommunist voter attitudes but also to consolidate his power by winning two gubernatorial elections, in 1995 and 1999. However, voter preferences manifested themselves in the fact that in the 1996 legislative elections, the KPRF nominees won thirteen of thirty-five assembly seats, which enabled them to form a very sizable minority faction. One of them defected, so that by 1999, when Savchenko engaged in his reelection campaign, the KPRF faction numbered twelve members. During the campaign, the leaders of the party's regional branch endorsed the candidacy of a long-standing opponent of the governor. However, nine of the communist legislators, including deputy speaker of the assembly, defied party discipline and supported the candidacy of Savchenko instead.[84] It is possible that this influenced the outcome of the elections, won by Savchenko by a margin of more than 30 percent. In the aftermath of the elections, the faction continued to function as if nothing had happened.[85] A similarly large faction of the KPRF, ten of thirty legislators, was formed under the circumstances broadly similar to those of Belgorod in Omsk province. In the official publication of the party's national leadership the Omsk regional branch of the KPRF was explicitly criticized for "not being able to utilize these resources."[86] In a less euphemistic formulation, this meant that all the heads of agricultural enterprises elected on the KPRF ticket defected from the faction. Not surprisingly, the policy impact of the KPRF faction was estimated as negligible.[87]

In order to assess the impact of committee-structured assemblies upon the legislative behavior of party nominees, it is important to take into account an important characteristic of these legislatures previously unaddressed in this study. This characteristic needs to be discussed if only because in the comparative literature on the subjects, the legislators' ability to attain high levels of professionalism is often viewed as a decisive precondition for legislative autonomy (Fried 1966; Squire 1998). Among other things, Yeltsin's decree of December 22, 1993, stipulated that the share of full-time legislators in regional legislative assemblies could not exceed 40 percent. While this decree did not affect the first-cycle elections held in December 1993, which allowed the city of Moscow, Moscow province, and Tyva to create professional legislatures, this provision was fully consequential not only for the majority of the first cycle elections, but also, by setting a rule that was readily grasped by the legislatures themselves, for the further history of Russia's regional legislatures. Unfortunately, the data on the scope of regional legislators' full-time employment at my disposal are not comprehensive, which makes it imperative to rely upon two less than perfect procedures. One of them is the analysis of the deputies' occupational backgrounds reported in Table 5.4, where the category of "legislators" comprises just 8.8 percent of the 3,420 deputies elected in the second electoral cycle. This figure, however illuminating in the sense that it reveals the share of deputies who actually viewed legislative work as their major vocation, seems to underestimate the actual scope of deputies' full-time employment. Indeed, according to different regional laws, university professors, high school teachers, journalists, and perhaps most important, municipal leaders, could combine full-time employment in legislatures with their previous jobs. The Panorama group provides different and seemingly more robust information on the matter.[88] Unfortunately, the data published by Panorama are not synchronic, for they apply to the deputies' full-time employment in fifty-two first-cycle legislatures and thirty-four second-cycle legislatures; the sets of regions in the two selections do not overlap. Yet for all these deficiencies, the Panorama data source is apparently the best on the subject. For the first electoral cycle, the data reported in the source allowed me to establish that the average number of full-time deputies in an assembly was 12.4, while the average assembly size for the selection was 44.6. The average share of full-time deputies was 29.0 percent. There was substantial variation on the parameter, with the shares of full-time deputies varying from 100 percent in the three regions named above to 2.3 percent in Penza province. In the second electoral cycle, the average number of full-time deputies in an assembly dropped to 9.1, while the average assembly size dropped to 34.5. The average share of full-time deputies remained at approximately the same level, 30.1 percent, with variation from 100 percent in Koriak autonomous district to 4.5 percent in Marii El.

Thus the number of full-time deputies in regional legislative assemblies was as a rule small but not negligible. At the same time, the role played by full-time deputies in the legislative activities of the assemblies was understandably greater than that of part-time deputies. The speakers and deputy speakers of the assemblies invariably worked full-time, and the chairpersons and deputy chairpersons of the committees only rarely worked part-time. It is important to note that the presence of party nominees was more pronounced among full-time deputies than it was among part-time deputies. This happened for two reasons. First, as it can be inferred from Table 5.4, party nominees were overrepresented among those deputies who were already professional politicians (such as legislators, aides to national and regional deputies, leaders of public and political organizations, and the like) for whom taking paid positions in the regional assemblies was therefore only logical. Second, for those deputies whose occupational backgrounds did not involve politics, some of the old professions could be profitably changed. A high school teacher, a university professor, or in most cases a journalist could tremendously enhance his or her material well-being by receiving a salary as a professional legislator. At the same time, an industrial enterprise director or a high-standing state official had little if any incentive to become a professional legislator. On the one hand, such an exchange did not promise anything good in monetary terms. On the other hand, and more important, these deputies already belonged to regional elites. They simply consolidated their previously acquired statuses by winning regional legislative elections, but of course, exchanging these statuses for full-time legislative employment was hardly rational. But as demonstrated in the previous chapter, the shares of party nominees within the elite categories of deputies were very low. Thus, in fact, party nominees were at an advantage on the assembly floor. By taking full-time legislative jobs, they could enjoy immediate benefits provided by wider access to the key positions within assembly structures. More than this, they received an opportunity to develop policy expertise unavailable to part-time deputies. Does this mean that parties were at an advantage too?

One of the most well-established findings in the comparative legislative studies literature is that the stronger the committees, the less party discipline among their members (Olson 1994: 66–67). It seems that this generalization fully applies to Russia's regional legislatures. Party nominees do enter legislative leadership in increasing numbers, but this privilege comes with a price attached: what they are expected to do as legislative leaders is to work on bills, not to promote their parties' political goals. From this perspective, it is not surprising that KPRF members could be found in positions of power in the assemblies of those regions where the party itself was neither appealing to voters nor influential enough to set its own policy agenda. For instance, the only communist in the Murmansk provincial legislature elected in 1994 served as its chairperson.[89] Similarly, the only left-wing deputy in the legislature of Nizhnii Novgorod province elected in 1998 served as a deputy head of the committee on social policy.[90] An even more telling example is Yamal-Nenets autonomous district, an oil- and gas-rich region that gained tremendously from the collapse of the distributive Soviet economy and that was therefore consistently noncommunist in all manifestations of its political life. In 1996–2000 the legislature of the region had a Communist Party member, Andrei Artiukhov, as its chairman. Moreover, after the 2000 elections, Artiukhov—who was not reelected as the leader of the legislature—received a new appointment as the deputy head of the Tiumen provincial administration.[91] It is quite clear that the appointment came as a reward for political loyalty, not for a record of opposition to the regional executive authorities. Therefore, committee-structured assemblies with their strong emphasis on professional legislative work provide disincentives for partisanship.

*   *   *

Due to the specific configuration of external and internal political influences during the period when their constitutions and statutes were crafted, the regions of Russia assumed a variety of constitutional forms, from "pure" presidentialism to rather clear-cut instances of president-parliamentary and even premier-presidential regimes. Rather than facilitating party development, this exacerbated the regional executives' will to place legislatures under their political control and thereby made conditions for party development even worse. On the one hand, the regional executives found institutional ways of preventing party development, as exemplified by the use of bicameralism and administrative-territorial electoral districts in many of the republics. On the other hand, the political mechanisms of establishing executive control over the assemblies involved political parties only rarely. While being prone to external political control, the regional assemblies are nevertheless capable of achieving certain degrees of legislative autonomy. To this end, however, they develop committee structures rather than party structures, which makes party affiliation irrelevant on the assembly floor. Thus the institutional design of Russia's regions impedes party development.

Notes

1. Itogi sessii cheliabinskogo oblsoveta, *Kommersant-Daily*, November 13, 1992.

2. Vologodskii oblsovet narodnykh deputatov prinial reshenie, *Piatnitsa* (Vologda), May 21, 1993.

3. Ekstrennoe zasedanie malogo soveta Vologodskoi oblasti, *Moskovskie novosti*, October 10, 1993.

4. V Irkutske razrabatyvaetsia proekt ustava oblasti, *Nezavisimaia gazeta*, August 1, 1992.

5. "Poetapnaia konstitutsionnaia reforma" kak obraz zhizni, *Segodnia*, May 6, 1995.

6. Rubikon pereiden, *S toboi* (Kemerovo), June 26, 1997.

7. Mestnaia vlast: Mezhdu politicheskimi ambitsiiami i interesami dela, *Rossiiskie vesti*, August 31, 1995.

8. Oblast oboidetsia bez ustava do vyborov, *Molva* (Vladimir), May 18, 2000.

9. Amurskii oblsovet—samyi sovetskii v mire, *Rossiiskie vesti*, March 20, 1996.

10. Nazad k sovetam, *Rossiiskie vesti*, November 5, 1996.

11. See however Gel'man 2000.

12. www.legislature.ru.

13. One more regime, parliamentarism, is essentially outside this framework because of the lack of directly elected presidents.

14. For an extensive treatment of one of the executives' legislative powers, see Carey and Shugart 1998. For a different approach to what constitutes a regional regime in Russia, see Gel'man 1999a.

15. The power to confirm the appointment of the prime minister is quite an important power, for it impacts the composition of the executive as a whole. Yet it is clear that an assembly is much stronger if it directly confirms the appointment of individual ministers and members of administration as well.

16. Separate prime ministerial positions were established not only in the majority of republics, but also in some other regions, such as in Sverdlovsk and Nizhnii Novgorod provinces.

17. Ispolnitel'naia vlast v Tatarstane stala zakonodatel'noi, *Rossiiskie vesti*, March 17, 1995.

18. Vybory dolzhny byt spravedlivymi, *Ekspress-khronika*, July 26, 1999.

19. Tatarstan bez parlamenta ne ostanetsia, *Vremia i den'gi* (Kazan), November 22, 1999.

20. Lish odin raionnyi glava ne proshel v parlament, *Izvestia*, January 12, 2000.

21. Adygei, slaviane! *Izvestia*, February 8, 2001.

22. Prioritet—federal'nomu zakonu, *Yuzhnyi Federl'nyi* (Rostov-na-Donu), March 5, 2001.

23. Adygeia: Vybornyi marafon s prepiatstviiami zavershilsia, *Severnyi Kavkaz* (Nal'chik), April 11, 2001.

24. In the December 1993 regional legislative elections in Moscow, the federal party of power, Russia's Choice, won an outright majority. At that time, however, Russia's Choice could not be considered as a party controlled by city authorities.

25. The third-cycle cases, Bashkortostan and Kemerovo, are discussed in Chapter 8.

26. Komu zhivetsia veselo, vol'gotno na Rusi, *Izvestia,* July 28, 1998.

27. Aman Tuleev: Ubezhdenii nikogda ne menial, *Rossiiskii Kto Est Kto,* December 7, 1995.

28. See, for instance, My spasaem Rossiiu, *Vsiakaia vsiachina* (Krasnodar), April 7, 1997.

29. Vlast doverena patriotam, *Sovetskaia Rossia,* November 24, 1998.

30. Nas vybrali rabotat, a ne shtampovat reshenia plenumov, *Izvestia Yug* (Rostov-na-Donu), December 17, 1998.

31. Aman Tuleev poidet svoim putem, *Vremia MN,* January 29, 1999.

32. I lichno Aman Gumirovich, *Novye izvestia,* April 10, 1999.

33. Volgogradskaia bitva, *Tribuna,* December 12, 1996.

34. Novyi gubernator Volgogradskoi oblsti, *Vse vesti* (Volgograd), January 6, 1997.

35. Patrioty "mladentsem" dovol'ny, *Oblastnye vesti* (Volgograd), July 4, 1997.

36. Pered shturmom Gosdumy, *Novye izvestia,* February 10, 1999.

37. V Volgograde schitaiut luchshe, chem vo Floride, *Obshchaia gazeta,* December 21, 2000.

38. *Informatsionnyi biulleten KPRF,* April 15, 1998; cited in March 2001: 287.

39. Neuvol'niaemyi Vitalii Mukha, *Trud—7,* August 23, 1996.

40. Vitalii Mukha, *Rossiiskii Kto Est Kto,* July 28, 1999.

41. Zhiriuganovtsy idut! *Molodost Sibiri* (Novosibirsk), June 28, 1996.

42. Pobedil Viktor Tolokonskii, *Vechernii Novosibirsk,* December 28, 1999.

43. Ekaterinburg: Duma na grani rospuska, *Ekspert,* July 27, 2001.

44. Ne pora li davat zanaves? *Oblastnaia gazeta* (Ekaterinburg), October 9, 2001.

45. V nashem monastyre svoi ustavy? *Vechernii Ekaterinburg,* November 15, 2001.

46. Eduarda Rosselia pustili na tretii srok, *Kommersant,* December 28, 2001.

47. Lebedinaia pesnia? *Versty,* March 2, 2002.

48. "Spisok Luzhkova": Kazhdoi tvari po pare, *Moskovskii komsomolets,* November 11, 1997.

49. Seans chernoi magii s popytkami razoblachenia, *Russkii telegraf,* December 25, 1997.

50. V "Bitve za Moskvu" Luzhkov nagolovu razbil supostatov, *Russkii telegraf,* December 16, 1997.

51. Spisochnaia volna nakryvaet izbiratelei s golovoi, *Nevskoe vremia* (St. Petersburg), December 18, 1998.

52. Piterskie vybory, *Kommersant,* December 22, 1998.

53. Itak, predstavitel'naia vlast v gorode i oblasti izbrana, *Bereg* (Voronezh), March 30, 2001.

54. Vybory v Lenoblasti: Pobedila stabil'nost, *Peterburgskii Chas pik* (St. Petersburg), December 19, 2001.

55. Zakonotvortsy rvutsia k rabote, *Slovo,* December 21, 2001.

56. Gubernskie kandidaty v deputaty zakonodatel'nogo sobrania, *Kommercheskie vesti* (Omsk), December 26, 2001.

57. Kommunisty opredelilis, *Stavropol'skaia pravda* (Stavropol), October 18, 2001.

58. Smenilo svoe nazvanie na novoe obshchestvennoe dvizhenie "Yuzhnyi Ural," *Cheliabinskii rabochii* (Cheliabinsk), March 22, 1994.

59. Vladimir Utkin, kandidat ot rabochego Urala, *Kontakt* (Cheliabinsk), December 22, 1995.

60. Stanovlenie rossiiskogo parlamentarizma: Regional'nyi aspect, *Vlast,* July 26, 2001.

61. *Vybory v organy gosudarstvennoi vlasti sub"ektov Rossiiskoi Federatsii 1997–2000: elektoral'naia statistika* (Moscow: Ves Mir, 2001), pp. 39–42.

62. Alevtina Aparina, pervyi sekretar Volgogradskogo obkoma KPRF, *Pravda KPRF,* December 8, 2000.

63. Mesto dlia shaga vpered, *Podmoskov'e-Nedelia,* December 26, 2001.

64. Gubernatoru budet opponirovat "kremlevskaia" partia, *Viatskii nabliudatel* (Kirov), July 6, 2001.

65. Partiinye spiski, *Ezhenedel'nik Monitor* (Nizhnii Novgorod), April 29, 2002.

66. "Velikolepnaia semerka" Zaksa, *Delovaia Panorama* (St. Petersburg), November 11, 2000.

67. Politicheskii sovet Vserossiiskogo obshchestvenno-politicheskogo dvizhenia "Nash dom—Rossia," *Rossiskaia gazeta,* April 26, 1997.

68. NDR koordiniruet svoiu deiatel'nost na vsekh urovniakh, *Segodnia,* November 24, 1997.

69. See, for instance, NDR gotovitsia k s"ezdu, *Birobidzhaner Shtern* (Birobidzhan), February 25, 1997.

70. NDR perestaet byt "partiei gubernatorov," *Nezavisimaia gazeta,* January 21, 1998.

71. "Edinstvo nezavisimykh deputatov regiona," *Kaliningradskaia pravda* (Kaliningrad), January 19, 2000.

72. Podrobnosti, *Murmanskii vestnik* (Murmansk), April 5, 2001.

73. "Edinaia Rossia" opredelilas s vyborom, *Tverskaia zhizn* (Tver), March 22, 2002.

74. Bumazhnyi kandidat, *Novye izvestia,* November 16, 2001.

75. "Velikolepnaia semerka" Zaksa, *Delovaia Panorama* (St. Petersburg), November 11, 2000.

76. Vypolniaia voliu izbiratelei, *Orenburzh'e* (Orenburg), November 21, 2002.

77. www.panorama.ru/works/zs/index.html.

78. Here and later, I discounted those committees that dealt exclusively with the internal organization of the legislatures, deputy conduct, and the like.

79. I left out of the "large" domains the committees on legislation. For a discussion of functions played by such committees in the national legislatures of post-communist countries, see Olson 1995: 58.

80. See, for instance, Opasny dlia okruzhaiushchikh, *Tiumenskie izvestia* (Tiumen), November 3, 2001.

81. Nikto ne khotel ustupat, *Sovetskaia Adygeia* (Maikop), January 20, 1996.

82. Professionalizm nachinaetsia s diskussii, *Sovetskaia Adygeia* (Maikop), February 24, 1996.

83. www.adygeya.maykop.ru/parlament/gshra/work/bulletin/iab_4/pr_4.htm.

84. Kto ne s nami, tot protiv nas! *Izvestia,* May 21, 1999.

85. "Yabloko" pokrasneet? *Belgorodskaia pravda* (Belgorod), November 17, 2000.

86. Omskaia strategia proryva, *Pravda KPRF,* June 22, 2000.

87. Omskie politiki ochen khotiat, no poka ne mogut, *Novoe obozrenie* (Omsk), April 7, 1999.

88. www.panorama.ru/works/zs/baza.html.

89. Dekabr na vyborakh, *Sovetskaia Rossia,* December 9, 1997.

90. Deputatskii koeffitsient poleznogo deistvia, *Nizhegorodskie novosti* (Nizhnii Novgorod), December 15, 2001.

91. O dosrochnom prekrashchenii deputatskikh polnomochii, *Tiumenskie izvestia* (Tiumen), October 17, 2001.

7

The Effects of Electoral Systems

The flourishing literature on the relationship between electoral systems and party systems tends to be focused primarily on the roots of political fragmentation (Rae 1967; Taagepera and Shugart 1989; Lijphart 1994; Ordeshook and Shvetsova 1994; Amorim-Neto and Cox 1997), and on the impact exerted by electoral rules upon the organizational properties of political parties (Katz 1980; Carey and Shugart 1995). Yet in Russia, the central question is neither the number of important political parties nor the degree of their organizational cohesion but rather the lack of important parties as such. This chapter deals with this question by analyzing the political consequences of those electoral systems that have been used in regional elections in 1993–2003. While the concept of an electoral system is quite inclusive, the principal aspects to be addressed in this chapter are the consequences for party formation entailed by different electoral formulas, and to a lesser extent by the forms of candidate nomination. Indeed, the diversity of electoral rules employed in Russia's regional assembly elections is striking enough to allow for such a research agenda. At the same time, variations in many other variables are largely controlled because all electoral systems were applied in the same country within a limited time span. Methodologically, therefore, my approach fits into the category of "comparable-cases strategy" (Lijphart 1975). In the first section of the chapter, I provide basic factual information about Russia's regional electoral systems. In the second section, by analyzing some of the findings established in comparative electoral system research and juxtaposing them with Russia's political reality, I state the theoretical expectations regarding the effects of different electoral formulas upon party formation in the country. I then proceed to set out my methodological framework and variable construction. In the final section I present the results of this analysis. Since the findings tend to differ from many of the previously stated expectations, my major task is to explain the idiosyncrasies.

Electoral Systems in the Regions of Russia

In the previous chapter I dealt extensively with federal influences upon the models of separation of powers adopted by different regions. The role of such influences in shaping regional electoral systems should be examined as well. Starting from scratch, that is from the 1936 constitution, which legitimized the direct election of soviet deputies, all elections in the Soviet Union, including those to regional soviets, in theory had to be held in a uniform way by a majority system (Carson 1955; Latov 1974)—that is, by a system in which a candidate is required to win at least 50 percent of the valid votes cast, plus one vote, to be elected. Like in many other countries, the Soviet variant of this system was one with a majority runoff, in which a second round is held between the top two candidates of the first round. This variant of the majority system is often called two-round majority (TRM). Throughout most of Soviet history the provision for the second round was quite inconsequential simply because normally there was only one candidate on the ballot paper. Theoretically again, the voters could cross this candidate's name out, which would render elections void, but such occasions were unusual, to say the least. Starting with 1989, however, TRM was fully implemented in national and regional soviet elections (Urban 1990; Kiernan 1993). The first law on the election of the heads of administrations in regions other than republics adopted by Russia's national legislature in October 1991 also required these elections to be held by TRM. Practically, however, this law was used in few regions, namely in those that subjected Yeltsin-appointed governors to election procedures in April 1993.

The 1993 national legislative elections constituted a major threshold in Russia's history of electoral system development. As described in Chapter 2, the 1993 elections were held by a complex combination of rules. For the first time since 1917, half of the lower chamber of the legislature was to be elected by proportional representation (PR). The other half was elected by a plurality system in single-member districts, in this analysis referred to as single-member plurality (SMP). Finally, the upper chamber of the national legislature was elected by plurality rule in two-member districts, with each elector possessing the number of votes equal to that of contested seats. This system can be defined as multimember plurality (MMP). In contrast to PR and even SMP, MMP was a system not entirely alien to Soviet electoral practices, but before 1993 it was used only at the subregional level.[1] It is worth noting that according to Yeltsin's October 1993 decrees, the majority of the regions were required, and the republics recommended, to hold fresh legislative elections either concurrently with the national elections or in the first half of 1994. One would expect that under such conditions, it was only natural for the regions to grasp electoral systems that were used for national elections. One circumstance that intervenes with this line of reasoning is the fact that on October 27, 1993, Boris Yeltsin issued a decree that approved a document titled "The Basic Regulations of Elections to the Representative Organs of State Power of Territory, Province, Federal City, Autonomous Province, and Autonomous District." In Article 3.2 the document stipulated that regional legislative elections had to be held "as a rule, on the basis of a majority system in single-member (one district, one member) electoral districts drawn on the basis of the norm of representation." Russian legal vocabulary does not make a distinction between majority and plurality systems. However, given that in Article 35 the regulations explicitly defined the winning candidate as the one "who received the largest number of valid votes," it is clear that the drafters of the document meant SMP. At the same time, in Article 3.3 the document stipulated that on the approval of the Central Electoral Commission of Russia, regional authorities could make a decision on holding elections by what, this time quite consistently with the scholarly use of the term, was called a "mixed" electoral system—that is, a system involving a PR tier.

Similar to the rules used for the 1993 national legislative elections, the regulations provided electors with the opportunity to vote against all candidates. Thus the right theoretically possessed by voters in the Soviet era was retained under the new order, even though it had to be exercised not by crossing out the names of disapproved candidates but rather by making a mark in a special box on the ballot paper.[2] The regulations stated that in order to win, the leading candidate had to receive more votes than cast "against all." Otherwise, election results would be declared invalid, and by-elections would follow. Besides, the regulations stipulated that for elections to be valid, voter turnout had to exceed 35 percent. While this aspect of Russia's electoral systems is not of primary importance for this analysis, it must be briefly addressed insofar as it had a direct impact on party representation in regional legislative assemblies. Following the federal regulations, the regions were quick to set turnout requirements at 35 percent or even higher, sometimes at 50 percent. As a result, many regions in 1994 entered a marathon series of by-elections caused by insufficient turnout. Political parties suffered from this process because turnout tended to be higher in the countryside and lower in urban areas, where the majority of party candidates in the first electoral cycle actually ran. In the second electoral cycle, however, this factor largely lost its importance. On the one hand, political parties, especially the Communist Party of the Russian Federation (KPRF) and the Agrarian Party of Russia (APR), successfully penetrated the rural areas. On the other hand, from 1994 until 2002, federal law did not set specific turnout requirements, while the regional legislators used their ability to learn from error by lowering these requirements or abolishing them altogether. Indeed, during the first electoral cycle one of the major handicaps in the activities of regional legislative assemblies was their inability to reach a quorum.

Retrospectively, it can be said that the regulations were not a masterpiece of electoral legislation. Some of their provisions, in fact, were impossible to implement. For instance, while making it imperative that electoral district borders be drawn in accordance with the "norm of representation," an aspect addressed in the previous chapter, the regulations also required that they be drawn in a way that would allocate at least one mandate to each of the administrative districts (Article 7.1.V). Given that another decree, as mentioned in the previous chapter, required the regional legislatures to have no more than fifty members, in many regions district borders were drawn either in correspondence to the administrative borders or on the basis of the norm of representation, not in both ways simultaneously. Thus the regulations indirectly legitimized the use of administrative-territorial districts. True, in November 1993 Yeltsin issued a decree that excluded Article 7.1.V from the regulations. Yet judging from how district borders were actually drawn in the first electoral cycle, the regional authorities largely overlooked this second decree. This brings us to a more important question, the extent to which the 1993 regulations were implemented regionally. In fact, rather than stipulating for direct implementation, the document charged the regional authorities with using it as a basis for developing regional regulations. Curiously enough, Article 3.1 of the document defined the regional authorities charged with this undertaking in two ways: first, as the representative bodies of power, and second, in those regions where these bodies were dismissed as requested by one of the Yeltsin's previous decrees, as the heads of regional administrations.

Indeed, the regional regulations on holding legislative elections came from different quarters. An analysis of more than thirty such documents conducted by Petrov (1996) allowed him to conclude that the heads of administrations exercised their right to draft them in approximately half of the regions. In several regions, especially but not exclusively in republics, the soviets were not actually dissolved and thus remained in full capacity to draft the regulations. In other regions, the soviets were dissolved but, with the permission of the heads of administration, provisional bodies were created to carry on legislative work. In two regions, Moscow city and Moscow province, electoral regulations were introduced by a special decree of the federal executive. Perhaps the most unusual course of action was taken in Belgorod province, where the regulations were drafted by a specially convened constituent assembly.[3] Comprehensive factual evidence on the institutional choices made by the drafters of the regional regulations will be presented below. Here, it is sufficient to say that quite in keeping with the decree of October 27, 1993, only a few regions—precisely three—opted for mixed electoral systems in the first electoral cycle. Two of them, Marii El and Tyva, held their legislative elections concurrently with the national elections in December 1993. While little is known about the political contexts in which they adopted mixed electoral systems, I would speculate that they mimicked national legislation without giving much thought to the consequences. The prospects for switching to mixed electoral systems were actively discussed in two republics, Tatarstan[4] and Karelia (Tsygankov 1998), where the local elites apparently viewed such institutional arrangements as important symbols of their sovereignty. As a result of these discussions, however, Tatarstan abandoned the idea altogether, while in Karelia it was implemented for electing the city council of the republic's capital, not the regional legislature. In Saratov province, in contrast, the adoption of a mixed system reflected both the pressure from local political activists[5] and the deliberate political choice of the regional executive (Ryzhenkov 1997). The vast majority of regions opted for plurality/majority formulas. It seems that in choosing the variants of such formulas, the regions felt largely unconstrained by the provisions of the 1993 regulations. While it is true that most regions obeyed the regulations by adopting SMP systems, the cases of MMP were quite numerous too. In addition, several regions, mostly republics, stuck to TRM systems inherited from the Soviet past. In St. Petersburg, Mayor Anatolii Sobchak first enacted electoral regulations that stipulated for an SMP formula,[6] but then, fearing that a thus elected legislature would be controlled by his political rivals, switched to TRM in the midst of the electoral campaign.

Thus by the end of the first electoral cycle, the set of electoral formulas in use in regional legislative elections emerged largely as a product of the regions' choice, not as a result of pressures from Moscow. This set, including SMP, MMP, TRM, and mixed electoral systems involving PR, remained largely unchanged throughout the 1993–2003 period. The federal law "On the Basic Guarantees of Citizens' Electoral Rights," enacted in December 1994, established quite a loose legal framework for holding regional elections, especially as far as electoral formulas are concerned, by permitting all four formulas to be used if stipulated by regional law. Unlike the 1993 regulations, the 1994 law did not contain any reservations regarding the use of mixed electoral systems in the regions. Similar to the 1993 regulations, but this time with more consistency, the law excluded administrative borders as a basis of electoral districting. True, some of the republics continued to use administrative-territorial districts in clear contradiction to the law, while others employed bicameralism as a loophole. In regions other than republics, however, administrative-territorial districts started to disappear. One way to eliminate the problem was, of course, to create equal-size single-member districts. An alternative way permitted by the 1994 law was to leave some of the previously existing single-member districts intact while transforming others, namely those with large populations, into multimember districts in accordance with sizes of voting populations. This is one of the reasons for a visible increase in the number of regions employing MMP in the second electoral cycle. Mixed systems, in contrast, remained out of demand. All three regions that used them in the first electoral cycle abandoned them. Of those five regions that switched to mixed systems in the second electoral cycle, two autonomous districts, Koriak and Ust-Ordynskoe Buriat, could have made such institutional choices partly in order to implement the norm of representation as required by the federal legislation, even though it should be immediately added that they were in position to meet this requirement in different ways. Both of them reverted to plurality systems in the third electoral cycle. At the same time, the authorities of three other regions, Krasnoiarsk territory and Kaliningrad and Sverdlovsk provinces, apparently sought to achieve certain political goals by electoral system reform. In these regions mixed systems proved to be sustainable. Pskov province joined them in the third electoral cycle. The political motives for switching to mixed systems will be discussed below. Here it is important to mention that in 1994–2002, federal authorities and federal law neither encouraged potential switches to mixed systems nor discouraged them. Those few switches that did take place occurred because of institutional choices made independently in the regions.

The 1994 law served as a basis for new regional electoral laws that gradually replaced the provisional regulations of late 1993 through 1994. In 1997 the federal legislature adopted a new federal law titled "On the Basic Guarantees of Citizens' Electoral Rights and the Right to Participate in Referenda." The new law was different from its predecessor in that it regulated electoral procedures in much more detail, but speaking of basic formulaic structures, it did not bring about any significant innovations. In this particular respect, the only additional limitation imposed by the new law was that the magnitude of multimember plurality districts—that is, the number of seats to be allocated in each of them—must not exceed five. Quite probably, such a provision came as a reaction to the 1994 elections in Ingushetia, where all the members of legislature were elected at large in a single twenty-seven-member district. Some of the observers considered this to be a gross violation of voter rights, arguing that it was impossible to meaningfully cast as many as twenty-seven votes. Convincing or not, this logic produced a legal provision that, in addition to Ingushetia, made it imperative to change electoral systems in four other regions, Kalmykia, Krasnodar territory, Jewish autonomous province, and Khanty-Mansi autonomous district.

The second important federal intrusion into the use of MMP in Russia's regions took place in March 2000, when the Constitutional Court of Russia ruled that the numbers of votes available to voters in any given elections had to be equal. The judiciary justified this decision by arguing that having different numbers of votes in the same election violated the principle of voter equality. The ruling legally eliminated the previously widespread practice in which some of the deputies were elected in single-member districts and others in multimember districts of different magnitudes, which happened in Orenburg province—the case on which the Constitutional Court made its judgment. As a result of the 2000 ruling, some of the regions switched to "pure" SMP systems, which partly explains why the number of MMP systems in the third electoral cycle decreased. At the same time, several regions switched to "pure" MMP systems with equal-magnitude districts instead. The third and most unusual option was to retain old district magnitudes but to endow each of the voters, irrespective of district magnitude, with only one vote. This course of action was taken in two third-cycle regional legislative elections, in Murmansk and Tver provinces. Curiously, by doing so, the regional legislators brought to life a distinct electoral formula that is internationally known as single nontransferable vote (SNTV). By all appearances, this was an unintentional result of the regional legislators' attempts to satisfy the requirements of the federal law without redrawing district borders. The 2000 ruling left intact the use of regionwide MMP districts in parallel with SMP districts of smaller size, as well as the use of MMP for electing individual chambers of bicameral legislatures.

The sweeping reform of the electoral systems of Russia's regions that was initiated in 2002 will be discussed at length in Chapter 8. Here, it is sufficient to say that major innovations concerning electoral formulas were not to be enacted before July 14, 2003. Thus throughout the first three electoral cycles, and despite the minor attempts at federal regulation discussed above, the regions were largely free to choose formulas for their legislative elections from a rather large set of available options. The second aspect of primary importance for this analysis, candidate nomination, was also not subjected to extensive federal regulation. As discussed previously in this book, very few regions, exclusively in the first electoral cycle, did not mention party nomination in their electoral regulations. Such an omission was in fact illegal from the point of view of the 1993 federal regulations and the 1994 law. In the vast majority of regions in the first electoral cycle and invariably thereafter, political parties and blocs, alongside groups of voters, individual voters, and candidates themselves, could perform as candidate-nominating entities. The only exception is the 1994 elections in Kalmykia, which in addition to nineteen "regular" single-member districts involved a nine-member district where candidate nominations could be made exclusively by the president of the republic. The oddity of this provision was further exacerbated by the fact that in this district, 25 percent of the vote sufficed to win. By the beginning of the second electoral cycle, however, the right of political parties to run their candidates in regional elections became recognized in all regional electoral laws. In 1997 the national legislature amended the 1994 federal electoral law by introducing a narrow definition of "political public associations" that made most of the interest advocacy groups ineligible for electoral participation and required those parties that wanted to retain their eligibility to obtain fresh registration with the Ministry of Justice. However, none of the nationally or regionally important parties were affected.

In those regions that used mixed electoral systems, candidate nomination in their PR tiers was made available exclusively to political parties. Besides, there were two regions where only political parties could nominate candidates in multimember plurality districts, a system referred to in this analysis as party multimember plurality (PMMP). One of them, North Ossetia, used a very unusual electoral system that combined seventy single-member plurality districts with the election of five deputies in a plurality district under the following conditions: each of the electors was to have five votes, only political parties were entitled to nominate candidates, and each party could nominate only one candidate. Theoretically, this curiosity can be viewed as a real-life instance of a hypothetical "every-party-gets-a-seat" electoral system (Taagepera and Shugart 1989: 33–34). Koriak autonomous district, when switching from a mixed electoral system in 2000, allowed for electing four of its twelve legislators by MMP with exclusive party nomination and without any limitations on the number of candidates nominated by any single party. In both regions, the explicitly stated goal of these innovations was to encourage party development. It seems that in North Ossetia, a more proper term would be "token representation." As far as Koriak autonomous district is concerned, PMMP was more of a price paid for switching from the mixed electoral system.

The second question applying to candidate nomination concerns who could be nominated. In the vast majority of regions throughout the period, the answer to this question was unproblematic because virtually nobody was excluded. At the same time, there were several regions in which candidate nomination in certain electoral districts was reserved for specific societal categories. Dagestan, a republic where the possibility of ethnic conflict was strong, used an elaborate scheme of group representation in its legislative elections. In 1994, when it was used for the first time, the scheme combined forty-eight single-member majority districts open to all candidates, with seventy-three districts where candidates had to belong to certain ethnic groups, to have certain educational backgrounds, or to be female (Kisriev and Ware 2001). In several districts, only candidates combining some of these characteristics were allowed to run. Despite its complexity, the system apparently worked well enough to ease ethnic tensions, if not to improve the educational and gender compositions in the legislature. While subject to criticism from different quarters, the system survived into the next electoral cycle, even though in a revised form because in early 1999 the Constitutional Court of Dagestan ruled out gender-based districts.[7] For the 2003 elections, Dagestan's legislators invented an even more unusual electoral system. It combined sixty-eight single-member districts with nineteen multimember districts of varying magnitudes. Elections in the single-member districts were to be held by TRM. Multimember district elections were distinctive in two ways. First, there were ethnic quotas in these districts. For instance, in a three-member district, two of the elected deputies had to represent ethnic groups specified by the law, while the remaining mandate (locally referred to as an "open mandate") was to be allocated irrespective of the winning candidate's nationality. Second, while multimember elections were to be held by SNTV in the sense that each of the voters had only one vote, Dagestan's legislators also introduced a majority requirement. In order to make this provision logically compatible with SNTV, they defined "majority" as a product of dividing 50 percent by district magnitude. This meant that in a five-member district, the front-runner had to receive at least 10 percent of the vote in order to win. Otherwise, the second round of voting had to be held.[8] I refer to this unusual electoral system as SNTV with a majority requirement (SNTVM).

In addition to Dagestan, several autonomous districts used ethnicity-based nomination practices to ensure the representation of their "titular nationalities," which also happened to be ethnic minorities. This was achieved by creating regionwide multimember districts in which everybody could vote but only ethnic minorities could run. Such provisions of the regional laws, however benevolent, had to confront the harsh reality of voter attitudes, though. While the system seemed to work well when initially implemented, in the third electoral cycle the Russian voting majorities of Yamal-Nenets and Khanty-Mansi autonomous districts effectively got rid of it by casting votes against all candidates, so that ethnic representatives could not be elected anyway.[9] In general, it can be argued that such provisions suppressed party development by inducing ethnicity-based electoral mobilization instead. This reasoning, however, does not take into account that seats reserved for ethnic representation could be contested and won either by ethnic-based organizations, such as Yamal to the Descendants in Yamal-Nenets autonomous district, or by parties of cross-ethnic appeal, such as the Communist Party of the Republic of Dagestan. Thus in the analysis below I do not address the effects of special provisions for ethnic representation at any length.

By two major criteria identified above, electoral formula and candidacy form, the universe of systems used for regional legislative elections in Russia can be divided into seven substantively different yet unequally spread categories: TRM, SMP, MMP, SNTV, SNTVM, PMMP, and mixed systems involving PR. Before reporting factual evidence on their spread in the regions of Russia, it is important to make several remarks about their technical characteristics. All the mixed systems but one belong to the category of mixed-superposition systems (Massicotte and Blais 1999), which means that each elector has two sets of representatives, one of them elected in a PR district, and the other, most often, in a plurality district. Krasnoiarsk territory in 1997 and Koriak autonomous district in 1996 elected certain numbers of their deputies by TRM and MMP respectively. One region, Sverdlovsk province, elected the whole lower chamber of its assembly by PR. Yet in this case too, PR elections were almost invariably held concurrently with SMP elections to the upper chamber, which makes it possible to treat this system as a special case of SMP-PR superposition. Speaking of the characteristics of the PR tiers of Russia's regional elections, all of them were closed list systems used in regionwide districts, their magnitudes varying from four to twenty. The mode of seat allocation was invariably Hare quota and largest remainders. The legal thresholds of representation are normally the same as in national legislative elections, 5 percent of the vote. A curious situation occurred in Koriak autonomous district when its legislators, apparently seeking to avoid political fragmentation, introduced a 25 percent threshold of representation in the 1996 elections. Three parties, the KPRF, Our Home Is Russia (NDR), and the Association of Aboriginal Small Nationalities of the North, contested the elections. Many votes were cast against all lists. As a result, only one party, the KPRF, crossed the threshold and was thus eligible to claim all seats allocated by PR. Yet the Communists, apparently not expecting such a "sweeping victory" in a region with predominantly noncommunist voter attitudes, nominated a list of only three candidates, one of whom refused to take his seat because he immediately received an offer for a high-standing position with the regional executive.

While the combinations of different plurality/majority formulas are not normally considered mixed electoral systems, the ways of combining their components can be described in the same terms. From this perspective, the available set of mixtures includes not only the cases of superposition (when single-member and multimember districts overlap) and bicameralism, in both of which every voter has two sets of representatives, but also those of coexistence, in which different parts of the territories are subjected to different rules. General information about electoral systems employed for legislative elections in the regions of Russia in 1993–2003 can be found in Table 7.1, with "+" referring to various ways of combining electoral system components.[10] I distinguish among the categories involving combinations of different systems by a rather transparent criterion of the particular rule applied to the election of the majority of deputies. One region, Kabardino-Balkaria, used SMP and MMP rules for electing equal-size chambers of its

Table 7.1   Electoral Systems in the Regions of Russia, Percentage Shares by Electoral Cycle, 1993–2003

	1st Electoral Cycle	2nd Electoral Cycle	3rd Electoral Cycle
Plurality/Majority			
TRM	8.2	7.1	6.0
TRM + SNTVM	—	—	1.2
SMP	65.9	60.0	72.6
SMP + MMP	8.2	10.6	4.8
SMP + PMMP	—	1.2	—
SMP + SNTV	—	—	1.2
MMP	8.2	7.1	7.1
MMP + SMP	5.9	8.2	—
MMP + PMMP	—	—	1.2
SNTV + SMP	—	—	1.2
Mixed			
TRM + PR	—	1.2	—
SMP + PR	3.5	3.5	4.8
MMP + PR	—	1.2	—
Total	99.9[a]	100.1[a]	100.1[a]

Note: a. Does not sum to 100.0 percent because of rounding.

assembly. I arbitrarily assigned this electoral system to the SMP + MMP category. As follows from the table, the distribution of basic electoral system types across regions remained relatively stable despite numerous switches in individual regions. The share of majority systems gradually decreased, while the share of systems involving MMP increased from the first to the second electoral cycles and then declined again. Most visibly, not only was SMP the most widespread system throughout the 1993–2003 period, but its domination consolidated over time as well.

Understandably, electoral systems used for regional executive elections were much more uniform. Indeed, the regions elected their executives by only two systems, TRM and SMP. As discussed by Lijphart (1994: 18), all TRM systems employed in the regions of Russia are majority-majority systems in the sense that only two top candidates from the first round enter the second round, even though the provision for voting against all candidates makes it possible that a candidate can win without receiving a majority of the vote. One more clarification is that several regions modified their SMP systems by allowing for second rounds. Second rounds are held if none of the candidates receive more than a specified share of the vote below 50 percent, such as 35 percent or 25 percent. I assign such modifications to the category of SMP. Taking this into account and excluding Chechnya again, it can be reported that in the second and third electoral cycles, SMP was employed in 28.1 and 34.1 percent of regional executive elections respectively, with the remaining regions using TRM. It can be argued that the small increase in the number of regions that employed SMP was politically motivated. Vulnerable incumbents used SMP for converting their modest electoral assets into electoral victories. For instance, the governor of Pskov province initiated a switch from TRM to SMP in order to escape a very possible defeat in the second round.[11] The strategy worked perfectly well, as testified to by the fact that the incumbent gained reelection with only 28 percent of the vote. Given the negligible role played by political parties in regional executive elections, it would be difficult to expect that TRM and SMP produce varying effects on the levels of party candidate success, and indeed my statistical analysis revealed no such effects whatsoever. The empirical evidence for my analysis comes from regional legislative elections.

Theoretical Expectations and Findings

Empirically, the problem of electoral system effects upon party formation may seem too simplistic to deserve scholarly treatment. Indeed, such a basic feature of proportional representation systems as the list form of candidacy can be easily identified as a principal determinant of party formation because, even though it may be absolutely insufficient for full-scale party institutionalization, it mechanically excludes independents from electoral competition, thus making party formation unavoidable.[12] However, this analysis is empirically focused on less permissive institutional environments where list candidacy either does not exist or plays a secondary role. If not mechanically induced by the list form of candidacy, political parties emerge as a product of politicians' self-interest. Within the context of regional legislative elections the desired outcome is, of course, an assembly seat. Political parties can be expected to form wherever they help to achieve this end. The principal questions in this regard are, first, how many additional votes come along with party affiliation, and second, whether the addition of this many votes to a candidate's total is likely to produce a victory. It is the second question that brings the electoral system into the calculus of a self-interested politician, yet the first question is of course more important. Candidates, irrespective of their affiliations, win if they obtain the amounts of votes that earn them seats within the most favorable competitive contexts (the threshold of inclusion or representation) and within the least favorable ones (the threshold of exclusion). From this perspective, it is important to note that judging from the results of national legislative elections by party lists, only three parties could provide their candidates with a vote surplus greater than 20 percent: in 1995–2003 the KPRF, in 1993–1995 the Liberal Democratic Party of Russia (LDPR), and in

1999–2003 Unity. The LDPR, however, was not organizationally developed enough to actively participate in regional politics during the heyday of its electoral appeal, while Unity remained inactive in regional elections throughout most of the period. Of course, more parties were successful in individual regions, but the general picture still points to the uniqueness of the KPRF in terms of its ability to secure sufficient numbers of votes for its nominees. In different electoral systems, the values of effective thresholds vary. At this moment, leaving quantitative specifications for further analysis, it is important to mention that the value of the threshold of inclusion depends on the number of candidates contesting each seat.

A long-established property of the single-member plurality system is that it tends to lead to two-party competition, thus decreasing the level of party system fragmentation. This "law," first formulated by Duverger (1954), has been tested empirically in numerous studies, many of which found it to be correct (Rae 1967; Taagepera and Shugart 1989; Lijphart 1994). While political fragmentation is not of primary concern for this analysis, Duverger's law and the related debates are still important for assessing the impact exerted by SMP upon party formation. Under SMP, third parties tend to be gradually eliminated because they fail to cross the effective thresholds. The threshold of exclusion under this system is invariably 50 percent of the vote, while the threshold of inclusion varies depending on the competitive context: its value can be obtained by dividing 100 percent by the number of candidates. From the figure reported above, one may infer that the average threshold of inclusion in Russia's regions that employ SMP is roughly 20 percent of the vote. Judging from the levels of voter support gained in national elections, this means that during the period under observation none of Russia's parties had been able to supply its nominee with the amount of votes sufficient to cross the threshold of exclusion, while the threshold of inclusion was within the reach of the KPRF. Yet even this ability was fairly limited. Hence there are reasons to expect that the impact of SMP upon party formation in Russia's regions is negative.

The effects of multimember plurality are less well known than those of SMP because MMP is less widespread. In their fundamental treatment of electoral system effects, Taagepera and Shugart (1989: 23) briefly state that MMP tends to "lead to extreme disproportionality" and then leave this "increasingly rare" system aside. In fact, as of 1999, MMP was employed for national elections in thirteen countries with populations of more than 500,000 (Rose 2000). There are several historical instances of national elections by SMP-MMP combinations in major democracies (Lijphart 1994: 19–20). By 1998, thirteen states in the United States used MMP for electing their legislatures (Wasserman 2000). U.S. subnational elections are indeed the most extensively researched instance of MMP (Engstrom and McDonald 1986; Gerber, Morton, and Rietz 1998). The most commonly attained finding is that such systems tend to suppress minority representation. This happens because of these systems' ability to produce a "sweep effect," manifesting itself in that "any party, slate-making organization, ethnic group etc. that can get a bare majority (or plurality in any election that permits plurality winners) will tend to win all or most of the seats at stake" (Weaver 1984: 193). The existence of the sweep effect has been noticed in some cross-national studies too (Reynolds and Reilly 1997: 36). If this effect does take place in Russia, then the impact of MMP upon party formation can be expected to be a reinforced version of SMP: it strongly supports strong parties and strongly suppresses weak parties, thus producing single-party domination. Given that in 1993–1999 the strong KPRF effectively emerged as the principal agency of party development in the regions of Russia, the overall impact of MMP upon party formation may be positive. It is doubtful, however, that Russia's nascent political parties, including the strongest of them, are strong enough to enjoy a bonus produced by this system. In fact, this system makes the threshold of exclusion even higher than under SMP: $(100 \text{ percent} \times M) / (M + 1)$, where M is district magnitude (Rae, Hanby, and Loosemore 1971). This yields 66.7 percent for two-member districts, 75 percent for three-member districts, and so on. Of course, the threshold of exclusion is calculated for the conditions of minimal competitiveness, with the number of candidates in the district as small as $M + 1$. If two candidates contest each of the seats, the threshold of exclusion is the same as in two-candidate races under SMP: 50 percent irrespective of district magnitude.

When studying the effects of MMP in Hungarian local elections, Benoit (2001: 217) observed that the overall numbers of candidates in multimember districts tended to increase in comparison with single-member districts. This is hardly an unexpected finding, yet theoretically the proliferation of candidates alone may account for bringing down the threshold of inclusion, thus creating more permissive environments for weak party candidates. But for this hypothesis to be true, an important condition has to be fulfilled. The formula that establishes the value of the threshold of inclusion for MMP is essentially identical to that for SMP—that is, if expressed as a percentage, $(100 \text{ percent} \times M) / n$, where M is district magnitude and n is the number of candidates. Thus the threshold of inclusion becomes lower only if the number of candidates contesting every seat, not only every district, becomes greater than under SMP. But there is no apparent theoretical reason to believe that this is the case. My expectations regarding the impact of MMP upon party formation are therefore mixed. While, due to the higher threshold of exclusion, it may be that MMP suppresses all parties irrespective of their relative size, there are two different reasons—the sweep effect and empirical evidence from Hungary—to expect a more positive effect.

The two-round majority formula has long been in use for parliamentary elections in one of the major democracies, France. Other instances of TRM, both historical (Carstairs 1980) and contemporary (Rose 2000), are quite numerous. TRM is often praised for its capability to "encourage the formation of bargains among the parties in between rounds" (Taagepera and Shugart 1989: 22). This is achieved by excluding those parties that, however strong, are not disposed for bargain making (Hermens 1984: 25–26). One may expect that the TRM-induced mechanisms of exclusion apply primarily to the KPRF, a strong yet rather rigid party ideologically. Speaking of other parties, a reasonable expectation would be that they are too small to gain at the expense of the KPRF. Indeed, the thresholds of exclusion and inclusion in the second round of TRM elections are as high as 50 percent, which is unlikely to help small parties. Hence it can be hypothesized that the overall effect of TRM upon party formation in the regions of Russia is entirely negative, as the KPRF is damaged no less than its political opponents.

Mixed electoral systems can be expected to support party formation simply because their proportional tiers exclude independents. In addition, they yield very low thresholds of exclusion and inclusion, which makes one logically expect that they support not only strong but also weak parties, quite in line with the voluminous literature dealing with PR effects upon party system fragmentation. Indeed, there is some cross-national evidence that such systems facilitate the survival of minor parties (Shugart and Wattenberg 2001). Yet these expectations apply primarily to what results from the allocation of proportional seats. Given that the proportional tiers of Russia's regional electoral systems are invariably smaller than nonproportional tiers, a more important question is what happens in plurality/majority districts under the impact of "mixing" them with PR. Regarding this question, there is not too much empirical evidence to rely upon. Moser (1997, 1999), who has established that the plurality tier of Russia's national legislative elections tends not to significantly constrain the number of electoral competitors, relates this finding to the massive presence of independent candidates—that is, to the lack of progress in party formation. Such an explanation, while very plausible in itself, is difficult to build into the explanatory logic of this analysis. A useful cue can be derived from a phenomenon dubbed the "contamination effect." The presence of a party candidate often enhances the fortunes of the given party in the proportional tier of elections in the given district, which makes parties nominate more candidates than possible in a "pure" plurality or majority system (Golosov and Yargomskaya 1999; Herron and Nishikawa 2001; Cox and Schoppa 2002). This naturally increases the overall share of party candidates. Not all of them are necessarily weak, performing as tokens of party presence. On the one hand, parties themselves are interested in recruiting stronger candidates. On the other hand, the increased visibility of parties in the given electoral arena may push toward party affiliation those personally resourceful candidates who would otherwise maintain nonpartisanship. Hence it can be expected that under mixed electoral systems, party formation is stimulated not only by the effects of their PR tiers, but also by the contamination effect as described above.

When testing the expectations stated above empirically, I follow Lijphart (1994) in using electoral systems rather than individual elections or individual regions as the basic units of analysis. Such a research strategy seems to be consistent with the goals of my study. The overall number of thus-defined observations in the study is 162, which corresponds to 254 elections observed in 88 regions. Ordinary least squares (OLS) estimation is used for all models.[13] My definition of electoral system change, which allows for characterizing systems consequently employed in the same region as different, includes the following components. The first and most important of them is any shift from one of the seven basic systems identified above (SMP, MMP, TRM, SNTV, SNTVM, PMMP, or PR) to another, or in case of their mixtures, any increase of the share of deputies elected by one of them at the expense of another. The second component, radical redistricting, can be subdivided into two categories. One of them is the change of assembly size, which occurred quite frequently and sometimes on an impressive scale. The other category is the change of principles according to which district borders are drawn, which involves switches between "regular" and "administrative-territorial" districts and, on a smaller scale, occasional experimentation with minority representation as described above. The cases when district borders were redrawn without a shift from one principle of representation to another were not considered as constituting new electoral systems, even though sometimes the scope of such a redistricting was quite sizable. In addition to the 1996–1997 elections in Chechnya, I had to exclude three elections that, for different reasons, were held on nonpartisan bases.[14] I also excluded the 2002 elections in Sverdlovsk province, which in contrast to all previously held elections in the region and uniquely in the history of regional legislative elections in Russia, were held exclusively by the PR system. This happened because the upper chamber of the regional legislature elected in 2000 extended its term to four years, while the lower chamber did not and thus was subjected to fresh elections. Leaving this case in my selection would have created a less than desirable outlier produced exclusively by the mechanical effects of the party-list form of candidacy. The values of all variables are defined either on a single-observation basis or as averages for two or three observations.

My principal dependent variable is the percentage share of party nominees elected to the regional assembly. Given that my theoretical expectations regarding the impact of electoral systems upon party development vary depending on party size, I employ two additional dependent variables, the share of elected KPRF nominees, which for the purposes of this study includes the nominees of the other parties belonging to the KPRF conglomerate, and the share of elected nominees of noncommunist parties. An important substantive problem can be related to the fact that within my research design, the effects of PR have to be distinguished from the effects of mixing it with plurality/majority rules. I sought to solve this problem by using two sets of dependent variables, one of them including proportional seats won by the parties under consideration, and the other excluding them. Turning to the construction of independent variables, it is important to note that most recent empirical research on the effects of electoral systems tends to concentrate on one variable that is justly considered to be central, district magnitude (Ordeshook and Shvetsova 1994; Amorim-Neto and Cox 1997). In particular, district magnitude was employed to distinguish between plurality/majority formulas and PR. Yet in this study it is important to take into account more subtle distinctions among different varieties of plurality/majority rules. In order to overcome this difficulty, I used a three-step procedure, each step resulting in the introduction of an independent variable. First, I distinguished between SMP and TRM on the one hand, and systems employing MMP and SNTV on the other hand, by constructing a variable defined as the average magnitude of plurality/majority districts (AMPMD). Its values equal 1 for SMP and TRM, and they are always greater than 1 for MMP and SNTV. The advantage of a variable constructed in this manner is that it takes into account both the shares of deputies elected by MMP and district magnitudes. My model does not estimate the effects of SNTV primarily because of the very limited use of this system in the regions of Russia: elements of SNTV were involved in only 3 of 162 electoral systems in my study.[15] A theoretical rationale for such an approach will be provided further in this chapter.

The second step was to bring in TRM by introducing a variable defined as the percentage share of deputies elected by this system. Since TRM is only rarely used in combination with other systems, its values in my data set are 0 or 100, which makes the variable almost dichotomous, with an exception for one region that "mixed" it with PR and another that "mixed" it with SNTVM. Finally, PR itself is introduced in exactly the same way, as a percentage share of deputies elected by this system. The use of an obvious alternative, PR district magnitude, could have brought very similar results statistically,[16] but it seems plausible to suggest that the consequences of the presence of a four-member PR district are greater in a twelve-member assembly than in a thirty-member assembly. And, to state it once more, my purpose is not to assess the effects of PR as such, for its positive impact upon party formation is self-evident, but rather to estimate the results of "mixing" it with plurality/majority systems. One more clarification is that for the purposes of statistical analysis, I rather arbitrarily assigned two electoral systems involving PMMP to the category of mixed electoral systems. The magnitudes of multimember districts are not entered into my calculations of AMPMD, but they are taken into account when establishing the values of the PR variable for these two systems. Such an approach can be justified with reference to the fact that PMMP not only mechanically guarantees certain levels of success to party nominees but also, and related to this property, can be expected to produce something similar to the "contamination effects." The shares of deputies elected by PMMP are so small that such a categorization, correct or not, does not significantly influence the results of my analysis.

The effects of electoral systems upon party formation in the regions of Russia are estimated in Table 7.2. The effects of PR are most clearly as expected. It emerges as the strongest predictor of party development if PR seats are taken into account, but even if they are not, a strong positive influence is still evident, even though the parameter estimate is considerably smaller. At the same time, multiple regression analysis brings about two largely unexpected results. First, in total contradiction to my expectations, TRM does not seem to suppress party formation. In fact, it seems that this electoral system produces no effect on party formation whatsoever. Second, the effects of MMP upon party formation turn out to be positive irrespective of how the dependent variable is constructed. When stating my theoretical expectations regarding the possible role of MMP, I presented two alternative explanations of why it may support party formation, the sweep effect and the lowering of the threshold of inclusion consequential upon the mul-

Table 7.2   Electoral Systems and Party Representation in Russia's Regional Legislative Assemblies, 1993–2003

| Variables | PR Seats Included | | PR Seats Excluded | |
	Parameter Estimate	T-value	Parameter Estimate	T-value
Intercept	4.76* (2.59)	1.84	4.20 (2.65)	1.59
AMPMD	6.92*** (1.65)	4.21	7.19*** (1.68)	4.27
TRM	–0.02 (0.05)	–0.46	–0.02 (0.05)	–0.34
PR	1.17*** (0.15)	7.71	0.65*** (0.15)	4.22
N	162		162	
R-squared	0.32		0.18	
Adj. R-squared	0.31		0.17	

Notes: The dependent variable is the share of seats won by all party nominees. Parentheses indicate standard errors.
  * Significant at 0.1.
  ** Significant at 0.05.
  *** Significant at 0.01.

tiplication of candidacies. In order to test whether the former explanation is true, it is sufficient to look at multiple regression results for two additional dependent variables. Multiple regression results for the KPRF dependent variable are reported in Table 7.3. Very small values of R-squared suggest that the level of the party's representation only marginally depends on electoral systems. The consequences of PR are far less pronounced, and they seem to be more complex than in the previous case. It appears that the KPRF does benefit from PR by winning PR seats, yet when these seats are excluded from analysis, the gains turn out to be insignificant. As a partial compensation for this idiosyncrasy, TRM behaves almost as predicted. It does suppress the strong, ideologically rigid party, even though the effect is less than statistically significant. The effects of MMP apparently support the sweep-effect hypothesis. However, before making conclusions regarding the presence of the sweep effect in Russia's regional legislative elections, it stands to reason, first, to take a closer look at electoral returns in those regions that actually use MMP, and second, to examine how it influences noncommunist parties.

Multiple regression results presented in Table 7.4 add several important clarifications to the findings reported above. The positive effects of PR upon the formation of noncommunist parties are much stronger than in the previously observed case, and they do not fade away upon the exclusion of seats allocated by proportionality rules. This means that when forced to enter the electoral arena under the influence of PR, noncommunist parties are capable of finding ways to recruit relatively strong candidates. A more

Table 7.3   Electoral Systems and Representation of the KPRF Conglomerate in Russia's Regional Legislative Assemblies, 1993–2003

Variables	PR Seats Included			PR Seats Excluded		
	Parameter Estimate		T-value	Parameter Estimate		T-value
Intercept	3.21*	(1.91)	1.68	3.24	(1.90)	1.70
AMPMD	3.66***	(1.21)	3.02	3.58***	(1.21)	2.96
TRM	−0.05	(0.04)	−1.47	−0.05	(0.03)	−1.47
PR	0.31***	(0.11)	2.79	0.11	(0.11)	0.99
N	162			162		
R-squared	0.11			0.08		
Adj. R-squared	0.09			0.06		

Notes: The dependent variable is the share of seats won by the KPRF conglomerate nominees. Parentheses indicate standard errors.
  * Significant at 0.1.
  ** Significant at 0.05.
  *** Significant at 0.01.

abstract explanation could be that by stimulating party candidate nomination in SMP/MMP districts, PR helps to enhance the overall number of candidates, thus bringing down the threshold of inclusion. However, the difference between the average numbers of district candidates per seat in the mixed and nonmixed systems of Russia's regions is statistically insignificant. In contrast to noncommunist parties, the KPRF is already present in the majority of regional elections, but it is worse equipped for luring personally resourceful candidates under its banner. It is thus not surprising that it gains little from the contamination effect. Speaking in more general terms, it is worth mentioning that within the specific context of Russia's regional elections, PR fully adheres to its reputation as a formula that supports political fragmentation. The primary gainers from the effects of PR— not only from its own effects induced mechanically but also from the political effects of "mixing" it with plurality/majority formulas—are small parties. Some of the elections held by mixed electoral systems in the regions of Russia brought about spectacular examples of political fragmentation. For instance, in the 1993 elections in Marii El, eight PR seats were distributed among seven parties. In the 2000 elections in Kaliningrad province, five PR seats were allocated to five different parties. Of course, it may be argued that an assembly that contains five party deputies, each of them belonging to a separate party, does not really contain parties at all. Thus small magnitudes of PR districts in combination with high levels of political fragmentation serve as an additional impediment to party development.

Table 7.4   Electoral Systems and Representation of Noncommunist Parties in Russia's Regional Legislative Assemblies, 1993–2003

	PR Seats Included		PR Seats Excluded	
Variables	Parameter Estimate	T-value	Parameter Estimate	T-value
Intercept	1.56 (1.80)	0.87	0.96 (1.78)	0.54
AMPMD	3.27*** (1.14)	2.86	3.61*** (1.13)	3.19
TRM	0.03 (0.03)	0.89	0.03 (0.03)	1.06
PR	0.86*** (0.11)	8.15	0.54*** (0.10)	5.21
N	162		162	
R-squared	0.32		0.19	
Adj. R-squared	0.30		0.17	

Notes: The dependent variable is the share of seats won by nominees of noncommunist parties. Parentheses indicate standard errors.
 * Significant at 0.1.
 ** Significant at 0.05.
 *** Significant at 0.01.

Explaining Electoral System Effects

Two findings reported in Table 7.4, the effects of TRM and MMP upon the development of small noncommunist parties, are quite unexpected. The effect of MMP is positive and strong; the effect of TRM, while statistically insignificant, is positive too. It seems that the sweep effect is not the only factor that can be held accountable for the observed performance of MMP. In fact, small parties gain from this system more than the relatively strong, well-organized KPRF. Is it possible to explain these findings with reference to the effective thresholds? Prior to looking for a theoretical answer to this question, it seems useful to examine in depth several cases of elections held by MMP. The 1998 legislative elections in Krasnodar territory can be viewed as perhaps the most salient manifestation of the sweep effect in the electoral history of Russia's regions. The elections were held in twelve multimember districts of different magnitude, from two to five. The overall number of seats to be allocated was fifty. In addition to the left-wing/nationalist regional movement Fatherland, led by the governor, Nikolai Kondratenko, ten other parties took part in the elections. Five of them nominated too few candidates to be named here. Three others were national parties—Yabloko, the NDR, and the LDPR. A former LDPR leader who built his campaign rhetoric on anticommunism and the issues of fighting crime and corruption led a local entity called the Bloc of Boris Vavilov.[17] Several individuals previously unnoticed in the political arena of the region created the second local group, the Socialist Party. Perhaps their major goal was to split the left-wing electorate of Fatherland. The majority of candidates, however, were independents. After the elections many observers estimated their results as astonishing, given that Kondratenko's party took thirty-eight of fifty seats in the legislature. In order to test whether Fatherland fared equally well in terms of voter support, I aggregated electoral returns in eleven multimember districts.[18] The results are reported in Table 7.5. Obviously, MMP worked very well for Kondratenko's movement by allowing it to gain a share of seats more than twice as large as the share of the vote. Thus the sweep effect was in place.

However, in order to characterize the huge overrepresentation of Fatherland in Krasnodar's regional assembly as a consequence of the systemic properties of MMP, it has to be assumed, first, that SMP is unable to produce similar levels of dominant parties' overrepresentation, and second, that they are invariably produced by MMP. It seems that none of these assumptions holds. Consider the 1998 regional legislative elections in Volgograd province. Unfortunately, detailed district-level data for these single-member plurality elections are not available. Two pieces of information that are available are, first, the share of seats won by the KPRF, 68.8 percent (eleven of sixteen), and second, the shares of the vote gained by those

Table 7.5   **Candidates, Votes, and Seats in the 1998 Elections in Krasnodar Territory**

	Number of Candidates	Percentage Share of the Vote	Percentage Share of Seats Gained
Independents	276	54.9	20.0
Fatherland	44	36.7	77.8
Yabloko	9	2.7	2.2
NDR	10	0.1	0.0
LDPR	11	0.6	0.0
Bloc of Boris Vavilov	24	1.8	0.0
Socialist Party	13	0.7	0.0
5 other parties	17	2.5	0.0
Total	404	100.0	100.0

Note: MMP, 50 seats contested.

candidates who won seats. It is also known that the KPRF ran candidates in all sixteen districts. On the assumption that in each of the districts that returned noncommunist deputies, the KPRF candidates lost on 5 percent margins, I estimated the average share of the vote received by KPRF candidates as 33.2 percent. Given that district borders in Volgograd province were drawn in keeping with the norm of representation, this figure can be viewed as a reasonable approximation of the share of the vote actually won by the KPRF. Thus similar to MMP in Krasnodar territory, SMP in Volgograd province allowed the dominant party to gain a share of seats more than twice as large as the share of the vote.

Let us now turn to the second aspect of the problem under discussion, whether the sweep effect mechanically occurs whenever MMP is in use. Perhaps the most spectacular counterexample comes from the 1994 legislative elections in Krasnodar territory. The average magnitude of districts used in 1994 was even larger than in the 1998 elections discussed above, 7.1 against 4.2. While the 1994 elections did produce a party-structured legislature (forty of the fifty elected deputies were party nominees), there was nothing reminiscent of single-party domination. As a proof of that, the effective number of legislative parties, if calculated on the generous assumption that all ten independents constituted one party, was 4.6. Unfortunately, district-level electoral returns for these elections are not available. They are available, however, for the 2001 legislative elections in Kamchatka province held in three-member districts. There were three parties in these elections. One of them was an electoral bloc that comprised the local left-wing movement Comrade and a nationalist group called Slavic National Patriotic Union, with the local branch of the LDPR as an informal participant. The official label of the bloc was Rally in Support of the

Governor.[19] The local branches of Yabloko, the Union of Right Forces (SPS), and Fatherland formed the second bloc, For Kamchatka, as a major electoral tool of the governor's opposition.[20] The local branch of Unity stood in the middle ground. The results of the elections are reported in Table 7.6. The largest party is still at an advantage, but this advantage is far less "sweeping" than in the 1998 Krasnodar elections. In fact, the major opposition party's share of seats is larger than its share of the vote, too. While Unity is slightly underrepresented, this would not have been the case if it had gained two seats instead of one. The independents' joint share of seats almost perfectly corresponds to their share of the vote. What we have in the end is a multiparty legislature with individual parties being represented quite in correspondence with their levels of voter support. The sweep effect just does not occur.

Is it possible to explain the observed electoral system effects with reference to effective thresholds? To answer this question, it is important to test whether candidate proliferation is conducive to increased party success under SMP. To achieve this, I measured the association between the numbers of candidates per seat/district and the percentages of elected party nominees in 78 "pure" SMP systems used in the first and second electoral cycles.[21] The two parameters turn out to be positively associated at 0.26 (the Pearson's r correlation coefficient is significant at 0.05). The more candidates per seat, the lower the threshold of inclusion; and the lower the threshold of inclusion, the more party nominees gain seats. In order to test whether the same logic explains the observed difference between the effects of SMP and MMP, I looked at the numbers of candidates per seat in 114 electoral systems, including 78 SMP systems and 36 cases of "pure" MMP or its combinations with SMP. In fact, the average numbers of candidates per seat in SMP and MMP systems turned out to be 5.1 and 4.6

Table 7.6   **Candidates, Votes, and Seats in the 2001 Elections in Kamchatka Province**

	Number of Candidates	Percentage Share of the Vote	Percentage Share of Seats Gained
Independents	162	62.8	61.5
Rally in Support of the Governor	33	17.9	25.6
For Kamchatka	21	9.7	10.3
Unity	6	4.5	2.6
Against all candidates	—	5.1	—
Total	222	100.0	100.0

Note: MMP, 39 seats contested.

respectively, which if statistically significant could have indicated higher thresholds of inclusion in multimember districts. Similarly, it has been found that the average magnitude of plurality/majority districts correlates with the average number of candidates per seat at as low as 0.06 (Pearson's *r* is insignificant). Then when applied to the case of MMP, the candidate proliferation hypothesis does not hold.

In his analysis of strategic voting patterns, Cox (1997: 146–147) notes that under MMP, these patterns vary depending on whether electors can partially abstain from casting all their votes. In the regions of Russia, they can. What are the consequences? If in each of the multimember districts all votes are cast, then what we have is a system with high thresholds of exclusion and inclusion. But if some of the voters cast fewer votes than district magnitude allows, then what we have is a system that approximates the so-called system of limited vote, or if brought to the extreme, when each voter uses only one vote, SNTV. The general formula for the threshold of exclusion under limited vote is $(100 \text{ percent} \times v) / (v + M)$, where M is the district magnitude and v is the number of votes each voter can cast (Lijphart, López Pintor, and Sone 1986: 157–158), which for two-member districts yields 33.3 percent, lower than under SMP and twice as low as under MMP. But perhaps the most striking feature of the limited vote system is that its threshold of inclusion is unusually low. As Lijphart (1994: 40) puts it, "the most extreme example in, say, a three-member district would be one candidate receiving all but two of the votes, and hence obviously being elected, and two other candidates receiving one vote each—and also winning seats!" Then it may be so that the MMP systems of Russia's regions support small parties because, in effect, these systems operate as something between MMP as such and limited vote. But to claim this with confidence, it is necessary to establish empirically whether Russian voters are inclined to cast fewer votes than they are entitled to. Unfortunately, the data at my disposal are insufficient for running such an empirical test on a comprehensive basis. However, some illustrative evidence can be derived from the 1994 elections in Tambov province, and from the 2001 elections in Amur, Kamchatka, Kirov, and Tomsk provinces, all of which were held under MMP systems. As follows from the data presented in Table 7.7, in none of the regions were voters scrupulous enough to use all their votes. Moreover, it seems that the number of those partially abstaining increases as district magnitude becomes greater.

While this claim obviously needs further empirical verification, it can be theoretically justified with reference to the fact that the more candidates who are to be assessed by the voter, the more information the voter needs to collect in order to avoid partial abstention. Since rational voters are rarely motivated to invest massive effort into making choices at the polls (Downs 1957), it stands to reason to expect that many votes will remain unused in

Table 7.7   Total Percentages of the Vote Cast in Multimember District Elections in Five Regions of Russia

Regions	Minimum	Maximum	Mean
Tambov, 1994 (2)	153.7	188.1	170.9
Kirov, 2001 (2)	129.3	158.5	142.9
Tomsk, 2001 (2)	145.4	166.4	161.4
Amur, 2001 (3)	185.0	225.0	209.8
Kamchatka, 2001 (3)	193.7	244.8	225.1

Note: Parentheses indicate district magnitudes.

large multimember districts. And the more votes remain unused, the lower the effective thresholds, which produces quite favorable conditions for small parties. Applying the limited vote formula to the five regions in my sample by substituting v with the average total percentages of the vote cast in the districts, it can be calculated that the thresholds of exclusion were 46.1, 44.7, 42.9, 41.7, and 41.2 percent in Tambov, Tomsk, Kamchatka, Kirov, and Amur respectively.

In fact, the Downsian logic applied above helps to develop a more general model within which the idiosyncratic effects of MMP can be explained. It is only natural that MMP enhances the overall numbers of candidates per district if the number of candidates per seat remains about the same or even slightly smaller than under SMP, which in itself means that the threshold of inclusion does not become lower. Indeed, the average number of candidates per district was 10.3 in systems involving MMP against only 5.1 in "pure" SMP systems; the Pearson's r correlation coefficient between the average number of candidates and average district magnitude is 0.88 (significant at 0.001). The model consists of two parts. First, as the number of candidates in the district increases, the same happens with the value of any specific labels, including party labels, which may assist the voter in making his or her choice by providing additional information. Second, the more candidates who run in the district, the more voters fail to obtain relevant information about those candidates who are not labeled. On the one hand, this makes some of the voters partially abstain, which results in the lowering of the effective threshold. On the other hand, party nominees are additionally capacitated to pass the threshold due to their information advantage over nonpartisans. This logic may favor a single strong party, which produces the sweep effect, but it may also support relatively small parties in those cases when there is no single party enjoying superior levels of support across all districts. This explanatory logic can be applied to the results of regional legislative elections in Krasnodar territory and Kamchatka province as reported in Tables 7.5 and 7.6. In Krasnodar, all political parties but Fatherland, and to a much lesser extent Yabloko, were too weak in terms of voter support to deliver any advantages to their nominees. The candidates of Fatherland, when confronting either independents or those candidates whose party labels were of little vote-attracting value (it seems that, in fact, some of these labels worked against candidates who carried them), could supplement their shares of the vote with a monopolistically held information advantage. This, in turn, brought about the sweep effect. Quite the reverse, in Kamchatka there were several parties with labels of positive information value. As a result, none of these parties could find MMP as profitable as it turned out to be in Krasnodar, but none of them was at a disadvantage either. In fact, both Rally in Support of the Governor and For Kamchatka gained shares of legislative seats that were larger than their shares of the vote.

Paradoxically, it can be found that certain elements of this model apply to the even more puzzling case of TRM. One possible way to look at TRM is to divide its operation into two phases. If viewed separately, it is the second round that can be properly described as SMP in single-member districts with the number of candidates being limited to two, which sets both effective thresholds at the dangerously high 50 percent level. The first round is SNTV in two-member districts, with a 33.3 percent threshold of exclusion and a very low threshold of inclusion. Of course, electoral outcomes are decided in the second round, which punishes strong, ideologically rigid parties. Yet for small, ideologically acceptable parties the picture may be different. If the immediate prize is entry into the second round, then with district magnitude rising to two, more candidates have incentives to enter. Indeed, I have calculated that in the "pure" TRM systems in my selection, the average number of candidates per seat/district was 6.4 compared to 5.1 under SMP; the Pearson's r correlation coefficient between the number of candidates and the TRM/SMP dummy is 0.25 (significant at 0.05). Once they enter the electoral arena, party candidates hold an information advantage over independents, and they are assisted with lower effective thresholds. Hence they may enter the second round in sufficient numbers, too. Insofar as this happens, the principal question is the political standing of the opponent. If the second round is contested by two labeled candidates, then irrespective of what constitutes the label—party affiliation, a specific issue position, or some kind of personal resources—the party candidate may win if his or her label is more acceptable for the majority of voters. While punishing candidates of the KPRF, this logic does not necessarily impede the chances of non–communist party candidates, and it may be asserted that in the face-to-face contests with the communists they are likely to win. Therefore, TRM cannot be discarded as a system that invariably hinders party development. Nonpartisanship is not its unavoidable consequence.

Consider the 1998 regional legislative elections in St. Petersburg, mentioned previously in connection with the list of candidates endorsed by the incumbent governor, Vladimir Yakovlev. The list included both party nominees and independents. In general, the same can be said about the camp of opposition to Yakovlev as represented in the 1998 elections. In the course of the campaign, however, Yabloko emerged as a party that sought if not to unseat Yakovlev, then to control him by winning a comfortable majority in the fifty-member legislature.[22] An electoral bloc, Accord–The United Democrats of St. Petersburg, formed by the regional branch of Democratic Russia's Choice (DVR) and two ideologically similar groups, took an explicitly anti-Yakovlev stance. After the first round Yabloko and Accord created a coalition, United Civic List, and as a result, Yabloko firmly located itself within the anti-Yakovlev camp.[23] The third important party in the 1998 elections was a bloc of the KPRF and the Russian Communist Workers Party (RKRP), the Communists of Leningrad. Some of the Communist candidates were apparently acceptable for the city's executive; at the same time, in contrast to most regions, neither of the communist parties was particularly popular with the electorate. Thirteen minor parties of different political leanings also contested the elections. The majority of candidates were independents. The striking peculiarity of the 1998 elections was the proliferation of candidates. The number of candidates nominated for elections was 837, and 574 of them remained on the ballot when the day of elections came. The average number of candidates per district was 11.5. Table 7.8 reports information on the electoral returns. I understand "winners" in the first round to mean both those six candidates who actually won seats by receiving more than 50 percent of the vote and those eighty-eight candidates who made it into the second round. Winners in the second round are those who gained the remaining forty-four seats. The data reported in the table make all too apparent the logic of party candidates' success under TRM as reconstructed above. The results of the first round are quite similar to those of the 2001 elections in Kamchatka. Independents and very small parties are at a small but sensible disadvantage. Larger parties, in contrast, convert their votes into second-round entrances on quite profitable terms, so that the larger the size of a party's electorate, the larger the bonus it gets. To put it a different way, larger information advantages become convertible into better seat-to-vote ratios. In the second round, however, the terms of conversion are entirely different and now unfavorable for political parties. Since the overall number of candidates decreased, Yabloko and the Communists became capable of faring better in terms of voter support than they did in the first round. But this time, the coalitions of voters assembled by them turned out to be insufficiently large for winning seats. As a result, Yabloko, Accord, and the Communists received smaller shares of seats than could be claimed on the basis of their vote shares. In contrast, independents with no party labels at all, as well as nominees of

Table 7.8   Candidates, Votes, and Seats in the 1998 Elections in St. Petersburg

	1st Round			2nd Round		
	Number of Candidates	Percentage Share of the Vote	Percentage Share of Winners	Number of Candidates	Percentage Share of the Vote	Percentage Share of Winners
Independents	460	60.9	55.3	48	54.0	70.5
Yabloko	29	14.8	25.5	23	22.8	15.9
Accord	16	3.8	4.3	4	3.3	2.3
Communists of Leningrad	26	8.4	11.7	11	9.2	6.8
13 other parties	43	3.6	3.2	2	2.8	4.5
Against all candidates	—	8.5	—	—	7.9	—
Total	574	100.0	100.0	88	100.0	100.0

Note: TRM, 50 seats contested.

small parties with labels of almost no information value but generally positive connotations, such as the Regional Union or For Justice, were at an advantage. If the 1998 elections were held exclusively by SNTV in two-member districts—that is, without the second round—then the share of party nominees in the assembly would have been 42.0 percent.[24] The actual share of party nominees in the assembly was 28.0 percent, though. Thus the mechanics of TRM support party candidates in the first round but punish them in the second.

From the analysis above, it becomes apparent that SMP is actually the worst electoral system from the point of view of its impact upon party development. Any of the alternatives ever used in the regions of Russia fared better. This conclusion sheds new light on two findings previously reported in this study: first, the increasingly negligible role played by political parties in regional executive elections, and second, the gradual but quite visible process of replacing non-SMP systems with SMP in regional legislative elections. Regional executive elections are held either by SMP or by TRM. Two interrelated aspects of these elections differentiate them from the legislative elections, and each of them places a party candidate at a disadvantage. First, executive elections are more important. This means that candidates in these elections tend to be individually resourceful, high-profile personalities. Even if they are not, the very fact that they succeed in obtaining registration brings them to the level of publicity unattainable in regional legislative elections. As a result, the information value of party labels becomes relatively low. Second, executive elections are more difficult to take part in. This filters out insignificant candidates and thereby raises the threshold of inclusion. Given that none of Russia's political parties can deliver large numbers of votes to its candidates, the result is, again, a lower level of party candidate success. Thus SMP works against political parties.

The case of TRM is admittedly more complex. While the two aspects of party disadvantage in executive elections, as identified above, are obviously not alien to TRM, both, at least arguably, may be less pronounced than under SMP. On the one hand, party candidates may run in TRM elections not so much in order to win but rather to be better equipped for bargaining with the leading candidates between the two rounds. On the other hand, the first round, with its properties of SNTV in two-member districts, facilitates the proliferation of candidates and thereby increases the information value of party labels. These theoretical considerations, however, have to be juxtaposed with the political realities of regional executive elections. The bargaining proposition works only if the prospective winner is likely to stick to the terms of contract after coming to power—that is, if a minor participant in the contract possesses effective sanctions against free-riding. In the majority of regions, however, this is not the case. As demonstrated in the previous chapter, the institutionally embedded and/or politically ensured prominence of regional executives is such that on their part, "winner takes all" is an adequate approach. Of course, the information advantage proposition works only if the proliferation of candidates under TRM actually takes place, which can be tested empirically. For the time span of 1995 to the end of 2002, the average numbers of candidates in 55 SMP and 119 TRM regional executive elections were 5.2 and 6.2, which is a sizable but not very pronounced difference. Apparently, the TRM's ability to support candidate proliferation largely fades away in the arena of executive elections.

True, regional executive elections provide little space for institutional engineering in the sense that the set of available options is fairly limited; one-person offices can be filled either by SMP or by TRM. In regional legislative elections, however, there are several alternatives. From this perspective, it is noteworthy that from the second to the third electoral cycle, the share of regions employing "pure" SMP increased from 60.0 to 72.6 percent, while the shares of regions employing MMP (including its combinations with different formulas) and mixed electoral systems decreased from 27.1 to 13.1 percent and from 5.9 to 4.8 percent respectively. Institutional reasons for the decline in the use of MMP have been described at the beginning of this chapter. In several regions, however, the political motivation for electoral system change was observable too. The most abrupt change of this kind took place in Krasnodar territory, which switched from MMP to SMP in 2002. The official motivation for an electoral system change, as vocalized by the governor who actually initiated the reform, was to provide each of the region's administrative districts with at least one legislative representative.[25] Yet it seems that the real motivation concerned changing political conditions in the region. In 2000, Nikolai Kondratenko announced that he would not run for a second term and endorsed a communist and former political rival, Duma deputy Aleksandr Tkachev, as his successor.[26] In addition to being a member of the KPRF, Tkachev was also a member of Kondratenko's Fatherland movement.[27] The outgoing governor, however, made it clear that he would retain the position of the movement's sole leader. Given that Fatherland controlled a sizable majority of seats in the legislature, and that Kondratenko also took a Federation Council seat as an early retirement payoff, the ex-governor remained a potentially important actor in regional politics. External control over the legislature, however, was hardly consistent with Tkachev's own plans. The extent of his control over the local branch of the KPRF was also insufficient. Then it was only logical to eliminate institutional conditions that made one-party domination in the assembly possible. In the 2002 regional legislative elections in Krasnodar territory there were 307 claimants for 70 seats—that is, 4.4 candidates per seat against 10.1 candidates per seat in the previous elections held by MMP. Fatherland did not officially nominate candidates but it endorsed its members on a personal basis,[28] while the KPRF nominated 33 candidates, 28 of whom actually participated in the elections. All of them were also endorsed by Fatherland. As a result of the elections, only 28 endorsees of Fatherland, including 13 communists, gained assembly seats. Thus the performance of the left-wing parties was rather poor in comparison with 1998. The left-wing governor, however, was apparently happy with the result. In an interview given in the immediate aftermath of the elections, he estimated quite positively that the majority of deputies were now industrial and agricultural managers and optimistically concluded: "I am sure that with these people we will be able to continue fruitful and constructive work."[29] Thus the legislative assembly of Krasnodar territory, after a long period of party domination, got back to normal. It seems that electoral system change played a role in this transformation.

Multimember plurality does not necessarily support party formation, but mixed electoral systems do. Therefore it stands to reason to take a closer look at those regions that experimented with electing part of their deputies by PR. There were nine such regions, but only four of them retained mixed electoral systems by the end of the third electoral cycle. One way to look at the effects of these institutional arrangements is to examine the political trajectories of those nine chief executives under whose leadership mixed electoral systems were enacted. The most striking finding is that only one of them, Sherig-ool Oorzhak in Tyva, survived executive elections that followed the first legislative races held by a mixed electoral system. The Yeltsin-appointed governor of Saratov province did not participate in the 1996 gubernatorial elections because he was dismissed briefly before the event. The incumbent chief executives of Marii El, Ust-Ordynskoe Buriat and Koriak autonomous districts, Krasnoiarsk territory, and Kaliningrad and Sverdlovsk provinces did run but lost. The ninth governor, Evgenii Mikhailov in Pskov province, introduced a mixed electoral system in his region late in the third electoral cycle, yet Mikhailov is recognizably one of the least politically resourceful regional leaders. It remains highly probable that when subjected to elections in 2004, he will follow in the footsteps of earlier chief executives who experimented with the idea of proportional representation. Thus the survival rate among chief executives of the regions that employ mixed electoral systems is much lower than in "normal" regions.

Why? Given that the legislative assemblies are not primary players in Russia's regional politics, it would be implausible to suggest that elections held by mixed electoral systems invariably produced assemblies that were strong enough to unseat the governors. It seems that the real-life dynamics of the process are more related to the causes of switches to mixed electoral systems than to their political consequences. Namely, only those incumbent senior executives who already felt themselves fundamentally endangered had two major incentives for switching to mixed electoral systems in regional legislative elections. One of these incentives is very transparent. If you feel that the chances for losing your current position are high, then a logical way to ensure some political future for yourself is to create an alternative power base outside of the executive. Independent deputies belonging to the local economic and managerial elite may be easily controllable insofar as you are in office, but once you are out, they all have an incentive to offer their loyalty to your successor. In contrast, party-list deputies—if, of course, you have a party to rely upon—are more likely to remain loyal even upon your departure from executive power. The second incentive concerns the patterns of executive control over the legislatures. Vulnerable executives are generally those who have to deal with strong oppositions emerging from within regional elites. Under such conditions, an exclusively elite-based legislative assembly is less than desirable, for it naturally serves as an institutional site where the antiexecutive opposition can consolidate. Then it stands to reason, first, to complement the composition of the assembly with some nonelite groups, and second, to make the assembly as politically fragmented as possible. Both targets can be reached by switching to a mixed electoral system.

Consider the only region that switched to a mixed electoral system in the third electoral cycle, Pskov province. The 1998 legislative elections, held by a plurality system in single-member and two-member districts, produced an assembly that was generally, even though not very consistently, hostile to the governor, Evgenii Mikhailov.[30] His own party, the LDPR, won only two seats, and four seats came to a KPRF-led bloc, People's

Power. The remaining sixteen seats were distributed mostly among the industrial and agricultural managers of the region. In 1999, Mikhailov defected from the LDPR and became a very enthusiastic supporter of the new party of power, Unity.[31] This did not help him to drastically improve his position in the region, even though he was able to win the 2000 gubernatorial elections by a minimal margin. Moreover, defection from the LDPR had a price attached: Mikhailov had to fire one of his close political allies, Mikhail Gavunas, previously an all-powerful deputy head of administration in charge of economic policy.[32] This further exacerbated the ongoing intraelite conflict in the region. In particular, one of the influential clients of Gavunas, a national Duma deputy and a wealthy businessman, Mikhail Kuznetsov, abandoned Mikhailov's team and started to play on his own. He even ran against Mikhailov in the 2000 elections. While Kuznetsov lost, many in the region considered him a prospective winner in the 2004 elections, as a result of which few regional legislators who were previously supportive of Mikhailov defected to his new rival. Against these unfavorable backgrounds, the endangered governor announced that he would support holding the 2002 legislative elections by a mixed electoral system.

This proposal, while enthusiastically supported by the KPRF and other parties registered in the region, was less than favorably received by the local elite, including the chairman of the assembly.[33] To oppose the idea, Kuznetsov organized a vocal political movement, Partii.net ("no parties"). Most probably, Mikhailov would have never pushed new electoral legislation through the regional assembly on his own. It was only after the federal authorities openly came out in his support and apparently exerted direct pressure upon Kuznetsov and several other oppositionists that the legislature reluctantly approved electoral system reform.[34] Yet it came in a circumscribed form: despite Mikhailov's proposal to elect half of the deputies by PR, the legislature agreed to only a third. Thus under the new electoral system, twenty-two deputies were to be elected by SMP and eleven by PR. On March 31, 2002, the Pskov voters had to choose among three major party lists: the KPRF, Unity (which effectively served as Mikhailov's party), and the opposition bloc, Kuznetsov–Polozov–Savitskii: Together for the Sake of the Future (KPS). Five other parties on the ballot paper, including the LDPR, the SPS, Yabloko, the Democratic Party of Russia (DPR), and the People's Party of the Russian Federation (NPRF), were not regarded as serious alternatives. In party-list competition, the KPRF placed first with 27.6 percent of the vote, and Unity placed second with 26.2 percent. The KPS, with its 15.1 percent of the vote, came a distant third. These vote shares were converted into four, four, and three seats respectively. The KPRF and Unity were also able to win two district seats each, and four previously independent deputies joined the Unity faction after being elected.[35]

For different reasons, plurality elections did not return deputies in four districts. Thus the assembly included ten loyalists, six communists, three non-communist oppositionists, and ten independents mostly belonging to the region's managerial elites. It was now a fragmented legislature with two possible pro-Mikhailov majorities, Unity plus the Communists (in fact, the KPRF supported several Unity nominees in single-member districts) or Unity plus independents. An opposition majority comprising the KPRF and independents could be safely ruled out. Thus electoral reform worked very well for Mikhailov.

The problem with this path to electoral reform is that chief regional executives as vulnerable as Mikhailov are few. Moreover, as we have seen, the incumbency advantage has tended to consolidate over time. Strong executives, however, normally do not need political parties for controlling legislatures, or for any practical ends whatsoever. When Yurii Belykh in Saratov province initiated an experiment with PR in 1994, much of his motivation was apparently similar to that of Mikhailov. In 1996, however, he was dismissed and replaced with Dmitrii Aiatskov, a local strongman whose chances of winning the executive elections scheduled for the same year seemed unbeatable. Correspondingly, Aiatskov was very explicit in his rejection of Belykh's experimentation. However, the new governor could not abolish the mixed system at his own will. This could be done only by the legislature itself, but more than half of its deputies were party nominees elected either on a list basis or in single-member districts. To overcome this difficulty, Aiatskov started a comprehensive process of luring party deputies out of the legislature by offering them attractive positions with the executive. Thus the local leader of the APR was appointed as a deputy head of administration in charge of agriculture, and the leader of a right-wing group became head of the department of international and interethnic relations; overall, in the first months of Aiatskov's governorship more than half of the deputies either left the legislature altogether or received part-time jobs with the executive.[36] As a result, it became easy to reinstall SMP in Saratov province. Ironically, in 2002, when Aiatskov's position in the region became vulnerable in connection with the emergence of a nationally acclaimed political leader of Saratov origin, the maverick governor proposed to revert to a mixed electoral system. This time, however, he was not in a position to convince the deputies.[37] The case of Omsk province is also quite revealing. As far back as December 1995, the region's legislators adopted a statute stipulating that a third of them, fifteen, should be elected by a proportional formula.[38] Changing regional statutes is often no less difficult than changing the 1993 federal constitution, so the provision remained intact for a long time thereafter. Yet proportional elections never took place. They were delayed twice: officially, for a variety of technical reasons such as the lack of funding, and effectively, because the governor's analysts calculated that this provision, if implemented, would have brought the number of KPRF nominees in the assembly to fifteen (Novikov 1998). Clearly, yielding a substantial share of assembly seats to the opposition was not very advantageous for the governor, Leonid Polezhaev, who was politically resourceful enough to comfortably coexist with the incumbent deputies. But it was equally disadvantageous for the loyal deputies who, being in a legislative majority, were entitled to make the decision. The presence of a meaningful opposition would have made their lives a lot more complicated.

Thus it is not by accident that by the end of the third electoral cycle, SMP established itself as the prevalent system in regional legislative elections. In fact, the "pure" plurality system prevailed because it was the most advantageous for the executive elites. The MMP and TRM systems may be profitable for highly consolidated elites and highly popular executive incumbents, but the former becomes risky when a relatively strong party plays on the opposition side, while the latter maximizes risks posed by an opposition party with a relatively high coalition potential. Taking this into account, the risk-aversion properties of the plurality system can be explicated with reference to its well-established ability to produce binary formats of electoral competition (Duverger 1954). Under the specific conditions of party underdevelopment in Russia, the two competitors most visibly supported by the plurality formula are the proexecutive independent and the nominee of a major opposition party, if not a nonparty oppositionist. This can be illustrated by the results of the 2002 regional legislative elections in Saratov province, reported in Table 7.9. The effects of votes-to-seats conversion upon the representation of the KPRF are self-explanatory. Note, however, that while Unitary Russia nominated few deputies, they were not at a disadvantage at all. This happened because they belonged to the regional elites themselves, while the candidates of the KPRF did not.

Table 7.9   Candidates, Votes, and Seats in the 2002 Elections in Saratov Province

	Number of Candidates	Percentage Share of the Vote	Percentage Share of Seats Gained
Independents	74	67.7	90.0
KPRF	14	9.2	0
Unitary Russia	5	7.3	10.0
4 other parties	5	1.8	0
Against all candidates	—	13.9	—
Total	98	99.9[a]	100.0

Notes: SMP, 35 seats contested, 30 deputies returned.
a. Does not sum to 100.0 percent because of rounding.

By converting advantages associated with the insider status into substantial electoral gains, the plurality formula tends to make the "bosses" better equipped for success.

*   *   *

Which is the best electoral system from the point of view of its impact upon party formation? Findings presented above indicate that single-member plurality is the worst. Overall, each of the observed alternative modifications of plurality/majority rules performs better. It is not surprising that list PR supports party formation. Yet this effect stems not only from the mechanical exclusion of independents from the electoral arena, but also, in mixed systems, from the interaction of their plurality/majority and proportional tiers. More unexpectedly, I found that even such unlikely candidates for party-friendly behavior as two-round majority and multimember plurality are actually not the worst options. While the effects of the former are dubious, as it suppresses strong, ideologically rigid parties while opening the window of opportunity for small and flexible ones, the latter exerts a consistently strong positive impact upon party formation. These findings cannot be explained with reference to the theoretically expected properties of TRM and MMP. Rather, the key system for understanding their unexpected behavior is single nontransferable vote. While almost invisible in my data set, this system uncovers itself both in MMP (because of vote wasting) and in TRM (in the first round). That is why in their actual operation in Russia, MMP and TRM tend to lower effective thresholds and to enhance the information value of party labels, thus facilitating the entry of party candidates and their electoral success. At the same time, this explains why SMP gradually became a prevalent electoral system in regional legislative elections. To state it briefly, SMP was a system that throughout the whole period under observation remained consistent with the dominant political interests in the regions of Russia.

Notes

1. See, for instance, *Sostav deputatov, ispolnitel'nykh komitetov, postoiannykh komissii i rezervnykh deputatov mestnykh sovetov narodnykh deputatov, 1987 g.*, Moscow, 1987.

2. Some of the republics continued to use Soviet-type ballot papers. See Löwenhardt and Verheul 2000.

3. Oblastnoe uchreditel'noe sobranie, *Belgorodskaia Pravda* (Belgorod), January 18, 1994. McFaul and Petrov (1998: 183) mistakenly attribute this oddity to Lipetsk province.

4. Gazeta pomeshchaet otchet, *Izvestia Tatarstana* (Kazan), June 26, 1994.

5. V Saratove sostoialos koordinatsionnoe soveshchanie, *Saratovskie vesti* (Saratov), January 19, 1994.

6. Anatolii Sobchak urezaet polnomochia budushchikh zakonadatelei, *Segodnia,* January 12, 1994.

7. V Dagestane, *Vremia MN,* January 27, 1999.

8. Mnogomandatnye izbiratel'nye okruga, *Dagestanskaia Pravda* (Makhachkala), November 22, 2002.

9. Tri mandata vmesto odnogo, *Slovo neftianika* (Noiabr'sk), April 28, 2000; Liubov Chistova, *Tiumenskie izvestia* (Tiumen), July 21, 2001.

10. The 1996 and 1997 legislative elections in Chechnya were held by different electoral systems. Of them, Table 7.1 refers to the 1997 elections because they produced a longer-lasting legislature (the 1996 legislature was elected in June 1996 only to be ousted from the republic in August 1996).

11. Pskov i Kaluga primer dlia Ameriki, *Rossia,* November 14, 2000.

12. Technically speaking, PR systems do not necessarily involve the list form of candidacy (the single transferable vote system does not), nor do plurality/majority systems necessarily presuppose individual candidacy (list candidacy is used in the multimember plurality/majority systems of Cameroon, Chad, Côte d'Ivoire, Ecuador, Singapore, Thailand, etc.). The effects of these modifications of electoral rules are not addressed in this study.

13. The problem with treating elections as observations while using the OLS model is that two elections in the same region are not independent of each other. This led me to use the Huber-White estimator as a technique for calculating "robust" standard errors, which did not produce results significantly different from those reported in this chapter.

14. The 1994 elections in Ingushetia and Rostov province, and the 1999 elections in Komi. See Chapter 4.

15. For a detailed analysis of SNTV effects in a cross-national perspective, see Grofman et al. 1999.

16. Thus constructed PR variables are highly intercorrelated, Pearson's $r = 0.95$.

17. Bazarnyi den nakanune vyborov, *Kommersant-Vlast,* November 24, 1998.

18. One of the five-member districts was omitted for a technical reason related to data availability. For similar reasons, I had to discount the votes cast against all deputies. Thus percentages reported in Table 7.4 are shares of total valid vote cast for individual candidates.

19. "Zakamchattsy," "podderzhanty" i mechtateli, *Novaia kamchatskaia pravda* (Petropavlovsk-Kamchatskii), November 15, 2001.

20. Vse—za. Kto protiv? *Vesti* (Petropavlovsk-Kamchatskii), October 11, 2001.

21. The bivariate analysis reported here and later was performed on a data set that included 133 electoral systems used in the first and second electoral cycles. The complete data on candidate nomination in some of the elections are not available.

22. Peterburg pered vtorym turom, *Russkaia mysl* (Paris), December 17, 1998.

23. Proigrysh "naperstochnikov," *Vremia MN,* December 28, 1998.

24. In this calculation I took into account six second-runners in those districts where seats were allocated in the first round. Characteristically, all of them were independents.

25. Kogda zakon i pravo, *Krasnodarskie izvestia* (Krasnodar), May 24, 2002.

26. Kto stanet "bat'koi" na Kubani? *Parlamentskaia gazeta,* November 11, 2000.

27. Teatr odnogo aktera, *Itogi,* October 3, 2000.

28. V ZSK prishli promyshlenniki, khoziaistvenniki i politiki, *Kubanskie novosti* (Krasnodar), November 29, 2002.

29. Predvaritel'nye itogi vyborov, *Kubanskie novosti* (Krasnodar), November 26, 2002.

30. Oblastnoe sobranie—1998, *Pskovskaia gubernia* (Pskov), February 21, 2002.

31. When explaining the reasons for his defection from the LDPR, Mikhailov said: "In the early 1990s, Zhirinovsky was the only visible patriotic leader, but nowadays, first, everyone is a patriot, and second, there is such a figure as Putin." See Nelegkii vybor byl u pskovichei, *Novgorodskie vedomosti* (Novgorod), November 17, 2000.

32. Pravda Zhirinovskogo, *Kommersant Sankt-Peterburg,* December 28, 2000.

33. Kak nashi vlasti "istolkovali" kruglyi stol, *Novosti Pskova* (Pskov), June 3, 2001.

34. Severo-zapadnyi dialog v kontekste, *Veche* (Pskov), September 28, 2001.

35. KPRF v Pskove sil'na "Edinstvom," *Novgorodskie vedomosti* (Novgorod), April 3, 2002.

36. Blesk i nishcheta saratovskogo gubernatora, *Krasnoe znamia* (Syktyvkar), February 19, 1997.

37. Nachalo kontsa dlia D.F., *Nastoiashchii Saratov,* April 19, 2002.

38. V poiskakh stabil'nosti, *Pravda—5,* October 5, 1996.

8

Political Engineering vs. Party Underdevelopment

This chapter pursues two goals. First, it brings together different factors identified in this book as exerting influence upon party development in the regions of Russia in order to develop and statistically test overall explanatory models for the three electoral cycles under examination. This is the subject of the first section. Second, I examine the reactions of Russia's political actors, both on the national and regional levels, to the situation of party underdevelopment. Starting in 2000, Russia's federal authorities launched a comprehensive campaign aimed at inducing political parties to spread into the country's peripheries by means of political engineering. Their motivation for this undertaking, as well as its early phase associated with the adoption of the 2001 law on political parties, are examined in the second section. Then I discuss the 2002 electoral reform as the principal tool used by the federal authorities to accelerate party formation in the regions. In this connection I examine the institutional mechanics of the reform, and the strategies and counterstrategies of the involved political actors. In the third section, I examine regional reactions to the reform by identifying several strategies of adaptation to the changing institutional environments, and on this basis briefly discuss the prospects for party formation in the regions of Russia.

The Causal Model of Party
Underdevelopment in the Regions of Russia

In this book I have identified several causal factors that influence the formation of political parties in the regions of Russia. However, it is important to assess the relative weight of these factors. The standard statistical procedure that allows for such an assessment is multiple regression analysis (ordinary least squares [OLS] for all models below). The principal dependent variable is the share of seats won by party nominees in regional legislative elections. Like in Chapter 7, I use two additional dependent variables, the share of nominees from the Communist Party of the Russian Federation

(KPRF) conglomerate, and the share of non–communist party nominees.[1] This time, however, the unit of analysis is not the individual electoral system but rather the individual region. I run separate regressions for each of the three electoral cycles. Such an approach seems to be necessary for tracing the dynamics of the process of party formation. The number of observations in each of the regression equations equals that of regional legislative elections in which political parties were legally entitled to participate.[2]

While the primary purpose of multiple regression analysis is to develop causal explanatory models,[3] its additional advantage is that it makes it possible to introduce environmental control variables. Indeed, one would argue that before political and institutional influences upon party formation come into effect, and independently from these influences, the speed of the process in individual regions could be determined by their basic socioeconomic characteristics. The impact of two such characteristics, on theoretical grounds, can be expected to weigh especially heavily. One of them is simply population size. Dahl and Tufte (1973) advance a theory that small polities manage without parties because in such polities the need for formal, impersonal means of expressing political conflicts is negligible; the conflicts themselves, due to societal homogeneity, are not very intense; and the prospects for forming opposition parties are vague because a dissenter may fail to rally a sufficient number of supporters. Indeed, a recent empirical study demonstrated that those six democracies without parties that do exist in the contemporary world are all small, with an average population size of 45,000 (Anckar and Anckar 2000: 232). Thus my first control variable is population size in millions (POP). The second control variable has comparably sound theoretical credentials. Huntington (1968), when advancing his notion of political parties as necessary channels for political participation in modern and modernizing societies, emphasized that rural turf is not fertile for party development. Modern political parties are the product of urban elites; when established in the cities, parties start to penetrate the countryside, not vice versa. Hence the second control variable, the percentage share of urban dwellers in the population of the region, URB.

The second group of variables pertains to the political preferences of the voters as expressed in national electoral returns. Like in the previous case, the logic behind the introduction of these variables is quite transparent. It may be so that regional electoral arenas, rather than displaying causal dynamics of their own, are simply epiphenomena of voter attachment to (or in this case, detachment from) national political parties. If this is the case, then the levels of party representation in regional legislative assemblies can be expected to replicate national electoral returns in the respective regions. Taking into account the two-tier structure of Russia's national electoral system, this expectation can be empirically tested in two different ways. Obviously, the clearest manifestation of voter attitudes toward political parties in national legislative elections is the vote for party lists in the nationwide district. The major difficulty with taking this factor into account is that the voters have no choice but to vote for political parties. Yet arguably some parties are more partylike than others. In Chapter 3 I identified those national political parties that were meaningfully present in regional legislative elections (Tables 3.9–3.11). It is only logical to suggest that those electors who abstain from voting for these parties' lists in national legislative elections, either by casting their votes for the lists of other parties or by voting against all lists, transfer their preferences to independents in regional legislative elections. Hence I construct the first independent variable pertaining to national elections, party vote (PVOTE), in the following way. If the dependent variable is the share of party nominees in regional legislative assemblies, then PVOTE is the joint percentage share of the vote received by the lists of all parties identified in Tables 3.9–3.11.[4] If the dependent variable is the share of KPRF conglomerate nominees, then PVOTE is the share of the vote received by the KPRF alone. If the dependent variable is the share of other parties' nominees, then PVOTE is the share of the vote jointly received by all parties represented in the regional electoral arenas with the exception of the KPRF. The second variable pertaining to national elections, parties in single-member districts (PSMD), is the percentage share of party nominees elected to the national legislature in a given region. For example, if a region returned four deputies, including two independents, a KPRF nominee, and a nominee of a different party, then the values of PSMD entered into the three regressions with different dependent variables as identified above are 50.0, 25.0, and 25.0.

The third group of independent variables used for statistical analysis pertains to intraelite conflicts at the regional level and to the role of political parties in these conflicts. In Chapter 5, I introduced these variables for the second and third electoral cycles. CHELS is the percentage share of the vote received by a successful challenger in the single or second round of voting in regional executive elections held in a given electoral cycle; ENC is the effective number of parties in the single or first round of regional executive elections; and PNI and PNC are the respective percentage shares of the vote received in the single or first round of voting by party-nominated incumbents and, jointly, by party-nominated challengers. If the dependent variable is the share of party nominees in the regional legislative assemblies, then the values of PNI and PNC are based on the vote for all party nominees in regional executive elections. If the dependent variable is the share of KPRF conglomerate nominees in the regional assemblies, then the values of PNI and PNC are based on the shares of the vote received by the candidates of the KPRF conglomerate. If the dependent variable is the share of other parties' nominees, then PNI and PNC are based on the shares of the vote jointly received by all noncommunist party-nominated candidates. Since the KPRF did not nominate any incumbents in the second electoral cycle, PNI is omitted from the corresponding regression equation. In those few cases when regional executive elections were not held in a given electoral cycle, I used the data from the last elections held in the previous electoral cycle. Special cases are Dagestan and Udmurtia, the former of which did not hold direct executive elections at all, and the latter of which did not hold direct executive elections in the second electoral cycle. In order to keep these regions in my selection of cases, I assigned values of 0, 1, 0, and 0 to the missing CHELS, ENC, PNI, and PNC respectively. The rationale for such assignments is quite transparent, taking into account that the minimum effective number of candidates is one, not zero.

Of course, these independent variables cannot be used for the analysis of the first electoral cycle simply because of the short supply of regional executive elections. To overcome this difficulty, I employed data from elections that, being national in their scope, had a well-articulated regional dimension too—the direct Federation Council elections of December 1993. As mentioned in Chapter 2, the Federation Council elections were held by a plurality system in two-member districts. According to the 1993 constitution, the Federation Council was expected to serve as a chamber of regional authorities, both executive and legislative. One of the reasons why the implementation of this constitutional provision was postponed was that by the end of 1993, few regional legislatures were actually in place. In this conjunction, the regional executives were subjected to elections too, even though they could choose to abstain from running without losing their jobs. The independent variable referring to this process, the Federation Council elections (COFED), is a dummy assuming the value of 0 if the incumbents either won or abstained from running, and the value of 1 if they participated and lost. The second variable, party members in the Federation Council (PMFC), is intended to express the role of parties in these elections. Like those of several variables introduced above, the values of PMFC are constructed in a way that takes into account the nature of the dependent variable. If the dependent variable is the share of party nominees in the regional legislative assemblies, then the value of PMFC is the number of all party nominees returned to the Federation Council in a given region. If the dependent variable is the share of KPRF conglomerate nominees in the regional assemblies, then the value of PMFC is the number of KPRF nominees elected to the Federation Council. If the dependent variable is the share of other parties' nominees, then the value of PMFC is the number of non–communist party nominees elected to the Federation Council.[5]

The independent variables of the fourth group pertain to electoral system effects. The construction of these variables, the share of deputies elected by proportional representation (PR), and the average magnitude of plurality/majority districts (AMPMD), has been discussed at length in Chapter 7. The effects of two-round majority systems are too weak to be entered into my analysis at this stage. I also skip one of the dependent variables used in Chapter 7, the share of party nominees elected by plurality/majority systems. While this obviously overemphasizes the mechanical effects of the form of candidate nomination inherent to PR, an advantage of comprehensive multivariate analysis is that it allows for weighting these effects against those of many other factors. Finally, I use a variable that seems to be essential for assessing the causal dynamics of the process of party formation, continuity (CONT). While it can be argued that the regional electoral arenas of the first electoral cycle emerged from scratch, such an argument is obviously inapplicable to the subsequent electoral cycles. On the contrary, it may be so that the formation of political parties is a process driven by its own inertia rather than by the exogenous factors identified above: once political parties take root in some regions, they continue to develop there, and they do not form in those regions where they were absent at the time of the arrival of competitive electoral politics. In correspondence with this reasoning, the values of CONT for the second and third electoral cycles are identical to the values of the dependent variables for the first and second electoral cycles respectively. Similar to these dependent variables, they assume different values for all parties, the KPRF conglomerate, and noncommunist parties.

Some of the factors identified in this book, such as the availability of alternatives to party-related resources, resisted my attempts to incorporate them into statistical models because they were too difficult to operationalize. The data at my disposal are insufficient to study the impact of candidates' occupational backgrounds upon the representation of political parties in regional legislative assemblies, even though such a research agenda could be feasible and potentially fruitful. The effects of institutional design have been tested statistically and found negligible throughout the second and third electoral cycles, which is why I do not report the corresponding regression results. Indeed, the argument presented in Chapter 6 leaves little theoretical ground to believe that institutionally strong assemblies in the regions of Russia are likely to become party-structured, but there is no apparent reason to believe that they are particularly party-resistant either. An additional variable in the third-cycle regression equation is LAW2002, a dummy assuming the value of 1 for eight regions that held legislative elections in December 2002–April 2003. The label of the variable refers to the fact that to conduct these elections, the regions had to amend their electoral regulations by incorporating some of the provisions of two federal laws adopted in 2002, the amended versions of the national electoral law and of the law on the principles of organization of state power of the regions. These provisions, generally favorable for political parties, will be discussed in the following section of this chapter. Here, it is sufficient to say that the effects of the LAW2002 variable can be interpreted in terms of institutional engineering.

The results of multiple regression analysis for the first electoral cycle are reported in Table 8.1. As follows from the table, environmental variables differed in their impact upon party formation in the regions. As far as urbanization is concerned, Huntington's theory does not seem to apply to Russia. An obvious explanation is, of course, the early emergence of rural party activism in the form of the Agrarian Party of Russia (APR). Yet it is also worth mentioning that other left forces, primarily the KPRF, were quite successful in penetrating the rural peripheries too (McFaul and Petrov 1997). Population size, in contrast, emerges as a significant determinant of party formation. However, it does not seem to affect the KPRF whatsoever, which suggests that the Communists were equally able to penetrate small and large regions. Turning to the second group of variables, the extent to which the pattern of regional party formation replicates national electoral trends seems to be strikingly small. Party vote in the proportional tier of the national electoral system is entirely unrelated to the levels of representation in regional legislative assemblies achieved by all parties and by noncom-

Table 8.1   Factors of Party Development in the Regions of Russia, First Electoral Cycle, 1993–1995

Variables	All Parties			KPRF Conglomerate			Other Parties		
	Parameter Estimate		T-value	Parameter Estimate		T-value	Parameter Estimate		T-value
Intercept	−54.90	(36.66)	−1.50	0.44	(3.96)	0.11	−17.43	(14.29)	−1.22
POP	3.02**	(1.21)	2.50	−0.03	(0.58)	−0.06	3.44***	(0.95)	3.63
URB	−0.04	(0.10)	−0.43	−0.06	(0.05)	−1.12	0.02	(0.09)	0.23
PVOTE	0.56	(0.42)	1.33	0.20*	(0.11)	1.83	0.09	(0.21)	0.45
PSMD	0.08*	(0.05)	1.81	0.04	(0.04)	0.91	0.08**	(0.04)	2.13
COFED	7.94**	(3.20)	2.48	1.57	(1.60)	0.98	6.54**	(2.67)	2.45
PMFC	5.58	(3.37)	1.65	7.45***	(2.26)	3.30	4.62	(3.68)	1.26
AMPMD	7.64***	(1.82)	4.21	3.18***	(0.90)	3.52	4.42***	(1.51)	2.93
PR	1.21***	(0.34)	3.60	0.23	(0.16)	1.38	0.97***	(0.28)	3.50
Number of observations	83			83			83		
R-squared	0.47			0.37			0.46		
Adj. R-squared	0.41			0.31			0.40		

Notes: The dependent variable is the percentage share of party nominees in regional legislative assemblies. Parentheses indicate standard errors.

* Significant at 0.1.
** Significant at 0.05.
*** Significant at 0.01.

munist parties. The association between the KPRF vote and the level of its representation in regional assemblies is positive but very weak. Perhaps even more striking, the levels of party representation in the single-member tier of the national electoral system match the levels of party representation in regional legislative assemblies to a very limited degree. However, a closer look at the data reveals that while the lack of correspondence is indeed apparent in the case of the KPRF, noncommunist parties did secure a certain level of symmetry between their national and regional representation. Intraelite conflict, as expressed in the Federation Council election results, seems to exert a sizable impact upon party formation. The COFED variable is positively associated with the regional representation of all parties and noncommunist parties, while the KPRF achieved higher levels of representation in those regions where its members were elected to the Federation Council. In the case of the KPRF, the lack of association between the dependent variable and COFED can be related to the fact that communists tended to win Federation Council seats in those regions where the incumbent chief executives lost or abstained from running. Thus the impact of PMFC simply overshadows the influence of COFED. At the same time, the impact of intraelite conflict seems to be generally weaker than that of the electoral system. Indeed, the strongest independent variable in the first-cycle regression equation is AMPMD, while the impact of PR is quite sizable too. When comparing multiple regression results for the KPRF and noncommunist parties, the difference between the effects of different electoral systems surfaces. The representation of the KPRF is overwhelmingly associated with AMPMD but only marginally with PR. The representation of noncommunist parties, in contrast, is associated more strongly with PR than with AMPMD, even though the impact of the latter remains sizable enough.

Turning to the second electoral cycle regression results, as reported in Table 8.2, we find quite a different picture. The impact of environmental controls almost entirely withers away. The representation of the KPRF seems to be greater in more populated regions, but the association is too weak to render interpretation. At the same time, noncommunist parties emerge as primarily urban formations. Rather than viewing this as a confirmation of political modernization theories, I would speculate that most of them were simply unable to penetrate the countryside, while the only noncommunist party with a rural following, the APR, declined in comparison with the previous electoral cycle. Similarity between national and regional election results is much greater than previously. In particular, national party-list vote emerges as a strong predictor of party representation in regional legislative elections. However, it seems that the only party that was able to translate voter support, as manifested in national elections, into regional legislative seats was the KPRF. It gained both in those regions

Table 8.2   Factors of Party Development in the Regions of Russia, Second Electoral Cycle, 1995–1999

Variables	All Parties			KPRF Conglomerate			Other Parties		
	Parameter Estimate		T-value	Parameter Estimate		T-value	Parameter Estimate		T-value
Intercept	−85.39***(25.18)		−3.39	−16.06	(10.34)	−1.55	−4.35	(7.07)	−0.62
POP	0.09	(0.14)	0.65	0.20*	(0.11)	1.77	−0.08	(0.06)	−1.32
URB	0.13	(0.12)	1.08	−0.05	(0.11)	−0.51	0.12**	(0.05)	2.16
PVOTE	0.97***(0.30)		3.17	0.53**	(0.20)	2.60	−0.09	(0.12)	−0.75
PSMD	0.08*	(0.04)	1.72	0.11**	(0.05)	2.15	0.03	(0.02)	1.15
CHELS	0.16**	(0.06)	2.54	0.11*	(0.06)	1.93	−0.01	(0.03)	−0.28
ENC	1.39	(1.88)	0.74	0.17	(1.75)	0.09	2.10**	(0.92)	2.29
PNI	0.24**	(0.11)	2.15	—		—	0.09*	(0.05)	1.79
PNC	0.11	(0.11)	1.02	0.17	(0.12)	1.49	0.07	(0.10)	0.77
AMPMD	6.95**	(3.12)	2.23	7.94***(2.98)		2.66	−0.57	(1.37)	−0.41
PR	1.24***(0.23)		5.29	0.29	(0.21)	1.42	0.83***(0.10)		8.06
CONT	0.17	(0.10)	1.59	0.02	(0.22)	0.11	0.31***(0.06)		4.99
Number of observations	83			83			83		
R-squared	0.54			0.42			0.68		
Adj. R-squared	0.47			0.34			0.63		

Notes: The dependent variable is the percentage share of party nominees in regional legislative assemblies. Parentheses indicate standard errors.
    * Significant at 0.1.
    ** Significant at 0.05.
    *** Significant at 0.01.

where its national list enjoyed voter support and in those where its nominees won State Duma seats. In contrast, the noncommunist parties gained regional representation in absolute isolation from national electoral returns. Intraelite conflict contributed to party development in the regions too. In general, party representation is greater in the presence of strong challengers and party-nominated incumbents. True, the association between CHELS and KPRF representation seems to be weak, but my additional inquiry into the nature of this idiosyncrasy revealed that it stems from a strong statistical association between CHELS, PVOTE, and PSMD. Indeed, it is only logical that strong communist challengers emerged in those regions where the communists' positions in national elections were strong enough. In regression employing the share of all party nominees as the dependent variable, these interaction effects wither away, which allows the effects of CHELS to be revealed. Thus it can be inferred that despite the apparently weak association, KPRF did receive enhanced representation in those regions where strong challengers were in place. Noncommunist parties, in contrast, formed in those regions where there were high levels of electoral fragmentation in executive elections, irrespective of whether incumbents won. In addition, noncommunist parties received a boost in regions with party-nominated incumbents. As argued in Chapter 5, party-nominated incumbents tended to lose the second-cycle executive elections to left-wing challengers. This explains why the association between PNI and overall party representation is stronger than its association with the representation of noncommunist parties. Electoral system effects remain strong, but in a way quite different from the first electoral cycle. This time, the overall impact of PR is decisively stronger than that of AMPMD. Noncommunist parties do not gain from AMPMD at all, but they gain tremendously from PR. The KPRF, in contrast, does not gain from PR, yet its representation continues to be positively influenced by the presence of multimember districts.

In the third electoral cycle, the impact of environmental controls is small. As reported in Table 8.3, the association between URB and KPRF representation becomes positive and statistically significant. This is a very

Table 8.3   Factors of Party Development in the Regions of Russia, Third Electoral Cycle, 1999–2003

Variables	All Parties			KPRF Conglomerate			Other Parties		
	Parameter Estimate		T-value	Parameter Estimate		T-value	Parameter Estimate		T-value
Intercept	−17.26	(41.19)	−0.42	−9.27*	(4.77)	−1.95	−3.35	(11.83)	−0.28
POP	−0.37	(1.16)	−0.32	−0.99*	(0.52)	−1.90	0.42	(0.95)	0.44
URB	0.15	(0.10)	1.49	0.10**	(0.05)	2.03	0.10	(0.08)	1.21
PVOTE	−0.04	(0.47)	−0.09	−0.04	(0.11)	−0.40	−0.14	(0.18)	−0.74
PSMD	0.06	(0.04)	1.38	0.00	(0.03)	0.18	0.07	(0.05)	1.52
CHELS	−0.04	(0.07)	−0.60	−0.02	(0.03)	−0.67	−0.04	(0.06)	−0.65
ENC	3.64***	(1.37)	2.66	1.37**	(0.62)	2.21	2.18*	(1.12)	1.95
PNI	0.08	(0.10)	0.76	0.21*	(0.11)	1.86	−0.03	(0.09)	−0.28
PNC	0.12	(0.18)	0.65	0.10	(0.09)	1.11	0.37	(0.33)	1.12
AMPMD	0.89	(3.63)	0.25	1.00	(1.65)	0.60	−0.13	(3.01)	−0.04
PR	0.78***	(0.19)	4.06	0.12	(0.08)	1.61	0.78***	(0.17)	4.50
CONT	0.39***	(0.09)	4.33	0.46***	(0.05)	9.03	0.18	(0.14)	1.24
LAW2002	29.70***	(5.23)	5.68	3.73	(2.36)	1.58	24.25***	(4.23)	5.73
Number of observations	83			83			83		
R-squared	0.67			0.68			0.63		
Adj. R-squared	0.61			0.62			0.56		

Notes: The dependent variable is the percentage share of party nominees in regional legislative assemblies. Parentheses indicate standard errors.

    * Significant at 0.1.
    ** Significant at 0.05.
    *** Significant at 0.01.

novel trend. My explanation is that by the beginning of the third electoral cycle, the regional authorities became strong enough to uproot the KPRF in the subregional structures of political and economic power. With the disappearance of the KPRF-affiliated local "bosses," the party lost both credible candidates and resources to support them. In the cities, the resourcefulness of the "bosses" is sometimes matched by the programmatic appeal of the oppositionists, as a result of which the KPRF becomes more urbanized than previously. In contrast to the second electoral cycle, the influence of the national electoral arena upon the regional arenas almost entirely disappears. At the same time, the influence of intraelite conflict remains strong. Of the variables pertaining to the concept, ENC exerts a decisive impact. Like in the previous electoral cycle, intraelite conflict emerges as a factor conducive primarily to the success of the KPRF conglomerate. At the same time, there is no significant association between CHELS and party representation, and if there is any, it is negative. This reflects a combination of two circumstances: first, strong challengers came to be in much shorter supply than they were in the previous electoral cycle, and second, fewer of them were affiliated with political parties. It seems that only weak challengers sought party nomination. The role of parties in executive elections remains a weak predictor of their legislative representation. However, it seems that the few incumbents affiliated with the KPRF or local left-wing movements contributed to the representation of the party. Electoral system effects remain strong. But while the impact of one of the variables, PR, is quite articulated, another, AMPMD, fades away. Intriguingly in the light of the theoretical reasoning presented in this book, AMPMD supports neither noncommunist parties nor the KPRF, even though in the latter case the association is still positive. My interpretation would be that by the beginning of the third electoral cycle, regional elites have learned enough of the specific effects of multimember plurality system to get rid of them as opportune. In those regions where it effectively resisted elite nonpartisanship, such as in Krasnodar territory, it was abolished. It was allowed to stay either in regions where the pattern of elite nonpartisanship was absolutely predominant, such as in Amur province, where no party nominees participated in the 1997 and 2001 legislative elections, or in regions where the rationale for maintaining it was securing ethnic minority representation, such as in some of the autonomous districts. PR proved to be more resistant to such manipulations. Yet another very strong influence upon party representation in regional legislative assemblies started to be exerted by its previous level, CONT. This factor, however, affects only the KPRF conglomerate. In contrast, the variable related to institutional engineering, LAW2002, emerges as the strongest determinant of the overall party representation and of the representation of noncommunist parties, but not the KPRF.

In the third electoral cycle, party representation in Russia's regional legislative assemblies stabilized, but at a very low level. Perhaps most important, the previously observable interaction between the national and regional electoral arenas withered away. In this sense, the regions succeeded in developing fairly autonomous, if not isolated, political systems with a very limited space for political parties. As demonstrated by the analysis above, political parties were still able to claim some moderate gains in those regions where the levels of elite fragmentation were unusually high. Indeed, both the increased intensity of intraelite contestation and the related decrease of the effective thresholds of representation invited political parties as useful electoral tools. In other contexts, however, political parties remained out of demand, and it is clear that such unfavorable contexts existed in the vast majority of regions. In the third electoral cycle, incumbent executives became less vulnerable than ever before, and they consolidated their control over the regional political arenas. Of the electoral systems favorable for party formation, the use of multimember plurality became circumscribed to a narrow circle of regions where it did not support party formation, while PR continued to be used in a handful of regions, most of which had introduced it before. Of course, these institutional developments were not accidental. After nonpartisan elites consolidated their control over regional electoral arenas, which in itself rendered political parties irrelevant, they proceeded to create institutional environments that solidified the pattern of party extinction. By doing so, they created optimal conditions within which regional power could be easily gained if subjected to voter choice, and easily maintained if challenged by nonelite contenders. In the majority of regions, the internal forces supportive of party development became eliminated or reduced to political negligibility, which naturally doomed political parties to ultimate extinction unless an external intervention took place.

Political Engineering

In July 2000, when delivering his first annual address to the Federal Assembly, president Vladimir Putin energetically criticized the shortcomings of Russia's party system.[6] As emphasized by Putin, "Russia needs parties that enjoy mass support and sustainable authority. [Russia] does not need just another set of officials' parties that lean to power or more than this, substitute for it. Judging by experience, such formations perish immediately after they get from the hothouse conditions into competitive environments." The president urged the legislators to accelerate their work on a new law on political parties and party activities, unexpectedly adding that "perhaps candidates for the post of the head of state have to be nominated only by public political associations." Another topic that featured quite prominently in Putin's address was federalism. Putin said that "federal relations in Russia are incomplete and underdeveloped. Regional autonomy is often understood as an approval of state disintegration. We have been talking permanently, for years, about a federation and strengthening it. But we must admit that so far, we have not had a full-fledged federal state. I must emphasize that what we have had, what we have created is a decentralized state." Putin suggested several remedies that were expected to "strengthen federalism." One of them was to create the so-called federal districts. Headed by the appointed plenipotentiary representatives of the president, the federal districts were to coordinate the activities of the federal bodies of power in the regions, and to ensure the regions' compliance with federal legislation. The second measure was to reform the Federation Council by switching the principle of representation from the ex officio membership of the elected chief executives and heads of legislative assemblies to the membership of their trusted representatives. Putin did not make any explicit connection between party reform and federal reform, but it did not take long for such a connection to become apparent.

It seems that the primary incentive for party reform, quite in accordance with Putin's reasoning cited above (but perhaps for practical rather than normative reasons), came from the national political arena. The 1999 national legislative elections sent threatening messages to Russia's political elites. True, the incumbent power-holders were lucky enough to find a credible replacement to Yeltsin and to "invent" Unity as a party that was able to achieve significant representation in the national legislature. Yet even as late as August 1999, none of these accomplishments could be taken for granted. Newly appointed as prime minister, Putin was as likely to fail on rallying popular support as his immediate predecessor, Sergei Stepashin, while Unity simply did not exist. The danger that Primakov and Luzhkov, whose aversion to many of Yeltsin's close associates was known all too well, would take over the national executive, while the KPRF would win a legislative majority, was perceived as very real. Hence it is not surprising that the federal authorities as put by a Russian political analyst, "would wish to bring more certainty, clarity, and predictability into political struggle."[7] Predictability seems to be a code word here, especially in the light of the persistent question of what happens when Putin, upon the completion of his second and last constitutionally allowed term, steps down as president. A deputy head of the presidential administration and a man often considered as the mastermind of party reform, Vladislav Surkov, delivered a picturesque description of how perilous this situation could be at a meeting of the activists of Unitary Russia in February 2002: "The president goes away—we can't keep him—what happens next? Both the extreme right and the extreme left might come to power. . . . We might make fools of ourselves and fail. We can't survive on artificial breathing."[8] Thus the first incentive for party reform was the idea that by institutionalizing party competition, the national political elite could decrease uncertainty and thus minimize risks related to electoral politics. Stable national political parties were the key.

At this point, however, regions had to be taken into account. Logically, it is difficult to expect viable national parties to form without territorial penetration. Indeed, the sustainable territorial network of the KPRF was often considered as the decisive source of its viability in the national electoral arena. In contrast, the "parties of power" proved to be generally inefficient. Moreover, one of the messages of the 1999 campaign was that elections were too prone to the influence of regional elites, which threatened the strategic goals of the national power-holders in two ways. On the one hand, as demonstrated by the history of Luzhkov's flirtation with regional authorities, the Kremlin could not take the loyalty of the regions for granted. In a situation involving a lame duck incumbent and a relatively popular challenger, they were likely to jump on the bandwagon. On the other hand, the dependence of "parties of power" on regional executives greatly enhanced their political resources vis-à-vis the federal authorities, as a result of which some of them could claim the role of national power-brokers for themselves. Those regional leaders who formed All Russia in 1999 proved this all too clearly, even though this particular attempt was not very successful. Taking this into account, the strategic goals of the reform can be described in the following way: (1) to create political parties not only in the opposition segment of Russia's political spectrum, where one such party already exists, but also in the progovernment segment; (2) to form these parties on a national rather than on a regional basis; and (3) to make these parties politically important and thereby viable. In order to implement these goals, the federal authorities launched new legislation on political parties and elections.

The Law on Political Parties, initiated by the president and passed without any serious complication by both chambers of the Federal Assembly, was adopted in June 2001. The most radical novelty of the law was its definition of political parties. In addition to defining a party as a public association with explicit political goals, which did not differ from the notion of "public political associations" already present in Russia's national legislation, Article 3 of the law set two major organizational thresholds that had to be passed by an organization seeking the status of a political party. First, a political party had to have branches in more than half of Russia's regions. Second, the overall membership of a party had to be no less than 10,000, on the condition that in no less than half of the regions it formed branches of no less than 100 members, while other regional branches had to have no less than 50 members each. In order to make parties comply with these regulations, the law required all previously existing "public political associations" to obtain fresh registration as "political parties" in the new legal meaning of the term. The same procedure had to be followed by new political parties. After holding its founding congress or a congress that officially transformed it into a political party, an association had to register its bylaws with Russia's Ministry of Justice. This, however, was only a preliminary registration. Within six months of the event, an association had to register branches in no less than half of regions with the local departments of justice and to present the list of thus-formed branches to the Moscow office of the ministry. Only after that was it officially recognized as a political party entitled to electoral participation. This entitlement was exclusive. According to Article 36 of the law, "a political party is the only kind of political associations entitled to independently nominate legislative candidates or lists of candidates, and candidates for other elected offices in the organs of state power." Political parties could nominate candidates either individually or by forming electoral blocs. To be sure, the law did not eliminate the legal basis for nonpartisanship because self-nomination and nomination by a group of voters remained possible. However, it drastically restricted the circle of organizations that could participate in elections. The law eliminated the notion of subnational, that is, regional or local, public political associations. They were deprived of electoral participation. National public political associations that opted not to transform themselves into political parties were still entitled for electoral participation, but only in blocs, which practically reduced them to junior partners of registered parties.

According to the law, electoral participation was not only an exclusive right of national political parties but also, in effect, their duty. Party registration could not only be obtained from the Ministry of Justice but also canceled by the Supreme Court of Russia, on the appeal of the ministry, if a party abstained from elections. Specifically the law stipulated that the ministry sustained registration of those parties that, in the course of five years, fulfilled one of the following conditions: (1) nominated its list in the proportional tier of national legislative elections, (2) nominated its candidates for no less than 5 percent of seats contested in the plurality tier of national legislative elections, (3) nominated its candidate for the Russian presidency, (4) nominated its candidates for chief executive positions in no less than 10 percent of the regions, (5) nominated its candidates in regional legislative elections in no less than 20 percent of the regions, or (6) nominated its candidates in municipal elections in no less than half of the regions. Political parties could meet these conditions either individually or by forming blocs. If, however, none of them were fulfilled, the Supreme Court could cancel registration. Moreover, the Ministry of Justice was charged with the regular scrutiny of political parties aimed at identifying those that ceased to meet membership and territorial spread requirements. Here again, if the requirements were not met, the ministry could bring the matter to the Supreme Court with a high likelihood of fatal consequences for the party in question. Political parties were also charged with providing the fiscal agencies and the Ministry of Justice with extensive information about their financial standing, sources of party funds, and political activities. The ministry, in turn, had to publish this information both in print and on the Internet, for which it created a special Internet site.[9]

As partial compensation for all these inconveniences, national political parties received a bonus in the form of state funding. However, as stipulated by Article 33 of the law, funding had to be provided not to all registered parties but only to those that managed to secure a certain minimum of success in national elections. First, state funding was to be provided to those parties that received no less than 3 percent of the vote in the proportional tier of national legislative elections. Second, state funding was extended to those parties that failed to cross this threshold but succeeded in electing no fewer than twelve deputies in single-member districts. Funds were to be provided annually. The amount of funding was to be determined by the number of votes received by party list or jointly received by successful party nominees, depending on what entitled the given party to enjoy state support. Finally, those parties that ran their candidates in presidential elections were entitled to receive state funding too, provided that the candidate received no less than 3 percent of the vote. These funds were to be paid out in a lump sum after each of the presidential elections. The law stipulated that each of the votes received by a party that qualified for state funding had to be converted into 0.005 percent of the legally established minimum salary, which is a standard way of calculating state charges in Russia. Many Russian political observers ridiculed such amounts as absolutely insufficient. As put by one of them, "funding is so miserable that it can serve neither as a serious bonus to large parties nor as a means of getting rid of the black cash and illegal sponsors."[10]

The major problem with the implementation of the law was, of course, that it legally eliminated those already existing political organizations that called themselves parties. For this reason, it simply could not be implemented immediately. As a result, Article 46 of the law established a two-year transitional period during which political parties had to be created. More specifically, by the end of the transitional period, all previously existing public political associations had to transform themselves into either political parties or public associations. Before the July 2003 deadline, however, both public political associations and new political parties, insofar as they received preliminary registration with the Ministry of Justice, remained entitled to electoral participation. The same applied to regional political associations. State funding of political parties was to come even later, starting in January 1, 2004. Thus the law did not have immediate consequences for regional elections. The transformation of public political associations into political parties did indeed start at the end of 2001, and it would be fair to say that four of the parties created (or rather re-created) in compliance with the law, the KPRF, Unitary Russia, the People's Party of the Russian Federation (NPRF), and the Union of Right Forces (SPS), became slightly more active in regional elections in 2002–2003 than the public associations from which they originated were in 2000–2001. The consequences of their activation, however, were counterbalanced by the fact that some of the previously active organizations, such as the Pensioners Party, were engaged in complex processes of refoundation that apparently distracted them from regional elections, while regional organizations became discouraged by the prospect of losing their political status.

It seems that, in fact, the drafters of party reform did not anticipate that it would come into effect immediately. While some of the politicians did express hope that the 2003 national legislative elections would be contested by "three or four large parties,"[11] the head of the Central Electoral Commission, the agency that actually drafted the 2000 law, anticipated that the number of political parties entitled to participate in the 2003 elections would be sixty,[12] which in retrospect can be viewed as a very sober estimation. When assessing this number, it has to be taken into account that the number of public political associations entitled to participate in the 1999 campaign was 139. Indeed, the provisions of the law were generally conducive to a decrease in the number of parties. First, the law made it more difficult to register a party. Second, the law supplemented registration with a new and perhaps less easily surmountable threshold, the necessity to sustain certain levels of membership and electoral participation. Electoral participation was an especially demanding requirement. Very few parties could meet this requirement by means of participation in the specified numbers of subnational electoral campaigns. Hence for a microparty, the only feasible way to survive for more than a five-year period was to participate in national legislative or presidential elections, which required it to collect a large number of signatures and otherwise invest in elections that it had little chance to win. Under such conditions, the label of a minor party becomes a liability rather than an asset, which means that in the long run—by approximately 2007–2008—such labels are likely to be skipped by their holders. Hence the principal target of the 2001 party reform can be related to the reduction in the number of parties. This can be characterized as a fairly rational strategy of supporting party development. If a commodity is in low demand, then reducing supply, when combined with increasing the value of the product, may be a feasible solution. As demonstrated in Chapter 4, the oversupply of party labels is an obstacle to party formation, and so is the low value of the existing party labels. However, my further analysis revealed that a stronger obstacle is the presence of easily available alternatives to party nomination. The 2001 law did not, in fact, eliminate these alternatives. Moreover, by reducing party supply and arguably increasing the costs of party affiliation, the new law could have made the alternatives, in the form of nomination by voters and self-nomination, more attractive to regional politicians. The demand side remained to be dealt with.

My analysis in the previous section of this chapter suggests that the demand for political parties in regional elections increases under two different conditions, intensive intraelite conflict and electoral systems supportive of party development. The latter condition was a lot easier to achieve by means of political engineering. But deliberation on the former option is in order here. In fact, Putin's strategy toward regions, irrespective of whether the proper description for it would be strengthening federalism, recentralization, or enhancement of state capacity, was inherently inconsistent with the existence of closed political arenas controlled by the regional executives. At the same time, the prospects for opening up these arenas were not very encouraging. A full-scale institutional reform such as the reinstitution of appointed governors remained a subject of lively political and journalistic debate throughout the 2000–2003 period and even received support from some of the governors themselves,[13] yet the implementation of this idea would have involved full-scale constitutional amendment, something Putin never agreed to do. Moreover, the appointment of senior executives, while being nothing new in the majority of regions, would have been a striking novelty in the republics. Both available alternatives, appointing the heads of republics at risk of ethnic unrest and making them appointment-exempt, with the reestablishment of asymmetrical federation as a logical consequence, could be scarcely acceptable. Other available means of institutional engineering, such as introducing parliamentary systems in the regions, were never even discussed. In fact, the evolution of the regions' institutional design took the exactly opposite direction of strengthening the executives. Since general solutions were in short supply, the federal executive's struggle for the opening of the political arenas of the regions took the shape of a series of ad hoc actions aimed at removing some of the most notorious and least compliant regional leaders. The institutional base for these actions was provided by the decreased dependence of federal bodies in the regions on the regional authorities, which was one of the consequences of the creation of federal districts. In particular, courts turned out to be quite resistant to regional strongmen.

One of the most notorious governors of the Yeltsin era, Aleksandr Rutskoi of Kursk province, was disqualified from running for a second term in 2000 for a formal reason. There was widespread speculation that the Kursk provincial court would have never dared to do that unless supported by the Kremlin. When asked to comment on the rumor, an influential political consultant who at that time often served as an unofficial spokesman for the presidential administration, Gleb Pavlovskii, said: "I think that in the situation with the Kursk governor Rutskoi's electoral disqualification the one who is to be blamed is Rutskoi himself, not the Kremlin. But the Kremlin certainly has to do with it too. In this case, a precedent has been created: the restoration of the authority of the court vis-à-vis the incumbent governor, the authority that turned out to be stronger than the executive power of the governor... This is a part of the federal center's strategy, a part of the dictatorship of the law."[14] A very similar story happened with the president of Sakha, Mikhail Nikolaev. While the reason for his disqualification from the 2001 regional executive race was, like in the previous case, provided by a court decision on formal grounds, the majority of local observers alleged that Russia's presidential administration was not only directly involved in but also decided the outcome.[15] The infamously authoritarian governor of Primorskii territory, Evgenii Nazdratenko, also had to leave his office after Putin's plenipotentiary representative in the Far East said that Nazdratenko's mismanagement rendered the necessity of "tough measures" against him.[16] Thus the strategy aimed at removing the least acceptable of the regional executives occasionally worked out. Yet it is quite clear that, as any ad hoc strategy, it had its limitations. Moreover, it tended to backfire. While Nikolaev's successor in Sakha was seemingly acceptable for the Kremlin, this was not the case with the man who won gubernatorial elections in Kursk province, the outspoken communist Aleksandr Mikhailov. The winner of the 2001 gubernatorial elections in Primorskii territory, Sergei Dar'kin, was a political outsider and a shadowy businessman with alleged criminal connections.[17] Closed political arenas are like this not only because all-powerful elite groups monopolistically control them but also because there are no groups capable of challenging the existing power. The ad hoc measures implemented by the Kremlin could eliminate the first but not the second component of this formula, which is why they opened a window of opportunity for extremists and political outsiders. Therefore, any systemic solution had to involve not only less favorable conditions for regional autocrats but also more favorable conditions for their opponents—that is, the possibility of an institutionalized opposition.

This makes it useful to revisit the relationship between the two causal components of party formation, intraelite conflict and electoral systems. The first years of Putin's centralizing efforts demonstrated that intraelite conflict could not be induced in the regions externally. Electoral system reform emerged as the only feasible way to stimulate party formation by regulating the demand side of the political marketplace. However, once formed, political parties could fix the deficiency that made the political arenas of the regions resistant to opening, the lack of viable opposition. Hence the chain of causality between electoral system reform and party formation

could be complemented with one more link, intraelite conflict, thus forming what could be called a virtuous circle of party formation. Choosing the
principal institutional site for party formation was less than problematic. As
in any presidential democracy, legislative assemblies could perform this
role. The direction of the reform was rather clear too. True, the evolution of
regional politics since 1993 suggested that in principle, proportional representation was not the only way to ensure party formation. Multimember
plurality could be an acceptable solution if reform strategists aimed at party
formation at any price. However, the political goals of the federal executive
were scarcely consistent with implementing an electoral system that gave
an advantage to the major national opposition party. Rather, the strategic
goal of the reform was to stimulate the development of noncommunist parties desirably loyal to the federal authorities and possibly in opposition to
the regional ones. As demonstrated in the previous section of this chapter,
the only electoral system that invited such parties and that, no less important, was not very favorable for the KPRF, was proportional representation.

In May 2001, two State Duma deputies, Boris Nadezhdin and Igor
Igoshin, initiated a bill that would introduce mixed systems into regional
legislative elections. The bill, shaped as an amendment to the law "On the
General Principles of Organization of the Legislative (Representative) and
Executive Organs of State Power of the Subjects of the Russian
Federation," was quite remarkable already because of the bipartisan composition of its initiators: Nadezhdin was an SPS party-list deputy, while
Igoshin entered the Duma on the list of the KPRF and was delegated to the
satellite Agro-Industrial deputy group. At their first joint press conference,
Nadezhdin and Igoshin stated that the domination of single-member district
systems in regional legislative elections placed legislatures under the control of the executives. Proportional representation, reasoned the drafters of
the bill, would allow for making legislative assemblies more independent
and enhance the role of political parties in the regions.[18] Later, Nadezhdin
elaborated in the following way: "By passing this law, we make the governors face opponents of equal strength. Now, under single-member district
systems, there are no such opponents. Under a party list system, the governors will confront organizations that are localized not in individual districts
but rather in the regions as a whole, and moreover, with federal-level politicians beyond them. Each of the governors will have to do with actors
whose resources are comparable with the governor's own."[19] Nadezhdin
discarded the naïve hope that regions themselves would initiate a reform
that would allow "alien" federal parties to claim power in their territories.[20]
That is why, he insisted, only federal law could implement the reform. At
the same time, the drafters of the bill were not very confident that the
Federation Council would pass it. To make a bitter pill sweeter, the bill set
rather modest levels of party representation. First, the share of the deputies

to be elected by party lists was defined as no less than 15 percent, and there was no apparent reason to believe that many regions would opt for increasing it. While Nadezhdin estimated this to be the minimum measure that would allow for "creating new federal centers of gravity in the regions,"[21] his preemptive readiness to compromise was indicative that he did not foresee an easy passage of the bill. The second compromise norm of the bill was that mixed electoral systems were to be implemented only in the regions with numbers of voters in excess of 1 million. This exempted from mixed systems all autonomous districts, the autonomous province, twenty-one provinces, and perhaps most important, sixteen republics—overall, forty-eight regions. Thus the majority of the regions, and by implication the majority of the Federation Council members, had nothing to worry about.

The Nadezhdin–Igoshin bill was passed by the State Duma in the first reading, on July 13, 2001. The second reading did not take place until April 2002. In the interim, however, a new turn of events arrived. In October 2001 the Duma adopted in the first reading a new version of the law "On the Basic Guarantees of Citizens' Electoral Rights and the Right to Participate in Referenda." The bill recommended that half of the deputies to the regional legislative assemblies be elected by party lists. This norm was not obligatory. Regions themselves could decide whether to comply. From this perspective, it was even more harmless than the proposals of Nadezhdin and Igoshin. At the same time, the chairman of the Central Electoral Commission, Aleksandr Veshniakov, introduced the bill to the Duma on behalf of the president of Russia. This not only elevated the status of the bill in comparison with that of Nadezhdin–Igoshin but also signaled that the Kremlin viewed the idea of electoral reform quite favorably. When asked to comment on this change of fortune, Nadezhdin explained the reasons beyond the national executive's decision to support regional electoral reform in the following way: "I think one of the reasons is that in fact, Putin is a consistent liberal, and he understands all too well that a civil society cannot be created without political parties. The second reason is that the Kremlin's managers led by Surkov are confident that the processes going on in the country will be more manageable if parties become stronger, so that when dealing with a situation in an individual region, it would be sufficient to call one person, the party boss, and to softly advise what is the right way for the region."[22] While this is obviously an interpretation, not a factual statement, the fact is that by the spring of 2002, Veshniakov changed his position regarding the way in which mixed electoral systems were to be implemented regionally. If earlier he was "generally supportive" of the idea,[23] which corresponded all too well to the original intention to leave the issue for resolution at the regional level, the draft of the law on the basic guarantees that was prepared for the second reading made this norm obligatory.

This, in turn, stimulated the Duma to get back to the Nadezhdin–Igoshin bill. In its amended form, the bill increased the minimum share of seats to be filled by proportional representation to 50 percent, extended the norm to all regions, and made its implementation imperative two months after the enactment of the law. In this form, the bill evoked little controversy among the Duma deputies. The only legislator who questioned it was a single-member district deputy and a defector from the Russian Communist Workers Party (RKRP), Oleg Shein. He argued that political parties in the regions were not developed enough to take half of the seats in the legislatures. Another deputy, Elena Mizulina of Yabloko, responded by stating that party systems in the regions "will never form if we let the regions themselves decide."[24] The bill was adopted by an overwhelming majority and sent to the Federation Council, which not unexpectedly vetoed it on April 24, 2002. Ironically, the decision on the bill evoked as little controversy in the Federation Council as it did in the State Duma. Apparently speaking for all Federation Council members, the chairman of the upper chamber's committee on the issues of federation stated that setting regional electoral systems was an exclusive prerogative of the regional authorities, and that by passing the Nadezhdin–Igoshin bill, the State Duma attempted "not to regulate the general principles but rather to dictate how regions must hold their elections."[25]

In the meantime, the Duma proceeded with the new version of the law on the basic guarantees of electoral rights. Despite the position of the Federation Council that was expressed two days earlier, the draft prepared for the second reading left intact the norm according to which half of the regional legislators, or a half of the members of one of the chambers of bicameral assemblies, were to be elected by party lists. However, when speaking to the deputies of the State Duma, Veshniakov advocated two amendments that, in his view, could have made the bill acceptable to the members of the Federation Council. Both amendments were related to the 2001 law on political parties. First, reasoned Veshniakov, the law on political parties had to be enacted in full on July 14, 2003. It would be only logical to postpone the introduction of mixed electoral systems to the same date, so that only full-fledged national political parties could run their candidates in regional legislative elections.[26] The second amendment made exempt from introducing mixed electoral systems those regions where there were less than three registered branches of national political parties. Indeed, by April 2002 only a few parties registered their regional branches, and there was a widespread expectation that the process of territorial penetration would take time. Thus the amendment could be viewed as a compromise.[27] With these amendments, the State Duma unanimously approved the bill in the second reading, on April 26, 2002, and then, less than a month later, in the third and final reading. Then it was the Federation Council's turn. The upper chamber scheduled its deliberations on the bill for May 29, 2002.

Well aware that the members of the upper chamber had little if any reason to approve the bill, its supporters prepared the ground for a favorable outcome by inviting Putin himself. On May 21, 2002, Putin argued that party-list systems "will allow political parties to advance candidates who are better prepared for [legislative] work. Under such systems, voters will be able to choose among ideas, not among attractive faces and persons."[28] Veshniakov and several representatives of the presidential administration attended deliberations on the bill in the committees of the upper chamber in order to ensure its preliminary approval. Ultimately, these heavy preparations paid off, but the passage of the law was anything but easy. Discussion took as long as one and a half hours, which in itself was unusual for the Federation Council.[29] Moreover, the vast majority of the participants in the discussion recommended either to veto the law or to postpone voting. Interestingly enough, among the most vocal critics of the law were not only representatives of those regions where political parties actually did not exist, such as Khanty-Mansi autonomous district, but also representatives of the regions where party nominees already constituted legislative majorities, such as Krasnoiarsk and Krasnodar territories.[30] Veshniakov, who took the floor closer to the end of discussion, was careful enough to state that he was acting not in a personal capacity but rather as a trusted representative of the president. While his emotional advocacy of party development in the regions apparently did not impress the Federation Council members, this statement, combined with the reminder that most regions would have to implement mixed systems in no sooner than four years, could be convincing enough. In his turn, the chairman of the Federation Council and a member of Putin's "inner circle," Sergei Mironov, reminded the members of the council about the compromise decision to postpone the implementation of mixed systems to July 2003, and recommended to adopt the law. The carefully orchestrated deliberations resulted in the approval of the law by ninety-six to thirty-six votes, with fourteen abstentions, an unusually poor result for a law initiated by the president. At the same time this was a victory. The Nadezhdin–Igoshin bill was amended in correspondence with the law on the basic guarantees of electoral rights and passed by the Duma on June 26, 2002, to be quietly approved by the Federation Council two weeks later.

In addition to mixed electoral systems in regional legislative elections, the 2002 laws introduced three norms that could be expected to influence regional electoral politics in general and the role of political parties in particular. In contrast to the provision for mixed electoral systems, all three norms were to be implemented immediately upon the enactment of the laws. First, Article 71 of the law on the basic guarantees of citizens' electoral rights made it imperative to use two-round majority systems in regional executive elections; single-member plurality was legally eliminated. In line with the argument presented in Chapter 7, it is possible to believe that in the long run political parties will benefit from the resulting reduction of the effective thresholds in the first round. Second, the same law stipulated for only two forms of nomination, nomination by a political party (or by a bloc of parties) and self-nomination. The previously dominant form in the majority of regions, nomination by a group of voters, was no longer legally acceptable. Given that self-nomination was often considered a somehow inferior form,[31] this symbolically elevated the status of party nomination. At the same time, the perceived inferiority of self-nomination stemmed from the reluctance of most resourceful independents to use this form. Once nomination by a group of voters is not an available option, self-nomination may easily improve its credentials if used by resourceful candidates. Perhaps the most important innovation was introduced as an amendment to Article 12 of the law "On the General Principles of Organization of the Legislative (Representative) and Executive Organs of State Power of the Subjects of the Russian Federation." The amendment, passed by the Duma on April 10, 2002, stipulated that a deputy elected to a regional legislative assembly could not combine his duties with employment as a state official or an elected municipal officer. Given the role of state officials and municipal leaders in downgrading the role of political parties in regional legislative elections as described in Chapter 5, this was a truly revolutionary amendment, and it came into effect immediately after the law was enacted on May 7, 2002. It was applied to all regional legislative elections held in December 2002 and henceforth. In theory, state officials and municipal leaders were not deprived of their right to contest legislative elections. In practice, however, few of them would possibly exchange their positions of power for assembly seats. This created a new structure of opportunities for candidates belonging to less resourceful occupations, and to party nominees in particular. It must be kept in mind, however, that the third category of resourceful candidates, the businesspeople, remained in complete capacity to go on with "assembly colonization."

In the end it would be fair to say that the proponents of electoral reform demonstrated remarkable tactical skills. In order to make the Federation Council approve what the overwhelming majority of its members intensively disliked, they masterfully used two bills containing the same norm, one of them enacting it almost immediately and another with a substantial delay. The scope of change initially proposed in the Nadezhdin–Igoshin bill was quite modest, but it allowed for making the case for reform. Then the presidential administration came out with an even more modest proposal that, however, originated from a much more authoritative source. After that, the Nadezhdin–Igoshin bill became radical enough to be bluntly rejected by the Federation Council. By doing that, the upper chamber demonstrated its political will and independence, which cleared the way for a compromise on conditions set by the presidential administration. In fact, the level of support for reform in the State Duma was high enough to override the veto of the Federation Council, which meant that the law could be signed by the president and enacted without the upper chamber's consent. Such an outcome, however, would have been less than optimal for both sides. Not only would the Federation Council have lost outright, but also it would have possibly had the reform implemented immediately. At the same time, the implementation of a major regional political reform without the explicit consent of the Federation Council promised nothing good to the Kremlin both because in this case the reform would have been viewed as illegitimate by the regional elites, and because thereby the obstacles to change would have mounted. Thus the proponents of the reform won in the first round. The outcome of the second round, however, was to be decided in the regions.

Regional Reactions to Reform and Its Possible Consequences

The complex maneuvering that surrounded the movement for electoral reform in Moscow was viewed by regional elites with anxiety. The deputy mayor of Moscow, Valerii Shantsev, reacted by claiming that party lists were "a threat to democracy." He elaborated: "We are against bringing politics into the City Duma, we are against voting from the positions of party discipline rather than from the positions of the voter. Indeed, when political struggle is going on, then the normal economic structure falls apart, because the economy depends on politics."[32] A very characteristic discussion took place in Nizhnii Novgorod province in April 2002.[33] Of the participants in the discussion, local politicians, academics, and journalists, only two supported the idea of the reform unambiguously, claiming that a party-list system would decrease the influence of money upon election outcomes. The remaining eight participants were more or less skeptical, citing such reasons as the lack of strong political parties in the regions, the inability of party deputies to deliver constituency service, and their dependence on Moscow party elites who allegedly sought to take over the regions. A factor that definitely contributed to appeasing the regional elites was that by May 2002 the majority of regions were to have their legislative elections no sooner than within three or four years. Yet as mentioned above, there were several important exceptions. In particular, the Nadezhdin–Igoshin bill, if passed by the Federation Council, would have made it imperative to elect the legislative assembly of St. Petersburg by a mixed system. This caused a panic among the incumbent legislators. In an attempt to prevent the threat, a group of deputies introduced a bill according to which fresh elections had to be held not in December, when assembly powers actually expired, but rather in September, which would have allowed them to legally set an election date before the enactment of the new law. When arguing for the bill, its initiators were quite explicit that their only goal was to get rid of party-list elections.[34] It was only after the Federation Council vetoed the Nadezhdin–Igoshin bill that the legislators of St. Petersburg, apparently relieved from their worst fears, duly scheduled fresh elections for December.

Other regions that held their legislative elections in the second half of 2002 or in the first months of 2003 faced a different problem. As mentioned in Chapter 3, they were legally entitled to postpone their elections so that they could be held concurrently with the federal elections—that is, in December 2003. It seems that in the beginning of 2002, this idea was viewed quite favorably by the majority of regional elites, executive and legislative alike, while their opponents were generally inclined to demand holding elections as early as possible. However, after the federal law made it unavoidable to use mixed electoral systems after June 2003, the picture radically changed. Even in those regions where it was firmly decided to postpone elections, such as in Udmurtia,[35] it suddenly turned out that time-ly elections were important. When discussing the matter at the plenary session of the republic's legislature in September 2002, its chairman argued that holding elections by party lists was impossible because, according to the results of a public opinion poll cited by the chairman, 70 percent of the population was unfamiliar with the activities of the regional branches of political parties. When commenting on this argument, an observer promptly added that "elections by the old system in 'well-fed' single-member districts would have meant almost guaranteed re-election for the majority of deputies, more or less wealthy businessmen."[36] Not surprisingly, this time there were few vocal proponents of delaying elections, most of them KPRF members. To achieve this goal, the KPRF formed an otherwise unlikely alliance with the regional branch of the SPS.[37] The alliance, however, was unable to mobilize anything close to a legislative majority.

An alliance of party politicians for a mixed electoral system in Sakha joined together the KPRF, the SPS, and Unitary Russia.[38] The alliance's campaign was simply ignored by the legislature of the republic. In North Ossetia, a similar coalition was formed by as many as sixteen organizations, again from the KPRF to the SPS. Rather than articulating the issue of electoral system choice, party politicians argued that holding concurrent elections in December 2003 would have relieved the republic's budget from the costs of one of the campaigns. However economical, this option was rejected outright by the chairman of the republic's electoral commission. In essence, he said, it was not about saving money but rather about having party-list elections. And party-list elections "are being induced artificially and prematurely."[39] In the end, the legislature of North Ossetia not only scheduled elections for May 2003 but also abolished the previously existing five-member district in which only parties could nominate candidates. Overall, of those twelve regions that were entitled to postpone their elections from December 2002–April 2003 to December 2003, only three, Ingushetia, Kabardino-Balkaria, and Volgograd province, actually did so. In Volgograd, however, this decision was made in 2001, when the prospect for implementing mixed electoral systems regionally was anything but clear. Ingushetia and Kabardino-Balkaria, in contrast, apparently made their choices in awareness of the possible consequences. In this connection, it is worth mentioning that the 1999 national legislative elections in Ingushetia brought a stunning result of 88 percent of the party-list vote to Fatherland–All Russia, with 1.0 percent for Unity and 1.8 percent for the KPRF. The distribution of the 1999 party list vote in Kabardino-Balkaria was more balanced: 34.7 percent for Fatherland–All Russia, 20.6 percent for Unity, and 23.9 percent for the KPRF. Hence the solution to the puzzle of the republics' willingness to adopt mixed systems is easy: their elites had every reason to believe that they would secure acceptable results under any electoral system. Under such conditions, postponing elections was expedient in the sense of economizing on election-related costs and, perhaps more important, in the sense of providing an additional safe year to the regional legislators.

For the majority of the regions, however, having early elections was not an available option. Some of the regional leaders started a crusade against the new law soon after it was adopted. A group of its most vocal critics included the mayor of Moscow, Yurii Luzhkov. In October 2002 he charged the lawyers employed by the city government to carefully examine whether the provision stipulating for mixed electoral systems in the regions of Russia was constitutional.[40] In a similar vein, the legislature of Astrakhan province initiated the process of amending the laws that provided for mixed electoral systems in the regions by making the norm a recommendation, not a requirement. Apparently aware that the amendments had very little chance to be adopted by the Duma, the chairman of the Astrakhan legislature stated that if the Duma would decline to support the move, the case would be brought to the Constitutional Court of Russia.[41] Hence it seems that the opponents of the reform started to view the Constitutional Court as their last resort. However, the chances of the court ruling against mixed electoral systems are not very good. In Article 77, the 1993 constitution states that "the systems of the state organs . . . are being established by the subjects of the Russian Federation independently, in accordance with the foundations of the constitutional system of the Russian

Federation and the general principles of organization of the representative and executive organs of state power as established by federal law." Since the 2002 laws define mixed electoral systems as one of the general principles according to which the representative bodies of power in Russia's regions shall be organized, it is difficult for the regions to claim the legal right to determine whether to implement electoral reform. Even though it remains possible to argue that the provisions of the 2002 laws are too detailed to qualify as general principles, this argument seems to be insufficiently specific to render a court ruling against the reform.

Thus the majority of the regions, even though slowly and reluctantly, entered the phase of public deliberations regarding how to cope with the reform imposed upon them. In the majority of cases, these deliberations mostly concerned the question of whether to double the number of deputies by simply supplementing the existing single-member districts with proportional representation districts equal in magnitude to previous assembly sizes, or to engage in comprehensive redistricting aimed at keeping previous assembly sizes intact. These deliberations, however interesting in themselves, are not of primary interest for this analysis. However, one aspect related to the institutional structure of regional legislative assemblies deserves to be mentioned here. The federal laws of 2002 established that mixed electoral systems had to be used for electing no less than 50 percent of the deputies. In bicameral legislatures, however, regions were allowed to limit the number of party-list deputies to half of one of the chambers. In the last months of 2002, the idea of switching to bicameralism became increasingly popular in the regions, including where such an idea had never surfaced before. In October 2002 the legislative assembly of Perm province discussed several proposals for bicameralism.[42] The assembly included forty members. One of the proposals was to keep the district structure intact and to comply with the requirements of the law by creating a ten-member upper chamber that would be elected by party lists, which would have reduced the overall share of party deputies to 20 percent. This idea was rejected because it presupposed giving some exclusive powers to the upper chamber, for which the Perm legislators were apparently unprepared. The second proposal was to make the lower chamber consist of twenty district deputies and twenty list deputies, and to supplement this structure with a twenty-member upper chamber elected in single-member districts. Thus the share of the list deputies increased to one-third, but they would not have had exclusive control over any of the chambers. This, however, raised the question of districting. In the end, the legislators agreed on a unicameral structure. Comic as it was, the Perm discussion revealed some of the possibilities actually available to regional institutional engineers. In 2002 the idea of switching to bicameralism was under discussion in several regions, including Tambov and Tula provinces.[43]

Thus institutional engineering started to be viewed as a possible means of local resistance to the reform imposed upon the regions by Moscow-based institutional engineers. Yet it is generally clear that the challenge can be met by political means too. In the remainder of this chapter, I will discuss several alternative strategies that can be employed by regional elites in order to accommodate the changed institutional environments. While being unavoidably speculative in many important respects, such a discussion nevertheless seems to be necessary for assessing the prospects for party formation in the regions of Russia. My reasoning on the subject is built upon several assumptions that need to be explicated. First, and related to the previous analysis presented in this book, I assume that the principal elite actors of Russia's regional politics are chief executives. Second, I assume that their political goals can be reduced to two major components, winning elections and controlling legislative assemblies. Third, I assume that in the changed institutional environments, they have stronger incentives to use political parties for achieving these goals, yet disincentives stemming from their unwillingness to carry the costs of party affiliation remain as strong as ever. Proceeding from these assumptions, I will describe and assess the possible strategies of chief executives. These strategies are dubbed "small-party capture," "party purchase," and "large-party capture." Then I will assess the consequences of each of the strategies for party formation in the regions.

Before discussing some of the strategies identified above, it is important to take into account that purely regional political parties are no longer useful for electoral purposes. To run its candidates, an organization has to be registered as a national political party. Then the first question to be addressed is whether such parties are available at all. It seems that they are. While, as mentioned in the first section of this chapter, the adoption of the new law on political parties did evoke hopes (and sometimes fears) that creating parties would become a formidably difficult task, these expectations proved to be groundless. As of June 2003, Russia's Ministry of Justice had registered as many as fifty-one parties. Forty-one of them had already registered their branches in more than half of the regions, thus becoming fully eligible for electoral participation. While the set of the newly registered parties included such veterans of Russia's political scene as the KPRF, the Liberal Democratic Party of Russia (LDPR), and Yabloko, and of course the new party of power in the form of Unitary Russia, it also featured a plethora of previously inactive or marginal groups such as the Conservative Party of Russia and the New Communist Party, led by a grandson of the Soviet Union's late leader Leonid Brezhnev. The question of how these entities managed to register their regional branches was partly addressed in Chapter 4. The task was relatively easy. Thus the supply of parties did not become scarce to an extent that only strong parties were available. Small parties survived.

The strategy of small-party capture takes place when a regional executive either creates a national party for his or her own needs or takes over an already existing party. In the electoral history of the regions of Russia, Aleksandr Lebed in Krasnoiarsk territory achieved the closest approximation to this strategy. The political organizations of Lebed, Honor and Motherland and the Russian Popular Republican Party (RNRP), lost national political significance after their founder became absorbed by regional politics in 1998. However, they retained their national status and, in the capacity of national political associations, contested the 2001 regional legislative elections in the territory as components of the pro-Lebed bloc. In the course of the third electoral cycle, two other governors took over national political parties. One of them, Mikhail Prusak of Novgorod province, took many observers by surprise when in September 2001 a congress of the Democratic Party of Russia (DPR) elected him as the leader of the party by an overwhelming majority.[44] Once the best-organized group of anticommunist "informals" that was still able to win representation in the 1993 State Duma, the DPR experienced a long period of decay, high leadership turnover, and intraparty struggles, eventually to become reduced to a small and politically impotent group. Still, it maintained some presence in the regions of Russia. When trying to make sense of the story, most observers came to the conclusion that Prusak was going to use the DPR as a tool to pursue a career at the federal level.[45] In particular, there was some speculation that the Kremlin encouraged Prusak to take over the DPR in order to create a pro-Putin right-wing party as a credible alternative to the Union of Right Forces.[46]

Similar explanations were offered concerning the conversion of the governor of Samara province, Konstantin Titov, into the leader of a social democratic party. Unlike Prusak, who thoroughly avoided any party activities before becoming a party leader, Titov had a long history of flirtation with different political groups, including the SPS. After the right-wing coalition refused to endorse his candidacy in the 2000 national presidential elections, Titov broke away from the SPS but took with him one of its original components, the politically insignificant Russian Party of Social Democracy. After taking over the party, Titov proceeded to merge it with a more important entity, the Russian United Social Democratic Party, led by Mikhail Gorbachev.[47] The founding congress of the new Social Democratic Party of Russia elected Titov as its chairman, while Gorbachev retained the position of the leader of the party.[48] A local political observer in Samara was quick to notice that in this way, Titov greatly enhanced his standing in the national, and perhaps even the international, political arena. In particular, the observer speculated: "The interests of the united party of Russian Social Democrats in the Socialist International will be advocated by their legitimate chairman, Konstantin Titov. In this position, he may safely count on the status of one of the most respected lobbyists in Russia."[49]

While it does seem that the primary motivation for taking over parties came from Prusak's and Titov's aspirations to pursue national political careers, such moves may have profound consequences for regional politics. True, the DPR and the Social Democrats did not contest the third-cycle legislative elections in the regions where their leaders were in power. This, however, may change in the new institutional context. Once half of the seats in a regional assembly become available only to party nominees, a party controlled by the governor naturally becomes instrumental in the governor's quest for a loyal legislative majority. Even though the electoral appeal of the party itself may be weak, and its own resources absolutely insufficient, the support of the governor may drastically improve its standing. In Samara the regional branch of the Russian Party of Social Democracy was formed only after Titov became the national leader of the party. However, such high-profile figures as the rector of the local university, several enterprise directors, and heads of local administration immediately became the party's card-carrying members. Moreover, it took only weeks to create party organizations in a majority of the districts of Samara province.[50] Thus it is not difficult to imagine a situation when a party, being nationally registered but more or less fictitious in nearly all those regions where it has its branches, nevertheless becomes strong enough in an individual region, with its strength stemming from its role as the incumbent chief executive's political instrument. Consider the 2002 mayoral elections in Velikii Novgorod, the capital of Novgorod province. The acting mayor, Sergei Lobach, broke with Governor Prusak and started to pursue his own political agenda, allegedly aimed not only at winning mayoral elections but also, ultimately, at replacing Prusak as a governor.[51] In this undertaking, he received support from the regional branches of the national parties of power, Unitary Russia and the NPRF.[52] Prusak responded by endorsing the candidacy of a vice governor, Nikolai Grazhdankin. Not surprisingly, Prusak's personal party, the DPR, nominated Grazhdankin, who thoroughly emphasized his party affiliation during the campaign. The opening words of Grazhdankin's preelection manifesto were: "Pre-election manifesto of the Democratic Party of Russia that nominates Nikolai Ivanovich Grazhdankin as a candidate for the post of the mayor of Velikii Novgorod. We are the Democratic Party of Russia. Our leader is Mikhail Mikhailovich Prusak. Our programmatic slogan is Democracy, Patriotism, Development."[53] Grazhdankin won election with 40.1 percent of the vote.

The strategy of small-party capture can be described as creating regional political parties disguised as national ones. This strategy, if implemented regionally, can pay off in several ways. First, incumbent governors fully control their parties, which reduces the political costs of party affiliation to a minimum. Second, incumbent governors receive an additional tool that helps to solidify their grasp over regional elites. Third, when retiring, governors may enjoy some residual political influence due to party leadership. At the same time, this strategy involves costs related to forming and sustaining party organization. First, federal authorities would rather prefer governors to support a national party of power, not small parties of their own choice. And falling out of the Kremlin's favor is something only few governors can afford to do. Second, even the activists of a small party may have interests different from those of the regional strongman who captures the label. In February 2003, Prusak was expelled from the DPR by the national convention of the party. When explaining this decision, a spokesman for the party mentioned that Prusak, rather than actively preparing the DPR for independent participation in the 2003 national legislative elections, planned to join a coalition with other right-wing parties.[54] While obviously beneficial for Prusak himself, this strategy promised little to the activists of the DPR who could not expect to occupy high positions on the coalition's list.

Given the costs of small-party capture, governors may engage in a different strategy, party purchase. This strategy, while it does not promise payoffs associated with sustaining permanent party organization at the regional level, allows for avoiding the related costs, and it may be more acceptable for the Kremlin. Indeed, one of the major concerns of the federal authorities is to secure favorable results of the national elections held in the region—that is, to make sure that governors invest their authority and material resources into encouraging their populations to vote for the national party of power. From this point of view, the major peril of the strategy of small-party capture is that governor-controlled parties will run in national elections and jointly capture significant portions of the vote. The difference made by the party purchase strategy is that there is no permanent connection between governors and individual parties. Once governors need a party to nominate a list of candidates fully loyal to them in regional legislative elections, they contact the national leadership of a small party and, probably after some bargaining, receive a party label in exchange for favors. The presumably material nature of these favors is reflected in how I dub this strategy. In certain contexts, it may be even more expedient to purchase two small parties and to create an electoral bloc with a descriptive label indirectly referring to the fact that the governor supports it.[55]

It is only natural that my discussion of the party purchase strategy is largely speculative. Its full-scale implementation will become possible only after electoral reform in the regions gains momentum. However, the history of the few regional elections already held by mixed electoral systems suggests that party purchase is quite feasible. As described in Chapter 7, one of the major participants in the 2002 legislative elections in Pskov province was an opposition bloc called Kuznetsov–Polozov–Savitskii: Together for the Sake of the Future. Clearly, the bloc derived its electoral appeal from the popularity of the individuals named in its label. However, to be formed officially, it also needed organizational components, and they were quick to arrive in the form of three organizations, one of them regional, the Provincial Public Political Organization of Pensioners, and two national, the All-Russian Movement of the Greens "Motherland" and the Russian United Social Democratic Party. Local observers alleged that the regional leaders of all three organizations simply sold their labels to the Pskov oppositionists.[56] In this connection, it is worth mentioning that in 2001–2002, different groups of the Greens became increasingly active in regional legislative elections. For instance, the 2002 elections in St. Petersburg were contested by as many as three parties featuring the word "Greens" in their labels, but only one of them could be viewed as a sincere expression of environmental concerns. Two others apparently rented their labels to different political forces, including the left-wing bloc Science, Industry, Education, which served as an umbrella for some of the KPRF-supported candidates.[57] Indeed, it seems that the "Green" label is an ideal commodity in the political marketplaces of Russia's regions. Carrying no specific policy stance but a substantial concern shared by many urban dwellers, it may be useful for politicians of any programmatic standing. Not surprisingly, the Ecological Party of the Greens "Cedar" successfully propelled itself into the future as a newly registered national party.

To an extent, each of the strategies described above carries costs and benefits of its own. At the same time they share a problem that is rather difficult to solve. It is undeniable that some of the regional executives enjoy substantial and relatively stable levels of voter support. The problem is that for controlled or purchased parties to be useful, these levels of support have to be transferred to party lists. However, this may be difficult to achieve. The compositions of contestants in regional executive and legislative elections are different. In executive elections, governors run in person against their political rivals, whose personal qualities and backgrounds are to be compared with their own. National political parties may nominate their candidates, but the programmatic standings and national political prominence of these parties are, at best, intervening factors. In legislative elections, if held by mixed electoral systems, the real national political parties—not those purchased by governors or controlled by them—become primary players. Under such conditions, governors' parties are likely to capture only a portion of the vote that could be easily gained by the governors themselves. Novgorod province provides a piece of hard evidence to support this argument. In October 2002, during the mayoral campaign described above, a public opinion poll conducted by a local agency revealed that voter support to individual parties was distributed in the following way: the KPRF, 17 percent; Yabloko, 11 percent; the LDPR, 8 percent; the DPR, 7 percent; Unitary Russia, 5 percent; and the SPS, 3 percent.[58] At the same time, a national poll conducted by the Public Opinion Foundation (Moscow) revealed the following distribution: Unitary Russia, 28 percent; the KPRF, 23 percent; the LDPR, 6 percent; the SPS, 5 percent; and Yabloko, 4 percent.[59] According to the national poll, the DPR was supported by less than 1 percent of the respondents. Thus Governor Prusak's affiliation with the DPR did contribute to the popularity of the party, yet not to the extent that would allow it win a majority of seats in the regional legislature. Of course, it can be safely assumed that if the campaign had been focused on the DPR itself, not on Grazhdankin as its candidate, it could have performed better. Even with this necessary correction, the level of popularity achieved by the DPR was very low in comparison with that of its national leader, who won the 1999 gubernatorial elections in Novgorod province with 91.6 percent of the vote. Thus the strategies aimed at establishing executive control over small parties may backfire by producing progovernor factions too small to rely upon.

In the ideal world of Russia's regional executives, their parties would add to the levels of support enjoyed by the governors themselves, not subtract from them. The only way to achieve such an ideal state of affairs would be to place the regional branches of major national parties under the control of the governors. Hence the third conceivable strategy, large-party capture. As demonstrated in Chapter 6, some of the governors successfully implemented this strategy long before the idea of the electoral reform surfaced. Their primary target was the KPRF. At the same time, my analysis revealed that this strategy was difficult to pursue and costly. At least one of the regional branches of the KPRF, in Volgograd province, not only resisted the pressure but also succeeded in using the region's chief executive as its political tool. In those regions where party capture did take place, the executives captured the KPRF by trapping its regional branches into regional political movements. Electoral reform, however, made such movements irrelevant. I would therefore speculate that the strategy of capturing the KPRF is unlikely to survive into the next phase of Russia's political development. This does not mean that the KPRF-nominated candidates will not be able to win regional executive elections. Yet these candidates' relations with the party are likely to be much more balanced than the term "party capture" can possibly allow. It seems that a reasonable strategy for a left-leaning governor who seeks the support of the communist electorate is not to attempt capturing the KPRF but rather to avoid being captured by it.

However, it is far from certain that regional executives will not be capable of capturing the party of power, Unitary Russia. Its predecessor,

Our Home Is Russia (NDR), was rarely targeted by regional executives simply because within the institutional context of 1995–1997, they could cope with the task of controlling legislatures by supporting loyal independent candidates. Even if completely dependent on the regional executives, the NDR remained out of demand. With the arrival of mixed electoral systems, the executives' need of political parties naturally increases. Hence it is only logical to expect that the party of power will be not only captured by the executives but also used by them for the purpose of gaining reelection and creating legislative majorities. Consider the 2003 executive elections in Mordovia. In the previous elections, held in 1998, Nikolai Merkushkin won a landslide with 90.9 percent of the vote. Both the incumbent and his only rival ran as independents. In 2003, Merkushkin chose to run as a party nominee. Apparently, this change of mind occurred for two reasons. On the one hand, since federal law eliminated the possibility of nomination by a group of voters, the only available alternative to party nomination was self-nomination, a form previously embarked upon mostly by political outsiders. Using self-nomination could have symbolically diminished Merkushkin's standing in the electoral arena. On the other hand, establishing a firm connection between Merkushkin and Unitary Russia was important from the point of view of preparations for regional legislative elections that had to be held by a mixed electoral system in December 2003. Besides, Merkushkin's major rival in the 2003 elections was a KPRF nominee, which made it useful to present Merkushkin as a programmatic candidate with broad societal appeal. As a result, the entity that nominated Merkushkin for election, an electoral bloc called simply For Mordovia, consisted of three components: Unitary Russia, the APR, and the republic's Council of the Veterans of War, Labor, Armed Forces, and Law Enforcing Agencies.[60] While the participation of Unitary Russia clearly identified Merkushkin as a candidate of the national party of power, the presence of the APR and the veterans council was clearly aimed at splitting the left-wing electorate. It seems that Merkushkin did not find it difficult to recruit the regional branch of Unitary Russia into this unlikely alliance. A member of the Supreme Council of the party, the incumbent head of Mordovia firmly established himself as an indisputable leader of its regional branch. With his blessing, the party was able to establish its organizations in all twenty-six districts of the republic and proceeded to create local cells, as many as 400 of which were in operation by September 2002.[61] Merkushkin won the elections by a margin of almost 80 percent.

Of course, it is quite likely that party nomination did not contribute too much to Merkushkin's successful reelection. What is important in this story is Merkushkin's ability to place the regional branch of Unitary Russia under his full control. A better example of the regional executive's ability not only to control Unitary Russia but also to use it for political ends was provided by the 2003 regional legislative elections in Bashkortostan. The president of Bashkortostan, Murtaza Rakhimov, played an important role in the formation of the All Russia movement in 1999. Since Rakhimov's tough leadership left little space for independent political activism in the republic, the regional branch of Unity could only be founded on the basis of All Russia, which practically meant that the executive did not even need to capture the party: it was captured from the very beginning. At the same time, Rakhimov's remarkable ability to deliver a substantial share of the republic's vote in national legislative elections to any party he was affiliated with made him a very important ally for the Kremlin. As a result, the federal authorities were apparently inclined to view quite favorably Rakhimov's firm grasp on the regional branch of Unitary Russia. When visiting Bashkortostan, the chairman of the General Council of Unitary Russia identified the republic as a "cornerstone region" of the party.[62]

The 2003 regional legislative elections proved that Rakhimov needed Unitary Russia too. The need stemmed from some of the institutional changes imposed upon the regions by the federal legislation of 2002, and it was strongly exacerbated by the fact that these changes eliminated the principal mechanisms of executive control over the legislature that were safely relied upon in Bashkortostan throughout the previous period. As described in Chapter 6, Rakhimov controlled the legislature by filling it with state officials and especially municipal leaders who won in administrative-territorial districts. Once the candidates of these occupational categories became effectively ineligible to run in regional legislative elections, administrative-territorial districts became unnecessary and they were indeed abolished. This, however, made it necessary to use an alternative mechanism of securing control over the legislature, and it is not surprising that Rakhimov used Unitary Russia precisely for this end.[63] The regional branch of the party nominated as many as 106 candidates, most of them businesspeople previously unnoticed in party activism, who won 87 seats in the 120-member assembly. Interestingly, Rakhimov was careful enough to provide token representation to other parties that could be considered as loyal, such as the NPRF, the APR, and the SPS. Of the 36 candidates nominated by the major opposition party, the KPRF, only 26 were able to obtain registration, allegedly because of the biased approach of district electoral commissions,[64] and none of them won.

An even more impressive case of party capture could be observed in the 2003 elections in Kemerovo province. After defeating his opponents in the 1999 elections, Governor Aman Tuleev regained full control over the regional left-wing movement, People's Power.[65] At the same time, he managed to take over the regional branch of Unity by filling its leadership with his loyalists, including a vice governor.[66] This made it possible to create an electoral bloc joining the left, represented by People's Power, and the party of power, represented by Unitary Russia and the NPRF, on the platform of unlimited support to Tuleev. At the conference of People's Power, some of the local leaders of the KPRF sharply objected to the idea, but their objections went in vain, and the bloc, called Serve to Kuzbass, came into existence.[67] Of the thirty-four nominees of the bloc, only two identified themselves as KPRF members, and two others as members of Unitary Russia. The regional branch of the KPRF nominated four candidates who ran against the nominees of Serve to Kuzbass. The Kemerovo city committee of the KPRF, however, preferred to offer its support to Tuleev's loyalists.[68] Unitary Russia did not display any signs of disobedience. As a result of the elections, Serve to Kuzbass won thirty-four seats in the assembly.

Thus some regional executives prove to be fully capable of capturing the branches of Unitary Russia, and there is little doubt that more examples of the strategy of large-party capture will arrive upon the full implementation of the electoral reform. The problem is that the Kremlin seems to be generally disinclined to view Unitary Russia as a political instrument that would allow the regional executives to consolidate their already firm control over the regional political arenas. In fact, as argued in the previous section of this chapter, the principal goal of party reform is exactly the opposite: to open the regional political arenas, to induce viable noncommunist oppositions, and thereby to place the regions under the firmer control of Moscow. As put by Vladislav Surkov, "Unity will become a true party only after its local branches will cease to be headed exclusively by the governors' people. This is because the regional branch of Unity does not have to stand for or against this or that governor; it has to stand for or against this or that political line."[69] In March 2002 the chairman of the general council of the party vocally criticized the regional strategies of capturing Unitary Russia: "Some of the heads of the subjects of the Russian Federation, sensing the great potential of Unitary Russia, immediately tried to find their place in the party, which is why in certain cases the establishment of the regional branches looked like the formation of new departments of regional administrations. . . . The lack of understanding provoked the regional authorities to meddle into the party's business and to use party members against each other."[70] Starting in 2002, the leaders of the party made it increasingly clear that the organizational structure of Unitary Russia would totally depart from that of its predecessors, Unity and Fatherland. In contrast to them, Unitary Russia had to be a strictly centralized organization based on committed party activists, not on incumbent office-holders.[71] Of course, the cases of Mordovia, Bashkortostan, and Kemerovo suggest that the wishful thinking of the leaders of Unitary Russia had to be balanced against the regions' political realities. In many regions, and especially in republics, it is both practically impossible and politically inexpedient to separate Unitary Russia from the regional executives. Yet it is also clear that due to the long-term goals of the party reform, the strategy of party capture may become more difficult to implement as the reform gains momentum.

Therefore, it seems that none of the conceivable strategies of the regional elites can be viewed as a warranted means of neutralizing the political consequences of the reform. The principal problem of party purchase and small-party capture is that these strategies do not guarantee the translation of the executives' electoral appeal into sufficient shares of the vote in regional legislative elections. Large-party capture, while eliminating this deficiency, is much more difficult to implement. This allows for a modestly optimistic conclusion that the opening of the regional electoral arenas may be achieved after all. It is possible to envision a situation in which the regional executives, rather than capturing political parties or manipulating them, consider joining them as crucial means of their own political survival, and therefore willingly pay the costs of party affiliation: obeying party discipline and sharing the parties' programmatic agendas. In the long run, this may give rise to a stable party system consisting of Unitary Russia, the KPRF or its successor, and several smaller parties of different ideological standings. Given the use of proportional representation in national and regional legislative elections, the extinction of these parties is unlikely. Such a system of moderate pluralism would perfectly address the Kremlin's need for "stability" and "predictability." However, for such a scenario to materialize, a principal condition has to be fulfilled. Namely, Unitary Russia has to be successful in the 2003 national legislative elections. The regional elites will not subject themselves to a party that is not able to perform its primary function—that is, to deliver the vote. Instead, they will be strongly motivated to embark upon the strategies discussed in this chapter. Each of these strategies, if it becomes dominant, may bring quite predictable consequences for the further development of Russia's party system. The discussion of these consequences, however, would have brought us too far into the realm of pure theoretical speculation. After all, the perceived failure of party reform may motivate the Kremlin to initiate a counterreform by eliminating the legal provisions introduced in 2002. In this case, however, the possible result is too easy to predict: political parties in the regions will ultimately vanish. Democracy will remain unclaimed.

Notes

1. I used averages for those regions that held two legislative elections in any given electoral cycle.

2. Regions excluded from my analysis: Adygeia, Chechnya, Ingushetia, Khakasia, Rostov, and Ul'ianovsk in the first electoral cycle; Chechnya,

Karachaevo-Cherkesia, Komi, Mordovia, Tatarstan, and Taimyr in the second electoral cycle; Chechnya, Ingushetia, Kabardino-Balkaria, Kalmykia, North Ossetia, and Volgograd in the third electoral cycle.

3. The predictive value of OLS models using percentage shares as dependent variables is limited (Katz and King 1999), which is why I refrain from discussing the substantive significance of the reported unstandardized coefficients.

4. Such parties are the Agrarian Party of Russia (APR), the Democratic Party of Russia (DPR), the KPRF, the Liberal Democratic Party of Russia (LDPR), the Party of Russian Unity and Accord (PRES), the Russian Movement for Democratic Reforms (RDDR), Russia's Choice (VR), and Yabloko in the first electoral cycle; the APR, Communists–Workers Russia–For the Soviet Union, the DVR–United Democrats, the KPRF, the Congress of Russian Communities (KRO), the LDPR, Our Home Is Russia (NDR), Power to the People, the Party of Workers Self-Government (PST), and Yabloko in the second electoral cycle; and Communists–The Workers of Russia–For the Soviet Union, Fatherland–All Russia, the KPRF, the Pensioners Party, the Union of Right Forces (SPS), Unity, Yabloko, and the Zhirinovsky Bloc in the third electoral cycle. Thus in addition to the vote against all party lists, I discount the vote for five, thirty-three, and eighteen parties in the 1993, 1995, and 1999 elections respectively. Yabloko remains in the first-cycle selection because even though it was not present in the regional elections, its major component, the Republican Party of the Russian Federation (RPRF), was. The same can be said about the relationship between Power to the People and the Russian All-People's Union (ROS). The Communists' coalitions in the 1995 and 1999 elections were organizationally identical to the Russian Communist Workers Party (RKRP), and of course the Zhirinovsky Bloc was not very different from the LDPR.

5. When establishing the values of PMFC, I took into account those parties that not only won Federation Council seats but also were present in the first-cycle regional legislative elections, the APR, the KPRF, the PRES, the RDDR, and the VR. As exceptions from this rule, I also took into account the Union of Communists of Karelia, an entity virtually identical to the KPRF, and two parties that officially participated in the VR bloc, Democratic Russia and the Peasants Party of Russia.

6. Kakuiu Rossiiu my stroim, *Rossiiskaia gazeta,* July 11, 2000.

7. Partia vlasti ili vlast partii, *Vek,* October 13, 2000.

8. Odinokii parovoz, *Ekspert,* February 25, 2002.

9. party.scli.ru.

10. Sgoniaem partiiu, *Versty,* November 1, 2001.

11. Soobrazim na troikh? *Versty,* August 29, 2000.

12. Ukrupnenie partii, *Vesti,* December 26, 2000.

13. Kotorye tut izbrannye? *Rossiiskaia gazeta,* February 15, 2001.

14. Gubernatorami politicheskaia elita prirastat ne budet, *Podmoskovnye izvestia,* October 31, 2000.

15. Troe v lodke, ne schitaia Kremlia, *Nashe vremia* (Yakutsk), December 14, 2001.

16. Primor'e: Teplovoe bessilie vlasti, *Novye izvestia,* December 27, 2000.

17. Dar'kin s moria, *Profil,* July 16, 2001.

18. Regional'nye parlamenty budut vybirat po-novomu, *Kommersant,* June 6, 2001.

19. "Poliana" rastet proportsional'no, *Novoe vremia,* November 11, 2001.

20. V regiony partiiam doroga poka zakryta, *Nezavisimaia gazeta,* August 4, 2001.

21. Novosti, *PR v Rossii,* August 31, 2001.

22. "Poliana" rastet proportsional'no, *Novoe vremia*, November 11, 2001.

23. Povyshenie bar'era pogubit demokratiiu, *Vremia MN*, November 10, 2001.

24. *Gosudarstvennaia Duma. Stenogramma zasedanii*, April 10, 2002.

25. V senate ne liubiat partii, *Vremia novostei*, April 25, 2002.

26. *Gosudarstvennaia Duma. Stenogramma zasedanii*, April 26, 2002.

27. Sovet Federatsii otlozhil reformu regional'nykh vyborov, *Kommersant*, April 25, 2002.

28. Tekushchaia informatsia, *Advokat*, June 24, 2002.

29. Sovet Federatsii proiavil kharakter, *Nezavisimaia gazeta*, May 30, 2002.

30. Sovet Federatsii odobril novyi izbiratel'nyi zakon, *Kommersant*, May 30, 2002.

31. Liubliu. Tseluiu. Prusak, *Nezavisimaia gazeta*, March 3, 2003.

32. Partiinye spiski—ugroza demokratii, *Nezavisimaia gazeta*, June 23, 2001.

33. Partiinye spiski, *Ezhenedel'nik Monitor* (Nizhnii Novgorod), April 29, 2002.

34. Sentiabristy protiv oktiabristov, *Novaia gazeta* (St. Petersburg), April 18, 2002.

35. Deputaty respublik obmenivaiutsia opytom, *Udmurtskaia pravda* (Izhevsk), June 26, 2002.

36. Partia dala porulit, *Ekspert-Ural* (Ekaterinburg), September 23, 2002.

37. "Pravye" i "levye" ediny… *Udmurtskaia pravda* (Izhevsk), October 23, 2002.

38. Daesh partiinye spiski! *Yakutia* (Yakutsk), June 18, 2002.

39. Perenosa sroka parlamentskikh vyborov ne budet, *Severnaia Ossetia* (Vladikavkaz), December 21, 2002.

40. Bespartiinaia sistema, *Vedomosti*, October 30, 2002.

41. Sistemu vyborov nado reformirovat, *Vsia Rossia—Novosti regionov*, December 11, 2002.

42. Vtoroi "etazh" ubrali, *Novyi kompan'on* (Perm), October 15, 2002.

43. Vlast narodu ili narod dlia vlasti, *Tambovskaia zhizn* (Tambov), October 23, 2002; Spiski—ne dogma, *Tul'skie izvestia* (Tula), March 15, 2002.

44. Nash chelovek v DPR, *Novgorodskie novosti* (Velikii Novgorod), September 28, 2001.

45. Partia novgorodskogo gostia, *Rossiiskie vesti*, September 26, 2001.

46. Pravyi zapasnoi, *Moskovskie novosti*, October 2, 2001.

47. Eshche odna novaia partia, *Nezavisimaia gazeta*, March 14, 2000.

48. Eta partia otkryta dlia vsekh, *Trud*, December 4, 2001.

49. Sotsial-demokraty stali ediny, *Delo* (Samara), December 4, 2001.

50. Est u nas svoi "kapital,", chelovecheskii, *Samarskie izvestia* (Samara), October 6, 2000.

51. Vse dzhipy, mersedesy i primknuvshie k nim chinovniki, *Novaia novgorodskaia gazeta* (Velikii Novgorod), November 6, 2002.

52. Prusak riskuet poteriat Novgorod, *Nezavisimaia gazeta*, November 14, 2002.

53. Vybory mera Velikogo Novgoroda, *Novgorod* (Velikii Novgorod), November 21, 2002.

54. V "sosnakh" zabludivshiesia, *Novaia novgorodskaia gazeta* (Velikii Novgorod), March 13, 2003.

55. The 2002 law on the basic guarantees of citizens' electoral rights legally eliminated the possibility to use personal names and the names of state offices in the official labels of electoral blocs.

56. Nikogda ne govori "nikogda,", *Pskovskaia gubernia* (Pskov), February 14, 2002.

57. Na pritsele—Smol'nyi, *Vremia MN,* November 15, 2002.

58. Storonnikam "Edinoi Rossii" ne nravitsia "Rossia," *Novaia novgorodskaia gazeta* (Velikii Novgorod), October 30, 2002.

59. www.fom.ru/survey/dominant/659/1410/5069.html.

60. Tsentrizbirkom RM informiruet, *Izvestia Mordovii* (Saransk), January 14, 2003.

61. "Edinaia Rossia" sozdaet novye pervichki, *Mordovia 7 dnei* (Saransk), September 11, 2002.

62. Bashkortostan stanovitsia opornym punktom "Edinoi Rossii," *Respublika Bashkortostan* (Ufa), August 1, 2002.

63. In fact, Rakhimov was so confident in his ability to win legislative elections in the republic that he even proposed to reinstate a parliamentary system, an idea that did not materialize seemingly because federal authorities objected to it. See Bashkiria reshila izbavit'sia ot prezidenta, *Kommersant,* October 11, 2002.

64. Za "chestnye" i "chistye" vybory pod rukovodstvom "Edinoi Rossii," *Pravda Rossii,* April 2, 2003.

65. Reshenia Narodovlastia, *Kuzbass* (Kemerovo), July 17, 2002.

66. Sibirskii meridian "Edinoi Rossii," *Kontinent Sibir* (Novosibirsk), February 21, 2003.

67. Sluzhu Kuzbassu! *Trud—7,* February 6, 2003.

68. Podderzhat, no ne bezdumno, *Kuzbass* (Kemerovo), March 13, 2002.

69. Tak vot, ia vam govoriu: Demokratia neischerpaema, *Kommersant-Vlast,* July 18, 2000.

70. "Edinaia Rossia" nedovol'na pravitel'stvom, *Nezavisimaia gazeta,* March 5, 2002.

71. Bol'shaia partiinaia mechta, *Vremia novostei,* March 4, 2002.

References

Afanas'ev, Mikhail. 1997. *Klientelizm i rossiiskaia gosudarstvennost*. Moscow: MONF.

Aldrich, John H. 1995. *Why Parties? The Origin and Transformation of Political Parties in America*. Chicago: University of Chicago Press.

Alexander, Herbert E., and Rei Shiratori, eds. 1994. *Comparative Political Finance Among the Democracies*. Boulder: Westview Press.

Amorim-Neto, Octavio. 2002. "The Puzzle of Party Discipline in Brazil." *Latin American Politics and Society* 44, 1: 127–144.

Amorim-Neto, Octavio, and Gary W. Cox. 1997. "Electoral Institutions, Cleavage Structures, and the Number of Parties." *American Journal of Political Science* 41, 1: 149–174.

Anckar, Dag, and Carsten Anckar. 2000. "Democracies Without Parties." *Comparative Political Studies* 33, 2: 225–247.

Ansell, Christopher K., and M. Steven Fish. 1999. "The Art of Being Indispensable: Noncharismatic Personalism in Contemporary Political Parties." *Comparative Political Studies* 32, 3: 283–312.

Barnes, Andrew. 1998. "What's the Difference? Industrial Privatization and Agricultural Land Reform in Russia, 1990–1996." *Europe-Asia Studies* 50, 5: 843–857.

Bartolini, Stefano. 1995. *Electoral Competition: Analytical Dimensions and Empirical Problems*. Robert Schuman Center for Advanced Studies Working Paper no. 95/06. Badia Fiesolana, Italy: European University Institute.

Bartolini, Stefano, and Peter Mair. 1990. *Identity, Competition, and Electoral Availability: The Stabilization of European Electorates, 1885–1985*. Cambridge: Cambridge University Press.

Beck, Paul A. 2000. *Party Politics in America*. 9th ed. New York: Longman.

Belin, Laura. 1997a. "All Sides Claim Victory in 1996 Gubernatorial Elections." *Transition* 3, 3: 25–26.

———. 1997b. "Russia's 1996 Gubernatorial Elections and the Implications for Yeltsin." *Demokratizatsiya* 5, 2: 165–184.

Belin, Laura, and Robert W. Orttung. 1997. *The Russian Parliamentary Elections of 1995: The Battle for the Duma*. Armonk, NY: M. E. Sharpe.

Benoit, Kenneth. 2001. "District Magnitude, Electoral Formula, and the Number of Parties." *European Journal of Political Research* 39, 2: 203–224.

Beyle, Thad. 1995. "Gubernatorial Report Cards: Summer 1994." *Spectrum: Journal of State Government* 68, 2: 14–20.

Bowler, Shaun, David M. Farrell, and Richard S. Katz, eds. 1999. *Party Discipline and Parliamentary Government*. Columbus: Ohio State University Press.

Brader, Ted, and Joshua A. Tucker. 2001. "The Emergence of Mass Partisanship in Russia, 1993–1996." *American Journal of Political Science* 45, 1: 69–83.

Brovkin, Vladimir N. 1990. "The Making of Elections to the Congress of People's Deputies (CPD) in March 1989." *Russian Review* 49, 4: 417–442.

Brown, Archie. 2001. "Vladimir Putin and the Reaffirmation of Central State Power." *Post-Soviet Affairs* 17, 1: 45–55.

Brown, J. David. 1996. "Excess Labor and Managerial Shortage: Findings from a Survey in St. Petersburg." *Europe-Asia Studies* 48, 5: 811–835.

Brown, Ruth. 1998. "Party Development in the Regions: When Did Parties Start to Play a Role in Politics?" *Journal of Communist Studies and Transition Politics* 14, 1–2: 9–30.

Brudny, Yitzhak M. 1993. "The Dynamics of 'Democratic Russia,' 1990–1993." *Post-Soviet Affairs* 9, 2: 141–170.

———. 1997. "In Pursuit of the Russian Presidency: Why and How Yeltsin Won the 1996 Presidential Election." *Communist and Post-Communist Studies* 30, 3: 255–275.

Bunce, Valerie. 1999. *Subversive Institutions: The Design and the Destruction of Socialism and the State.* Cambridge: Cambridge University Press.

Byzov, Leontii. 1995. "Rossiiskie natsional-patrioty i ikh elektorat." In A. I. Ioffe, ed., *Analiz elektorata politicheskikh sil Rossii,* pp. 46–61. Moscow: Moscow Carnegie Center.

Carey, John M. 2000. "Parchment, Equilibria, and Institutions." *Comparative Political Studies* 33, 6–7: 735–761.

Carey, John M., Frantisek Formanek, and Ewa Karpowicz. 1999. "Legislative Autonomy in New Regimes: The Czech and Polish Cases." *Legislative Studies Quarterly* 24, 4: 569–603.

Carey, John M., and Matthew S. Shugart. 1995. "Incentives to Cultivate a Personal Vote: A Rank Ordering of Electoral Formulas." *Electoral Studies* 14, 4: 417–439.

———, eds. 1998. *Executive Decree Authority.* Cambridge: Cambridge University Press.

Carson, George B. 1955. *Electoral Practices in the U.S.S.R.* New York: F. A. Praeger.

Carstairs, Andrew M. 1980. *A Short History of Electoral Systems in Western Europe.* London: Allen and Unwin.

Cassileth, Barrie R., and Vasily V. Vlassov. 1995. "Health Care, Medical Practice, and Medical Ethics in Russia Today." *JAMA: Journal of the American Medical Association* 273, 20: 1569–1573.

Colton, Timothy J. 1995. "Boris Yeltsin: Russia's All-Thumbs Democrat." In T. J. Colton and R. C. Tucker, eds., *Patterns in Post-Soviet Leadership,* pp. 49–76. Boulder: Westview Press.

———. 2000. *Transitional Citizens: Voters and What Influences Them in the New Russia.* Cambridge: Harvard University Press.

Colton, Timothy J., and Michael McFaul. 2000. "Reinventing Russia's Party of Power: 'Unity' and the 1999 Duma Election." *Post-Soviet Affairs* 16, 3: 201–224.

Coppedge, Michael. 1997. "District Magnitude, Economic Performance, and Party-System Fragmentation in Five Latin American Countries." *Comparative Political Studies* 30, 2: 156–185.

Cox, Gary W. 1986. "The Development of a Party-Oriented Electorate in England, 1832–1918." *British Journal of Political Science* 16, 2: 187–216.

————. 1987. *The Efficient Secret: The Cabinet and the Development of Political Parties in Victorian England.* Cambridge: Cambridge University Press.

————. 1997. *Making Votes Count: Strategic Coordination in the World's Electoral Systems.* Cambridge: Cambridge University Press.

Cox, Karen E., and Leonard J. Schoppa. 2002. "Interaction Effects in Mixed-Member Electoral Systems: Theory and Evidence from Germany, Japan, and Italy." *Comparative Political Studies* 35, 9: 1027–1053.

Dahl, Robert A., and Edward R. Tufte. 1973. *Size and Democracy.* Stanford: Stanford University Press.

Dasgupta, Partha, and Ismail Serageldin. 2000. *Social Capital: A Multifaceted Perspective.* Washington, DC: World Bank Group.

DeBardeleben, Joan. 1997. "The Development of Federalism in Russia." In P. J. Stavrakis, J. DeBardeleben, and L. Black, eds., *Beyond the Monolith: The Emergence of Regionalism in Post-Soviet Russia,* pp. 35–56. Baltimore: Johns Hopkins University Press.

Dogan, Mattei, and Dominique Pelassy. 1990. *How to Compare Nations: Strategies in Comparative Politics.* 2nd ed. Chatham, NJ: Chatham House.

Downs, Anthony. 1957. *An Economic Theory of Democracy.* New York: Harper and Row.

Dunleavy, Patrick, and Françoise Boucek. 2003. "Constructing the Number of Parties." *Party Politics* 9, 3: 291–315.

Dunlop, John B. 1993. *The Rise of Russia and the Fall of the Soviet Empire.* Princeton: Princeton University Press.

Duverger, Maurice. 1954. *Political Parties: Their Organization and Activity in the Modern State.* New York: Wiley.

————. 1980. "A New Political System Model: Semi-Presidential Government." *European Journal of Political Research* 8, 2: 165–187.

Elgie, Robert, ed. 1999. *Semi-Presidentialism in Europe.* Oxford: Oxford University Press.

Engstrom, Richard L., and Michael D. McDonald. 1986. "The Effect of At-Large Versus District Elections on Racial Representation in U.S. Municipalities." In B. Grofman and A. Lijphart, eds., *Electoral Laws and Their Political Consequences,* pp. 203–225. New York: Agathon Press.

Epstein, Leon D. 1964. "A Comparative Study of Canadian Parties." *American Political Science Review* 58, 1: 46–59.

————. 1966. "Political Parties in Western Democratic Systems." In E. H. Buehrig, ed., *Essays in Political Science,* pp. 97–130. Bloomington: Indiana University Press.

————. 1986. *Political Parties in the American Mold.* Madison: University of Wisconsin Press.

Evans, Alfred B., Jr. 2000. "Economic Resources and Political Power at the Local Level in Post-Soviet Russia." *Policy Studies Journal* 28, 1: 114–133.

Evans, Geoffrey, and Stephen Whitefield. 1995. "Economic Ideology and Political Success: Communist-Successor Parties in the Czech Republic, Slovakia, and Hungary Compared." *Party Politics* 1, 4: 565–578.

————. 1998. "The Evolution of Left and Right in Post-Soviet Russia." *Europe-Asia Studies* 50, 6: 1023–1042.

Fiorina, Morris P. 1981. *Retrospective Voting in American National Elections.* New Haven: Yale University Press.

Fish, M. Steven. 1995. *Democracy from Scratch: Opposition and Regime in the New Russian Revolution.* Princeton: Princeton University Press.

————. 1997. "The Predicament of Russian Liberalism: Evidence from the December 1995 Parliamentary Elections." *Europe-Asia Studies* 49, 2: 191–220.

Flikke, Geir. 1999. "Patriotic Left-Centrism: The Zigzags of the Communist Party of the Russian Federation." *Europe-Asia Studies* 51, 2: 275–298.

Fried, Robert C. 1966. *Comparative Political Institutions.* New York: Macmillan.

Friedgut, Theodore, and Jeffrey Hahn, eds. 1994. *Local Power and Post-Soviet Politics.* Armonk, NY: M. E. Sharpe.

Gallagher, Michael, and Michael Marsh, eds. 1998. *Candidate Selection in Comparative Perspective: The Secret Garden of Politics.* London: Sage.

Garand, James C., and Kenneth Wink. 1993. "Changing Meanings of Electoral Marginality in U.S. House Elections, 1824–1978." *Political Research Quarterly* 46, 1: 27–48.

Geddes, Barbara, and Artur Ribeiro Neto. 1992. "Institutional Sources of Corruption in Brazil." *Third World Quarterly* 13, 4: 641–661.

Gel'man, Vladimir. 1998. "The Iceberg of Russian Political Finance." In P. Burnell and A. Ware, eds., *Funding Democratization,* pp. 158–179. Manchester: Manchester University Press.

————. 1999a. "Regime Transition, Uncertainty and Prospects for Democratisation: The Politics of Russia's Regions in a Comparative Perspective." *Europe-Asia Studies* 51, 6: 939–956.

————. 1999b. *Transformatsia v Rossii: Politicheskii rezhim i demokraticheskaia oppozitsia.* Moscow: Moscow Public Science Foundation.

————. 2000. "Subnational Institutions in Contemporary Russia." In N. Robinson, ed., *Institutions and Political Change in Russia,* pp. 85–105. London: Macmillan.

Gel'man, Vladimir, and Grigorii V. Golosov. 1998. "Regional Party System Formation in Russia: The Deviant Case of Sverdlovsk Oblast." *Journal of Communist Studies and Transition Politics* 14, 1–2: 31–53.

Gel'man, Vladimir, Sergei Ryzhenkov, and Michael Brie, eds. 2000. *Rossia regionov: Transformatsia politicheskikh rezhimov.* Moscow: Ves Mir.

Gel'man, Vladimir, and Ol'ga Senatova. 1994. "Politicheskie partii v regionakh Rossii." In V. Gel'man, ed., *Ocherki rossiiskoi politiki,* pp. 16–30. Moscow: IGPI.

Gel'man, Vladimir, and Inessa Tarusina. 2000. "Studies of Political Elites in Russia: Issues and Alternatives." *Communist and Post-Communist Studies* 33, 3: 311–329.

Gerber, Elisabeth R., Rebecca B. Morton, and Thomas A. Rietz. 1998. "Minority Representation in Multimember Districts." *American Political Science Review* 92, 1: 127–144.

Golosov, Grigorii V. 1995. "New Russian Political Parties and the Transition to Democracy: The Case of Western Siberia." *Government and Opposition* 30, 1: 110–119.

————. 1996. *Modes of Communist Rule, Democratic Transition, and Party System Formation in Four East European Countries.* Donald W. Treadgold Paper in Russian, East European, and Central Asian Studies no. 9. Seattle: Henry M. Jackson School of International Studies, University of Washington.

————. 1997. "Russian Political Parties and the 'Bosses': Evidence from the 1994 Provincial Elections in Western Siberia." *Party Politics* 3, 1: 5–21.

————. 1998. "Who Survives? Party Origins, Organisational Development, and Electoral Performance in Post-Communist Russia." *Political Studies* 46, 3: 511–543.

————. 1999a. "From Adygeya to Yaroslavl: Factors of Party Development in the Regions of Russia, 1995–1998." *Europe-Asia Studies* 51, 8: 1133–1165.

————. 1999b. "Political Parties in the 1993–1996 Elections." In V. Gel'man and G. V. Golosov, eds., *Elections in Russia, 1993–1996: Analyses, Documents, and Data*, pp. 99–126. Berlin: Edition Sigma.

————. 2000. "The Spanish Right and the Russian Left: Party Organization, Ideology and Electoral Success." *Revista Internacional de Estudos Políticos/International Journal of Political Studies* 2, 2: 325–353.

————. 2001. "Political Parties, Electoral Systems, and Women's Representation in the Regional Legislative Assemblies of Russia, 1995–98." *Party Politics* 7, 1: 45–68.

————. 2002. "Party Support or Personal Resources? Factors of Success in the Plurality Portion of the 1999 National Legislative Elections in Russia." *Communist and Post-Communist Studies* 35, 1: 23–38.

Golosov, Grigorii V., and Edward Ponarin. 1999. *Regional Bases of Party Politics: A Measure and Its Implications for the Study of Party System Consolidation in New Democracies*. Robert Schuman Center for Advanced Studies Working Paper no. 99/25. Badia Fiesolana, Italy: European University Institute.

Golosov, Grigorii V., and Nataliya Yargomskaya. 1999. "The Impact of Russia's Electoral System on the Competitive Strategies of Political Actors in the Duma Elections." In V. Gel'man and G. V. Golosov, eds., *Elections in Russia, 1993–1996: Analyses, Documents, and Data*, pp. 150–171. Berlin: Edition Sigma.

Gorenburg, Dmitry. 2001. "Nationalism for the Masses: Popular Support for Nationalism in Russia's Republics." *Europe-Asia Studies* 53, 1: 73–104.

Gorfinkel, Il'ia, and Natalia Rusakova. 1995. "Vybory gubernatora: Kul'minatsia sistoialas." *Ural: Politika, ekonomika, pravo*, No. 3 (12): 6–9.

Grofman, Bernard, Sung-Chull Lee, Edwin Winckler, and Brian Woodall, eds. 1999. *Elections in Japan, Korea, and Taiwan Under the Single Non-Transferable Vote: The Comparative Study of an Embedded Institution*. Ann Arbor: University of Michigan Press.

Gunlicks, Arthur B., ed. 1993. *Campaign and Party Finance in North America and Western Europe*. Boulder: Westview Press.

Hahn, Gordon M. 1994. "Opposition Politics in Russia." *Europe-Asia Studies* 46, 2: 306–314.

Hahn, Jeffrey. 1994. "Conclusions: Common Features of Post-Soviet Politics." In T. Friedgut and J. Hahn, eds., *Local Power and Post-Soviet Politics*, pp. 270–280. Armonk, NY: M. E. Sharpe.

————. 1997. "Regional Elections and Political Stability in Russia." *Post-Soviet Geography and Economics* 38, 5: 251–263.

Haspel, Moshe. 1998. "Should Party in Parliament Be Weak or Strong? The Rules Debate in the Russian State Duma." *Journal of Communist Studies and Transition Politics* 14, 1–2: 178–200.

Haspel, Moshe, Thomas F. Remington, and Steven S. Smith. 1998. "Electoral Institutions and Party Cohesion in the Russian Duma." *Journal of Politics* 60, 2: 417–439.

Helf, Gavin, and Jeffrey Hahn. 1992. "Old Dogs and New Tricks: Party Elites in the Russian Regional Elections of 1990." *Slavic Review* 51, 3: 511–530.

Hermens, Ferdinand A. 1984. "Representation and Proportional Representation." In A. Lijphart and B. Grofman, eds., *Choosing an Electoral System: Issues and Alternatives*, pp. 15–30. New York: Praeger.

Herron, Erik S., and Misa Nishikawa. 2001. "Contamination Effects and the Number of Parties in Mixed-Superposition Electoral Systems." *Electoral Studies* 20, 1: 63–86.

Higley, John, and Michael Burton. 1989. "The Elite Variable in Democratic Transitions and Breakdowns." *American Sociological Review* 54, 1: 17–32.

Hinich, Melvin J., and Michael C. Munger. 1994. *Ideology and the Theory of Political Choice.* Ann Arbor: University of Michigan Press.

Hopkin, Jonathan. 1999. *Party Formation and Democratic Transition in Spain: The Creation and Collapse of the Union of Democratic Center.* New York: St. Martin's Press.

Hughes, James. 1994. "Regionalism in Russia: The Rise and Fall of Siberian Agreement." *Europe-Asia Studies* 46, 7: 1133–1161.

———. 1997. "Sub-National Elites and Post-Communist Transformation in Russia: A Reply to Kryshtanovskaya and White." *Europe-Asia Studies* 49, 6: 1017–1036.

———. 2002. "Managing Secession Potential in the Russian Federation." In J. Hughes and G. Sasse, eds., *Ethnicity and Territory in the Former Soviet Union: Regions in Conflict,* pp. 36–68. London: Frank Cass.

Huntington, Samuel P. 1965. "Political Development and Political Decay." *World Politics* 17, 3: 386–430.

———. 1968. *Political Order in Changing Societies.* New Haven: Yale University Press.

Hyde, Matthew. 2001. "Putin's Federal Reforms and Their Implications for Presidential Power in Russia." *Europe-Asia Studies* 53, 5: 719–743.

Ingram, Alan. 1999. "A Nation Split into Fragments: The Congress of Russian Communities and Russian Nationalist Ideology." *Europe-Asia Studies* 51, 4: 687–704.

Ishiyama, John. 1996. "The Russian Proto-Parties and the National Republics: Integrative Organizations in a Disintegrating World?" *Communist and Post-Communist Studies* 29, 4: 395–411.

———. 1999. "Sickles into Roses: The Communist Successor Parties and Democratic Consolidation in Comparative Perspective." *Democratization* 6, 1:52–73.

———. 2000. "Candidate Recruitment, Party Organization and the Communist Successor Parties: The Cases of MSzP, the KPRF, and the LDPR." *Europe-Asia Studies* 52, 5: 875–898.

———. 2001. "Party Organization and the Political Success of the Communist Successor Parties." *Social Science Quarterly* 82, 4: 844–864.

Ishiyama, John, and Ryan Kennedy. 2001. "Superpresidentialism and Political Party Development in Russia, Ukraine, Armenia, and Kyrgyzstan." *Europe-Asia Studies* 53, 8: 1177–1191.

Ivanchenko, Aleksandr. 1996. *Izbiratel'nye komissii v Rossiiskoi Federatsii: Istoria, teoria, praktika.* Moscow: Ves Mir.

Jacobs, Everett M., ed. 1983. *Soviet Local Politics and Government.* London: Allen and Unwin.

Jasiewicz, Krysztof. 1993. "Polish Politics on the Eve of the 1993 Elections: Toward Fragmentation or Pluralism?" *Communist and Post-Communist Studies* 26, 4: 387–411.

Jewell, Malcolm. 1982. *Representation in State Legislatures.* Lexington: University of Kentucky Press.

Kahn, Jeffrey. 2000. "The Parade of Sovereignties: Establishing the Vocabulary of the New Russian Federalism." *Post-Soviet Affairs* 16, 1: 58–88.

Karl, Terry Lynn. 1990. "Dilemmas of Democratization in Latin America." *Comparative Politics* 23, 1: 1–21.

Kartsev, Vladimir P. 1995. *! Zhirinovsky !* New York: Columbia University Press.

Katz, Jonathan, and Gary King. 1999. "A Statistical Model for Multiparty Electoral Data." *American Political Science Review* 93, 1: 15–32.

Katz, Richard S. 1980. *A Theory of Parties and Electoral Systems.* Baltimore: Johns Hopkins University Press.

Kempton, Daniel R. 1996. "The Republic of Sakha (Yakutia): The Evolution of Centre-Regional Relations in the Russian Federation." *Europe-Asia Studies* 48, 4: 587–613.

Key, V. O. 1964. *Politics, Parties, and Pressure Groups.* New York: Thomas Y. Crowell.

Kharkhordin, Oleg, and Theodore P. Gerber. 1994. "Russian Directors' Business Ethic: A Study of Industrial Enterprises in St. Petersburg, 1993." *Europe-Asia Studies* 46, 7: 1075–1107.

Kholmskaia, Marina. 1994. "Komdvizhenie v Rossii: Organizatsionnyi etap." *Vlast* no. 12: 24–28.

Khrushchev, Sergei. 1994. "The Political Economy of Russia's Regional Fragmentation." In D. W. Blum, ed., *Russia's Future: Consolidation or Disintegration?* pp. 91–107. Boulder: Westview Press.

Kiernan, Brendan. 1993. *The End of Soviet Politics: Elections, Legislatures, and the Demise of the Communist Party.* Boulder: Westview Press.

Kiernan, Brendan, and Joseph Aistrup. 1991. "The 1989 Elections to the Congress of People's Deputies in Moscow." *Soviet Studies* 43, 6: 1049–1064.

Kirkow, Peter. 1995. "Regional Warlordism in Russia: The Case of Primorskii Krai." *Europe-Asia Studies* 47, 6: 923–947.

———. 1998. *Russia's Provinces: Authoritarian Transformation Versus Local Autonomy?* London: Macmillan.

Kiselev, Konstantin. 1996. "Stilistika predvybornoi kampanii." *Ural: Politika, ekonomika, pravo* no. 1 (16): 129–133.

Kisriev, Enver, and Robert B. Ware. 2001. "Dagestan People's Assembly Election, 1999." *Electoral Studies* 20, 3: 463–501.

Kitschelt, Herbert. 1992. "The Formation of Party Systems in East Central Europe." *Politics and Society* 20, 1: 7–50.

Kitschelt, Herbert, and Regina Smyth. 2002. "Programmatic Party Cohesion in Emerging Postcommunist Democracies: Russia in Comparative Context." *Comparative Political Studies* 35, 10: 1228–1256.

Korguniuk, Yurii G., and Sergei E. Zaslavskii. 1996. *Rossiiskaia mnogopartiinost: Stanovlenie, funktsionirovanie, razvitie.* Moscow: INDEM.

Kostelecký, Tomáš. 2002. *Political Parties After Communism: Developments in East-Central Europe.* Washington, DC: Woodrow Wilson Center Press.

Koval, Boris I., ed. 1991. *Rossia segodnia: Politicheskii portret v dokumentakh, 1985–1991.* Moscow: Mezhdunarodnye otnoshenia.

Kullberg, Judith S. 1994. "The Ideological Roots of Elite Political Conflict in Post-Soviet Russia." *Europe-Asia Studies* 46, 6: 929–953.

Kurilla, Ivan. 2002. "Civil Activism Without NGOs: The Communist Party as a Civil Society Substitute." *Demokratizatsiya* 10, 3: 392–400.

Laakso, Markku, and Rein Taagepera. 1979. "Effective Number of Parties: A Measure with Application to West Europe." *Comparative Political Studies* 12,1: 3–27.

Lapidus, Gail W. 1999. "Asymmetrical Federalism and State Breakdown in Russia." *Post-Soviet Affairs* 15, 1: 74–82.

Latov, Vitalii S. 1974. *The Soviet Electoral System.* Moscow: Novosti Press.

Lehmann, Hartmut, Jonathan Wadsworth, and Alessandro Acquisti. 1999. *Crime and Punishment: Insecurity and Wage Arrears in the Russian Federation.* IZA Working Paper no. 65. Bonn: Institute for the Study of Labor.

Lewis-Beck, Michael S. 1988. *Economics and Elections: The Major Western Democracies.* Ann Arbor: University of Michigan Press.

Lijphart, Arend. 1971. "Comparative Politics and Comparative Method." *American Political Science Review* 65, 3: 682–693.

———. 1975. "The Comparable-Cases Strategy in Comparative Research." *Comparative Political Studies* 8, 2: 158–177.

———. 1994. *Electoral Systems and Party Systems: A Study of Twenty-seven Democracies, 1945–1990.* Oxford: Oxford University Press.

Lijphart, Arend, Rafael López Pintor, and Yasunori Sone. 1986. "The Limited Vote and the Single Nontransferable Vote: Lessons From the Japanese and Spanish Examples." In B. Grofman and A. Lijphart, eds., *Electoral Laws and Their Political Consequences,* pp. 154–169. New York: Agathon Press.

Linz, Juan. 1990. "The Perils of Presidentialism." *Journal of Democracy* 1, 1: 51–69.

———. 1994. "Democracy, Presidential or Parliamentary: Does It Make a Difference?" In J. Linz and A. Valenzuela, eds., *The Failure of Presidential Democracy: The Case of Latin America,* pp. 3–87. Baltimore: Johns Hopkins University Press.

Lipset, Seymour M. 2000. "The Indispensability of Parties." *Journal of Democracy* 11, 1: 48–55.

Liubarev, Arkadii. 2001. *Vybory v Moskve: Opyt dvenadtsati let, 1989–2000.* Moscow: Biblioteka Rossiiskogo ob"edinenia izbiratelei.

Loewenberg, Gerhard, and Samuel C. Patterson. 1979. *Comparing Legislatures.* Boston: Little, Brown.

Lohr, Eric. 1993. "Arkadii Volsky's Political Base." *Europe-Asia Studies* 45, 5: 811–829.

Löwenhardt, John, and Ruben Verheul. 2000. "The Village Votes: The December 1999 Elections in Tatarstan's Pestretsy District." *Journal of Communist Studies and Transition Politics* 16, 3: 113–122.

Luchterhandt, Galina. 1998. *Parteien in der Russischen Provinz: Politische Entwicklung in den Gebieten des Ural und der Wolgaregion.* Bremen: Edition Temmen.

Luntz, Frank I. 1988. *Candidates, Consultants, and Campaigns: The Style and Substance of American Electioneering.* New York: Basil Blackwell.

Lynn, Nicholas J., and Alexie V. Novikov. 1997. "Refederalizing Russia: Debates on the Idea of Federalism in Russia." *Publius* 27, 2: 187–203.

Mainwaring, Scott. 1993. "Presidentialism, Multipartism, and Democracy: The Difficult Combination." *Comparative Political Studies* 26, 2: 198–228.

———. 1999. *Rethinking Party Systems in the Third Wave of Democratization: The Case of Brazil.* Stanford: Stanford University Press.

Mainwaring, Scott, and Aníbal Pérez Linán. 1997. "Party Discipline in the Brazilian Constitutional Congress." *Legislative Studies Quarterly* 22, 4: 453–483.

Mair, Peter. 1997. *Party System Change: Approaches and Interpretations.* Oxford: Clarendon Press.

Makarkin, Andrei. 1996. *Kommunisticheskaia partia Rossiiskoi Federatsii.* Moscow: Tsentr politicheskikh tekhnologii.

March, Luke. 2001. "For Victory? The Crises and Dilemmas of the Communist Party of the Russian Federation." *Europe-Asia Studies* 53, 2: 263–290.

Massicotte, Louis, and André Blais. 1999. "Mixed Electoral Systems: A Conceptual and Empirical Survey." *Electoral Studies* 18, 3: 341–366.

Matsuzato, Kimitaka. 1997. "The Split and Reconfiguration of Ex-Communist Party Factions in the Russian Oblasts: Chelyabinsk, Samara, Ulyanovsk, Tambov, and Tver (1991–1995)." *Demokratizatsiya* 5, 1: 53–88.

———. 1999. "Local Elites Under Transition: County and City Politics in Russia 1985–1996." *Europe-Asia Studies* 51, 8: 1367–1400.

McAuley, Mary. 1997. *Russia's Politics of Uncertainty.* Cambridge: Cambridge University Press.

McFaul, Michael. 1993. *Post-Communist Politics: Democratic Prospects in Russia and Eastern Europe.* Washington, DC: Center for Strategic and International Studies.

———. 2001. "Explaining Party Formation and Nonformation in Russia: Actors, Institutions, and Chance." *Comparative Political Studies* 34, 10: 1159–1187.

McFaul, Michael, and Nikolai Petrov. 1997. "Russian Electoral Politics After Transition: Regional and National Assessments." *Post-Soviet Geography and Economics,* 38, 9: 507–549.

———, eds. 1998. *Politicheskii Al'manakh Rossii 1997.* Moscow: Moscow Carnegie Center.

Melvin, Neil J. 1998. "The Consolidation of a New Regional Elite: The Case of Omsk 1987–1995." *Europe-Asia Studies* 50, 4: 619–650.

Miller, Arthur H., Gwyn Erb, William M. Reisinger, and Vicki L. Hesli. 2000. "Emerging Party Systems in Post-Soviet Societies: Fact or Fiction?" *Journal of Politics* 62, 2: 455–490.

Miller, Arthur H., and Thomas F. Klobucar. 2000. "The Development of Party Identification in Post-Soviet Societies." *American Journal of Political Science* 44, 4: 667–685.

Mitchneck, Beth, Steven L. Solnick, and Kathryn Stoner-Weiss. 2001. "Federalization." In B. A. Ruble, J. Koehn, and N. E. Popson, eds., *Fragmented Space in the Russian Federation,* pp. 123–156. Baltimore: Johns Hopkins University Press.

Molinar, Juan. 1991. "Counting the Number of Parties: An Alternative Index." *American Political Science Review* 85, 4: 1383–1391.

Morgenstern, Scott, and Benito Nacif, eds. 2002. *Legislative Politics in Latin America.* Cambridge: Cambridge University Press.

Moser, Robert G. 1997. "The Impact of Parliamentary Electoral Systems in Russia." *Post-Soviet Affairs* 13, 3: 284–302.

———. 1998a. "The Electoral Effects of Presidentialism in Post-Soviet Russia." *Journal of Communist Studies and Transition Politics* 14, 1–2: 54–75.

———. 1998b. "Sverdlovsk: Mixed Results in a Hotbed of Regional Autonomy." In T. Colton and J. Hough, eds., *Growing Pains: Russian Democracy and the Election of 1993,* pp. 397–430. Washington, DC: Brookings Institution Press.

———. 1999. "Independents and Party Formation: Elite Partisanship as an Intervening Variable in Russian Politics." *Comparative Politics* 31, 2: 147–165.

———. 2001. *Unexpected Outcomes: Electoral Systems, Political Parties, and Representation in Russia.* Pittsburgh: University of Pittsburgh Press.

Moser, Robert G., and Frank C. Thames, Jr. 2001. "Compromise Amidst Political Conflict: The Origins of Russia's Mixed-Member System." In M. S. Shugart and M. P. Wattenberg, eds., *Mixed-Member Electoral Systems: The Best of Both Worlds?* pp. 255–275. Oxford: Oxford University Press.

Neformal'naia Rossia. 1990. Moscow: Molodaia Gvardia.

Norris, Pippa, ed. 1997. *Passages to Power: Legislative Recruitment in Advanced Democracies.* Cambridge: Cambridge University Press.

Norton, Philip. 1988. "Opposition to Government." In M. Ryle and P. G. Richards, eds., *The Commons Under Scrutiny,* pp. 99–119. London: Routledge.

Novikov, S. 1998. *Omskaia oblast: Vybory—1998, Chernye stranitsy rossiiskoi demokratii.* Omsk: n.p.

Oates, Sarah. 1998. "Party Platforms: Towards a Definition of the Russian Political Spectrum." *Journal of Communist Studies and Transition Politics* 14, 1–2: 77–97.

Olson, David M. 1994. *Democratic Legislative Institutions: A Comparative View.* Armonk, NY: M. E. Sharpe.

———. 1995. "Parliament by Design." *East European Constitutional Review* 4, 2: 56–60.

Olson, David M., and Michael L. Mezey. 1991. "Parliaments and Public Policy". In D. M. Olson and M. L. Mezey, eds., *Legislatures in the Policy Process: The Dilemmas of Economic Policy,* pp. 1–21. Cambridge: Cambridge University Press.

Ordeshook, Peter C., and Olga V. Shvetsova. 1994. "Ethnic Heterogeneity, District Magnitude, and the Number of Parties." *American Journal of Political Science* 38, 1: 100–123.

Orttung, Robert W. 1992. "The Russian Right and the Dilemmas of Party Organization." *Soviet Studies* 44, 3: 445–78.

———, ed. 2000. *The Republics and Regions of the Russian Federation: A Guide to Politics, Policies, and Leaders.* Armonk, NY: M. E. Sharpe.

Ostrow, Joel M. 1998. "Procedural Breakdown and Deadlock in the Russian State Duma: The Problems of an Unlinked Dual-Channel Institutional Design." *Europe-Asia Studies* 50, 5: 793–816.

Pammett, Jon H., and Joan DeBardeleben. 2000. "Citizen Orientations to Political Parties in Russia." *Party Politics* 6, 3: 373–384.

Panebianco, Angelo. 1988. *Political Parties: Organization and Power.* Cambridge: Cambridge University Press.

Pedersen, Mogens N. 1979. "The Dynamics of European Party Systems: Changing Patterns of Electoral Volatility." *European Journal of Political Research* 7, 1: 1–26.

Petracca, Mark P. 1989. "Political Consultants and Democratic Governance." *PS: Political Science and Politics* 22, 1: 11–14.

Petrov, Nikolai. 1996. "Vybory organov predstavitel'noi vlasti regionov." *Mirovaia ekonomika i mezhdunarodnye otnoshenia* no. 3: 25–34.

Pirumova, M. N. 1986. *Zemskaia intelligentsia i ee rol v obshchestvennoi bor'be do nachala XX veka.* Moscow: Nauka.

Polsby, Nelson W. 1968. "The Institutionalization of the U.S. House of Representatives." *American Political Science Review* 62, 1: 144–168.

Portes, Alejandro. 1998. "Social Capital: Its Origins and Applications in Modern Sociology." *Annual Review of Sociology* 24: 1–24.

Pribylovskii, Vladimir. 1992. *Dictionary of Political Parties and Organizations in Russia.* Washington, DC: Center for Strategic and International Studies.

Pridham, Geoffrey. 1990. "Southern European Democracies on the Road to Consolidation: A Comparative Assessment of the Role of Political Parties." In G. Pridham, ed., *Securing Democracy: Political Parties and Democratic Consolidation in Southern Europe,* pp. 1–42. London: Routledge.

Privalov, Nikolai. 1995. *Osnovnye obshchestvenno-politicheskie organizatsii Urala.* Ekaterinburg: Tsentr demokratii i prav cheloveka.

Przeworski, Adam. 1975. "Institutionalization of Voting Patterns, or Is Mobilization the Source of Decay?" *American Political Science Review* 69, 1: 49–67.

———. 1988. "Democracy as a Contingent Outcome of Conflicts." In J. Elster and R. Slagestad, eds., *Constitutionalism and Democracy,* pp. 59–80. Cambridge: Cambridge University Press.

Putnam, Robert. 1993. *Making Democracy Work: Civic Traditions in Modern Italy.* Princeton: Princeton University Press.

Rae, Douglas W. 1967. *The Political Consequences of Electoral Laws.* New Haven: Yale University Press.

Rae, Douglas W., Victor J. Hanby, and John Loosemore. 1971. "Thresholds of Representation and Thresholds of Exclusion: An Analytic Note on Electoral Systems." *Comparative Political Studies* 3, 4: 479–488.

Ragin, Charles C. 1987. *The Comparative Method: Moving Beyond Qualitative and Quantitative Strategies.* Berkeley: University of California Press.

Remington, Thomas F. 1994. "Introduction: Parliamentary Elections and the Transition from Communism." In T. F. Remington, ed., *Parliaments in Transition: The New Legislative Politics in the Former USSR and Eastern Europe,* pp. 1–28. Boulder: Westview Press.

———. 2001a. "Putin and the Duma." *Post-Soviet Affairs* 17, 4: 285–308.

———. 2001b. *The Russian Parliament: Institutional Evolution in a Transitional Regime.* New Haven: Yale University Press.

Remington, Thomas F., and Steven S. Smith. 1995. "The Development of Parliamentary Parties in Russia." *Legislative Studies Quarterly* 20, 4: 474–475.

———. 1996. "Political Goals, Institutional Context, and the Choice of an Electoral System: The Russian Parliamentary Election Law." *American Journal of Political Science* 40, 4: 1253–1279.

Remington, Thomas F., Steven S. Smith, D. Roderick Kiewit, and Moshe Haspel. 1994. "Transitional Institutions and Parliamentary Alignments." In T. F. Remington, ed., *Parliaments in Transition: The New Legislative Politics in the Former USSR and Eastern Europe,* pp. 159–180. Boulder: Westview Press.

Reynolds, Andrew, and Ben Reilly. 1997. *The International IDEA Handbook of Electoral System Design.* Stockholm: International Institute for Democracy and Electoral Assistance.

Rhodes, Martin. 1997. "Financing Party Politics in Italy: A Case of Systemic Corruption." *West European Politics* 20, 1: 54–80.

Roeder, Philip G. 1991. "Soviet Federalism and Ethnic Mobilization." *World Politics* 43, 1: 196–232.

Roniger, Luis, and Ayse Gunes-Ayata, eds. 1994. *Democracy, Clientelism, and Civil Society.* Boulder: Lynne Rienner.

Rose, Richard, ed. 2000. *International Encyclopedia of Elections.* Washington, DC: Congressional Quarterly Press.

Rose, Richard, Neil Munro, and Stephen White. 2001. "Voting in a Floating Party System: The 1999 Duma Election." *Europe-Asia Studies* 53, 3:419–443.

Rose, Richard, and Evgeny Tikhomirov. 1997. "Understanding the Multi-Party Choice: The 1995 Duma Election." *Europe-Asia Studies* 49, 5: 799–823.

Rutland, Peter. 2000. "Putin's Path to Power." *Post-Soviet Affairs* 16, 4: 313–354.

Ryzhenkov, Sergei. 1997. "Saratovskaia Oblast (1986–1996): Politika i Politiki." In K. Matsuzato and A. Shatilov, eds., *Regiony Rossii: Khronika i Rukovoditeli,* vol. 2, *Rostovskaia Oblast, Saratovskaia Oblast,* pp. 83–331. Sapporo: Hokkaido University, Slavic Research Center.

Ryzhenkov, Sergei, and N. Vinnik, eds. 1999. *Reforma mestnogo samoupravlenia v regional'nom izmerenii.* Moscow: MONF and IGPI.

Sakwa, Richard. 1990. *Gorbachev and His Reforms 1985–1990.* Englewood Cliffs, NJ: Prentice Hall.

———. 1993. *Russian Politics and Society.* London: Routledge.

———. 1995. "The Russian Elections of December 1993." *Europe-Asia Studies* 47, 2: 195–227.

Samuels, David J. 2002. "Presidentialized Parties: The Separation of Powers and Party Organization and Behavior." *Comparative Political Studies* 35, 4: 461–483.

Sartori, Giovanni. 1986. "The Influence of Electoral Systems: Faulty Laws or Faulty Method?" In B. Grofman and A. Lijphart, eds., *Electoral Laws and Their Political Consequences,* pp. 43–68. New York: Agathon Press.

———. 1997. *Comparative Constitutional Engineering: An Inquiry into Structures, Incentives, and Outcomes.* 2nd ed. New York: New York University Press.

Schlesinger, Joseph. 1984. "On the Theory of Party Organization." *Journal of Politics* 46, 3: 369–400.

Schneider, Eberhard. 1995. *The Nationalist and Communist Parliamentary Groups in the Russian State Duma.* Cologne: Bundesinstitut fur Ostwissenschaftliche und Internationale Studien.

Sedaitis, Judith B., and Jim Butterfield, eds. 1991. *Perestroika from Below: Social Movements in the Soviet Union.* Boulder: Westview Press.

Shevchenko, Iulia, and Grigorii V. Golosov. 2001. "Legislative Activism of Russian Duma Deputies, 1996–1999." *Europe-Asia Studies* 53, 2: 239–262.

Shlapentokh, Vladimir. 2001. "Putin's First Year in Office: The New Regime's Uniqueness in Russian History." *Communist and Post-Communist Studies* 34, 4: 371–399.

Shlapentokh, Vladimir, Roman Levita, and Mikhail Liberg. 1997. *From Submission to Rebellion: The Provinces Versus the Center in Russia.* Boulder: Westview Press.

Shugart, Matthew S. 1996. "Executive-Legislative Relations in Post-Communist Europe." *Transition* 2, 25: 6–11.

———. 1998. "The Inverse Relationship Between Party Strength and Executive Strength: A Theory of Politicians' Constitutional Choices." *British Journal of Political Science* 28, 1: 1–30.

Shugart, Matthew S., and John M. Carey. 1992. *Presidents and Assemblies: Constitutional Design and Electoral Dynamics.* Cambridge: Cambridge University Press.

Shugart, Matthew S., and Martin P. Wattenberg, eds. 2001. *Mixed-Member Electoral Systems: The Best of Both Worlds?* Oxford: Oxford University Press.

Simonsen, Sven G. 1996. "Raising 'the Russian Question': Ethnicity and Statehood—Russkie and Rossiya." *Nationalism and Ethnic Politics* 2, 1: 91–110.

———. 2001. "Nationalism and the Russian Political Spectrum: Locating and Evaluating the Extremes." *Journal of Political Ideologies* 6, 3: 263–288.

Slider, Darrell. 1994. "Privatization in Russia's Regions." *Post-Soviet Affairs* 10, 4: 367–396.

———. 1996. "Elections to Russia's Regional Assemblies." *Post-Soviet Affairs,* 12, 3: 243–264.

———. 1999. "Pskov Under the LDPR: Elections and Dysfunctional Federalism in One Region." *Europe-Asia Studies* 51, 5: 755–767.

Smirniagin, Leonid, ed. 1995. *Rossiiskie regiony nakanune vyborov—95.* Moscow: Analiticheskoe upravlenie Prezidenta Rossiiskoi Federatsii.

Smith, Graham. 1996. "Russia, Ethnoregionalism, and the Politics of Federation." *Ethnic and Racial Studies* 19, 2: 391–409.

Smyth, Regina. 2002. "Building State Capacity from the Inside Out: Parties of Power and the Success of the President's Reform Agenda in Russia." *Politics and Society* 30, 4: 555–578.

Sobianin, Aleksandr A., ed. 1992. *VI S"ezd Narodnykh Deputatov Rossii: Politicheskie itogi i perspektivy.* Moscow: Organizatsionnyi Otdel Prezidiuma Verkhovnogo Soveta Rossiiskoi Federatsii.

Solnick, Steven L. 1995. "Federal Bargaining in Russia." *East European Constitutional Review* 4, 4: 52–56.

———. 1998. "The 1996–97 Gubernatorial Elections in Russia: Outcomes and Implications." *Post-Soviet Affairs* 14, 1: 48–80.

Solovei, Valerii. 1996. "Perspektivy russkogo natsionalizma v svete parlamentskikh vyborov." In L. Beliaeva, ed., *Partiino-politicheskie elity i elektoral'nye protsessy v Rossii*, pp. 29–36. Moscow: TsKSIiM.

Squire, Peverill. 1998. "Membership Turnover and the Efficient Processing of Legislation." *Legislative Studies Quarterly* 23, 1: 23–32.

Startsev, Yaroslav. 1999. "Gubernatorial Politics in Sverdlovsk Oblast." *Post-Soviet Affairs* 15, 4: 336–361.

Stepan, Alfred. 2000. "Russian Federalism in Comparative Perspective." *Post-Soviet Affairs* 16, 2: 133–176.

Stoner-Weiss, Kathryn. 1997. *Local Heroes: The Political Economy of Russian Regional Governance.* Princeton: Princeton University Press.

———. 2001. "The Limited Reach of Russia's Party System: Underinstitutionalization in Dual Transitions." *Politics and Society* 29, 3: 385–414.

———. 2002. "Central Government Incapacity and the Weakness of Political Parties: Russian Democracy in Disarray." *Publius* 32, 2: 125–146.

Strom, Kaare. 1990. "A Behavioral Theory of Competitive Political Parties." *American Journal of Political Science* 34, 2: 565–598.

Stuart, Robert C., ed. 1983. *The Soviet Rural Economy.* Totowa, NJ: Rowman and Allanheld.

Sungurov, Aleksandr. 1994. *Stanovlenie politicheskikh partii i organov gosudarstvennoi vlasti v Rossiiskoi Federatsii.* St. Petersburg: Strategia.

———. 1996. *Etiudy politicheskoi zhizni Peterburga.* St. Petersburg: Strategia.

Suny, Ronald G. 1993. *The Revenge of the Past: Nationalism, Revolution, and the Collapse of the Soviet Union.* Stanford: Stanford University Press.

Taagepera, Rein, and Bernard Grofman. 1981. "Effective Size and Number of Components." *Sociological Methods and Research* 10, 1: 63–81.

Taagepera, Rein, and Matthew S. Shugart. 1989. *Seats and Votes: The Effects and Determinants of Electoral Systems.* New Haven: Yale University Press.

Tolz, Vera, and Irina Busygina. 1997. "Regional Governors and the Kremlin: The Ongoing Battle for Power." *Communist and Post-Communist Studies* 30, 4: 401–426.

Treisman, Daniel. 1997. "Russia's 'Ethnic Revival': The Separatist Activism of Regional Leaders in a Postcommunist Order." *World Politics* 49, 2: 212–249.

———. 1999. *After the Deluge: Regional Crises and Political Consolidation in Russia.* Ann Arbor: University of Michigan Press.

Tsygankov, Anatolii. 1998. *Prishestvie izbiratelia: Iz istorii vybornykh kampanii v Karelii, 1989–1996.* Petrozavodsk: Karelia.

Umnova, Irina. 1996. *Sovremennaia rossiiskaia model razdelenia vlasti mezhdu federatsiei i ee sub"ektami.* Moscow: INION RAN.

Urban, Joan B., and Valerii D. Solovei. 1997. *Russia's Communists at the Crossroads.* Boulder: Westview Press.

Urban, Michael. 1990. *More Power to the Soviets: The Democratic Revolution in the USSR.* Brookfield, VT: Gower.

———. 1991. "Party Formation and Deformation on Russia's Democratic Left." In R. Hubert and D. Kelley, eds., *Perestroika-Era Politics: The New Soviet Legislature and Gorbachev's Political Reforms,* pp. 129–150. Armonk, NY: M. E. Sharpe.

———. 1992. "Boris El'tsin, Democratic Russia and the Campaign for the Russian Presidency." *Soviet Studies* 44, 2: 187–207.

———. 1994. "December 1993 as a Replication of Late-Soviet Electoral Practices." *Post-Soviet Affairs* 10, 2: 127–158.

———. 1997. *The Rebirth of Politics in Russia.* Cambridge: Cambridge University Press.

Urban, Michael, and Vladimir Gel'man. 1997. "The Development of Political Parties in Russia." In K. Dawisha and B. Parrott, eds., *Democratic Changes and Authoritarian Reactions in Russia, Ukraine, Belarus', and Moldova,* pp. 69–218. Cambridge: Cambridge University Press.

Verkhovskii, Aleksandr, and Vladimir Pribylovskii. 1996. *Natsional-patrioticheskie organizatsii v Rossii: Istoria, ideologia, ekstremistskie tendentsii.* Moscow: Panorama.

Vujacic, Veljko. 1996. "Gennadiy Zyuganov and the 'Third Road.'" *Post-Soviet Affairs* 12, 2: 118–154.

Wasserman, Scott. 2000. "Multimember Districts." www.senate.leg.state.mn.us/departments/scr/redist/red2000/ch4multi.htm.

Weaver, Leon H. 1984. "Semi-Proportional and Proportional Representation Systems in the United States." In A. Lijphart and B. Grofman, eds., *Choosing an Electoral System: Issues and Alternatives,* pp. 191–206. New York: Praeger.

Weigle, Marcia A. 1994. "Political Participation and Party Formation in Russia, 1985–1992: Institutionalizing Democracy?" *Russian Review* 53, 2: 240–270.

Weinberg, Robert. 1998. *Stalin's Forgotten Zion.* Berkeley: University of California Press.

White, Stephen, and Ian McAllister. 1996. "The CPSU and Its Members: Between Communism and Postcommunism." *British Journal of Political Science* 26, 1: 105–122.

White, Stephen, Richard Rose, and Ian McAllister. 1997. *How Russia Votes.* Chatham, NJ: Chatham House.

Wilson, Gary N. 2001. "'Matryoshka Federalism' and the Case of the Khanty Mansiysk Autonomous Okrug." *Post-Soviet Affairs* 17, 2: 167–194.

Young, John F. 1997. "At the Bottom of the Heap: Local Self-Government and Regional Politics in the Russian Federation." In P. J. Stavrakis, J. DeBardeleben, and L. Black, eds., *Beyond the Monolith: The Emergence of Regionalism in Post-Soviet Russia,* pp. 81–102. Baltimore: Johns Hopkins University Press.

Zaller, John R. 1992. *The Nature and Origins of Mass Opinion.* Cambridge: Cambridge University Press.

Index

About the Book

Political parties typically are assumed to be essential for contemporary democratic government and governance. Why, then, has the regime change in Russia failed to produce viable political parties? Grigorii Golosov addresses this question, exploring issues central to an understanding of Russian political development.

Golosov combines statistical and qualitative analysis, including many case studies, to explain why political parties have not yet taken hold in Russia's regions. His argument is bolstered by a uniquely comprehensive database of regional elections held from 1993 to June 2003. Moving from the late Soviet era to current efforts by the federal government to promote a viable party system at the regional level, his work is a pathbreaking contribution to both Russian studies and comparative politics.

Grigorii V. Golosov is associate professor of political science at the European University at St. Petersburg (Russia). His many publications include *Elections in Russia: Analyses, Documents, and Data* and *Partiinye Sistemy Rossii i Stran Vostochnoi Evropy* [Party Systems of Russia and East European Countries].